A Maritime History of Somerset

Volume Three

Somerset Archaeological & Natural History Society

A MARITIME HISTORY OF SOMERSET

VOLUME THREE

Adrian J. Webb

SOMERSET ARCHAEOLOGICAL AND NATURAL HISTORY SOCIETY

COVER ILLUSTRATION

Front and back: An early nineteenth-century watercolour of Minehead harbour, reproduced with permission of S.A.N.H.S.

The image for the backdrop for the title page is reproduced with kind permission of Mrs M.F. Webb from a painting of the harbour at Minehead by Harry Frier dated 1917

The views expressed in this volume are those of the authors and not those of the Somerset Archaeological and Natural History Society.

Typeset in Garamond.
Typeset and designed by Adrian Webb.
Printed by The Russell Press, Nottingham, 2017.

ISBN 978 0 902152 26 7

Contents

Abbreviations

A.O.D.	Above Ordnance Datum
B.A.	Bristol Archives, 'B' Bond, Bristol
B.L.	British Library, St Pancras, London
B.O.D.C.	British Oceanographic Data Centre
B.R.S.	Bristol Record Society
C.C.R.	*Calendar of Close Rolls*
C.D.E.P.N.	*Cambridge dictionary of English place-names*
C.F.R.	*Calendar of Fine Rolls*
C.I.M.	*Calendar of Inquisitions Miscellaneous*
C.P.R.	*Calendar of Patent Rolls*
D.C.R.S.	Devon and Cornwall Record Society
D.E.P.N.	*Concise Oxford dictionary of English place-names*, 4th edn
H.A.T.	Highest Astronomical Tide
L.A.T.	Lowest Astronomical Tide
M.H.S.	*Maritime History of Somerset*
M.H.W.N.	Mean High Water Neaps
M.H.W.S.	Mean High Water Springs
M.L.W.N.	Mean Low Water Neaps
M.L.W.S.	Mean Low Water Springs
O.D.N.	Ordnance Datum Newlyn
O.S.	Ordnance Survey
P.S.A.N.H.S.	*Proceedings of the Somerset Archaeological and Natural History Society*
P.S.M.S.L.	International Permanent Service for Mean Sea Level
S.A.N.H.S.	Somerset Archaeological and Natural History Society
S.D.N.Q.	*Somerset and Dorset Notes and Queries*
S.H.C.	Somerset Heritage Centre, Norton Fitzwarren, Taunton
S.R.S.	Somerset Record Society
T.B.G.A.S.	*Transactions of the Bristol and Gloucestershire Archaeological Society*
T.N.A.	The National Archives [of England and Wales], Kew
U.K.H.O.	United Kingdom Hydrographic Office, Taunton
V.C.H.	*Victoria County History*

Acknowledgements

COMPILING THIS third volume of new studies into aspects of Somerset's extensive and diverse maritime history has been a pleasure, although a protracted process. I am grateful to my fellow authors for their contributions, constructive criticisms and patience. Special thanks go to Dr Alston Kennerly for his patience and to Professor Mike Duffy for writing the foreword to this volume. I would like to thank my family for their support whilst working on this volume and not undertaking my full share of our collective domestic duties.

I am particularly grateful to the South West Maritime History Society for their financial contribution towards this volume. Also to an organisation, who wish to remain anonymous, who have generously supported the publication of this volume.

The reproduction permissions have been agreed between the copyright holders and the individual authors. Illustrations (as marked in the text) are reproduced with the permission of those individuals and organisations. I gratefully acknowledge the assistance of David Bromwich, Ian Coleby, staff at the Somerset Heritage Centre, and the United Kingdom Hydrographic Office, S.A.N.H.S. Publications Committee, Gary Holden, Louisa Webb, Margaret Webb and David Worthy. Special thanks go to Ian Coleby for his cartographic skills used to produce the maps in this volume.

A final note of thanks must go to Philip Ashford who has brought this project to the attention of many authors, read through numerous draughts and compiled the index of place-names. His enthusiasm has been a driving force behind these publications.

Foreword

AS ONE OF the editors of *The New Maritime History of Devon* I willingly assisted when asked to advise on the first volume of *A Maritime History of Somerset*, little dreaming that it would grow to three volumes with perhaps more to follow. This series now stands as a worthy partner alongside the maritime histories of Devon (1992, 1994) and Cornwall (2014) in providing the South West with by far the most extensive and authoritative study of a region's maritime history than any other of the United Kingdom. Somerset's place in this is significant in that although it lacked the large deep water harbours and plethora of ports of its western neighbours, its economy nevertheless still depended on maritime transportation until the coming of the railways and motorways and hence can show a thriving maritime past, while the latter facilitated the development of a new recreational maritime economy. This third volume gives further proof of the extent to which the sea has embedded itself in the life of the county and will surely stimulate the search for more examples which might appear in future volumes. The series editor, Adrian Webb and his contributors, deserves our thanks and congratulations for another magnificently produced volume.

Michael Duffy

Professor Michael Duffy
Research Fellow, University of Exeter
Formerly Head of History and Director of the Centre for Maritime Historical Studies

Introduction

VOLUME THREE in this series contains the widest range of studies of maritime history published by the Somerset Archaeological and Natural History Society to date. It is also the first of the volumes which includes aspects of Somerset's medieval trades. Since the publication of volume one in 2010, the interest in Somerset's maritime past has expanded. Chapters from the first two volumes are being cited by researchers and reviews of both volumes have been favourable. Subsequently, the profile of Somerset's maritime history and heritage has been significantly raised. When looking back slightly earlier this is no bad thing, as in 1990 (and again in 2000), the National Maritime Museum's *Guide to maritime Britain* contained nothing about Bridgwater or Watchet, and only one sentence for Minehead and two for Porlock Weir.[1] The good citizens of all the maritime areas of Somerset who were overlooked in this attractive book, in my opinion, can feel hard done by. Hopefully the publication of volumes one, two and three in the Maritime History of Somerset series will stir the authors of national studies to look at Somerset's maritime heritage more favourably. No longer is there an excuse for not having access to a wealth of detailed research.

It is possible for some people to overlook how Somerset was (and still is) reliant on the sea in days gone by, far more so than today. In this volume Dr David Pugh, an eminent marine scientist, has written

> It is easy to forget how on a daily basis Somerset is a county predominately under the influence of the sea: economically, geographically, socially, and above all as a result of its continual geological reshaping, by rivers, by tides and by currents. With so much of the county lying close to and just a few metres above mean sea levels, there is an ongoing battle between land and sea.

The chapters published in this series help to remind us of the economic, geographical and social factors that affected Somerset in days gone by. Even those people who did not live next to the sea relied upon it for a whole host of reasons, such as a source of food, entertainment, fuel, imports and exports. For example, Taunton, some 16 miles from the coast, was a place from which people journeyed in order to buy fish caught at sea, and there were four fish shambles in the town in 1630.[2] Fish was also bought from the south coast, for example in 1585.[3] How the sea affected the social lives of the thousands of people in Somerset who lived next to it has yet to be written. For example, absentee fathers could have been a reason for smaller families in coastal settlements than are found further in land. But were there more illegitimate births in coastal parishes compared to those parishes further inland? Perhaps these are themes for future volumes in this series.

Volume three in this series adds a significant amount to our knowledge of Somerset's maritime past. Some chapters in this volume are ground-breaking for different reasons, whilst others continue themes covered in volumes one and two. One of those ground-breaking studies involves the use of navigational texts, maps and nautical charts to help identify the origins of some of Somerset's more obscure maritime place-names. Although most of the texts and charts are from the seventeenth and eighteenth centuries, Professor Richard Coates and myself show how these can be used to clearly identify the origin of numerous placenames along Somerset's coast. Even more recent navigational publications have helped identify the dates when some names appear to have come into use, such as the change from Botestal Point to Hinkley Point. Other identifications have relied upon linguistic evidence to show the Scandinavian origin of names such as Anchor Head. This chapter shows how places were named throughout the period of written history and that spelling was not standardized and therefore inconsistent. It can also be seen how some names may have been forgotten, whilst other places were on occasion known by two different names. Others were incorrectly copied by publishers in the seventeenth and eighteenth centuries that remain on current publications in their incorrect form.

Rarely names appear in such publications that cannot be identified with modern equivalents. One such name that has not been included in this chapter is 'Com'. It appears on a map by Robert Adams, published in London in 1590, situated near the coast opposite the Holms about half way between Ilfracombe and Bristol.[4] This name raises two significant questions. To start with, why is there no other placename in the county of Somerset shown on this map apart from this one? And, what could the modern equivalent of this name be? The answer to the first question is due to the fact that the purpose of the map was to show the route of the Spanish Armada in 1588. As this armada did not venture into the upper reaches of the Bristol Channel there was little need for the mapmaker to include many names along this stretch of coast; this is also true for the coast of south Wales. Secondly, a modern equivalent could be Combwich. Or, less likely, it could be an abbreviation for the Latin word *Comitatus*, meaning county, which appears on Christopher Saxton's map of 1575.[5] If either of these possibilities is the case then the cartographer, or the engraver, may have simply made a mistake copying the name. It may have been the case that a single place-name was needed between Bristol and Ilfracombe for aesthetic purposes and the cartographer decided upon Combwich, simply because it was roughly half way between two larger ports.

Similarly, there are names which indicate a feature which was once 'new' but centuries later may have been called something different. These types of name can also be difficult to attach to an actual place. One such example occurs in the Patent Rolls in 1394 as the *Neweground.* Located somewhere in the 'Severne' but within the liberty of Bristol, it was the site of a shipwreck.[6] The question of whether this was the same feature as the one shown on charts in the early eighteenth century as *New Bank*[7] is not readily answerable. The persistence of *new* in names is not a problem, however; there are plenty of analogies for a 'new' feature being persistently called new, at least on land, as witness Newton near Bicknoller, recorded in Domesday Book, the mid-seventeenth century New Cut in the Fenland of Cambridgeshire, New College Oxford, founded in 1379, and Newcastle upon Tyne, whose castle was begun in 1080.

Continuing the theme of economic history found in previous volumes, especially volume one, there are chapters in volume three on the export of Ham Green Ware and Dundry stone during the medieval period, the people involved in the customs district of Bridgwater from 1320 to 1500, west Somerset's maritime stone trade from 1400 to 1900, and copper ore mining and shipping in west Somerset from 1791 to 1820. Each of these helps historians understand the complexities of different aspects of maritime trade.

From the north of the ancient county of Somerset, Philip Ashford has identified a maritime network with its origins in the twelfth century. This network stretched as far as Cork, Galway and Rathmullan, a distance of over 300 miles as the crow flies. But to make this journey by water, even if conditions were favourable and navigators knew enough about local tidal streams and dangers to navigation, the journey was more like one of 500 miles. This network also had commonality with shipments of raw commodities, such as Dundry stone, that were shipped over to Ireland where it was used to construct some fine ecclesiastical buildings. Whereas manufactured goods, such as pottery at Ham Green was completed before it was shipped. How Ham Green Ware was 'marketed' (to use a modern term) in Ireland, if at all, is a mystery. Did the potters of Ham Green simply rely upon local opportunities to sell their products? For example, local markets and fairs (especially those at Bristol) and passing ships may have been their main points of sale. If so, the extent of the distribution of Ham Green Ware was dependent on well established markets and the potters of Ham Green simply tapped into existing opportunities.

On the subject of stone, but for a much longer period, Ashford has identified a host of references in contemporary documentation for the trade from West Somerset. This industry involved Cornish slate, Plymouth limestone, Porlock pebbles, Watchet alabaster, Bristol sandstone, Dundry stone, and Pennant sandstone. The serviceability of various types of rock meant that it was used for buildings, for artistic and industrial usage such as in harbour construction, for pavements, as well as ballast in ships plying to and from Wales. One irony of this trade being that on the one hand stone was used for construction but, on the other, when it was quarried from coastal locations it made this part of the landscape vulnerable to erosion. What was given in one hand was taken away in another. Nevertheless, some small parts of Somerset have been exported overseas and to areas of Britain that have become part of the fabric of important buildings, as well as part of the manmade landscape, hopefully to remain so for generations to come.

Fortunately, archaeological excavations have (literally) unearthed numerous locations showing the geographical extent to which Ham Green Ware reached, whereas evidence for the geographical reach of exports of Dundry stone can be seen above ground at locations across Ireland. The potters of Ham Green were undoubtedly part of a wider mercantile community. An example of a mercantile community within Somerset was the one centred on the busy port of Bridgwater. Ashford has reconstructed a picture of the complexities of that community located in the customs district of Bridgwater from 1320 to 1500. He shows that the customs district stretched along the coast from the Devon/Somerset border in the west to the River Axe, north of Brean Down, encompassing the vast majority of Somerset's ports and harbours, namely Minehead, Dunster, Watchet, Bridgwater, Combwich and 'Axewater'. It had connections with mainland Europe, further into Somerset and its adjacent counties.

Bridgwater became a central location for the export of cloth to Gascony and the Iberian Peninsula, especially during the late fourteenth and early fifteenth centuries. Also, there were many factors at work concerning the appointment of officers who served within this district. Combined with its connections with Ireland, its location between other trading centres in Somerset, local families through marriage, and the farming and clothmaking industries, the Bridgwater customs district was a vibrant and important catalyst for Somerset's economy. It is hard to imagine these days the effort involved in transporting goods for any great distance, however, Dr Andrew Butcher has identified an agreement in the early fifteenth century for cloth to be transported by cart along Somerset's roads from Crowcombe, on the south side of the Quantocks, to Bridgwater.[8] Was this some of the cloth that was destined, via a local ship, for the Iberian peninsula during the fifteenth century? Were these cloths known as 'Crowcombes', 'Tauntons' or 'Bridgwaters', or simply as broadcloths?

A microcosm of economic history can be seen in Dr Peter Skidmore's chapter on the link between investors, mining, transport, manufacturing and point of sale. The fortunate survival of letters to the landowner of the copper mine at Dodington (the Marquis of Buckingham) from his estate agent, initially Richard Camplin and later Scrope Bernard, letters between the estate agent and the mining agent William Jenkin, and between Jenkin and the various mining captains reveals the arrangements between those involved in this process. Although the quantities shipped from Combwich were insignificant when compared with the amounts shipped from some of the Cornish ports, mining provided employment for many people in this area of west Somerset. Employment not just at Dodington, but for those who transported the ore to Combwich, stored it at the warehouses there, loaded it onto the ships and for those who worked the boats over to Wales and back again.

The remainder of this volume covers new aspects in this series on the subjects of wrecks, geology, welfare and tidal history. Collectively these chapters cover thousands of years of history and show how varied maritime history can be. Detective work by Serena Cant, a national expert on wrecks, examines three wrecks showing differing aspects of trade and shipping some 200 to 250 years ago. The three wrecks are rare survivals considering there are more than 11,000 documented wreck events in England, of which only some 40 wreck sites have so far have been identified. Wrecks of this era in the archaeological record are rare, especially for this size of vessel. The name of the vessel wrecked at Minehead, despite the detailed research undertaken to identify her, still remains elusive. Hopefully the publication of this chapter may bring forward more information or avenues for establishing its true identity.

Professor Eric Robinson uses a geologist's perspective to identify aspects of the construction of west Somerset ports. With an introductory section by Ashford touching on documentary sources, Robinson's wealth of experience has unravelled the complexities of harbour construction, something that rarely happened during one short period of time.

These two aspects of research combined together help to explain to visitors how ports and harbours developed over many centuries and continue to do so in many cases. Perhaps there is much to be learned from applying this approach elsewhere in the Bristol Channel and even further afield.

Occasionally tantalising references come to light that touch upon the subject of stone from the coast but are not sufficiently detailed to show their true meaning. Three such entries can be found in the Stogursey churchwardens' accounts in 1526-7, 1527-8 and 1533-4. In the 1520s stone was purchased and delivered from 'the sey'; at the same time a quantity of lime appears in the accounts. In 1533-4 a further 12d was paid for 'bryngyng off the stonys to the bot' and 12d to 'men that brothe home the stonys' to the church. An action that suggests, but is not totally clear, that stones may have been imported by boat. Was this stone imported, or simply brought from a different part of the Somerset coast? The churchwardens of Nettlecombe, much further in-land, paid 21d in 1523-3 for 'gathering the stonys to gether at see syd'.[9] Perhaps some part of Stogursey and Nettlecombe churches are constructed from these consignments of stone recorded just before the Reformation.

Dr Alston Kennerley has written on a subject that local historians often overlook, *i.e.* social welfare. It is something that maritime communities relied upon that existed outside of the established religious and parochial or government backed welfare and education provision. It was specifically established for maritime purposes and found a niche with a small number of maritime folk who did not conform with such long established institutions and looked elsewhere for support. Two men founded the provision of that support for mariners living along Somerset's coast. Their names were the Reverend John Ashley and the Reverend George Charles Smith. Kennerley's chapter on seamen's religious and social welfare, 1817-1983, shows just how much Somerset was involved in the various facets of welfare provision; a situation comparable to other parts of the British Isles. Today, although much of charitable social welfare provision for seafarers has been assumed by the welfare state, the Mission to Seafarers (as it is known today) continues this essential work.

The final chapter in this volume concentrates on the science behind an event that was catastrophic for (potentially) thousands of people in Somerset. Two international experts from the world of marine science, Dr David Pugh and Dr Kevin Horsbrough, have combined resources and along with numerous contemporary records researched by Philip Ashford, show how the great flood of 1606/7 was not a tsunami as suggested by Bryant and Haslett.[10] The science behind the event combined with contemporary evidence shows how a combination of factors caused the greatest recorded flood in the documented history of Somerset. It is highly likely that the flood was caused by the worst combination of high spring tide and locally generated surge in the Bristol Channel. And, if it happened once in the early seventeenth century, it could have happened before but no contemporary written record survives to prove such a theory. This is not surprising, as in certain parts of Somerset flooding was so common an event that it was not unusual enough to have troubled someone to record its occurrence.

One man who did record such events, albeit in more recent times, was the Reverend William Holland. A country parson (whose diary was made famous by Jack Ayres), noted such an event on 9 February 1809 how: 'the oldest man living does not remember such great floods and so much water'. He observed further from Over Stowey how 'Everything beyond Bridgwater is like a sea'.[11] How much of this was due to poor sea defences, poor drainage, and / or excessive rain is not known. But shortly after this event the Brue drainage scheme came into place, and that would have included much (if not all) of the area witnessed by Holland.

One thing often leads to another. As a result of the publication of earlier volumes in this series, information has been passed to the editor which expands our knowledge of certain aspects of maritime history published in those books. One item of note relates to Somerset's seaside history published in volume two. In 1704, John Cannon, who left a fascinating diary cum commonplace book, recorded in some detail a trip to the seaside:

> several of our company with me rode down to the seaside for our pleasure and the sight of the sea; and riding along the strand to a large promontory or down called Brean Down by Brent, Berrow and other places, we came to this down, at that time a large coney warren and well stocked with coneys. It happened the warrener was absent being gone to a

> fair, and left none at home but children which we finding right for our purposes: viz. we all agreed to get some of the coneys clandestinely, which we did with our dogs and staves planting ourselves between the hill on our left hand and the meadow on our right, wherein they being got out in great numbers we opposed their passage to their burrows. Whilst we were on the down, my mother fainted away, occasioned by the vapours and breezes of the sea but soon recovered, In the evening we returned and the next day went again, but the warrener being at home prevented our second design intended as before, yet on request permitted us to take some with his feretts and netts, which we liberally gratified him for.[12]

Is this the first account of someone visiting the Somerset coast purely for 'pleasure' (albeit with an ulterior motive)? The lure of the sea was something that the diarist Holland could also not resist. Living at Over Stowey, overlooking the Bristol Channel, he often noted the view, ships and people associated with this maritime world. Like Cannon he was also lured to its waters for pleasure and to obtain supplies of food, as well as coal.[13]

As well as of great value to historians, there are aspects of this volume that have an appeal to visitors to Somerset's coast. Visitors wishing to see the wreck at Minehead, or marvel at the geology of the walls of Watchet and the rocks in Minehead harbour will not be disappointed. Visiting the small church of Kingston Seymour with its reminder of the great flood is a worthwhile journey, noting the origins and changes of name at nearby Weston-super-Mare, and coastal defences at Uphill, remind us how aspects of maritime history are still visible and not simply pages in dull volumes of academic papers.

The ability of visitors to access important but previously relatively inaccessible stretches of the Somerset coast has recently been enhanced by the opening of two high specification cycle ways. One route follows the coast from Dunster to Blue Anchor, whilst another from Weston-super-Mare to the fort at the end of Brean Down. The track crosses the Axe at a sluice gate and means that the glories of Brean Down can now be approached from Uphill to the north of the Down and not just from Brean to the south. Hopefully this increased accessibility to the coast will cause more people to be inspired by the sea and thus to read these volumes concerning Somerset's vibrant maritime past.

But what is the future for Somerset's maritime history? When the range of subjects that have appeared in this series is compared to their modern equivalents, it is difficult to see in some cases how some can be written about in the future. This may be hampered by unforeseen developments, such as tidal energy lagoons, if they become a reality in Bridgwater Bay. For example, what exists today to compare with Somerset's maritime trade of centuries past? By sea, for coastal trade, the answer is insignificant, but by land there are innumerable business connections by road and rail with tons of goods delivered to Somerset, and vice versa. A comparison of the customs districts shows that there is a modern equivalent thanks to the continuing role of Her Majesty's Revenue & Customs. Through Royal Portbury Dock comes millions of GBP, so much so that following the privitisation of Bristol Docks in 1991, some '£475 million has been invested to create a modern, thriving business offering the full range of shipping, distribution and logistics services'.[14] This provides plenty of material to be researched, analysed and published in the future.

A comparison can also be made with subjects published in July 2017's issue of *Somerset Life* for potential topics for the future. Will historians in future generations be writing about beachcombing? The spoils of the sea can be seen littered along Somerset's coast. Amongst the tons of plastic waste are many treasures, but combing the beach for such spoils is nothing new. Windsurfing, kayaking, jet skiing, and who knows what other new technologies will be exploited for pleasure purposes may be the subject of future chapters. Conversely much has been written about tourism, which appears to be one area that continues to grow. This growth is partly fuelled by the large number of housing developments in places like Bridgwater, Portishead, Taunton and Bristol whose residents are attracted to the coast. Combined with an increasing number of leisure opportunities will this be something that will promote maritime history, or just another reduction of unprotected natural coastal habitats? Only time will tell.

Adrian Webb
Taunton
August 2017

References

1 K. Wheatley, *National Maritime Museum guide to maritime Britain* (London, 2000), 137.

2 S.H.C., DD\DP/66/14 lease, 1630.

3 S.H.C., DD\WO/53/3/12 receipt, 1585.

4 National Maritime Museum, PBD8529(2) chart of Great Britain in R. Adams, *Expeditionis Hispanorum in Angliam vera descriptio anno domini MDLXXXVIII* (London, 1590). I am grateful to Megan Barford for access to an image of this chart.

5 C. Saxton, *Somersetensem comitat[um] ... ponit tabula* (London, 1575).

6 G.J. Morris, ed., *Calendar of the Patent Rolls, Richard II, 1391-1396*, 5 (1905), 433. I am grateful to Jennifer Scherr for this reference.

7 A.J. Webb, *Charts and surveys of the Somerset coast, c.1350-1824*, Somerset Record Society (hereafter S.R.S.) 97 (2014), facsimiles 6 and 7.

8 S.H.C., DD/TB/12/1, m.22-23. I am grateful to Dr Andrew Butcher for this reference.

9 R.W. Dunning and M. MsDermott, eds, *Church accounts 1457-1559*, S.R.S. 95 (2013), 57, 132, 134, 144.

10 E. Bryant and S. Haslett, 'Catastrophic Wave Erosion, Bristol Channel, United Kingdom: Impact of Tsunami?' in *Journal of Geology* 115 (2007) , 253–70; E. Bryant and S. Haslett, 'Was the AD 1607 Coastal Flooding Event in the Severn Estuary and Bristol Channel (UK) Due to a Tsunami?' in *Archaeology in the Severn Estuary* 13 (2002), 163-7.

11 S.H.C., A\BTL/2/29 diary of William Holland, book 62.

12 S.H.C., DD/SAS C795/PA/191 diary of John Cannon.

13 J. Ayres, ed., *Paupers and pig killers: the diary of William Holland, a Somerset parson, 1799-1818* (Stroud, 1984).

14 The Bristol Port Company, 'Our History' https://www.bristolport.co.uk/about-us/our-history, accessed August 2017.

List of Illustrations

List of Tables

List of Figures

Chapter One

Two Medieval Somerset Exports: Ham Green Ware and Dundry Stone

Philip Ashford

Introduction

IN 1959, ONE OF THE few medieval pottery kiln sites found so far in south-west England was discovered in a field next to what was then Ham Green Hospital on the edge of the current village of Pill, Somerset, and within metres of Hung Road on the River Avon. Archaeologists found thousands of wasted sherds of cooking pots and jugs which provided enough information to reconstruct pottery forms. The pottery, which consists of two main forms, jugs and jars, were hand-built with characteristic applied, rouletted or grooved decoration and distinctive fabric. These criteria help to identify the ware when found at other sites and among old collections in museum stores. A report was subsequently written by Ken Barton on the kiln and the pottery and published in 1963.[1] Crockern Pill, referred to as 'Creocham' in the second half of the twelfth century and 'Crockerspull' in 1268, derives from the fact that it was a source of pottery, the term 'crocker' commonly used to denote 'potter'.[2] Since Barton's publication in 1963, Ham Green Ware has become the best-known medieval ware in the west of Britain in terms of its widespread occurrence on excavated archaeological sites.

Illustration 1.1: A Ham Green Ware jug (© Bristol Museum and Art Gallery, G2632)

Ham Green Ware and the understanding of its distribution, 1965-1985

Petrologically, there are two principal Ham Green pottery fabrics; a red-firing ware with fine quartz sand temper used for jars and an off-white firing ware with similar sand but clay pellets and some light clay inclusions used for green-glazed jugs. The jug fabric is probably derived from coal-measure clay, while the jar fabric may be more local.[3] It is not known where the clay pits, the source of the material, are located. For practical and economic reasons it is thought the sources will not be far from Pill. It is suggested that the source of the jug clay was Bedminster which is part of the Bristol coalfield, but because of Pill's location on the banks of the Avon the clay could have been shipped in.[4] Another suggestion is that the mixture of geology in the fields of Chapel Pill farm, near to the Ham Green kiln, provided the range of inclusions in the pottery.[5] From Barton's work it is possible to distinguish Ham Green A jugs dating from the earlier twelfth century, from Ham Green B jugs, dating from the late twelfth and into the thirteenth century.[6]

A second potential kiln site was identified from a group of wasters found actually in Pill 1.5 miles (as the crow flies) from the Ham Green kiln site.[7] This find is significant in that a particular type of spoutless A-type jug was identified as well as jar wasters with sandier or no inclusions. The coarser ware with rounded quartz is often called 'proto-Ham Green' but in fact seems to be contemporary with Ham Green cooking wares. Sherds of this ware appear to be represented among the Pill wasters, suggesting it was made at Pill.[8] The wasters have been found on the banks of the Avon at Pill itself, so it is likely the kiln was very close to the shore.[9] Some of the output from this kiln, like Ham Green Ware, would have been loaded on boats for personal use and commercial reasons.

It is now accepted that the kiln was in operation during the twelfth and thirteenth centuries and pottery assemblages are dateable from *c.*1120 to *c.*1250.[10] It is thought that the kilns ceased to make pottery in the mid-thirteenth century when they were replaced by wheel-thrown ware made in Bristol at Redcliffe Hill and other Bristol sites where waste sherds have been found. Medieval-style pottery of this type was made in Bristol until the early sixteenth century. The presence of large numbers of Ham Green sherds in domestic waste from more recent periods does not mean that Ham Green Ware was still being made, but that these are old residual sherds caught up in later deposits. It is to be expected that brittle pots broke relatively easily, especially when used in cooking processes, and were readily discarded in some quantity. Since the identification of Ham Green Ware and the establishment of its period of manufacture, it has become a great help to the dating of archaeological deposits.

taken the few hundred yards to the cliffs of Hung Road and lowered directly into the holds of vessels anchored there, or transported down the hill the few hundred metres to vessels lying in the mud at the inlets of Pill, or Chapel Pill, along with the products of the kilns at Pill. No doubt both situations were possible but given the small size of vessels at the time, there is no reason why Hung Road, rather than

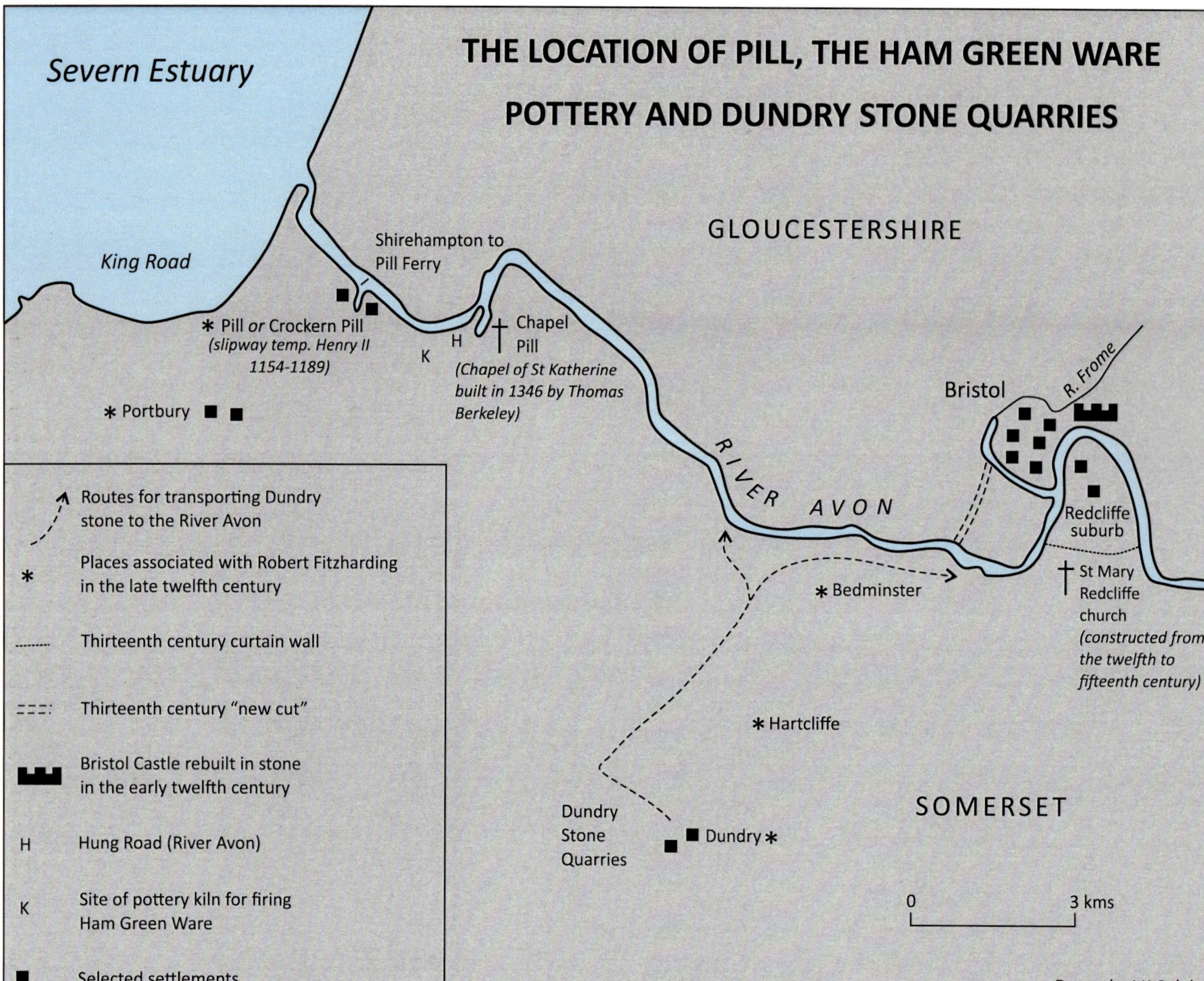

Illustration 1.2: Aspects of the twelfth and thirteenth century medieval landscape of north Somerset and south Gloucestershire including the locations of the Ham Green kiln and Dundry stone quarries (Philip Ashford, 2017)

It is clear from the distribution of finds outlined by Barton, that the pottery was transported by boats and ships, since many of the locations are coastal or riverine. Barton wrote that the market for the pottery was 'limited to the Severn traffic and byway rivers'.[11] In view of the location of the Ham Green kiln, it might reasonably be asked whether the pottery was

the Pills, was the favoured location. On the basis that throughout parts of the west of Britain and Ireland, several types of early medieval pottery are found associated with Ham Green Ware including on sites in Bristol, Alan Vince has argued that ships were loaded with all types of traded pottery in the Bristol itself.[12]

Vince, an expert on the medieval pottery of the Severn basin, does not take into account any maritime understanding of the historical importance of Hung Road, Pill or King Road as locations where freighted ships naturally waited for tides, and sometimes weeks for winds, as shown in several chapters in this series of volumes on the maritime history of Somerset. Thus, it is argued here, that whilst some Ham Green ware might have been loaded onto vessels in Bristol, there was ample opportunity to take on supplies, including Ham Green Ware, for use by merchants, or for trading, at Pill itself.[13] Indeed, Pill had some importance at the time, there being a ferry crossing and a slip present in the late twelfth century.[14] The general consensus amongst archaeologists is that pottery, including Ham Green Ware was never shipped as the only consignment on a vessel. Boats and ships carrying other marketable goods, military supplies or people would often have pottery loaded as well, either for the use of the people aboard or as additional cargo to be traded once the destination was reached.[15] Perhaps the pottery was stowed in baskets, or sacks, and packed in straw in an attempt to minimise breakages. (See illustration 1.4)

The quantity of sherds found at sites indicates the prolific business of the early medieval Pill potters. By 1984 Vince could say that at various sites in Chepstow, Ham Green Ware accounted for between 45% and 83% of all twelfth century pottery sherds found. Vince stated that though quantatively unimportant outside the Severn, Avon and Wye valleys, significant finds of Ham Green Ware had been discovered along the south coast of Wales and in south-east Ireland, all places accessible by boat, and lesser finds had been identified in east and north-east Wiltshire.[16] The current distribution of finds, illustration 1.22, is a significant development from the early map drawn by Barton in the 1960s and Vince's assess-ment of the distribution in the early 1980s. The details of the publications that relate to these finds are found in the appendices. Clearly, the evidence of a wide distribution of Ham Green Ware has much to say about the development of the port of Bristol and the reach of Bristol merchants in the twelfth and thirteenth centuries. This in itself should further stimulate research into the outgoing and incoming goods to and from Bristol during that period.

Illustration 1.3: A Ham Green Ware 'hunting jug' from an excavation at Peter Street, Bristol; the handle is missing. (© Bristol Museum and Art Gallery, Q1844)

Current understanding of the spread of Ham Green Ware and vessels used in its transportation

Much Ham Green Ware consists of jugs for decanting or pouring liquids perhaps mainly wine. Wine rather than beer was the preferred drink of the Normans, and, just like the activity of tea drinking requires a teapot, the drinking of wine needs a jug, a container to transfer the wine from the barrel, or tun, to the table where it can be poured into drinking cups. Thus, the spread of Norman culture during the twelfth and thirteenth centuries in the Great Britain and Ireland and the associated growth of the wine trade were important factors in the demand for jugs from the Ham Green Ware. Also, from the maritime perspective, the presence of pottery kilns explains why Pill was such a significant settlement during that period. However, jugs have been found on lower status sites where wine may not have been drunk, so their use may have been adopted by people more likely to drink beer.[17]

There appears to have been a steady spread of traded Ham Green Ware from about 1120. Sherds of Ham Green Ware found in the lower Severn valley, at Chepstow and Lydney for example, derived from the mid to late twelfth centuries, whilst some sherds from Bristol, dated by Mike Ponsford using dendrochronology, are from 1140 or earlier. This latter dating of sherds, found at Dundas Wharf, Bristol is crucial for the current understanding of an early date when the kiln at Ham Green functioned. Finds further afield, in Gloucester and Hereford, for example, are in contexts where the pottery was clearly in use in the mid thirteenth century.[18] Quite probably, therefore, new sales of the pottery occurred through recommendation by satisfied customers at increasing distances from Pill, as well as from merchants having stocks available for sale at local fairs and markets, thus extending the sphere of influence of the Pill potters.

The distribution maps of Ham Green Ware illustrating this chapter, pose the question as to the type of vessels that may have called at Pill to load the ware to be taken onwards to its destination. Bearing in mind pottery was probably never the sole cargo but part of more important consignments; the transport of pottery would therefore echo general trade by boat throughout the region. For example, Ham Green Ware may well have been moved as far as Bath in small river boats designed solely for work on the Avon. This would have avoided expensive transhipment to smaller craft at other locations. However, by 1276 there were sufficient weirs on the Avon between Bristol and Bath to stimulate an inquiry into these impediments to navigation; navigation by implication having occurred more easily in previous generations.[19] Though not date specific, it appears that riverine trade to and from Bath in the thirteenth century included the transportation of wine, wax, salt, wool, skins and cloth.[20] Pottery taken up the Severn to Worcester, or up the Wye to Hereford, may have been taken first in medieval non-decked trows, capable of navigating the turbulent waters of the Severn Estuary and the upper reaches of the Bristol Channel. Especially in the twelfth century, these vessels may well have looked a little similar to the double-ended clinker built vessels so favoured by the Viking and Norman traders of the time.[21] In the thirteenth century, trading vessels operating in the open waters would have been very similar to the 14 metre long, iron-ore and grain carrying Magor Pill vessel which was built in 1239-1240 and found in the 1990s.[22] Such vessels may have delivered Ham Green Ware to Berkeley and nearby Hill Flats, where sherds have recently been found.[23] The sherds found at Hill Flats may be associated with a small medieval landing place or quay and not necessarily a settlement. With regard to the movements of goods to the upper Severn (to the north of Worcester), barge traffic is recorded in 1198.[24] The free movement of boats and merchandise along the Severn was such an important matter in the first half of the thirteenth century that when there were issues between traders of Worcester and Gloucester, or Gloucester and Bristol, as there were in 1233 and 1241 for example, matters quickly came to the attention of the King to help resolve the situation.[25]

Similar vessels to the Magor Pill vessel would have taken goods to Uphill and Bridgwater. Perhaps pottery was off-loaded into smaller river craft for carriage over the final miles to its point of unloading. For example by the thirteenth century, inland from Uphill, along the Axe, there were a number of landing places fit for non-decked river vessels, at Bleadney, Northlode near Wedmore, Clewer and Hyth near Cheddar, Brinscombe, Axbridge, Lower Weare, Rackley and Rooksbridge, suggesting the amount of waterborne traffic was not inconsiderable.[26] The charter allowing the Bishop of

Illustration 1.4: An artist's reconstruction of a vessel taking on Ham Green Ware, as part of a cargo, at Pill. The scenario illustrated is a vessel, having come down the Avon from Bristol loaded with wine in 1250, has beached in order to take on local produce, Ham Green Ware and sheep, prior to sailing to Steep Holm, Bridgwater or further afield to South Wales. The location of the Ham Green kiln is illustrated by the twist of smoke rising above the trees in the central background. The vessel is modelled on artist's reconstructions of the recently discovered, mid thirteenth century, Magor Pill vessel. (Christine Molan, 2016)

Bath, who, at the time was Reginald Fitz Jocelin, to form the borough and port of Rackley, to the west of Axbridge was granted in 1189.[27] Finds of Ham Green Ware have been made at Bleadon, near Rackley, only a short distance from the Axe.[28] After the death in 1242 of another Jocelin, a subsequent Bishop of Wells, there was a two-year vacancy of the see between 1242 and 1244. Michael, abbot of Glastonbury seemed to take control over matters regarding navigation on the Axe between Rackley and Glastonbury at this point; in the early 1240s, his boats were used to break three fisheries.[29] Wooden fish traps 'blighted river transport' and their removal was foreseen in the Magna Carta of 1215.[30] Fisheries on the Axe affected the passage of vessels, and part of the economy of Glastonbury Abbey lands depended on riverine transport.

This event of clearing navigation obstacles in the Axe in the early 1240s has an interesting context. Jocelin had been Bishop of Bath since 1206. He had been a supporter of King John but sided with the Archbishop and Barons during the period of negotiations for Magna Carta, becoming one of the signatories. Clause 33 of Magna Carta orders the removal of fish traps from all English rivers. Jocelin would have known this but somehow did not, or was not able to have the Axe traps removed. After the death of King John in 1216, Jocelin was one of the ecclesiastical anointers of King Henry the Third in Gloucester Cathedral and helped the King restore the Crown's possessions. Henry updated and re-issued Magna Carta throughout his reign.[31] Yet the fish traps were built on the Axe. It is possible that the traps on the Axe and the Avon weir were erected after Jocelin had died and during the See inter-regnum of 1242-1244. Thus it fell to the Abbott of Glastonbury to remove the ones on the Axe and an Abbott of Keynsham was involved in the removal of the weir on the Avon in 1248.[32]

It is known that in the 1230s and 1240s, a tenant of the abbot, William Aurifaber, took care of the Abbott of Glastonbury's boats on rivers between Clewer, Mark and Glastonbury. During the 1250s, boats were used to transport corn along the Brue from the Meare area to the Abbot of Glastonbury's granaries, already and ancient river vessel route, the same waterway as was used by John of Glastonbury in 1091 to transport the bones of St Benignus from Mere to Glastonbury.[33] Furthermore, in a legal action of 1276 regarding the Abbot of Glastonbury's navigation rights on the Axe, it was recorded that boats commonly transported corn, stone and lime from near Cheddar to Glastonbury.[34] Rivers upstream of Glastonbury appear also to have been navigable. In the early thirteenth century Robert Malerbe, a tenant of the Abbot of Glastonbury was responsible for the transfer of the abbot's wine, made from local grapes, by boat, from Pilton to Glastonbury, as well as transporting the abbot and his cook or hunstsman and others in a boat capable of carrying eight people.[35] Pottery, though essential, remained an 'invisible' commodity because of its probable cheapness and lack of volume, and thus its transport is not mentioned in surviving texts but, unsurprisingly, Ham Green Ware is found at Glastonbury Abbey itself.[36] Illustration 1.22 shows a number of Ham Green find locations along the navigable length of the Axe. Perhaps the find of Ham Green Ware sherds at Brent Knoll, was associated with a medieval wharf, the remains of which have been found nearby.[37]

Illustration 1.5: The mouth of the River Axe at Uphill with Black Rock in the middle ground. Medieval cargoes from Bristol, probably including Dundry stone and Ham Green Ware would have passed this side of Black Rock. (Elliot Lowe, 2014)

Similarly, Magor Pill type vessels could have taken Ham Green Ware to the River Parrett to be distributed in the mid Somerset basin along the Parrett and Tone. There have been finds of Ham Green Ware at the aptly named The Old Ship Inn at Combwich,[38] multiple finds in Bridgwater including in the castle moat, Eastover and at the Friary,[39] as well as further up-river at Langport.[40] The construction of Bridgwater castle, St John's Hospital at the eastern end of Eastover, and Friary commenced in the early decades of the thirteenth century under the authority of the wealthy justice and baron, William Brewer (d.

1226) and his son, also William.[41] The importance of these Bridgwater buildings, the new bridge, and the growing town at that time would have increasingly caused ships to berth at the castle on the Parrett, and pottery, along with other goods, unloaded. The Langport find may well be associated with the medieval landing place at Stathe, four miles downstream of Langport mentioned in 1233.[42] The question arises as to whether goods including pottery were transhipped at Combwich or Bridgwater into specialised Parrett river craft. The answer is most probably yes, especially after the construction of Bridgwater's bridge in the very early thirteenth century. Also it is known that in 1280, the burgesses of Bridgwater argued that they had enjoyed the right of towing their boats (presumably by horse) upriver from Bridgwater to Langport 'from time immemorial'.[43] This certainly implies river craft working the Parrett south of Bridgwater rather than small sea-going craft working upriver as they may have sometimes done on spring tides in the twelfth century. However, passage of boats may well have been impeded by a weir constructed by William Brewer in the 1220s, presumably higher up the Parrett, since it prejudiced Somerton and Ilchester.[44]

Further evidence of the busyness of river transportation on the Parrett in the thirteenth century is the fact that at least six men drowned from boats in the river in 1242-43 in five or six separate incidents ranging from near the mouth to Langport. There were two further drownings from boats on the Tone near North Petherton when there were five passengers aboard, and another at Creech St Michael.[45] Some of the vessels from which people drowned on the Parrett and Tone may well have been used in the daily shipment in winter months of brushwood to Athelney Abbey on the Tone prior to 1250,[46] or in the Ham Hill stone carrying trade from 1245to 1249 when boats were used to carry the stone to Ruishton (on the Tone) from Ham Hill (on the Parrett) for construction work at Taunton Castle.[47] Ham Hill stone, from a quarry near Montacute was used extensively in church building in central Somerset. The overall distribution of churches using this stone is directly linked to the location of the Parrett and its navigable tributaries.[48] Thus, any Ham Hill stone used for church building in the twelfth and thirteenth centuries in central Somerset is quite likely to have been transported by river boat for as much of the journey as possible. Passengers were also conveyed on these rivers. For example, probably for many years prior to the late 1260s, there being a manorial duty to convey, by boat, officials from Athelney on the Tone, past Stathe and Langport on the Parrett to Ilchester at the times when justices were meeting.[49]

Illustration 1.6: Medieval seal of the reeves of Bridgwater, perhaps depicting a vessel similar to that of the Magor Pill vessel (T. Dilks, *Bridgwater borough archives 1200-1377*, S.R.S. 48 (1933), frontispiece)

Early thirteenth century Bridgwater craft and mariners were familiar with sailing across the Bristol Channel to Wales, to King Road and onwards up the Severn and back. These could have called at Pill and picked up pottery to bring back to Combwich or Bridgwater. Examples of other journeys from Bridgwater include one in 1233 when lead and timber from Bridgwater was transported up the 'Sabrina' (River Severn) to Tewkesbury.[50] Furthermore, prior to 1242, William Marsh of Huntspill's ship was impounded in Bristol. Gloucester authorities are also mentioned in the proceedings which commanded that the ship be released from Bristol and returned to Jordan Marsh, William's son, at Huntspill.[51] Bridgwater or Welsh ships brought millstones to Bridgwater's quay, often for use in the Bishop of Winchester's mills at Taunton. There are records of a Welsh stone arriving in Taunton in 1231-32 and in the 1250s Bridgwater is mentioned as the regular conduit of imported Welsh stones.[52] Whatever the informed speculation, it is clear that the distribution of Ham Green finds in Somerset is closely related to the vibrantly functioning inland waterways of the period, within which, the importance of Axbridge and Bridgwater as trans-shipment points must not be underestimated. Archaeological support for this latter statement derives from the fact that quantities of Ham Green Ware found in Somerset archaeological excavations decrease with increased distance from the riverine re-distribution points of Axbridge and Bridgwater.[53]

Ham Green Ware was also taken by sea-going vessels to Lundy, off the north Devon coast, and to the Isles of Scilly. In Barton's original article on Ham Green Ware, finds on Lundy were mentioned. Further finds in 'Pig's Paradise' on the Island have also been recorded.[54] Given that Lundy is often cast as a haunt of pirates and outcasts, the question arises as to what high status building or people living there made the importation of Ham Green Ware useful. It is tempting to associate the find with the outlawed Marisco family, who had been in conflict with the crown since 1155. They had plundered ships for some time and were a significant nuisance in the Bristol Channel. Then, in the 1230s they used the island to try and avoid being brought to justice for the murder of a minor Government official. The family may have been involved in a plot against King Henry the Third in 1238 who ordered an attack against the island and the Marisco fortified house at Bulls' Paradise in 1242; William de Marisco was captured and taken to London where he was hung.[55] Then, between 1242 and 1244, Henry ordered the building of a tower and curtain wall on the Island, and a constable, Richard de Especheleg, was appointed to manage the defence of the island.[56] Also, Bristol and Bridgwater authorities were charged with others, in 1242, with the safekeeping of the island.[57] All of which meant dozens of voyages of men and materials being shipped to the island.

Ham Green Ware was first identified on the small island of St Helen's, part of the Isles of Scilly, soon after the pottery was so named in the early 1960s, having been excavated in the late 1950s.[58] More recently Ham Green sherds have been found on the Island of Tresco and in the channel between Tresco and Bryher. The interpretation of the many pottery sherds found in the Tresco Channel is that two events where pottery was lost are involved: first an earlier twelfth century one where sherds from Ham Green, Normandy and western France were lost overboard; second a later thirteenth/early fourteenth century one where a large collection of south-western French pottery from the Saintonge was also lost overboard, probably as one event but not necessarily derived from a shipwreck. Both sherd groups were probably from ships bound for Wales and Ireland as an adjunct to the Gascon wine trade. It is notable that more Ham Green Ware has been found in the Scillies than any other English pottery type of the period.[59]

Vessels sailing from Pill past Devon and Cornwall to the Isles of Scilly may well have traded at Minehead, Ilfracombe, Barnstaple, Padstow and St Ives to name but a few locations, but there does not appear to be much Ham Green Ware to be found from west Somerset to Land's End. One explanation for this is that Devon wares were the dominant ceramic being traded in the above areas. Ham Green Ware found its greatest markets in areas which were without pitchers and jugs at the time. Having said this, small numbers of pieces of Ham Green Ware have been found on Lundy and at South Molton, Exeter, and in Cornwall.[60] It should be asked whether vessels which took Ham Green Ware from Pill to the Isles of Scilly were at their final destination, or on a longer passage to south-west France, or Iberia, in order to fetch wine. The answer is likely to have been that ships were breaking a longer journey coasting from the safety of one port to another. If this was the case, a further question is why Ham Green Ware has not turned up in archaeological excavations in the continental medieval ports like it has in the Isles of Scilly anchorage? The answer probably lies in the fact that the pottery was not traded to France and Spain as the areas were already well provided with good ceramics, so much so that French pottery was traded to England in competition with English pottery. Sherds of Ham Green Ware that might have been found by continental archaeologists have either not been recognised or were not present. English archaeologists, including Ken Barton, who have studied French pottery in depth, have so far not identified Ham Green Ware among collections of French pottery.[61] By the end of the Ham Green period, circa 1250, any pottery, whether taken on-board vessels at Bristol or Pill, about to trade as far as the Scillies, or onwards to France and Spain may well have been stowed in decked cogs which were coming into service at that time, and would have been a familiar sight anchored in Hung Road.[62]

Ireland

Considerable amounts of Ham Green Ware have been found in Ireland. See illustration 1.7. It is well known that Bristol had a trade with Ireland in the eleventh century, particularly with Dublin which was one of the main entrepots. The Norman 'invasion' of Ireland may well have been a further stimulus to trade and the spread of the use of Ham Green Ware. In 1171, King Henry the Second and his armies sailed from Bristol to Waterford and brought Leinster and Dublin under the control of the English crown. It is quite likely that elements of Ham Green Ware were taken to Ireland in this great expedition, as tens or even hundreds of vessels were provisioned at locations that must have included positions along the Avon from Bristol to Pill and in King Road. Furthermore, in 1172, Henry the Second granted the citizens of Bristol rights to inhabit Dublin and many Bristolians took this opportunity.[63] In the archives of the city of Dublin the names of citizens show that men from the Bridgwater area also moved there in the twelfth and thirteenth centuries, indicating a further Bridgwater maritime link of the time. Men such as Thomas of Quantock, Roger of Combwich, Walter of Petherton and John of Taunton are mentioned.[64] In fact 101 migrants from Somerset moved to Ireland, mainly to Dublin, between 1190 and 1265. Ten were from coastal towns such as Dunster and Clevedon, nine from settlements along the Parrett including Combwich and Bridgwater, nine from along the Axe and 24 from along the Avon including 18 from Bath. In addition, 20 came from Taunton which provided more migrants than any other Somerset settlement. In comparison 149 migrants moved from Bristol.[65] These migrations may well have increased the quantity of Ham Green Ware in use in the settlement. Moreover, the design of Ham Green Ware was so popular in Dublin that local potters, possibly from the Bristol area, quickly started to produce similar forms.[66] Such was the adoption rate of Ham Green Ware that Irish archaeologists like to quote the line that 'more sherds of Ham Green ware have been discovered in Ireland than in England'.[67]

Among the most considerable concentrations of the pottery in Ireland are those from the port towns of Waterford and Cork, two of the main ports of entry for traded goods. During archaeological excavations in Waterford in the 1970s, Ham Green Ware accounted for 46% of all medieval pottery found.[68] Since production stopped in the mid thirteenth century the concentration must be higher for the period 1100-1250. Ham Green Ware began to appear in Waterford in the second quarter of the twelfth century and became widespread in the town by 1150.[69] Excavations at Cork during the 1970s, found that 40% of medieval pottery finds were of Ham Green Ware.[70] Similarly to Waterford, Ham Green Ware seems to have arrived there by the mid twelfth century.[71] With reference to Dublin, at a particularly significant excavation a Wood Quay, 4.5% of over a million pottery sherds found were of Ham Green Ware.[72] This is a lower percentage than in Waterford and Cork, possibly indicating that Dublin's own potters, combined with a wider number of locations that traded with Dublin, had an influence on the relative importance of Ham Green Ware in that settlement. Pottery would have been moved inland along the navigable rivers in Ireland, just as it would have been in the Severn Basin and along Somerset's navigable rivers. The Ham Green Ware found in Bective Abbey and Trim may well have been taken up the Boyne from Drogheda. In 1194 a charter stated that the burgesses of Drogheda enjoyed free passage upriver to the bridge at Trim.[73] Likewise Ham Green Ware sherds found in excavations at Kilkenny may well have been transported along the navigable River Nore.[74] All this evidences the busy nature of trade from the River

Illustration 1.7: Ham Green Ware jug with distinct exterior design. (© Bristol Museum and Art Gallery, G289)

Illustration 1.8 (opposite): The distribution of mainly thirteenth-century Ham Green Ware finds in Ireland. Sources, references relating to Ireland and appendices 1 and 2. (Philip Ashford)

THE DISTRIBUTION OF HAM GREEN FINDS IN IRELAND

Avon in ceramic products from the Pill area, something that contributed toward the development of the regional economy from 1120-1250.

Trade in Dundry stone

Interestingly, another traceable twelfth and thirteenth century export from Somerset is Dundry stone, a Jurassic limestone, used in Bristol's thirteenth century defensive walls and St Mary Redcliffe Church which was within Somerset at the time. The stone was used for church building, especially between the Axe and the Yeo. Stone was shipped up the Axe and off-loaded at Rackley for use in the construction of Compton Bishop church, consecrated by Bishop Jocelin in 1236.[75] Dundry stone was also used for some of the carvings on the west front of Wells Cathedral, dated to 1235-1243, also built, of course, under the supervision of Bishop Jocelin.[76] The use of Dundry stone in Glastonbury Abbey, the 'great church' of which was completed about 1245, appears to date from an initial 'post fire' stage of 1184-1189. Other fire damaged Dundry stone, which has been found is interpreted as having been part of the pre 1184 Abbey construction.

Illustration 1.9: Walling from the inner north porch of St Mary Redcliffe constructed of Dundry stone with Blue lias columns. This is the oldest part of St Mary Redcliffe and was constructed *c.*1185. (Philip Ashford, 2016)

Illustration 1.10: The arch to the inner north porch at St Mary Redcliffe constructed of Dundry stone in the twelfth and thirteenth centuries. (Philip Ashford, 2016)

Like Ham Green Ware, there is the question as to whether the stone was purposefully traded. It could well have been used as ballast and off-loaded along the Axe in Somerset, or at the coast and riverine landing places in southern Wales or Ireland, from where it was put to other use.[77] Overall, the stone is also found in south-east Ireland with almost the same distribution as Ham Green Ware, a distribution first explored by D. Waterman in 1970.[78] The distribution stretches from Drogheda in the north to Cork in the south at all the usual coastal ports including Waterford and Youghal. Inland finds are, of course along the course of the navigable

Illustration 1.15: Stone quarrying along the River Avon, as it happens on the Gloucestershire bank. The tide is ebbing and a number of small vessels are depicted sailing downriver towards Pill. (J.C. Ibbetson, *A picturesque guide to Bath, Bristol, Hot-wells and the River Avon* (London, 1793), 184)

Reasons for maritime Ham Green Ware trade leading to Pill's importance

There seems to be four reasons why Ham Green Ware was taken onto boats and ships at Pill. First, both crew and passengers needed bowls and other pottery to eat and drink from whilst on board. If ware broke on the journey it would have been thrown overboard, so the bed of the Bristol Channel must be littered with it. If it broke whilst in port, archaeological excavations at quaysides have and will discover it, such those as Cardiff, Cork and Dublin.[90] Secondly, merchants, their servants, retainers and families on the move to, whether to Ireland, Gascony, Iberia or Iceland, may have owned and stowed Ham Green Ware for their new life, or bought it from the quayside when it arrived. When it broke, it would have been discarded, and so it has been found in the middens of their medieval merchant quarter residences abroad, within a hundred metres or so from the quayside in Cardiff, Swansea, Dublin and Drogheda for example.[91] Of course, it would not just have been those merchants which would have been the owners and users of Ham Green Ware sherds found at these or similar locations. Perhaps it is only a matter of time before Ham Green finds are confirmed in south-west France, northern Spain, Portugal and Iceland,[92] all locations in the sphere of Bristol's trade at the time.

Thirdly, quantities of Ham Green Ware would have been bought as un-customable goods, stowed on vessels and traded in the market towns, either along the rivers entering into the Severn estuary and the Bristol Channel coast, or in nearby market towns a short distance from landing places.[93] This would also apply to pottery taken to trade fairs in Ireland or continental ports. The discarded waste from this trade might be more widely distributed, not just in port towns but in or around the homes of people who came either to the quayside or to market to buy pottery.[94] With reference to this type of trade, one of the uses of Ham Green jugs was to for wine, often in ecclesiastical situations, not only in monasteries but also in bishops' palaces. Bristol's wine trade expanded in the thirteenth century. Named Gascon wine merchants were in Bristol in 1236 but one of the most significant importers in the 1250s was the Bishop of Worcester.[95] Furthermore, buildings belonging to Tintern Abbey, Monmouthshire, next to the Wye were used as warehouses for storing wine on its way to Monmouth Castle in 1258.[96] Unsurprisingly therefore, sherds of Ham Green jugs have been found in Worcester and at other ecclesiastical settings such as Tintern Abbey and around the Bishop's Palace in Wells.[97] In October 1207, the constable of Bristol was commanded to have two tuns of wine carried to a house of Jocelin, 'Bishop of Bath' in Bath itself.[98] This movement undoubtedly necessitated the use of boats. Then, in 1224 and 1225 Jocelin was allowed to purchase, in total, 10 tuns of wine out of King Henry the Third's wine stock in Bristol.[99] No doubt it too was moved east along the Avon to Bath for its purchaser.[100] Amongst many other markets, is clear that merchants of Ham Green Ware found opportunities for sale wherever there were Christian communities, be they Bishops' palaces, abbeys, friaries or chapels, throughout the south-west of England, Wales and also further afield in Chester and Kells, Ireland, for example.[101] It is not unlikely that some of the largest orders at Pill for Ham Green Ware for use in England were placed directly by church officials or their favoured merchants. The pottery may well have been transported on the same vessels which moved wine from Bristol to its regional ecclesiastical destinations along the Rivers Severn, Wye and Axe.

The development of the reach of Ham Green Ware came at the same time as the expansion of the influence of the Norman Christian church onto isolated Islands in the Bristol Channel and off Ireland where there had been Celtic Christian activity. For example, St Gildas is thought to have lived on Steep Holm in the sixth century and St Elidius on St Helens, Scilly Isles during the eighth century. One of the most unique Christian communities, dating from the sixth century, possibly founded by St Fionan, lived on the isolated island of Skellig Michael off County Kerry, Ireland. The later Priory of St Michael seems to have existed on Steep Holm from about the 1190s, but most of the brethren were moved off in about 1260. A chapel on St Helens, Scilly was enlarged in the Norman period and in the mid twelfth century given to Tavistock Abbey, after which pilgrimages to St Helens increased in the medieval period. The Skellig Michael church was enlarged sometime in the twelfth century but the community moved to the mainland in the late twelfth century. However, some sort of monastic community seems to have remained, connected to Ballinskelligs Abbey. In all three cases it seems that the small Christian communities had been and were the only permanent residents on the islands for some time. Ham Green Ware sherds, of the same time period as the Norman Christian expansion, have been found in association with the ruins of the ecclesiastical buildings or homes of the brethren at all three locations illustrating the spread of the pottery and the Norman influence on the Christian communities. It is but a small and logical leap of imagination to visualise the ships that brought supplies, including wine, and pottery from Pill to these Christian maritime locations.[102] Archaeological investigations have revealed that some of the rooves of Steep Holm Priory were constructed of Pennant sandstone,[103] Steep Holm itself being entirely Carboniferous limestone. The Pennant sandstone is likely to have been brought in vessels from south Wales, or the Bristol area, where it is found overlying coal measures. It might have arrived as ballast and been fashioned into stone tiles on Steep Holm.

Illustration 1.16: Steep Holm with the northern cliffs of Brean Down in the foreground. St Michael's Priory would have been visible on the skyline of Steep Holm in the twelfth and thirteenth century in weather conditions such as these. (Elliot Lowe, 2014)

Illustration 1.17: Some Ham Green sherds found at excavations near the summit of Steep Holm, near the site of St Michael's Priory, found by archaeologists in 2103 and 2014. (Garry Holden Photographics, 2015)

Fourthly, and mainly with respect to the English Marches, Wales and Ireland, Ham Green Ware would have been loaded onto vessels provisioning troops serving the English crown. Subsequently it would have made its way to castles and strong points in the disputed territories. Thus, Pill's pottery is often found at sites in and around the Norman castles of the Principality and in Ireland.[104] Even a cursory glance at Illustration 1.22 shows the cluster of medieval castles in west Wales, built to protect Anglo-Norman interests in Pembrokeshire, at which Ham Green Ware has been found. Many of the castles could be supplied by sea. Was Ham Green Ware aboard the vessel from Bristol that was ordered to carry wheat, barley oats and rye, cross-bow bolts and armour from Bristol to Carmarthen in 1233?[105] With respect to the English Marches, significant events took place in 1228 and 1232-34 which saw King Henry the Third campaigning against Welsh nobles and other Barons. In 1228 the action was centred around Montgomery and in 1233 near Monmouth.[106] In order to supply the Court and the King's administration in 1228, order after order came through to Bristol merchants to move with haste and in 'good barges' well over 100 tuns of mainly Gascon wine variously from Bristol to Hereford, Worcester and Monmouth. In 1232 large amounts were moved to Worcester and Gloucester, in 1233 30 tuns of Gascon and Anjou wine were moved from Bristol to Gloucester with some of it being re-located to Hereford, and in 1237 wine was moved from Bristol to Gloucester, Tewkesbury, Worcester and Kidderminster on the Severn and to Hereford on the Wye.[107] Large numbers of tun carrying ships and barges would have passed Pill on their journeys up the Usk, Wye and Severn, equally being able to pick up Ham Green jugs for dispensing wine. Given that some archaeologists maintain that most thirteenth century Ham Green Ware was used at high status locations, what higher status was there than the King's court? Thus, the hypothesis here is, that a significant amount of the current distribution of Somerset's Ham Green Ware from Pill, found in archaeological excavations in the Welsh Marches, are directly connected to wine drinking associated with King Henry the Third's campaigns of the 1230s.

Illustration 1.18: Ham Green Jug from the well at Bristol Castle. (© Bristol Museum and Art Gallery, G2634)

Having attempted to explain the distribution of Ham Green Ware and illustrate the distribution using maps, it is important to understand certain caveats before too many assertions are made. The distributions are squewed towards the locations where archaeologists have excavated. Funding is often availably to investigate castles and Christian sites and, thus, pottery is found at these types of location. It is important to realise that the ware is also

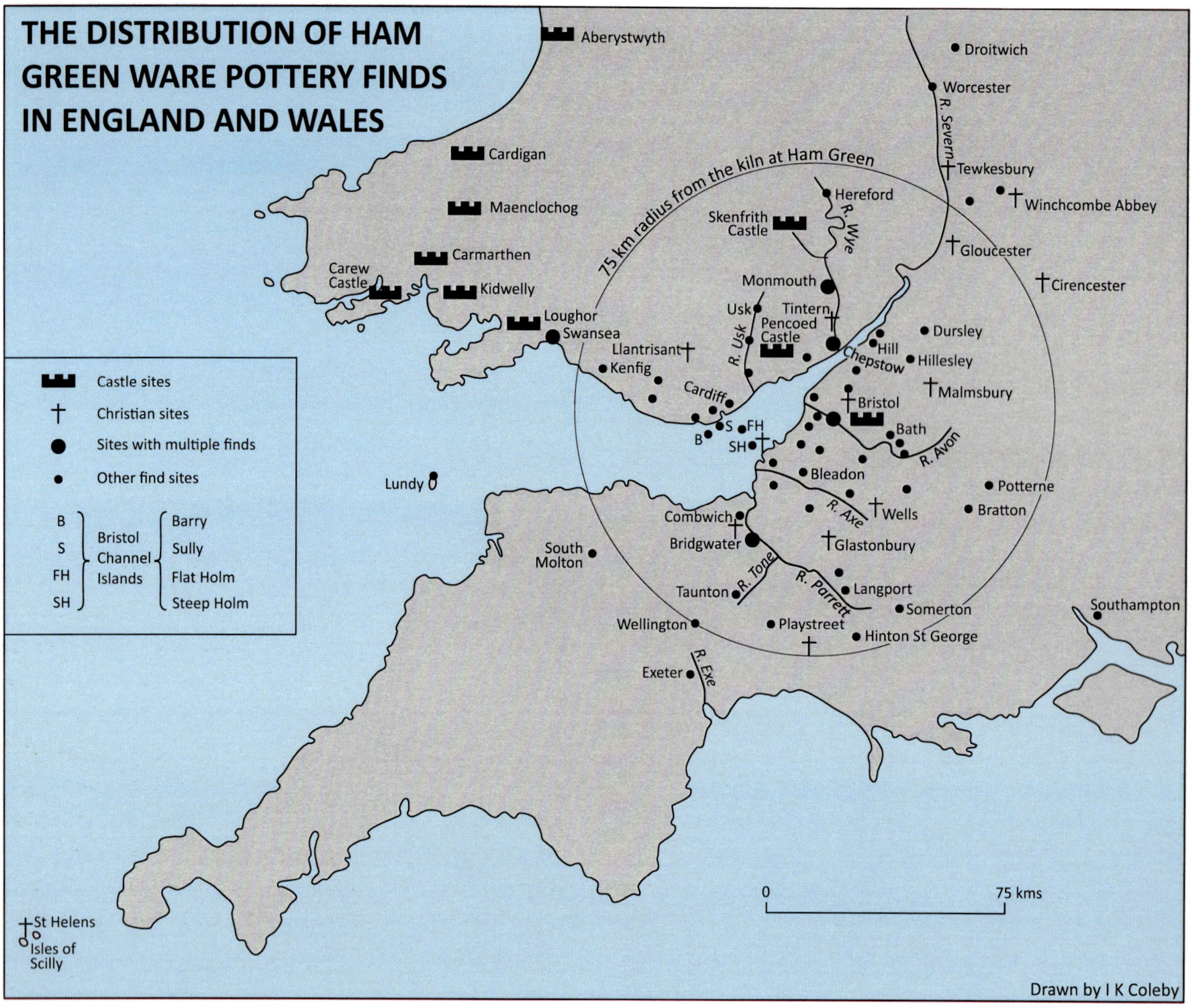

Illustration 1.19: The distribution of Ham Green Ware finds in England and Wales, sources, references relating to England and Wales and appendices 1 and 2. (Author)

found in rural or poorer domestic situations at medieval sites within Ham Green's distribution zone. There is a possibility that if more low class village locations are excavated, the impression might be that the ware was most commonly used in those lower class locations.

Furthermore, whilst it is clear that the distribution mirrors many of the maritime trade routes, meaning the pottery is a reflection of shipping at the time, the river valleys and the coastal plains were the main locations of human habitation, so the distribution of pottery reflects the distribution of people.[108] Having pointed this out, it is still abundantly clear that much of the Ham Green Ware, because of the location of the kilns at Ham Green and at Pill, at a strategic point in the region's maritime network, reached its point of usage via boats and ships operating in coastal and riverine situations.[109]

The end of a Somerset riverine pottery

A question remains as to why the Ham Green kiln closed down in the early to mid-thirteenth century and why, therefore, the importance and influence of Pill and its potters from this corner of Somerset declined. It is known that the ware was replaced by other Bristol wares including Redcliffe Ware.[110] But what caused this change? It was not the establishment of fairs in Bristol which led to the demise of pottery production at Ham Green. For example, the formalities of causing the income from the established St James's Fair, held in a churchyard to the south of St James's Priory, to go to that Priory, was completed *c.*1181, nearly a century before the demise of Ham Green Ware.[111] However, given the regional and international importance of Bristol, even at this juncture, it is not unlikely that the civic power of

Bristol authorities and its merchant guilds wanted pottery production inside the walls of Bristol, within the suburb of Redcliffe as it turned out. This allowed them to exercise more control over mercantile money making amongst the powerful. During the period of Ham Green production at Pill, 1120-*c.*1250 the merchants and civic authorities of Bristol were accumulating more power: Bristol's first charter of 1163 confirmed their existing privileges but enhanced trading and travel permits. In 1225 they gained greater control over town revenues and, during the late thirteenth century and very early fourteenth century, there was an intense, costly and bloody struggle over increasing their powers, including jurisdiction over the suburb of Redcliffe.[112] It is not unlikely that, during the later thirteenth century, some of the Pill potters moved to Bristol, and especially to Redcliffe, bringing their glazing and firing skills into the Bristol suburb, even if their hand throwing skills were marginalised by the improved technology of wheel thrown pottery.[113] Thus, the dynamic business of the rural Ham Green kiln at Pill faded in the face of the increasing power of the growing power of Bristol over the region.

Conclusion

The significant amount of Ham Green Ware that has now been found and its distribution shows the relative importance of Pill, a Somerset village, during the twelfth and thirteenth centuries. It is likely that boats and ships of the period visited and anchored there or nearby taking the opportunity to take on pottery and other provisions; the assertion that vessels were often anchored near Pill for long periods is based on an assumption regarding prevailing winds. Like today and from the eighteenth century when daily wind directions have been recorded, winds were predominantly westerly in the twelfth and thirteenth centuries. Such winds delayed vessels for days and weeks at Pill, so the same must have been true for the earlier vessels that picked up the pottery. Thus, in the late twelfth and early thirteenth century, it is likely that traders based in north Somerset, including Pill, were able to enjoy a fair degree of independence over the sale of Ham Green Ware to passing vessels, perhaps encouraged by Robert Fitzharding. It was not until September 1373 that the bounds of Bristol were officially designated as including the waters of the River Avon past 'Crokernpulle' and as far as Flat Holm and Steep Holm.[114] The growing evidence of the trade in ham Green Ware therefore continues to help change our perception of the role of the settlement of Pill, especially in the context of the history of the port of Bristol. The notion that it was solely a residence for pilots is incorrect. An understanding that it was a provisioning station for innumerable vessels, a foot passenger ferry port and a place of residence for those awaiting a vessel is now much clearer.[115] Having said this, the distribution of the two Somerset exports, Ham Green Ware and Dundry stone, in the early medieval period, would not have been so extensive if Bristol's mercantile and shipping activities had not been as developed as they were.

Ham Green Ware has now been found at considerable density within a 75 km radius of Ham Green, Pill, in the counties of Monmouthshire, Gloucestershire and Somerset. The distribution within this area shows that many of the find sites are associated with coastal and riverine trade routes in the twelfth and thirteenth centuries. The later twelfth century saw the commencement of the Anglo-Norman adventure into Ireland with the settlement of Bristol enhancing its trading links with the island. Thirteenth century England saw increases in population and prosperity and Norman domination in west Wales. With respect to the region served by Bristol, the thirteenth century saw an increase in maritime trade, including Dundry stone exports. Wine imports and re-distribution also expanded, especially during King Henry the Third's campaigns in the Welsh Marches in the 1230s. The Anglo-Norman church was expanding its influence in England, Wales and Ireland at the same time. Dundry stone passed Pill in boats and ships on its way to be used in abbeys churches and cathedrals in Somerset, Wales and Ireland. Wine was, and still is, used in the Christian Eucharist and was the beverage of choice in many higher class and ecclesiastical communities. The well positioned kiln at Ham Green in the north Somerset coast, producing cooking pots and wine jugs, amongst other items, was ideally placed to capitalise on these developments, supplying pottery to merchants who moved it from Pill in a variety of craft with a variety of cargos, including stone and wine, in order that it should reach its markets. So, Ham Green Ware rose to regional and international prominence as perhaps the most widely used English ware of the period. The expanding civic and economic muscle of Bristol and its merchants over the same period may have caused the kiln at Ham Green to close down. This in turn would have forced some potters, at least, to move to Bristol's southern suburb about 1250, allowing Redcliffe Ware to become a prominent replacement.[116]

Appendix 1. Academic websites with multiple references to Ham Green Ware sherd finds.

References to Ham Green Ware in the annual reviews of archaeology published by the Society for Medieval Archaeology.
There are more references to Ham Green Ware found in archaeological excavations at this one internet location than any other book or website searched by far. The references are found in the annual articles entitled *Medieval Britain and Ireland* and the years uploaded are from 1956-2005. All the following references are found at http://archaeologydataservice.ac.uk/archives/view/mbi/prev_vols.cfm?CFID=4344&CFTOKEN=AB930D55-D726-4326-A362C0038014EB5C accessed June 2015. Clearly, references to Ham Green Ware do not appear until the mid-1960s after Barton's article was published. The year of publication and the locations where the pottery has been found are as follows.
1965, Bratton, Wilts. 1967, St Oswold's Priory, Gloucester. 1969, Moat House farm Wraxall. 1970, Lewins Mead, Bristol; Upper Wick, Gloucestershire. 1976, Peter Street Bristol, the finds include a jug with a stag hunting scene. 1977, St Bartholomew's hospital, Bristol. 1980, Redcliffe Street, Bristol. 1982, Redcliffe Street Bristol; Pill itself, on the west bank of the stream that becomes Pill harbour. 1983, Lady Lane, Waterford, Ireland. 1984, St James Street, Drogheda; Kilcash, Tipperary; Deanery Gardens, Waterford, all Ireland. 1985, Buchanan's wharf, Bristol, Deanery Gardens, Waterford, Ireland. 1987, Peter Street and Lady Lane, Waterford, Ireland; Carew Castle Dyfed, Wales. 1988, Bristol and Waterford, Ireland. 1989, Main Street, Cashel, Ireland. 1990, St David's church, Naas; Dean Street Kilkenny, both Ireland. 1991, Marlwood Farm, Alveston, South Gloucestershire. 1992, Cathedral Hill, Downpatrick, Ireland. 1994, Bathampton. 1997, Kilkenny City. 1999, Christ Church Lane, Cork; Hannover Street Cork; Turkey Street, Cork; The Victoria Dairy, Monmouth. 2000, Hinton St George, Somerset. 2001, Monkswell Road, Monmouth; Trelech Farm, Trelech, Wales. 2002, Trellech Barns, Trellech; Caerphilly, both Wales. 2003, Kilkenny, Ireland. 2004, Chepstow; Monmouth comprehensive school; Castle Farm Barns, Bishton, Newport; Pencoed Castle, Llanmartin; Llantrisant; Salubrious Place, Swansea; Beechwood House, Sully, all Wales; South Main Street, Cork, Ireland. 2005, St Mary's Street, Monmouth, Wales.
References found on the British Museum Portable Antiquities Scheme where there are details of eleven different finds.
All finds on this site are sent in by amateurs who wish to have their finds checked by experts. Sometimes exact positions are not quoted as the amateurs do not wish others to know where they are finding coins, for example. The website is searchable and is found at https://finds.org.uk/ accessed June 2015.
Finds reported in Bath and North East Somerset, Wraxall, Somerset, Oldbury and other locations in South Gloucestershire, Worcestershire and Shropshire, the latter find awaiting confirmation.
References found at the "Somerset Historic Environment" website.
This website is found at http://webapp1.somerset.gov.uk/her/sop.asp?flash=true accessed June 2015.
12525, Fernhill Farm, Mudgley; 16479, High Ham; 54818, Langport; 57194, Eastover, Bridgwater.

Appendix 2. References to Ham Green finds, by county and country, used for map 2 and 3 but not referenced elsewhere in the chapter. (Sorted by area and date of publication).

Whilst every effort has been made to be thorough with this work, it is inevitable with such a large task that some finds have been missed. I can only apologise to the researchers for the omission of their work, a fault which is entirely mine.

Somerset
The distribution of Ham Green Ware found in Somerset prior to 1987 is mapped in C. Gerrard, Trade and settlement in medieval Somerset, PhD thesis for the University of Bristol, (1987), 165. These find locations are recorded on illustration 1.22

as is the find of Ham Green Ware in Taunton, T. Pearson, 'Medieval and post medieval ceramics' in P. Leach, (ed.), *The archaeology of Taunton: excavations and fieldwork in 1980* (Gloucester, 1984), 78.
Cotswold Archaeology, *Somerton reinforcement main, Somerset: Archaeological watching brief and recording* (Cirencester, 1998), 4, 21.
A. Vince, *The medieval and later pottery from SPA98-9* (Bath) (2002), 3, 8, 14. Found at http://archaeologydataservice.ac.uk/archiveDS/archiveDownload?t=arch-1000-1/dissemination/pdf/AVAC_reports/2002/avac2002085b.pdf accessed July 2015.
A. Vince, *Medieval pottery fabrics at Puxton, Somerset* (2005), 6-7.
S. Rippon, *Landscape, community and colonisation: The North Somerset levels during the first to second millennia A.D.* (2006), 135, 222, 225-6.
S. Milby, *Warleigh water main replacement, Bath and North-East Somerset* (Maperton, 2007), 10.
A. Vince, *Characterisation of medieval pottery fabrics from Evercreech, Somerset* (2008), 1, 21, 25.
Playstreet excavation results (2008), 9-10.
K. Powell 'Excavation of an early medieval site at West Wick, Weston-super-Mare' in *S.A.N.H.S.P.* 152 (2009), 172-4.
R. Austrums, *Geophysical survey Report: Farmborough, Bath and North-East Somerset* (Upton upon Severn, 2011), Appendix 2.
S. Joyce, *Land at Longforth Farm, Wellington* (Cirencester, 2011), 15, 31.
B. Bradbury, *Yatton archaeological research digs* (2012), 7, 11.

Bristol

A. Barber, *Land at castle Park, Bristol: Archaeological evaluation* (Cirencester, 2004), 7, 8, 16, 17.
A. Vince, *Assessment of the medieval pottery from 118-122 Jacob Street Bristol* (2004), 2.
Cotswold Archaeology, *The medieval and later pottery and ceramic building material from 3 Redcliffe Street, Bristol* (Cirencester, 2005), 2-4, 9-10.
A. Vince and K. Steane, *Assessment of the medieval and late pottery from Broad Quay/6-22 Marsh Street, Bristol (BQB06)* (Lincoln, 2007), 1-2.
N. Adam, *Land at the corner of Wine Street and Union Street, Bristol* (Cirencester, 2008), 5.
M. Brett, *Westmorland House, Stokes Croft Bristol: Archaeological evaluation* (Cirencester, 2009), 16.

Dorset

Ham Green Ware found at Sherbourne old castle. P. Spoerry, The chemical analysis of ceramic fabrics from medieval Dorset and its region, Dorset Institute of higher education, Phd thesis (1989), 253.

Gloucestershire

P. Ellis, 'Excavations in Winchcombe 1962-72' *T.B.G.A.S.* (1986), 104-5.
D. Wilkinson and A. McWhirr, *Cirencester Anglo-Saxon church and medieval Abbey* (Cirencester, 1998), 100, 105, 113-4, 121, 131, 133.
D. Enright and M. Watts, *A Romano-British and medieval settlement site at stoke road Bishops Cleeve, Gloucestershire* (Cirencester, 2002), 29.
K. Rodwell and J. Bertram, *Acton Court: The evolution of a Tudor courtier's house* (London, 2004), 295-96, 327.
T. Longman, 'The excavation of an early medieval field system at Hillesley Farm, Hillesley, Gloucestershire', *T.B.G.A.S.* 123 (2005), 110-11.
Severn Road (Avonmouth) Resource Recovery Centre (2009), chapter 13, cultural heritage, 11-12.

Hampshire

D. Brown, *Pottery in Medieval Southampton c.1066-1510* (London, 2002), 78.

Herefordshire

R. Shoesmith, *Hereford City excavations 3* (1985), 58 at http://archaeologydataservice.ac.uk/archiveDS/archiveDownload?t=arch-281-1/dissemination/pdf/cba_rr_056.pdf accessed July 2015.

Wiltshire

Ham Green Ware sherd, Bradford-on Avon museum. Found at www.bradfordonavonmuseum/archives/5627 accessed July 2015.
N. Davy, 'Medieval timber buildings in Potterne' in *Wiltshire Archaeological and Natural History Magazine* 83 (1990), 69.

Wales

S. Sell, 'Excavations at Little Wind Street Swansea 1976', *Gower* 32 (1981), 83.
P. Courtney, *Medieval and later Usk* 1 (Cardiff, 1994), 12, 44-45.
K. Howell, *61 Wind Street, Swansea: Archaeological watching brief* (Swansea, 2000), 14.
D. Schlee, *Maenclochog community excavation* (Llandello,

2007), 6.
Wessex Archaeology, *Harold's House, Portskewett, Monmouthshire, South Wales: Archaeological evaluation* (Salisbury, 2007), 20.
S. Clarke, *Land adjacent to Mill House, Llantrisant, Usk* (Monmouth, 2008), un-numbered penultimate page.
Monmouth Archaeology: Plot 1. Ridings Farm, Bishton Newport (Monmouth, 2012), no page numbers, but Ham Green Ware is recorded amongst the fabric series.
Wessex Archaeology, *Kenfig, Bridgend, Glamorgan, South Wales: Archaeological evaluation and assessment of results* (Salisbury, 2012), 13-14.
A. Forward, The ceramic evidence for economic life and networks from twelfth to seventeenth century settlement sites in South Glamorgan (2103), PhD in Archaeology from the University of Cardiff, 11, 158, 287-9, 346, 355, 360, 374. This significant work evaluates Ham Green finds at Loughor Castle, Cosmeston, Cowbridge, Quay Street Cardiff, Barry, Sully and Llantwit Major. Found at http://orca.cf.ac.uk/56805/1/2014forwardaphd.pdf accessed July 2015.

Ireland
T.B. Barry, ;Urban archaeology in the Republic of Ireland' in *Bulletin of the group for the study of Irish historic settlement* 5 (1978), 15, referring to John Street, Drogheda.
The Irish post medieval excavation database 1985-1995. Wood Quay, Dublin, 32; St David's church, Naas, 55; Dean Street Kilkenny, 56; Main Street Cashel, 58; High Street Dublin, 115; Dyer Street, Drogheda, 225 at www.science.ulster.ac.uk/crg/ipmag/IPMAG%20Post-Medieval%20Excavations.pdf accessed June 2015.
J. Kiely, *Archaeological excavations report: 26 Patrick Street Kilkenny* (Innishannon, 2000), 2, 17.
F. Myles, *Final excavation report: Tram Street and Phoenix Street, Dublin* (2002), 154-5 at www.rpa.ie/Documents/Archaeology/Red%20and%20Green%20Lines/12_Final_Report_Tram_Phoenix_St.pdf accessed July 2015.
J. Kiely, 'Final archaeological report for 56-60 South Main Street, Wexford' in *Eachtra Journal* 14 (2003), 21-2.
E. Fitzpatrick *et al*, *Archaeological investigations in Galway City 1987-1998* (Dublin, 2004), 376-74.
Post medieval Excavations 2001-2005: George Street Waterford, 67; Main Street Youghal, 86; Abbeygate Street Upper Galway, 135 found at www.science.ulster.ac.uk/crg/ipmag/post_medieval_2001.pdf accessed June 2015.
Cashel City walls management plan (2008), 6, found at www.heritagecouncil.ie/fileadmin/user_upload/Publications/Irish_Walled_Towns/Conservation_and_Management_Plans/Cashel_City_Walls_Management_Plan.pdf accessed June 2015.
C. Moloney *et al*, *Guide to the excavations at Ardreigh, County Kildare 2007-08* (Kildare, undated), 32.

Acknowledgements
I am particularly indebted to archaeologist Mike Ponsford, formerly curator of field archaeology at Bristol City Museum, a key factor for dating Ham Green Ware, for the considerable time and energy he put into this chapter to enable me to write tolerably archaeologically sound work. However, I take responsibility for any views expressed, however wrong, as well as for any mistakes in my interpretation of any archaeological data. I am also indebted to an anonymous referee, Dr Adrian Webb, Dr Joe Betty, David Dawson, Dr Flavio Miranda, Julia McDonald and staff at Bristol Museum and Art Gallery. Grateful thanks to Bristol artist, Christine Molan, who painstakingly reconstructed the scene of Ham Green Ware being loaded on to a vessel at Pill.

References

1 K. Barton, 'A medieval pottery kiln at Ham Green Bristol' in *T.B.G.A.S.* 82 (1963), 95-126. Barton, a medieval pottery expert and sometime conservator at Bristol Museum and Art Gallery and later curator of Worcester Museum, wrote of other Ham Green Ware finds in the vicinity of Bristol. For example, K. Barton, 'The excavation of a medieval Bastion at St Nicholas's Almshouses, King Street, Bristol' in *Medieval Archaeology* 8 (1964), 192; K. Barton, 'Pickwick Farm, Dundry, Somerset' in *Proceedings of the University of Bristol Speleological Society* 12 (1969), 103, 106, 110. Locations where Ham Green Ware finds were identified by Barton in the early 1960s and discussed in his 1963 article referred to above. **Bristol**: At least ten locations in the centre of the present city. **Somerset**: Chew Valley Lake; Pickwick Farm, Dundry; Moat Farm Failand; Axbridge; Steep Holm; Barrowmead, Cheddar; Brean Down and Butcombe. Museums at Weston-super-Mare, Wells, Glastonbury Wookey and Taunton contain Steep Holm sherds. **Devon**: Lundy. **Gloucestershire**: Mangotsfield; Frocester; Edge; two locations in Gloucester. **Herefordshire**: Hereford. Shropshire: Detton Hall. **Wales**: Cardiff; Newport;

Caerleon; Castel Taliorum; Laugharne; Grossmont; Merthyr; Caerphilly; Coity; Gregeen; Ogmore; Llantwit Major; Oxwich; Barry Island; Flat Holm. He made further comments in the distribution in K. Barton, 'A note on the distribution of Ham Green Pottery' in *T.B.G.A.S.* 86 (1967), 201-2.

2 Chapel Pill http://pillvillage.com/design-protocol/map-2/4-2/ accessed May 2015. 'Creocham' see *M.H.S.* 2, 125. 'Crokerespull', L. Landon (ed.), *Somerset pleas from the rolls of the itinerant justices*, S.R.S. 36 (1923), 65.

3 A. Vince, The medieval ceramic industry of the Severn valley, University of Southampton PhD thesis, 1984, chapter 2.

4 Information from Mike Ponsford, August 2015.

5 C. Gerrard, Trade and settlement in medieval Somerset, PhD thesis for the University of Bristol (1987), 155.

6 Initially, Barton, 'A medieval pottery kiln', 124, published that Philip Ratz dated Ham Green Ware to the thirteenth century. Since then, advances in dendrochronology and finds of the ware underneath foundations of buildings known to have been constructed in the twelfth century have caused a re-assessment of the dating to be from 1120-1300. See C. Sandes 'The re-dating of Ham Green Ware: some reflections in the Irish evidence' in *Trowel: The Journal of the Archaeological Society of University College Dublin* 4 (1993), 5-9 which considers evidence from Bristol, Somerset and Ireland; M. Ponsford, 'Dendrochronological dates from Dundas Wharf, Bristol and dating of Ham Green ware and other medieval pottery' in E. Lewis (ed.), *Customs and ceramics* (London, 1991), 81-103.

7 These sherds are in Bristol City Museums and Art Gallery's collections (accession no BRSMG 42/1982).

8 Ponsford, 'Dendrochronological dates', 81-103; A. Vince, 'Early medieval English pottery in Viking Dublin' in N. MacNiocaill and P. Wallace (eds), *Keimelia: studies in medieval archaeology in memory of Tom Delaney* (Galway, 1988), 258; A. Vince, 'The medieval pottery' in R. Shoesmith, *Excavations at Chepstow 1973–1974*, Cambrian Archaeology Monographs 4 (1991), 93-139.

9 Gerrard, Trade and settlement, 156-7, appendix 5.2 no. 22.

10 Ponsford, 'Dendrochronological dates', 81-103.

11 Barton, 'A medieval pottery kiln', 118.

12 Vince, The medieval ceramic industry, chapter 11.

13 This perspective was reached in 1987 by Gerrard, now Professor of Archaeology at Durham University (Gerrard, Trade and settlement, 162-3). Royston Griffey, chairman of the *Matthew* Trust, commented that a flow tide takes four hours, therefore outward bound ships waiting for the tide at Hung Road, during the medieval period 'would have ample time to load local items for export'. E-mail communication to Mike Ponsford, October 2015.

14 *M.H.S.* 2, 125.

15 Information from Mike Ponsford, August 2015.

16 A. Vince, The medieval ceramic industry, chapter 2. The Wiltshire finds were at Avebury and Highworth. An excavation at Milborne Port in Somerset, some way from the nearest navigable river, only turned up one sherd of Ham Green Ware out of a total of 573 pieces of medieval pottery (J. Schuster, S. Thompson and A. Powell, 'Medieval and post medieval occupation at Millbrook Mews, Milborne Port', *S.A.N.H.S.P.* 155 (2012), 61).

17 Information from Mike Ponsford.

18 A. Vince and K. Steane, *Tewkesbury Abbey meadow 1992: The pottery* (2006), 15; Ponsford, 'Dendrochronological dates', 81-103.

19 Edwards, 'The transport system', 336-7. An altercation between groups of men occurred in the early 1240s when a weir at Bitton was thrown down by a number of men including two fishermen. Presumably their fishing practices, as well as river navigation, were affected (C. Chadwyck-Healey, *Somersetshire pleas from the rolls of the itinerant justices* S.R.S. 11 (1897), 361-2).

20 R. Warner, *The history of Bath* (London, 1801), 167, 209. From this source Bath's charter seems to have been granted to its merchant guild in the first year of the reign of King Richard the First, that is, 1189-1190. Warner states that trade then began to prosper, leading to the riverine trade in the thirteenth century detailed in the text. This unreferenced statement is repeated by all the Bath guides of the first half of the nineteenth century. P. Davenport in his authoritative book, *Medieval Bath uncovered* (Stroud, 2002), quoting mainly from secondary sources, states categorically on page 110 that he considers medieval navigation on the Avon to Bath to be an invention of an eighteenth-century antiquarian. He backs this up by saying that there appear to be few business links between Bath and Bristol merchants in medieval times. Whilst Warner's assertion is unreferenced, it may be true since a further instance from 1411 stating that wine, corn, salt, wool skins, cloth and osiers were transported on the Avon to Bath is quoted in G. Boyes, 'The legislative history of river navigation and canals 1275-1603', *Journal of the Railway and Canal Historical Society*, 29:2, No. 136 (1987), 77.

21 E. Frankot, *Of laws of ships and shipmen* (Edinburgh, 2012), 6-7; P. Marsden, *Ships of the port of London: twelfth to seventeenth centuries* (London, 1996), chapters 1 and 2.

22 'Magor Pill boat-the design of the boat', found at www.s4c.cymru/hanescymruarmor/e_prog3_magwyrboat_design.shtml accessed June 2014; Magor Pill boat, Gwent www.selrc.org.uk/maplocation.php?location_id=36 accessed June 2015. In a recently published book, D. Hinton has made the connection between the Magor Pill boat and others of its type and the transportation of Ham Green Ware, though, disappointingly, no sherds were found associated with the wreck (D. Hinton, 'Archaeology and post conquest England' in A. Galloway (ed.), *The Cambridge companion to medieval English culture* (Cambridge, 2011), 76-7). However, Ham Green sherds have been found on the lower foreshore at Magor Pill (J. Allan and S. Rippon, 'Iron age to early modern activity and palaeochannels at Magor Pill, Gwent' in *The Antiquaries Journal* 77 (1997), 350).

23 J. Allan, 'A post-Roman pottery assemblage from Hill Flats south Gloucestershire: Trade and commerce by water in the Severn estuary' in *T.B.G.A.S.* 121 (2003) 201-12; interview with ceramic specialist Paul Blinkhorn 2013, 'Bristol dig Berkeley' found at http://bristoldigberkeley.blogspot.co.uk/2013/05/interview-with-ceramic-specialist-paul.html accessed may 2015.

24 J. Edwards, The transport system of Medieval England and

Wales, Ph.D. thesis for the University of Salford (1987), 330 found in full at http://usir.salford.ac.uk/14831/1/D083029.pdf accessed May 2015.

25 C.T. Martin, *Calendar of Close Rolls Henry III 1231-1234* (London, 1905), 542, 546-7; 1240-1, Henry III fine roll project, www.finerollshenry3.org.uk/ accessed June 2015 searching for 'Severn AND boat'.

26 S. Rippon, 'Waterways and water transport on reclaimed coastal marshland: The Somerset levels and beyond', chapter 8 in J. Blair, *Waterways and canal building in medieval England* (Oxford, 2007), 217.

27 Edwards, The transport system, 323. Two more recent doctoral theses which discuss medieval river transport on the Somerset rivers in some depth are D. Caffyn, River transport 1189-1600 (2010), University of Sussex D.Phil thesis, chapter 4 and Appendix A especially, and D. Greenfield, I.K. Brunel and William Gravatt 1836-1841, Ph.D for the university of Portsmouth (2011), chapter 5. The latter thesis discusses historical navigation on the Parrett in considerable detail prior to analysing nineteenth century navigation improvements.

28 D. Young, 'Iron Age, medieval and recent activity at Whitegate farm, Bleadon, North Somerset' in *S.A.N.H.S.P.* 151 (2008), 64.

29 Chadwyck-Healey, *Somersetshire pleas*, 237, 243. Details of the Bishops of Wells and Abbotts of Glastonbury are to be found at D. Greenway (ed.), 'Bishops' in *Fasti Ecclesiae Anglicanae 1066-1300: 7, Bath and Wells* (London, 2001), 1-6; D. Smith, *Heads of religious houses; England and Wales II 1217-1377* (Cambridge, 2001), 46-7.

30 D. Jones, *Magna Carta: the making and the legacy of the great charter* (London, 2014), 84. The itinerant and loathed King John was in Bridgwater, Wells, Ilchester and Wedmore in July 1204, Taunton in late August 1205 and Bridgwater, Glastonbury, Wells and Harptree in early September 1205, Wells on 16 September 1208 and Bridgwater on 19 September 1208, and Bridgwater and Stogursey in September 2010 (T. Hardy, 'Itinerarium Johannis Regis Angliae' in *Archaeologica* 22 (1829), 148 and http://neolography.com/timelines/JohnItinerary.html accessed July 2015). Did the King use Ham Green Ware on his travels in Somerset? He is likely to have stayed with the Bishop in Wells and the castle at Bridgwater, both locations where the ceramics have been found.

31 Jones, *Magna Carta*, 106, 132, 149.

32 Chadwyck-Healey, *Somersetshire pleas*, 361-2.

33 C. Elton, *Customaria of Glastonbury Abbey*, S.R.S. 5 (1891), 176-79, 204. The reference to transportation of the bones of St Benignus is from S. Rippon, 'Water and wetlands in medieval estate management: Glastonbury Abbey, Meare and the Somerset Levels in South West England' in J. Klapste (ed.), Water management in the medieval rural economy, *Ruralia V, Pamatky Archeologicke - Supplementum*, 17 (Prague, 2005), 104. Professor Rippon is probably the foremost current academic writing on the Somerset Levels in the medieval period. Page 95 of this article has a map of the estates of Glastonbury Abbey which indicates the necessity of transporting goods by river across the Levels. See also, S. Rippon, 'Making the most of a bad situation? Glastonbury Abbey and the exploitation of wetland resources in the Somerset Levels' in *Medieval Archaeology* 48:1 (2004), 91-130.

34 V. Russett, 'Hythes and bows: aspects of river transport in Somerset' in *Waterfront archaeology: proceedings of the third conference on waterfront archaeology held at Bristol* (1988), 63. No doubt the stone and lime were for the continuation of the development of the complex at Glastonbury Abbey.

35 M. Williams, *The drainage of the Somerset levels* (Cambridge, 1970), 71.

36 J. Allan, quoted in 'New light on Glastonbury Abbey's history' in *Bath Chronicle*, 12 May 2011.

37 D. Young, 'Excavation of an early medieval site at Brent Knoll' in *S.A.N.H.S.P.* 152 (2009), 113 for Ham Green Ware find. The medieval wharf is located at York Farm, East Brent and is mentioned in Somerset Historic Environment Record number 10051.

38 J. Brigers, *Report on an archaeological evaluation: The Old Ship Inn, Combwich* (Moorlinch, *c.*2005), 23.

39 Somerset Historic Environment Record number 57194 refers to Ham Green finds at Eastover; J. Wright and R. Chelu, 'The Franciscan Friary and civil war defences at Friarn meadows, Bridgwater' in *S.A.N.H.S.P.* 151 (2008), 103; D. Dawson, 'Bridgwater and pottery studies' (2013) found at www.bridgwaterarchaeology.org.uk/news/jubilee/dawson.pdf accessed June 2015 refers to sherds found in Bridgwater Castle's moat.

40 Somerset Historic Environment Record numbers 54818 and 16479. The latter find is of some Ham Green sherds along with other medieval pottery sherds scattered in a field at High Ham. The interpretation is they were delivered to the field in night soil from Langport.

41 The building of the 'new' castle began soon after 1200. St John's Hospital foundation involved Bishop Jocelin in 1219. The Greyfriars were in the town in the 1230s, building commenced in the 1240s but was continuing during the 1270s and 1280s (R.W. Dunning (ed.), 'Bridgwater' and 'Bridgwater Castle' in *V.C.H. Somerset* 6 (1992), 192-3, 206-7; W. Page, 'The Franciscans at Bridgwater' and 'St John the Baptist, Bridgwater' in *V.C.H. Somerset* 2 (1911), 151-2, 154-6).

42 Edwards, 'The transport system', 319.

43 L. Landon (ed.), *Somerset pleas from the rolls of the itinerant justices from 1280*, S.R.S. 44 (1929), 119-20.

44 Chadwyck-Healey, *Somersetshire pleas*, 134.

45 Perhaps the extreme tidal range of the Parrett was a factor causing so many deaths. There were only two other deaths from boats recorded in the year, Richard, a fisherman drowned on the Avon and a young man from the Hundred of Portbury, this death might have been a coastal accident (Chadwyck-Healey, *Somersetshire pleas*, 240, 254, 261-2, 292-3, 299-300, 314, 321).

46 William of Malmesbury (*c.*1095-*c.*1143) stated that Athelney Abbey was inaccessible, except by boat (Williams, *Draining*, 19, 30).

47 T. Hunt, 'Some thirteenth century building accounts for Taunton castle' in *S.A.N.H.S.P.* 115 (1971), 39-44.

48 Gerrard, Trade and settlement, 183-4.

49 H. Bates, *Two cartularies of the Benedictine Abbeys of Muchelney*

and Athelney, S.R.S. 14 (1899), 159.

50 C. Trice Martin, *Calendar of Close Rolls Henry III 1231-1234* (London, 1905), 343, 356.

51 R. Isaacson, *Calendar of Close Rolls Henry III, 1237-1242* (London, 1911), 385. Other Bridgwater mariners may well have been familiar with west Wales and its castles during the early 1200s. For example, in 1277 Bridgwater mariners, amongst those from Devon ports were charged with conveying corn and other victuals to the castles at Pembroke, Kidwelly, Carmarthen and Swansea, all locations where Ham Green Ware has been found (J. Black, *Calendar of Patent Rolls Edward I, 1272-1281* (London, 1901), 195).

52 Welsh millstones used in Somerset were cheaper than ones from France or even from Somerset quarries at Penselwood. In 1276/7 the price paid for a Welsh stone for Taunton mills was 8s whilst one from Penselwood was 37s and an overseas stone, probably from France via Southampton was 62s (D. Farmer, 'Millstones for medieval manors' in *Agricultural History Review* 40:2 (1992), 98, 106).

53 Gerrard, Trade and settlement, 164, 168.

54 J. Allan, 'The medieval pottery found at Pig's paradise, Lundy in 2001' in *Reports of the Lundy Field Society* 53 (2001), 138.

55 C. Harfield, 'Rebels and recluses: Lundy's history in context' in *Lundy Field Society* (1997), 40-1; Anon, *Lundy, the Marisco years*, found at www.landmarktrust.org.uk/lundyisland/discovering-lundy/history/the-mariscos1/ accessed June 2015. The latter website has a fine picture of Henry III's fortification on the island as a response to the Mariscos.

56 Henry III fine roll project, fully searchable in English and found at www.finerollshenry3.org.uk/ accessed June 2015. Search 'Lundy'.

57 Isaacson, *Close Rolls 1237-1242*, 446-7, 451, 470.

58 C. Johns (ed.), *Isles of Scilly historic environment research framework: resource framework and research agenda* (Truro, 2012), 140. The Ham Green sherds are now in the Isles of Scilly Museum.

59 For Ham Green sherds found on Tresco see S. Taylor, 'Dolphin Town playing fields, Tresco, Isles of Scilly: Archaeological watching brief' (Truro, 2004), 20, 30. For Ham Green sherds found in the Tresco Channel see C.I.S.M.A.S., *Tresco Channel, Isles of Scilly, survey project* (no place, 2011), 35-6.

60 A. Weale, *Great Hele Barton, South Molton, Devon* (Taunton, 2014), 6, mentions one piece of Ham Green Ware was found; J. Allan, *Medieval and post medieval finds from Exeter* (Exeter, 1984), 10, 76, 83; C. Thorpe, 'The pottery found in Cornwall and the Isles of Scilly' in *Cornwall archaeological society newsletter* 132 (2013).

61 A website relating to Pill and Easton-in Gordano, http://pillvillage.com/design-protocol/map-2/4-2/ accessed May 2015, states that Ham Green Ware has been found from the Algarve to Iceland. I consider this to be a genuine error deriving from the knowledge that during the twelfth and thirteenth century Bristol vessels traded with those destinations and places in between. Bristol Museum consulted Mike Ponsford and David Dawson, both experts on medieval pottery, who state that Ham Green sherds have not yet been identified on the continent. A Portuguese medieval maritime historian, Dr Flavio Miranda, consulted a number of archaeologists in Portugal and Ham Green finds in that country are not known.

62 E. Frankot, *Of laws of ships and shipmen* (Edinburgh, 2012), 7. This source describes the move to using cogs. Decking was a feature of larger trading vessels in the twelfth century, familiar to the Irish/Norman traders. These were, perhaps, built in the double-ended clinker tradition and not just a feature of cogs. See also W. Sayers, 'Twelfth century Norman and Irish literary evidence for ship-building and sea-faring techniques of Norse origin' in *A journal of early medieval north-western Europe* 8 (June 2005). However, the adapted Viking long-ship used for trade in the eastern Atlantic may only have had decks fore and aft with an open hold. See J. McCusker, 'Medieval mercantile shipping' in *Essays in the economic history of the Atlantic world* (Oxford, 1997), 20.

63 S. Kilfeather, *Dublin* (Oxford, 2005), 5.

64 A. Powell, *The ancient borough of Bridgwater* (Bridgwater, 1907), 188.

65 P. Connolly, Dublin guild merchant rolls 1190-1265, found at http://databases.dublincity.ie/dmgr/map.php accessed March 2017. This website contains digital images of the original document, full transcriptions and an interactive map from which all names of men from particular settlement can be found.

66 Information from Mike Ponsford.

67 M. Potterton, The archaeology and history of medieval Trim, County Meath, University of Ireland PhD thesis (2003), 160. In fact over 26,000 sherds of the ware have been recorded, where they have been counted in excavations in Ireland up to 2004, see A. O'Sullivan, F. McCormick, T. Kerr and L. Harney, 'Early Medieval Ireland: Archaeological excavations 1930-2004' (2009), 196-8, found at www.heritagecouncil.ie/fileadmin/user_upload/INSTAR_Database/EMAP_Progress_Reports_2009_4.pdf accessed June 2015.

68 P. Stevens, *Four excavations in Kilkenny City (1999-2001)*, (2000), 25.

69 M. Monk and J. Sheehan (eds), *Early medieval Munster, archaeology, history and society* (Cork, 1998) note 4, 175.

70 T. Barry, *The archaeology of medieval Ireland* (London, 1987), 97-8.

71 Monk, *Early medieval Munster,* 175.

72 C. McCutcheon, *Medieval pottery from Wood Quay, Dublin: the 1974-76 waterfront excavation* (Dublin, 2006), 48. I am indebted to Mike Ponsford for this reference.

73 M. Potterton, 'Medieval Trim: history and archaeology' (2005), 149 for the navigation charter and pages 64, 160 and 234 relate to Ham Green Ware. For Ham Green Ware found at Bective Abbey on the Boyne, see The Bective Abbey Project, 3.1 found at https://bective.files.wordpress.com/2012/11/archexbective2012.pdf accessed May 2015.

74 P. Stevens, *Four excavations in Kilkenny City (1999-2001): site reports and supporting documentation* (2000), 25. Reference to navigation on the Nore can be found in A. Cosgrove, *A new history of Ireland: medieval Ireland 1169-1534* (Oxford, 1987), 237.

75 Gerrard, Trade and settlement, 190-2.

76 C. Malone, *Façade as spectacle: ritual and ideology at Wells cathedral* (Leiden, 2004), 24; J. Sampson, Glastonbury Abbey: the post 1184 stone collection (2011), found at www.glastonburyabbeysymposium.com/summary.php?&id=1010&rpn=summaries accessed August 2015.

77 *Glastonbury Abbey Lady Chapel: polychromy survey* (1995, updated 2007).

78 The distribution was researched and published in D. Waterman, 'Somersetshire and other building stone in medieval Ireland *c.*1175-1400' in *Ulster Journal of Archaeology* 33 (1970), 63-75. The map consulted here is found in R. Stalley,' Masons and their materials in medieval Ireland' in V. Olson (ed.), *Working with limestone* (Farnham, 2011), 218.

79 D. Mortimer, *Cardiff: the biography* (Stroud, 2014), chapter 11.

80 *Welsh Stone Forum Newsletter* 14 (2014), 2-3.

81 J. Shipton, 'Newport and Neven, Pembrokeshire, 10th May 2014' in *Welsh Stone Forum Newsletter* 12 (2015), 13.

82 B. Hughes, 'Mapping the freestone of medieval ecclesiastical buildings in north Pembrokeshire' and J. Davies, 'Mapping building stone in churches across Wales: Part 2 Camarthenshire' in *Welsh Stone Forum Newsletter* 12 (2015), 3-4, 13.

83 C. Casey, *Dublin* (London, 2005), 20.

84 J. Cottrell, Leinster, South Wales, Bristol and Angevin politics 1135-1172, University of Bristol PhD thesis (2000), 179-80.

85 Berkeley Castle Minuments, BCM/A/2/68 documents relating to Bedminster hundred in the twelfth and thirteenth century.

86 Stalley, *Masons*, 219.

87 *Welsh Stone Forum Newsletter* 9 (2012), 11.

88 Hughes, *Mapping*, 13.

89 A. Grossart, *Lismore papers* 5 (London, 1886), 37. Considerable details of the maritime travels of the Boyle family relating to the Somerset coast is to be found in *M.H.S.* 2, chapter 1.

90 A. Forward, The ceramic evidence for economic life and networks from 12th to 17th century settlement sites in south Glamorgan, PhD in Archaeology, Cardiff University, 2013, 346 relates to finds at Cardiff Quay; T. Barry, *The archaeology of Medieval Ireland* (London, 1987), 97, details of finds at Wood Quay, Dublin; Finds at Kyrl's Quay Cork are detailed at A. O'Sullivan, F. McCormick, T. Kerr and L. Harney, *Early medieval Ireland: archaeological excavations 1930-2004* (Dublin, 2009), 196-8.

91 Forward, Ceramic evidence, 346 for Ham Green finds in Quay Street Cardiff. For two separate finds of Ham Green Ware within 200 metres of Swansea Quay in Wind Street and Little Wind Street see S. Sell, 'Excavations at Little Wind Street, Swansea, Gower' in *Journal of the Gower Society* 32 (1981), 83, also K. Howell, *61 Wind Street, Swansea: archaeological watching brief* (Swansea, 2000). With reference to Ireland see The Heritage Council's website showing significant unpublished Irish archaeological excavations from 1930 to 1997, fig 15.1 shows that Ham Green Ware was found within 100 metres of the Liffey in Winetavern Street, Dublin and section 17.1.1 shows that sherds were found in James Street Drogheda within 200 metres of the Boyne (http://heritagecouncil.ie/unpublished excavations/ accessed June 2015).

92 Mike Ponsford has informed me that one of his ex-colleagues stated that Ham Green Ware had turned up in Iceland but there is no formal publication of the find.

93 Interview with ceramic specialist Paul Blinkhorn 2013, 'Bristol dig Berkeley' found at http://bristoldigberkeley.blogspot.co.uk/2013/05/interview-with-ceramic-specialist-paul.html accessed may 2015; A. Vince, *Assessment of the Roman and medieval pottery from the Victoria works, Long Street Dursley* (2004), 7; D. Evans and A Hancock, 'Romano-British, late Saxon and medieval remains at the Old Showground, Cheddar' in *S.A.N.H.S.P.* 149 (2006), 114.

94 For example, Ham Green Ware from the later thirteenth century was found in the context of a two-roomed dry stone medieval home at Wraxall (D. Wilson and G. Hurst, *Medieval Britain in 1969* 14 (1970)).

95 Gascon merchants in Bristol are mentioned in the Henry III Fine Roll Project at www.finerollshenry3.org.uk/ search 'Bristol AND Gascony'. The Bishop of Worcester importing wine at Bristol can be found in M.D. Lobel and E.M. Carus-Wilson, *The atlas of Historic towns*, II (London, 1975), 1-6.

96 Edwards, The transport system, 340.

97 Ham Green jug sherds has been found in Worcester, A. Vince, *Provisional identification of some medieval pottery from Deansway, Worcester* (1998), 5, 9. Ham Green Ware found at Tintern Abbey includes 33 pottery items including many wine carrying jugs (P. Courtney, 'Excavations in the outer precincts of Tintern Abbey' in *Medieval archaeology* 33 (1989), 124, 132). Ham Green Ware waste has also been found in association with the Bishop's Palace at Wells (N. Payne and R. Hoggett, 'Test pits in the allotments of the Bishop's palace, Wells' (1999) University of Bristol, 9, found at www.rik-hoggett.co.uk/files/1999 wells testpits.pdf, accessed May 2015).

98 *Close Roll*, 9 John, m.14 quoted in Anon, 'The first Bishop of Bath and Wells: Jocelyn' found at http://fmg.ac/phocadownload/userupload/scanned-sources/tgb/Vol05-PDFs/S-2863-3.pdf accessed July 2015.

99 Henry III Fine Roll Project at www.finerollshenry3.org.uk accessed June 2015. Search 'Bath AND wine'.

100 If the wine was moved to Wells it may well have been taken to Uphill and up-river along the Axe.

101 Ham Green Ware finds in association with Christian establishments. **Cheshire**: Ham Green jug sherds, interpreted as having being used for wine have been found in the lesser religious houses of Chester see S. Ward, *Excavations at Chester: The lesser medieval religious houses* (Chester, 1990), 150, 192. **Ireland**: sherds of Ham Green Ware found at Kells Priory, founded 1193, see M. Clyne, *Kells Priory, Co. Kilkenny* (Dublin, 2007), 184; at Bective Abbey, county Meath see G. Stout, *The Bective Abbey Project, 3.1* (2012); a piece of Ham Green jug has been found at Clare Abbey, Co. Clare probably dating from when the Abbey was founded in the late twelfth century, see G. Hull and Sebastian Joubert, *Medieval monastic occupation and post-medieval military activity at Clare Abbey, C. Clare* (2008), 23, found at http://tvasireland.ie/Reports/clare.pdf accessed May 2015; a small number of Ham Green sherds were found in the graveyard of St. Canice's Cathedral Kilkenney, see C. O'Drisceoil, *Excavations and monitoring in St. Canices's graveyard* (2013), 167-8. **Bristol**:

R. Jackson, *Excavations at St James's Priory,* Bristol (Oxford, 2006), 123-4. **Somerset**: J. Wright and R. Chelu, 'The Franciscan Friary and civil war defences at Friarn meadows, Bridgwater', *S.A.N.H.S.P.* 151 (2008), 103. **Gloucestershire**: Vince and Steane, *Tewkesbury Abbey meadow 1992*; A. Barber and R. Riley, *Winchcombe Abbey, Winchcombe: archaeological evaluation* (Cirencester, 2014), 13-14, 26. **Wiltshire**: J. Hart and N. Holbrook, 'A medieval monastic cemetery within the precinct of Malmesbury Abbey: excavation of the old cinema site, Market Cross' in *Wiltshire Archaeological and Natural History Magazine* 104 (2011), 166-92. **Monmouthshire**: Large groups of cooking pots were recovered at Monmouth Priory in 2002 included Ham Green Ware, see 'Mission chapel, Caerleon: the medieval and later pottery fabric series' found at www.newport.gov.uk/stellent/groups/public/documents/planningdocument/cont621999.pdf accessed May 2015. No page numbers. **Carmarthenshire**: C. O'Mahoney, *Pottery, ridge tile and ceramic water pipe, excavations at Carmarthen Greyfriars* (1998), 10.

102 S. and J. Rendell, *Steep Holm pioneers* (Weston-super-Mare, 2003), 13-26. Some of the Ham Green Ware sherds found around the Priory have been reconstructed into partial jugs and are in Steep Holm Museum. The author has also seen sherds unearthed by archaeologists on Steep Holm during the 2013 and 2014 seasons that are stored on the island. For the ecclesiastical development on St Helen's from St Elidius see N. Orme, *The Saints of Cornwall* (Oxford, 2000), 111. For Ham Green Ware found on St Helen's see Johns, *Isles of Scilly*, 140; these Ham Green sherds are now in the Isles of Scilly Museum. Historic events on Skellig Michael found at http://whc.unesco.org/pg.cfm?cid=31&id_site=757 accessed May 2015. The Island is a U.N.E.S.C.O. world heritage site. Ham Green Ware in some quantity has been found at the site (E. Bourke, A. Hayden and A. Lynch, *Skellig Michael, Co. Kerry: the monastery and south peak archaeological report* (2011), 107, 132, 142, 144, 340-1, 370).

103 S. and J. Rendell, *Steep Holm*, 28-30.

104 **Castles in Wales**: D. Browne, Excavations at the first castle of Aberystwyth (2010), 35, found at www.coflein.gov.uk/pdf/ACE01_01_01/ accessed May 2015; Great Castle Head, Dale, Pembrokeshire found at www.dyfedarchaeology.org.uk/projects/GreatCastleHead.htm accessed May 2015; C. Caple, *Excavations at Dryslwyn castle 1980-1995* (2007) 108, 241; Ham Green Ware found at Cardigan Castle, see C. O'Mahoney, *Pottery, ridge tile and ceramic water pipe, excavations at Carmarthen Greyfriars* (1998), 10. N. Ludlow, *Carmarthen Castle: The archaeology of government* (Cardiff, 2014), chapter 6. **Castles in Ireland**: D. Sweetman. 'Archaeological excavations at King John's sastle, Limerick' in *Proceedings of the Royal Irish Academy* (1980), 211; Ballylough Castle, Northern Ireland found at www.iaasc.com/northern-ireland/ballylough-castle accessed May 2015; for Ham Green ware found at Rathmullan Castle see T. Barry, *The archaeology of medieval Ireland* (London, 1987), 99.

105 W. Stevenson, *Calendar of Liberate Rolls Henry III, 1226-1240* (London 2016), 205.

106 T. Tout, *The history of England from the accession of Henry the third to the death of Edward III, 1216-1377* (London, 1905), 37-8, 45-7.

107 Stevenson, *Calendar of Liberate Rolls, 1226-1240*, 66, 68, 95, 97, 101, 188, 192, 195, 217, 229, 254, 269 for example. Wine was transported by river along the Severn from Worcester to Shrewsbury in 1228 and from Bristol to Monmouth along the Wye in the same year and in the 1240s (Edwards, The transport system, 331, 340). Page 340 also conveys other thirteenth century incidents of wine being transported along the Wye.

108 I am grateful for discussion with Mike Ponsford regarding understanding of archaeological distributions.

109 I am indebted to Mike Ponsford for discussion leading to this statement.

110 Gerrard considered this very point, and even though he researched all known Somerset medieval pottery distributions both archaeologically and historically, he found no reason for the shift in pottery production from Ham Green to Redcliffe. (Gerrard, Trade and settlement, 149).

111 St James's Parade, 5, found at www.bristol.gov.uk/sites/default/files/assets/documents/st-james-parade-character-appraisal.pdf accessed May 2015. Interestingly, Ham Green sherds have been found in excavations at St James's Priory, R. Jackson, *Excavations at St James's Priory, Bristol* (Oxford, 2006), 123-4. Whether it was brought there for culinary, ecclesiastical or market reasons would be interesting to consider.

112 A. Harvey, *Bristol, a historical and topographical account of the city* (London, 1906), 27-37.

113 In an early but important article in 1968, which includes a case study of Somerset and the Pill pottery, no reference to potters' guilds in Bristol is mentioned (J. La Patoural, 'Documentary evidence and the medieval pottery industry' in *Medieval Archaeology* 12 (1968), 101-126). Again, in an important publication on medieval industry, including a chapter on potters, no reference to potters' guilds are mentioned but increasing urban control and guild control is a theme of the book (J. Cherry, 'Pottery and Tile' in J. Blair and N. Ramsey (eds.), *English medieval industries* (Cambridge, 1991), 189-210). There is reference to Bristol's 'reasonable guilds' in a charter of 1188, but overall there does not appear to be evidence that Pill or Redcliffe potters ever organised into functioning guilds (H. Cronne (ed.,) *Bristol charters 1378-1499*, B.R.S. 11 (1946), 25). Mike Ponsford considers that, in the middle of the thirteenth century, Ham Green potters did move to Redcliffe and used wheels there, since in discussion he has said "early Redcliffe looks very similar to late Ham Green". The kiln was on Redcliffe Hill outside the borough walls.

114 N. Harding, *Bristol Charters 1155-1373*, B.R.S. 1 (1930), 147-64.

115 *M.H.S.* 2 chapters 1 and 3.

116 Redcliffe was originally part of the Somerset manor of Bedminster, separated from Bristol by the River Avon. However, it became part of the county of Bristol when it was formed in 1373. The stand-off in the fourteenth century between Bristol authorities and the Berkeley's, who owned the manor of Bedminster, and Redcliffe's final legal sub-sumation into Bristol in 1373 is discussed in S. Seyer,

Memoirs historical and topographical of Bristol 2 (Bristol, 1823), 130-34. Thus, the development and spread of Redcliffe Ware from 1250-1373, via ships sailing from the Avon next to Bristol, is technically another chapter in Somerset's maritime history, yet to be written. Gerrard, however, has considered the distribution of Redcliffe Ware found in Somerset prior to 1987 (Gerrard, Trade and settlement, 165-7, appendix 5.2, no. 25 and accompanying map).

Chapter Two

Somerset's Maritime Place-Names

Richard Coates and Adrian Webb

Introduction

As SOMERSET IS A maritime county, it was inevitable that the sea, or the Bristol Channel, would influence the creation and development of place-names along its coast and the banks of its principal rivers. In addition to these names (such as *Burnham on Sea* and *Weston-super-Mare*) can be added those of a significant number of features lying below the mean high water mark (such as *Culver Sand*), or offshore (such as *Birnbeck*), or lying both above and below the high water mark (such as *Slut's Pill*). Such names are included in this chapter, as also are the names of certain landmarks, including many headlands, having great significance for mariners. Also included are a number of place-names in and along the two main navigable rivers of the county, *i.e.* the River Avon and the River Parrett; only those place-names up to the bridge at Bridgwater and the Rownham Ferry (connecting Somerset and Bristol) have been included. An arbitrary line running (approximately) half way between Somerset and Wales, or half way between Flat Holm and Steep Holm, has been used as the limit in this study. This chapter examines the naming of such features with reference to a wide variety of published and unpublished source material, including charters, depositions, surveys, maps, charts and sailing directions.

The inclusion of names that have appeared on maps and charts since the sixteenth century has been the main criterion for this chapter. Several names added to maps and charts in recent years have been ignored. It has not always been possible to identify all the names found on such documentary sources and these have been left out. For example, a 1468 charter recording the bounds of the borough of Bridgwater mentions 'the Rode called Seynt Andrew's pole . . . penyes dokke, mill pille, priorspill, Harfullpille . . . Pauletpille, Downendepille, Pagenspille, and Crowpille',[1] all significant places none of which appear on any modern charts. *Harfullpille* has an even earlier mention in the 1320s when the provosts, bailiffs and eight others petitioned the Crown because of the loss of customs to the town as vessels were unloading at Highbridge, in this instance *Harefeldspulle*.[2] Some 250 years later when a detailed chart of the River Parrett was published, only one of the named maritime features in the charter[3] was included on the chart.[4] Crow Pill survives on modern Ordnance Survey maps and has been included in this chapter; other place-names above Bridgwater Bridge have not. These lost names will require further research, and therefore remain outside of the scope of this chapter.

Cartographic evidence can at times provide unique spellings of place names. At other times it can be very misleading and should be used with caution. One example of this can be seen with the place-name *Birnbeck*. Cartographic evidence can be found that records the name as *Bearn Rock*, *Bearn Buck*, *Bairn bach* and *Bearn Island* from 1771 to 1839.[5] However, in property records from 1675 to 1790 the name only appears in two forms, either *Barnback* or *Birnback*.[6] The spelling variants were often made by surveyors who were not local men, but men who were told the names verbally, most likely by fishermen or pilots with a strong Somerset accent. This strongly suggests that the cartographers or map makers far too frequently got it wrong, from a local perspective. Other reasons for such errors are many and varied. One of the main reasons is incorrect copying. This can be seen in *Columsonde* which was incorrectly copied from a manuscript source recording *Colversonde*.[7] Similarly, cartographers, typesetters and engravers made copying errors. One that resulted in an error 200 years ago saw the name *Hurstone*, in the parish of Bossington, changed by a typesetter to *Hurlestone*.[8] This name has been incorrectly perpetuated in various guises to this day.

Following the publication of the first Admiralty charts and Ordnance Survey maps of the region in the early nineteenth century, there have been great efforts to standardise the spelling of place- names. The most recent versions of Admiralty charts and Ordnance Survey maps have been used to show the official or dominant current spelling. Hence the majority of references relating to variant spellings of place-names pre-date the early nineteenth century. Variant spellings are often a vital clue for the interpretation of the most obscure modern names; see for example *Denny Island*, *Hurlstone Point* and *Plotneys* (below). Unfortunately for those places offshore, the lack of sources before the latter part of the sixteenth century means there are only a handful of variant spellings for many of these features.

Scandinavian names

A problem of particular linguistic and historical interest in and around the Severn Sea is the occurrence of names of Scandinavian (Old Danish or Old Norwegian) origin. Scandinavian names in the Western and Northern Isles and the west and north coasts of Scotland, the Lake District, and much of eastern and East Midland England are a well-known and well-understood phenomenon whose distribution correlates with known waves of Scandinavian settlement from the ninth century onwards. The presence of such names for coastal features in the south-west of England and south Wales is more mysterious, given the complete absence of Scandinavian settlement names in Somerset, Monmouthshire and Gloucestershire, and their almost complete absence in Glamorgan. Such maritime names which are beyond reasonable doubt Scandinavian include especially those of islands such as the outlying *Lundy* and *Caldey*, and *Sker* Point and *Tusker* Rock in Glamorgan, the grange called *Meles* in Margam (Glamorgan; though the word *melr*[9] 'sand-bank, sand-dune' may have been borrowed into English, just as *holmr* 'small island' was), and a very small number of inhabited places in south Wales such as *Lamby* and *Womanby* (later *Homri*) in Cardiff.[10] In the inner Severn estuary, in the Aust narrows, we find the late-recorded but characteristically Scandinavian-looking *Leary* Rock (apparently from *leira* 'mudflat', or *leir(r)* 'mud', + *ey* 'island'), *Gruggy* (also apparently 'mud island'; compare *gruggóttr* 'muddy'), *Guscar* Rock (apparently from *gás* 'goose' + *sker* 'rock') and The *Scars* (an anglicized plural form of *sker* 'rock, skerry'). The existence of these names gives us confidence in interpreting other difficult names in the Severn region, including Somerset, as Scandinavian, such as the various *Dumbles* or *Dunballs* and the like representing occasionally overflowed

Illustration 2.1: Scandinavian place-names in the Upper Reaches of the Bristol Channel (Authors)

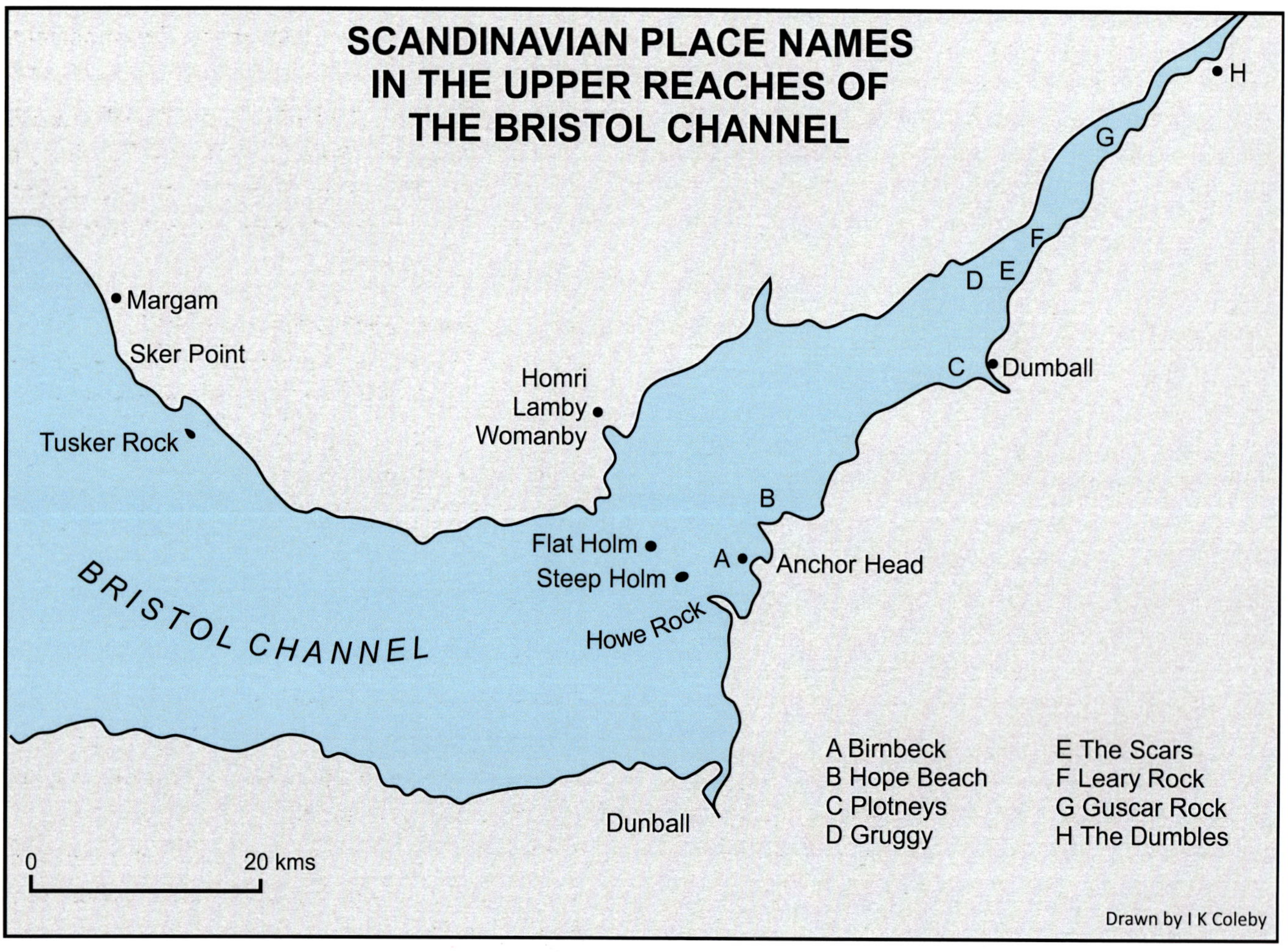

shoreline pasture (from *dunna* 'mallard' + *ból* 'lair, den');[11] Middle *Hope* Bay; *Plotneys* and the nearby mapped word *layer* (for which compare *Leary* above). *Flatholm* and *Steepholm* have often been thought Scandinavian, but *Flatholm* in particular offers uncertainties, and the account of their origin needs to be more nuanced; both are probably English. The original name of Anchor Head appears to be for the unrecorded but inferred Old Scandinavian **ankerissæti* 'anchorage'. A case, not watertight, but a case nevertheless, could also be made regarding *Birnbeck* and *Howe* Rock (Brean). The exact reason for the adoption and persistence of such alien maritime and coastal names in English- or Welsh-speaking territory is still not fully understood.

Arrangement

The maritime names of Somerset are listed alphabetically below, and the list is referred to as a gazetteer. The list is preceded by a short section on recurrent terms used as generic or classificatory elements in names. The linguistic background of these common general terms, such as *bay*, *head*, *pill* and *rock*, is explained. Many features in all of these categories include the names of coastal inhabited places, *e.g. Bossington Point*, and the origin of those place-names is also presented.

Notation and typographical conventions

In this chapter, references to words such as those mentioned above, and spellings of place-names in documentary evidence, are given in italics, as in: 'Before the Norman Conquest this river [Parrett] is recorded as *Pedredi(strem)* 725 (copy of about 1350), *Pedridan* 891, *Pedredan* 894; and after as *(la buche de) Pedredan* about 1140, *Peret* 1233 and frequently, *Paret* 1243, *Perret* 1253.'

Words preceded by an *asterisk are not actually on record, but their existence has been confidently inferred from other evidence, usually comparative data from related languages.

Symbols between /slashes/ represent phonemes (spoken sound-units, notated using the International Phonetic Alphabet), while symbols between <angle-brackets> represent letters of the writing system of the language in question. Units of speech and writing are related, of course, but should not be confused.

Place-names as headings of entries are in **bold**, as are cross-references. Any such names in ***bold italic*** are lost, in the sense that they have not been current in recent centuries, though their location may be known.

Generic terms and their history

anchorage: as in common usage.

bank: common term for a submerged feature raised above the general level of the sea-bed; in its basic English senses of 'raised ground', whether on land or under water, it is apparently an early copying ('borrowing') from Old Danish *banke* which has spread to all regions of England.[12]

bar: an obstruction, usually across the mouth of a river, which creates turbulence at some states of the tide but offers the prospect of smooth passage on its landward side.

bay: an indentation of any size in the coastline. The word was copied from French *baie* in the fourteenth century, and may or may not be related to the architectural sense of 'space between structural elements, recess'. It replaces older English words such as *bight*.

bluff: a broad, steep cliff face (originally American usage, but also in Britain from the nineteenth century).

channel: the hollow bed of a river or of the sea, especially the line of deepest flow of a river, or *thalweg*. The word was copied in the fourteenth century from Old French *chanel*, related to *canal*.

cliff: as in common usage.

clyce (in various spellings): a local term for 'sluice(-gate)', often preceded by a surname in the genitive case. The term in Middle English was *clūse*, which would regularly give modern **clouse* (/klauz/, *i.e.* rhyming with *rouse*). The Somerset word seems to have been influenced by the Dutch word *sluis* with the same meaning (pronounced in modern Dutch roughly like 'slice'), possibly used by Dutch engineers in the Levels. Both the Dutch and the English words are ultimately from Old French *escluse*.

cove: as in common usage for a small bay.

deep: term for an unexpectedly deep feature at a particular place, or for (a stretch of) the thalweg (line of deepest flow) of a river.

flat(s): general term for any level stretch of ground either permanently or intermittently exposed, as in *mudflats*, *sandflats*.

ground(s): a portion of the Earth's crust which may be submerged or above water, as in *spoil ground, middle ground, swampy ground, landing ground*;[13] such a feature on which a boat may *ground (run aground).*

head: a term used in names for headlands.

hole: usually self-explanatory for a depression in the sea-bed, but unclear in *Hole's Mouth.*

holm: an obsolete term for a small island, copied into Old English from Old Scandinavian, and seen also in *Skokholm* and *Grassholm* in Pembrokeshire and disguised in the Channel Islands *Jethou* and *Brecqhou*, all of which are of Scandinavian origin. But the word may well have been copied into Old English,[14] and there is therefore no linguistic barrier to the accompanying first element in, for example, *Flat Holm*, being either Old Scandinavian *(flatr)* or Old English *(flot)*. See the entry for Flat Holm for subtler discussion.

hook: any feature shaped like a hook when viewed from above, usually a bend in a river.

island: as in common usage.

ledge: a raised but level submerged feature.

mouth: the usual metaphorical term for where a river flows into a larger river or the sea.

patch: a term for a small feature of any kind; a maritime application of the general term defined in *Oxford English dictionary* as 'A part of a surface of recognizably different appearance or character from the rest; an irregular mark or spot.'

pill: a south-western dialect word for a saltwater creek, found mainly in coastal Somerset, Gloucestershire and Monmouthshire. The word descends from Old English *pyll*. This must be related in some way to Old English *pull*, found in place-names,[15] which may be copied from the Proto-Welsh word which gives rise to modern Welsh *pwll*. The plural stem of this word is *pyll-*; the modern pronunciation of the <y> in this differs from that in the Old English word, but in an older period of Welsh it might have been closer to the English and been substituted accordingly. The exact historical relation of these words to each other, and of any or all of them to Old English *pōl*, the source of *pool*, has never been convincingly worked out in detail.

point: a frequent word in names of coastal features significant as navigational aids. The word is of French origin and enters English in this sense in the fourteenth century.[16] Before that, prominent (especially long, narrow) features were called by the Old English words *ord* 'spear, point' or *steort* 'tail', or, more neutrally as regards shape, *hēafod* 'head'.

reach: a portion of a river, channel or lake which lies between two bends or which can be seen in one view.[17]

rhyne: the typical Somerset spelling of a south-western dialect word found elsewhere as *reen* (which accurately illustrates the pronunciation) or *rhine*, meaning 'drainage ditch', from Old English *ryne*. There is no evidence that this word is of Welsh origin, as sometimes claimed; it is paralleled by Old Frisian *rene*, and is therefore clearly Germanic. Welsh *rhewin* or *rhewyn* is said to be a word of western Welsh counties and is of unknown origin; it has nothing etymologically to do with *rhyne*.

road: general term for a roadstead or anchorage.

rock: the basic sense offered by the *Oxford English dictionary* is 'A large rugged mass of hard mineral material or stone forming a cliff, crag, or other natural feature on land or in the sea.' It may have been copied into Middle English from Norman French, or it may have been copied into Old English earlier from either Latin or early French. The older native English term is *stone*.

sand: as in common usage; also used as a general term in names of beaches. It can be used for offshore sandbanks that cover and uncover depending upon the tide, *e.g. Culver Sand.*

shoal: originally an adjective meaning 'shallow', now used as a general term for any place where the water is shallow; a sand-bank or bar.

spit: a long, narrow feature, especially one extending out from the shore; a metaphorical use of the term for a sharp rod or peg used in cooking.

stone: as in common usage.

strand: the traditional word of Germanic origin for 'beach', the latter word replacing it in general usage from the seventeenth century.

swatch or sometimes locally *swash*, elsewhere also *swatchway*: a term of uncertain origin for a passage or channel between sandbanks or between a sandbank and the shore.

warth: a local word seen in many Severnside minor place-names, typically denoting grazing land on the outward side of a seabank which floods occasionally (*i.e.* which is not strictly tidal saltmarsh); from Old English *waroð* 'shore', but often confused with the sometimes equally relevant *wharf* 'landing-place, quay, hythe, staithe'.

weir: in England a general term for a type of fish-trap, sometimes called more fully a *fish-weir*, 'a fence or enclosure of stakes made in a river, harbour, etc., for taking or preserving fish' (*Oxford English dictionary*), especially salmon. Such weirs were banned by Act of Parliament in 1861, but some names indicating their existence survive. For local weirs, both wooden and stone, see the works by Waters (1947), Crowther and Dickson (2008) and Jecock (2011).[18]

Gazetteer of the maritime place-names of Somerset

Anchor Head (Weston-super-Mare)

Anchor Head proves to be a problem. The further back in time we go, the more contradictory evidence we find as to exactly where this was. For the purposes of this chapter we have decided that it names the coastal area of the mainland pointing out to sea under the ancient hill fort at Worlebury. Just offshore is the island of Birnbeck. This position is not to be confused with that of Anchor Head as it appears on today's Ordnance Survey maps simply naming a small cove, mapped by name by Lieutenant Murdoch Mackenzie junior R.N. in the 1770s. That seems at first sight unlikely to be an anchorage, since the place is fully exposed to the south-west and Mackenzie junior did not mark it as a recommended anchorage.[19] But a string of very early forms reveals that the modern form, though distorting the etymology, enshrines the essence of its original meaning: for example, *Ankygsetyn* 'super mare' in 1480,[20] *Ankershed* in 1492,[21] *Ankershede* 1539,[22] *Ankresettal* in 1549, *Ankers Head* in 1572, *Ancros Head* in 1677 and *Anchors Head* in 1682.[23]

These, notably that of *Ankerseten* in 1496,[24] show that the original name is from Old (East) Scandinavian **ankerissæti* 'anchorage' (recorded in literary Old Norse as *akkerissæti*), influenced by the English word *head* as if the name were really that of the nearby headland. The forms in final <-n> might suggest the word was treated in Middle English as plural, or that the original Scandinavian name was rendered in Old English as **Ancorseten* (though *seten* is literally 'plantation').

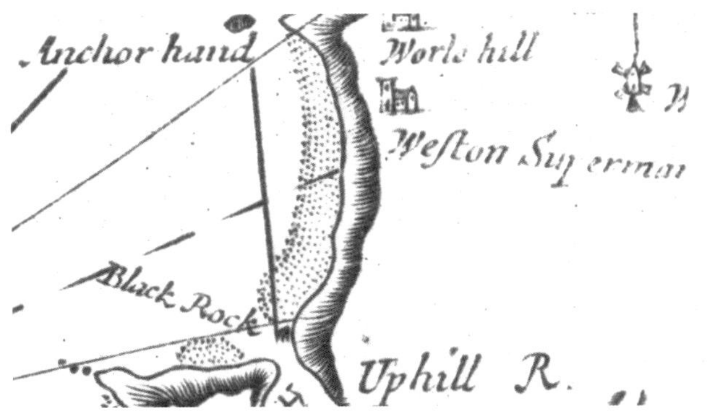

Illustration 2.2: In a chart by Captain Williams, of *c.*1706, he incorrectly named Anchor Head as *Anchor hand*. This was presumably an error by the engraver (Admiralty Library / Webb, *Charts*, facsimile 6)

Avill

This river-name appears to be a medieval alteration of *Avon*, but the change is not understood. It is recorded as both *Avene* and *Avele* in a Pipe Roll of 1202.[25] It is possible that an original *Avele* has been misunderstood as an example of the commoner river-name, but forms with <-n-> appear earlier than those with <-l->. If the <-l-> is original, the river-name could be understood as Old English **ā-fȳla* 'contaminator' or **ā-fylla* 'replenisher', but such names would have no parallels in English hydronymy.

Avon

Recorded in a Roman itinerary in the place-name *Abone*, taken to be that of the station and small port at Sea Mills.[26] This is an adaptation of British Celtic **abonā*, the normal word for 'river' (and the source of Welsh *afon* 'river'), and it was therefore not strictly a name, though that is what it has become for English-speakers. If it had a British Celtic proper name of its own, we do not know it.

Axe

This river-name dates back at least to the era of British Celtic. It duplicates the name of a river in Dorset and Devon. Ekwall takes it to be a variant form of *Exe*.[27] His careful philological argument to that effect is not easy or watertight, and the whole question of the etymology of *Exe* and similar names has been much discussed.[28] Ekwall's opinion on *Axe* has not been replaced by anything more convincing. If he was right, it represents British Celtic **iskā*, often taken to be a general term for 'water' in some remote period of Celtic (for which compare *Avon* for the sense, and Old Irish *esc* for the form) and used as a name. But an open mind is advisable about the detail. Watts notes that certain Old English spellings of *Axbridge* could suggest instead a connection with the unidentified and unexplained Romano-British place-name *Axium*, somewhere in southern Britain.[29]

Backhill Sands (Clevedon)
On current Ordnance Survey maps. Named from Back Hill (Walton in Gordano), with *back* probably in the sense of 'ridge'.

Banwell River
River name near Woodspring Priory shown on Admiralty chart 1152, deriving from the village of Banwell, inland from Weston-super-Mare, whose name is from Old English *bana* 'killer' + *wielle* or similar 'spring, stream'.

Batch
In 1700, when a grant was made by Henry Dod to Henry Gatchell of North Petherton, Dods Island was described as 'lately thrown up by sea in Burnham or Huntspill'.[30] There was also a *Dods Paddock* in Chilton Moor in 1710 part of the Corporation of Bridgwater's estate.[31] It is not known where this island was situated. The wording 'in Burnham or Huntspill' suggests that it was on the east bank of the Parrett. This feature is not named on a 1723 chart but it may be represented by Slab Island.[32] A detailed map of 1776 was drawn by local man William Locke. It is possible that Slab Island is shown to the south of Cures Island (owned by a man or woman with the surname *Sheldom*),[33] which is separated from the mainland by an area called *Huntspill Warth*. This Cures Island is probably Dunball, and the Batch (from the local term *batch* 'slope, hill, heap, pile') is the island with grass upon it,[34] being the *Slab Island* of 1723.[35] See also **Slab Island** (below).

Bathing Cove (north side of Worlebury Hill)
A secluded cove with a self-explanatory name. Sea-bathing began healthfully and fashionably in Brighton in the mid-eighteenth century, and took off in Weston from the early nineteenth; initially it was a private activity, hence the choice of this secluded place.

Battery Point (Portishead)
See **Portishead Point**.

Benhole Point (Stogursey)
From an unexplained farm-name, situated on the coast and recorded by the Ordnance Survey in 1809,[36] + *point*. The farm-name appears as *Penhote* on a map of 1820,[37] presumably in error for *Penhole*. The point is shown on Admiralty chart 1152 to the west of Hinkley Point.

Berrow Bay, Berrow Flats, Berrow Point and Berrow Swatch
From the place-name *Berrow*, recorded as *Berges* in 1196 and *Bergh* in 1249, from Old English *beorg* 'hill, mound, barrow, tumulus' or its plural *beorgas*. Since there is no known ordinary barrow or mound here, it is possible that the name was applied to the dunes.

Berrow Bay
From the place-name *Berrow* + *bay*. An unusual name in that it does not appear on maritime charts published before 1825[38] but is shown on sheet 20 of the first edition of the Ordnance Survey of 1809.[39] The Greenwoods also used the name in 1822.[40]

Berrow Flats
From the place-name *Berrow* + *flat* (plural). The *flats* are the far reaching sands, but the use of the term *flats* rather than *sands*, as elsewhere locally, is unexpected. From a charting perspective, the narrowness of Berrow Flats contrasts with the prominence of Gore Sand and results in their not being named on early charts.[41] Denham's 1832 survey of the River Parrett and surrounding area (published in 1839)[42] has an early record of the name.

Berrow Point
From the place-name *Berrow* + *point*. In the early 1770s Mackenzie junior used the term *Barra Point* (apparently influenced by the Hebridean island name *Barra*), but his use of *point* is hard to understand. There is no evident point here. The coastline is pretty straight and has no true headland, although it does bulge a little. It might be thought that there has been confusion with the prominent Brean Down over two miles to the north; against this is the fact that Berrow Point is mentioned by Richard Locke in the context of 'Burnham and Berrow Point' in 1790,[43] but in 1800 he refers specifically to 'Berrow Point'.[44] Locke was a local man and would hardly have confused the two locations, so the theory involving Brean Down is unlikely to be correct. The Greenwoods show

Berrow Point at the eastern edge of Gore Sand[45] but it is not shown on the Ordnance Survey six-inch series.

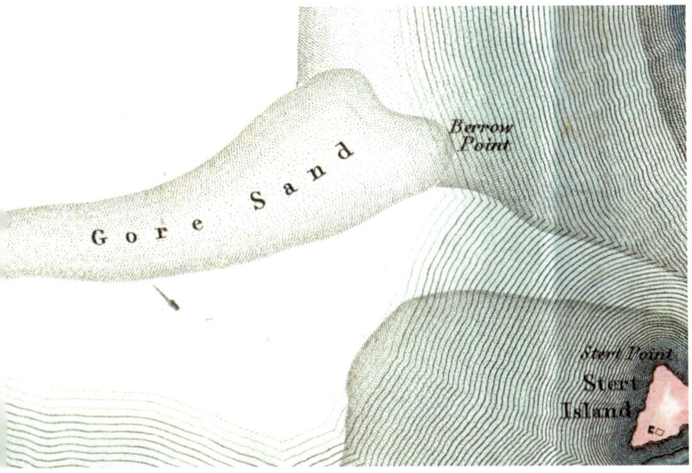

Illustration 2.3: Berrow Point as depicted in 1822 (C. and J. Greenwood, *Map of the county of Somerset, from actual survey made in the years 1820 & 1821* (London, 1822))

Berrow Swatch

From the place-name *Berrow* + *swatch*. Denham's 1832 survey of the River Parrett and surrounding area shows an early and unique record of the name.[46] No such feature is shown on earlier charts, which, considering the scale and detail shown on Payne's 1723 chart, suggests this may have not been in existence for very long before the 1830s.

Birnbeck (Weston-super-Mare)

The name of this island does not appear in very early records. This may be due to its being understood as part of Anchor Head (see above) and referred to accordingly in early documents. The area was a valuable fishery. A deed of 1549 mentions specific places at *Ankresettal*, such as *Owl Rock*, *Landrock* and *Brodestall* but not *Birnbeck* (in any of its variant spellings). When the coast was first charted in great detail by Mackenzie junior, in the early 1770s, he did not name it, merely referring to it as 'the small rocky isle that lies close to Anchor head, on the SW side of World Bay'.[47] The island has been mapped as *Bearn Rock* in 1771x1809,[48] *Bearn Buck* in 1809,[49] *Bairn bach* in 1831[50] and *Bearn Island* in 1839.[51] It was recorded in early-modern local deeds produced as evidence in Chancery in 1908 as follows: *Barne Back* in 1675, *Birnbeck* in 1690, *Bearneback* in 1754, *Birnbeck* in 1758 and *Barnback* as late as 1790.[52]

In 1805[53] and again in 1811, at the time of a local inclosure award, it was called *Bearn Back*.[54] Its closeness to the shore may explain why it is not mentioned in sailing directions for the Bristol Channel until 1821. In that year Barlow describes it as follows: 'Off Weston-head there is an Island, called Wearnback, marked on the chart Bearn-rock'.[55] In 1825 a print was published in which it is termed *Bearn Backs*.[56] It is recorded as *Bairn bach* in 1831 (see above) by Denham. He stayed at Weston whilst he was undertaking his survey in 1831, but when his sailing directions for the Somerset coast were published in 1839, he called it *Bearn Island*.[57] It was referred to as the *Isle of Bearnbeck* in 1845.[58] Travellers were advised that it was known as *Bearn Rock* or *Bearn Back* in the 1850s.[59] In 1855 it was reported that Birnbeck 'presented means of fortification, defence, harbourage, lading of vessels, and facilities of fishing not easily matched'.[60]

Illustration 2.4: An extract from a hydrographic survey, undertaken in 1848, showing *Bairn bach* (though it is hard to read) and the lines of fishing stakes (U.K.H.O., L7313/2 4e)

It is hard to know what to make of all this from the linguistic point of view. No sensible etymology has so far been proposed for the name, and none leaps out. That suggested by Stephen Robinson, 'the spring brook island', is hard to understand and in any case inaccurate.[61] There is a spring nearby on the mainland, but no brook. If *Bearn* is intended to rhyme with *earn*, it is surprising that it has never been written to match the familiar word *burn* (a pronunciation which the eighteenth-century and current spelling *Birn-* also suggests, again obliquely). If it is meant to suggest a diphthong (something like 'bee-arn'), as some local writers say, we have found no justification for this in any study of the dialect of Somerset, and in any case the dominant and earlier form in local documentation is *Barn-*. *Rock* appears to be an attempt to make sense of map-spellings like *Buck*, *Back* and the like, or derives from misreadings of them, but the dominant spelling type suggests that the second element is *back*. Some spellings of the type *bach* suggest the local word *batch* 'hill, slope, heap, pile', but they may simply be misspellings or misreadings of *back*.

Everything that follows is highly speculative. *Birnbeck* might be viewed as containing Old Scandinavian **bekk-* in the sense 'bench' attested in literary Old Norse as *bekkr*, but the same word-form with the more frequent meaning 'stream, brook' is not plausible here. **Bekk-* 'bench' has not been previously identified in English place-names. But if that is the origin, it is not clear what Scandinavian word might be represented by the first element. Alternatively, and perhaps with a better historical claim, the second element may be *back*, also most likely of Scandinavian origin, the word for a quay found for example in *Welsh Back* in Bristol and other local names, and fully discussed by Coates and Scherr (2011).[62] There are other Scandinavian names around the coasts of the Severn Sea (see Introduction). It is also conceivable that *Birnbeck* is for Old Irish **berna bec(c)* 'little gap', perhaps by metonymy (here, transfer from an adjacent place) from the narrow tidal channel separating Birnbeck from the end of Worlebury Hill, even though the expected Irish change of the first consonant of the adjective *bec(c)* from /b/ to /v/ appears to be absent. There is one indisputably Old Irish name in Somerset, *Beckery*, a former monastic establishment near Glastonbury, though this is from the grammatically different *Bec-Ériu* 'little Ireland'; the seventh or eighth-century Irish saint Indract was venerated at Glastonbury.[63]

No convincing explanation can be suggested. Given that it is unlikely to be English, the weight of other names in the Severn estuary suggests an Old Scandinavian origin is the most probable. Like Steep Holm and Flat Holm, Birnbeck is an island that could hardly have been overlooked by Scandinavian sailors looking for convenient maritime places to settle, or to operate from. If the name was descriptive of the island, the original landform it might describe is not easily recoverable, because of the works for the pier linking the island to the mainland, planned from 1845 and built in 1867. The list of formal possibilities for the first element, if it is Scandinavian, includes the following words, given in their Old Norse forms – let the reader evaluate their plausibility! – *barn* 'child'; *berg* 'rock, precipice' (though the <-n-> then needs explaining); *birna* 'she-bear'; *björn* 'bear', especially 'polar bear'.

Perhaps the least implausible, but hardly watertight, suggestion that can be made is *berg(a)-bakki* 'rock bank or quay'. This would be expected to give modern **Barback*, and the sprouting of the <-n-> would require explaining away in the history either of Scandinavian or of English. The partial resemblance to the English agricultural term *burnbake* 'denchering; improving the fertility of the ground by turning sods and burning them' must be coincidental.

Black Nore Point (Portishead)

From modern *black* + a name consisting of the truncated form of the Middle English definite article in the dative case + *ōr(e)* 'bank, hill with shoulder-shaped, convex, end', with *point* added for clarification when *ōr(e)* was no longer understood as being a descriptive word. Alternatively, but equivalently, if the name as it stands is truly ancient, the <-n-> might be from an inflected form of the Middle English adjective *blak* 'black', so 'the black bank'. The name appeared on maps and charts as *Blackmore*, in error, in *c.*1706 and 1736; the 1736 depiction may have been copied from the *c.*1706 publication.[64] Mackenzie junior called it *Blacknorth Point* in the early 1770s.[65] One London publisher mistakenly called it *Blacknose point* in the 1810s.[66]

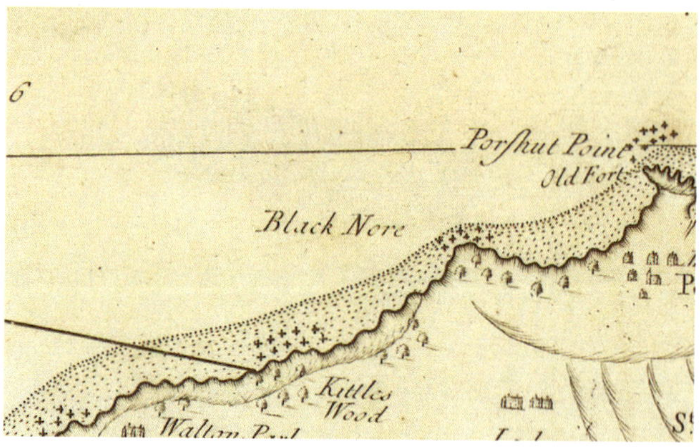

Illustration 2.5: Captain Holliday's chart, *c.*1712[67] (Adrian Webb Collection)

Black Rock (at the mouth of the River Axe; Kewstoke, to the north east of Birnbeck; in the River Parrett; and West Quantoxhead)

A common name for a rock which is either literally dark in colour or laden with dark seaweed. The age of such names is impossible to determine; they could have been formed with the modern result at any time during or since the Anglo-Saxon period, but Old English *rocc* (probably an early Romance borrowing) was buttressed by the borrowing of Norman French *roque* after the Conquest, and the name is probably medieval at the earliest.

(1) **Black Rock (at the mouth of the River Axe)**
This particular rock was of both navigational and legal significance. From a navigational perspective it was both named and depicted on a chart of *c.*1706.[68] From a legal perspective it marked the western extent of the royal forest of Mendip, mentioned in 1298 as *le Blacstone*.[69]

Illustration 2.6: Black Rock (in the foreground), from *The Westonian Guide* of 1829, was an important navigational landmark. Note the small craft sailing between it and Brean Down at high tide (S.A.N.H.S.)

(2) **Black Rock (Kewstoke)**
On the Ordnance Survey map of 1886 about 1,500 feet from the toll-gate near Birnbeck.

(3) **Black Rock (in the River Parrett)**
Possibly near Stretcholt or Pawlett, a salmon fishery in the River Parrett known as *Black Rock* was mentioned in a conveyance of 1797.[70]

(4) **Black Rock (West Quantoxhead)**
Shown on Admiralty chart 1152 at the low water mark in Saint Audrie's Bay.

Blackstone Rocks (Clevedon)
Shown on the first edition Ordnance Survey as *Blackston*.[71] It appears as *Blackstone Rocks* on today's Admiralty chart number number 1176 close to the shoreline at Clevedon;[72] compare **Black Rock** (1) at the mouth of the River Axe (above).

Blue Anchor Bay (Watchet) and Blue Anchor Road
From an extremely common name for a pub + *bay*. The earliest known pub so named is found in Lincoln in 1695.[73] There were 19 *Blue Anchors* in London alone in 1864, putting it only just behind the *Lord Nelson* and the *Britannia*, level with the *Prince Albert*, and ahead of the *Nag's Head* and the *Marquis of Granby*.[74] The anchor was a symbol of stability in a turbulent world and hence a symbol of hope or faith or both. Larwood and Hotten say that the *Blue* is merely to differentiate it from other *Anchors*,[75] but the actual lack of other *Anchors* with a colour term demands a better explanation. In the Middle Ages blue was seen as the colour of steadfastness, as opposed for example to green, symbolic of inconstancy. In *Against women unconstant*, attributed to Chaucer, we find: 'Ever in chaunging stant your sikernesse . . . In stede of blew thus may ye were al grene' which means 'Your faithfulness (security, constancy, etc.) is always changing … instead of blue you may as well wear all green.' So a blue anchor was gilding the lily, so to speak: double the ration of steadfastness, and an especially potent emblem in a port or on an exposed coastline.

Illustration 2.7: 'Blew Anchor' inn as depicted by Strachey in 1736; note the sign board hanging off the end of the building signifying an inn (S.A.N.H.S.)

In 1674 a burgage and brew house called *the Blew Anker* existed in Washford parish.[76] This was presumably the house called the *Blue Anchor*, probably already an inn, 'on the strand' beside the coast road from Watchet to Minehead by 1678,[77] though the modern village and railway station bearing the name are off to the west in the parish of Carhampton. The house continued in use until *c.*1860;[78] the current building of that name dates from later. Strachey names the place as *Blew Anchor* in his 1736 county map; he also shows an unnamed inn there.[79] The location was recorded by Mackenzie junior in the early 1770s as *Blue Anchor.*[80] Oddly, the *Victoria County History* states: 'North-west of Chapel Cleeve a sea-bathing resort was established in the late eighteenth century known as Cleeve Bay and later as Blue Anchor,' referring to Richard Warner's *Walk Thro' Western Counties* (published in 1800).[81] The name *Cleve Bay* does not appear on any contemporary maritime charts.[82]

Blue Anchor Road is from the place-name *Blue Anchor* + *road.* Shown on Admiralty chart 1152 as an anchorage off Blue Anchor.

Blue Ben (East Quantoxhead)

A promontory shown on Admiralty chart 1152 on the coast to the east of Saint Audrie's Bay. For the name, we only have folk-tales to go on, and the story has conflicting versions.[83] A dragon enslaved by the Devil and called *Blue Ben* lived at Kilve until he fell from one of the limestone pavements here and drowned in the mud of the foreshore. His skull (actually that of a fossil *Ichthyosaurus*) is on display in Taunton at the Somerset County Museum. The great parallel arcs of exposed resistant rock have been presented as Blue Ben's ribs. Perhaps they were really likened to the great arrays of roller-ends of a nineteenth-century carding-engine; in west Somerset in particular, *ben* was a word for 'that part of the frame of a carding-engine that serves to carry the various rollers parallel to the main drum or cylinder'.[84] *Blue* is used in older geological texts for slaty shades of grey, as would be appropriate here.

Bossington Beach and Bossington Point

From the place-name *Bossington* + *beach*, + *point.* The place-name means 'farm associated with [a man with the Anglo-Saxon name] *Bosa*'. The name is a relatively late addition to charts of the area appearing in the 1830s[85] and 1840s,[86] and does not appear at all before 1824,[87] although the name of Bossington village does appear on a chart from the early eighteenth century.[88] The name of the Point was usurped by *Hurlstone* or *Hurtstone Point*, which has a much more prolific appearance on maps and charts because of its navigational significance; see below.

Botestal Point (Stogursey)

Boat-stall + *point.* The *Middle English dictionary* defines a *stalbot* (literally 'place-boat') as 'a kind of fishing boat placed at anchor at the mouth of a river',[89] though what precisely it was placed there for is not suggested: perhaps to catch a certain sort of fish reliably found at a certain season or a certain state of the tide. But it does not seem unreasonable to suggest that a *botestal* was a place where a *stalbot* was placed. Other senses are possible: on Speed's map of Somerset in 1610 a manual ferry is marked in the River Avon in Bath and apparently named *The Boate stall.*[90] This survives in Boat Stall Lane.

Boats were also scuttled to block up rivers, letting nature leave deposits to fill the boat so that the land would eventually reclaim the river bed, and that seems the most likely interpretation here. Saxton recorded this place as *Botestall* in 1575.[91] The name *Botstall Point* appears on two charts of the English Channel published in 1693.[92] Although other variant names appear on published charts, it appears more often as *Botestal Point* after appearing on a chart of the River Parrett in 1723.[93] Replaced by **Hinkley Point**.

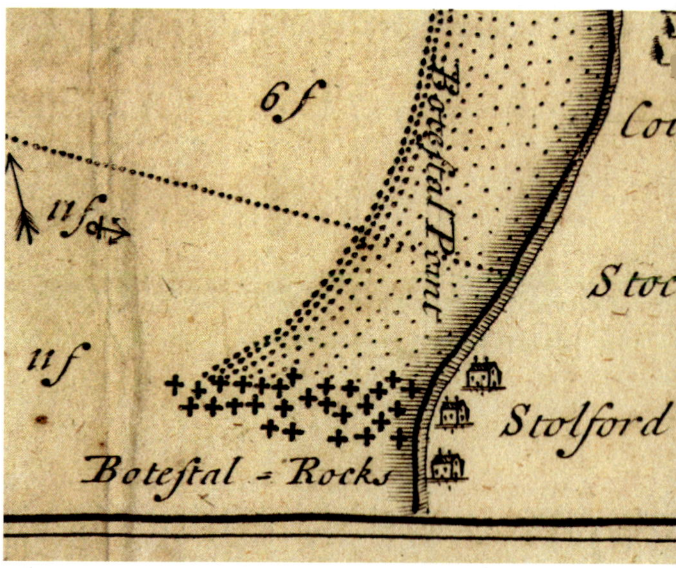

Illustration 2.8: Botestal Rocks and Botestal Point as drawn in 1723 (S.H.C., D/RA 9/9)

Botestal Rocks

See previous entry; + *rock(s).*

Brean Down
The striking headland at ST 2858, shown on Admiralty chart 1152. From the place-name *Brean* (*Brien* 1086, *Bren* 1212, *Breene* 1243, *Broen* 1254, *Breon* 1334, *Brayne* 1610)[94] + *down*. The village-name probably originally referred to the headland itself, recorded as *Brayne Downe* in 1723[95] and *Brean Down* in 1771.[96] It may derive either from an otherwise unknown OE **brēon* or **brēo*, ?nominative or dative plural form *brēon*, or from a derivative of British Celtic **brigā* 'hill' (compare Welsh *bre* 'hill'), + *down*, structured like *Bredon* (Worcestershire) and *Breedon* (Leicestershire) but of later formation.

Illustration 2.9: Brean Down, the mouth of the River Axe with Flat Holm in the background, *c.*1830 (S.A.N.H.S., A/DAS/1/439/4)

Bridgwater Bar, Bridgwater Bay and Bridgwater River
From the place-name *Bridgwater* + *bar*, + *bay*, + *river*. The base name is from Old English *brycg* 'bridge', distinguished by the addition of the Norman given name *Waltier* or *Wautier* 'Walter'. The manor was held by Walter de Dowai [Douai, Flanders] in the early post-Conquest period. Bridgwater's bridge was the lowest bridging point on the Parrett, and still is if we disregard the modern northern bypass (the present A39).

Bridgwater Bay appears on published navigational charts from 1723.[97] However *Bridgwater Bar*, located immediately north of Hinkley Point on Admiralty chart 1152, seems to be a later feature. It does not appear on maritime charts before 1825.[98] The new British Channel pilot book refers to the Gore Sand at the mouth of the River Parrett as being 'almost as a bar' into the river.[99] It appears on Denham's 1832 survey of the River Parrett and surrounding area (published in 1839).[100]

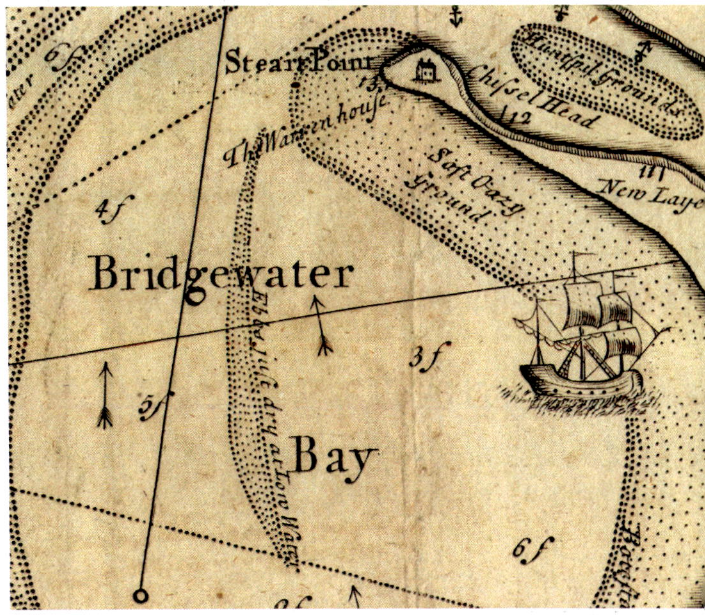

Illustration 2.10: Bridgewater Bay as drawn in 1723 (S.H.C., D/RA 9/9)

Bridgwater River is an unusual alternative name for the River Parrett, which first appears on a general chart of the English Channel published in 1693.[101] Its use on navigational charts after this time is very uncommon.[102]

Bristol Channel
From the place-name *Bristol* (see **Bristol Deep** below) + *channel*; a name first noted on seventeenth-century maps and charts, replacing the traditional Welsh *Môr Hafren* and its English equivalent *The Severn Sea*. The references below reflect how the different names, *Sabrina*, *Severn Sea*, *Severn or Bristol Channel*, and finally *Bristol Channel*, developed over the centuries. They have been arranged in order of their development and a few examples of their use are given.

(1) **Sabrina**
Gerald of Wales named the Bristol Channel as *Sabrina* in the late twelfth century[103] and Hereford Cathedral's famous *Mappa Mundi* of *c.*1300 shows *Sabina* (*sic*).[104] John Trevisa's translation of Ranulph Higden's fourteenth-century *Polychronicon* (as printed by William Caxton in 1480) mentions that:

the britons called the riuer babren [a printing error in picking up *habren* from the previous sentence] after the woman that was drowned therin / but by corrupt latyn it is called sabrina Seuarn in english Seuarn begynneth in the myddell of wales & passed first toward the eest vnto shrowesbury / and thenne torneth southward vnto briggenorth wircestre and gloucestre and falleth in to the west see besides bristowe and departed ['separated'] in somme place englond and wales … Seuarn is swyft of streme / fisshe craft is ther in / wodenes ['madness, turbulence'] of the swolewynge and of whirlyng water casteth vp & gadrith to hepe grete hepes of grauel / Seuarn ofte ariseth & ouerflowrth [sic] the bankes.[105]

The River Severn as we know it today was called *Sabrina* by George Lily on his map of 1546[106] and on Waghenaer's chart of the Bristol Channel 1589.[107] Its name was recorded in Roman times,[108] but its etymology is not known for certain.

Illustration 2.11: *Sabrina fluuius*, as depicted on Waghenaer's chart of 1589 of the Bristol Channel. Note how the name only applies to the area of what is known today as the River Severn[109] (Robin Bush Collection)

(2) **Severn Sea or River of Severn**

In 1480 William Worcestre referred to it as the *Severne*,[110] as did an unknown surveyor in 1539[111] and Michael Drayton in 1612,[112] to name but a few. A yeoman of Dunster called it *the river of Severne* in 1607 when aged 65, a name which he had most likely used for most of his life.[113] In 1637 Camden mentioned *the Severne Sea* some seven times when describing the waterway we know today as *the Bristol Channel*.[114] The term was used by various authors during the seventeenth century after Camden, notably by Captain Greenvile Collins in 1693 in his sailing directions.[115]

(3) **Severn or Bristol Channel**

These two names were often used together in either order. Williams used *Bristoll Channell or Severn sea* on his chart of *c*.1706.[116] Collins used *The Severn or Channell of Bristoll* in 1693,[117] whereas in 1728 Nathaniel Cutler, who re-worked the charts authored by Collins, called it *The Severn or Channel of Bristol*.[118] As late as 1795 the two names were being used jointly in one publication to describe the channel[119] which was most likely based only upon printed sources.

(4) **Bristol Channel**

In the early fourteenth century a navigator, probably from mainland Europe, referred to this as *kannele van brustouwe*.[120] Lucas Jansz Waghenaer, from the Netherlands, used *De Canael van Brostu* in 1589.[121] Probably in imitation of the Dutch cartographers, Holliday used *Bristol Channel* for his chart of the approaches to Bristol, *c*.1712.[122] After this date it became, and remains, the preferred option for naming the channel.

Bristol Deep

From the place-name *Bristol* + *deep*. *Bristol* is from Old English *brycg* 'bridge' + *stōw* 'place', typically denoting a place where there was gathering for a purpose, often at a site of religious importance.[123] It has been speculated recently that the name originally commemorated a shrine of St Jordan, companion of St Augustine of England on his mission beginning in 597 C.E.[124] Bristol, specifically the site of the present Bristol Bridge across the Avon (now the Floating Harbour) in the city centre, was the lowest bridging point on the Avon until modern times, until that honour was taken first by the Clifton Suspension Bridge and then by the M5 motorway bridge.

Bristol Deep lies in the approach to the mouth of the Avon between Welsh Grounds and English Grounds.[125] In the 1590s it was simply referred to as *The Channell betweene the groundes*.[126] It is a name that did not appear in printed sailing directions and charts until the 1970s.[127]

Brue

A pre-English (British Celtic) river-name derived from the ancestor of Welsh *bryw* 'brisk, vigorous'.[128]

Its course much further inland is referred to in a grant of *c.*1270 as the *Bryw*.[129] Since the late twelfth century the lower course of the river has been known variously as the *Fishlake*, the *Brent river* (from **Brent**; see above) and, since the later eighteenth century, the *Brue*.[130] It was shown as the *Brent River* on over half a dozen different maritime charts from 1693[131] to 1800. Day and Masters, in 1782, referred to it as the *River Brue*.[132]

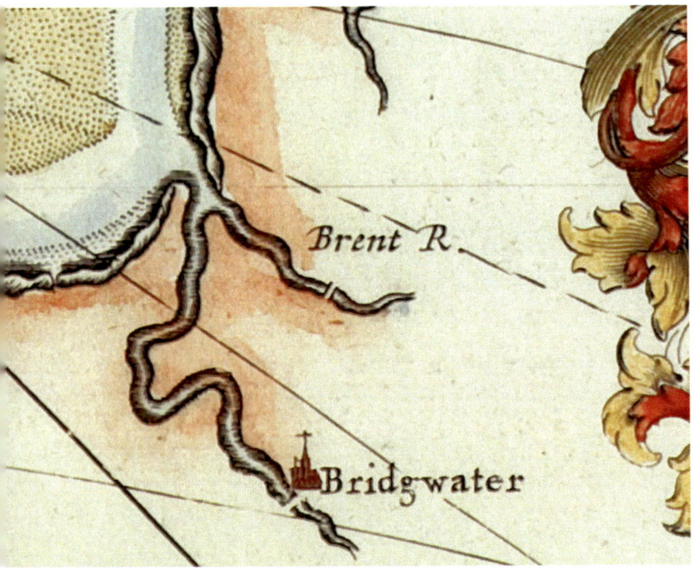

Illustration 2.12: Recorded as the Brent River by Captain Greenvile Collins in 1693[133] (Robin Bush Collection)

Burnham Reach

From the place-name *Burnham* + *reach*. Shown on Admiralty chart 1152 as a stretch of the channel into the River Parrett opposite Burnham on Sea. *Burnham* is apparently from Old English *burna* 'stream' + *hamm* 'land enclosed on two or more sides, hemmed in land, riverside land, (later) watermeadow'.[134] But *burna* 'stream' seems an inappropriate way of referring to the River Brue, at whose mouth the modern town stands, and it must refer to a lost feature at the town itself, perhaps a stream ancestral to Burnham Rhyne.

Calf Rock (Steep Holm)

Probably from the usage seen also in the *Calf of Man*, where there is an allusion to a smaller companion of a larger island. Shown on the 1886 Ordnance Survey map.[135]

Cannington Pill (Cannington)

From place-name *Cannington* + *pill*. The place-name is from Old English *Cantuc* 'Quantock' + *tūn* 'farm, village'.[136] The pill is shown on a chart of 1723.[137] Although not on modern Ordnance Survey maps, Cannington Brook runs into the River Parrett in the same vicinity at the modern-day Stallington's Clyce.[138]

Castle Rock (Steep Holm)

Shown on the 1886 Ordnance Survey map,[139] but changed to *Tower Rock* on the 1904 edition.[140] Both names are simply descriptive of the imposing feature.

Chapel Pill (Easton in Gordano and Portbury – eastern extremity of Easton parish)

From the medieval St Katherine's chantry chapel, founded by the Berkeley family, on the western side of the creek, now completely vanished, + *pill*. Historically the pill has also been referred to as *St Katherine's Pill*, which does not appear on any maritime charts but is better known as *Chapel Pill*[141] (as charted from 1693).[142] In 1833 it was recorded 'at the south-eastern extremity of the parish [of Easton-in-Gordano] there was anciently a chapel, the site of which is still called *Chapel Pill*',[143] which distinguishes this chapel from the one between Portbury church and King Road (see next entry).[144]

Illustration 2.13: A depiction of Chapel Pill (bottom left) on a chart of the River Avon by Greenvile Collins in 1693,[145] with north at the bottom (Robin Bush Collection)

Chapel Pill (Portbury and Easton in Gordano – western extremity of Easton parish)

The parish boundary between Portbury and Easton

in Gordano starts at the coastline at Chapel Pill. This was known as *Portebery pille* at the end of the sixteenth century.[146] Mapped as *Chapel Pill* for the first time on maritime charts in 1815 by Richard Thomas,[147] then by White in 1825.[148] In 1829 Rutter stated that the pill, located between King Road and Portbury, takes its name from 'a small Roman Catholic chapel, which stood in a field surrounded by elm trees; some vestiges of which still remain'.[149] The pill is clearly marked on an Admiralty chart of 1848[150] and Ordnance Survey mapping from 1884.[151] However, the matter is confused in 1840 when Portbury Pill is referred to as *Portishead Pill*,[152] which was clearly a mistake.

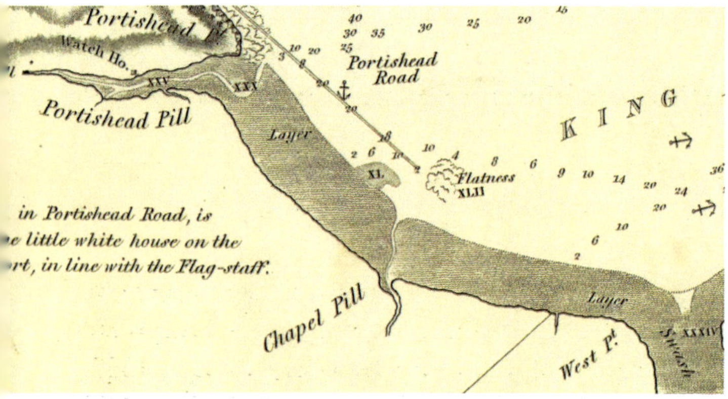

Illustration 2.14: An extract from a survey of the River Severn by Richard Thomas, 1815 (U.K.H.O., L3895)

Charlcombe Bay (Walton in Gordano)

From the place-name *Charlcombe* + *bay*. Shown on Admiralty chart 1176 immediately north of Walton Bay. [153] The place-name (*Cerlecume* 1086, *Cherlecumba* 1156), seen in Charlcombe House and Charlcombe Wood,[154] indicates that the name is genuinely local to Walton despite apparently recalling the better-known village of Charlcombe north of Bath. If it has the same origin as the Bath name, it must be from Old English *ceorla*, genitive plural of *ceorl* 'free peasant', + *cumb* 'valley (with a bowl-shaped upper end)'.

Chisel Rock (Huntspill)

From a medieval or modern *chisel*, ultimately from Old English *ceosol* 'gravel' (there are medieval references to *sand-chisel*) + *rock*. This dangerous rock, situated near the main channel at the mouth of the River Parrett, is not shown on Payne's detailed chart of 1723[155] or Mackenzie junior's work.[156] It appears not to have been named on navigational charts until the 1830s.[157]

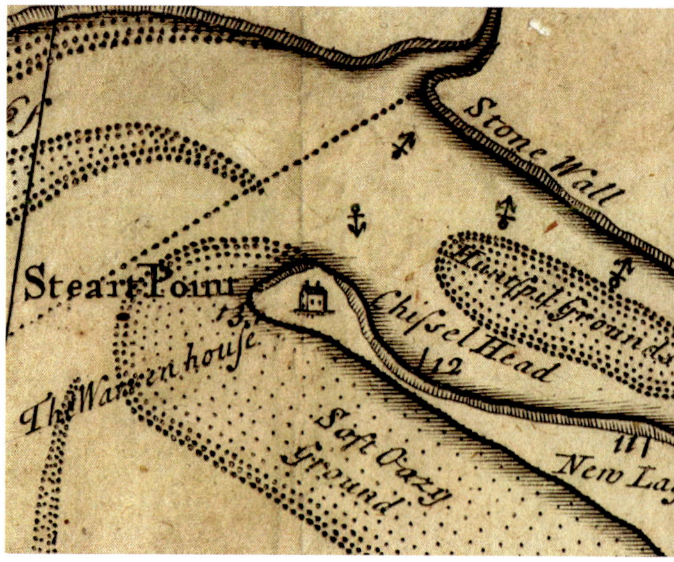

Illustration 2.15: Chisel Head (*Chissel Head*), on the channel side of the mouth of the River Parrett, just below the extremity of Stert Point, in 1723[158] (S.H.C., D/RA 9/9)

Cleve Bay (in Old Cleeve)

A former name, or possible former alternative name, for Blue Anchor. It does not appear on navigational charts before 1825.[159] *Cleeve* or *Cleve* is from an inflected form of Old English *clif* 'cliff', as in the second suggestion regarding **Clevedon**.

Clevedon Bay, Clevedon Flats, Clevedon Pill and Clevedon Point

From the place-name *Clevedon* + *flat* (plural), + *pill*, + *point*. The place-name, recorded as *Clivedone* 1086, *Clivedon* 1225, is either from Old English *clif* in the genitive plural form *clifa* + *dūn* 'hill', so 'hill of/with cliffs', or from a pre-existing place-name *Clife* 'at the cliff' + *dūn*, so 'hill at [the place called] *Clife*'.[160] The hill in question is the double feature Wain's Hill and Church Hill, the latter topped by St Andrew's church, at the western extremity of the present town.

Clevedon Bay

From the place-name + *bay*. Shown on the current Admiralty chart number 1176.[161]

Clevedon Flats

This name came into use on navigational charts in the 1770s. Murdoch Mackenzie senior defined an area, including the English Grounds, as *Clifton Flatts* on his chart published in 1775.[162] Various forms of the spelling of *Clevedon* occur on other charts published after Mackenzie senior's. Today this is known as the *Langford Grounds* (see **Langford**

Grounds below) and there was some confusion regarding the extent of both features before the nineteenth century. In 1825 Captain Martin White R.N. clearly delineated both features, with Langford Grounds further to the south.[163] Clevedon Flats is still named on today's Admiralty charts.[164]

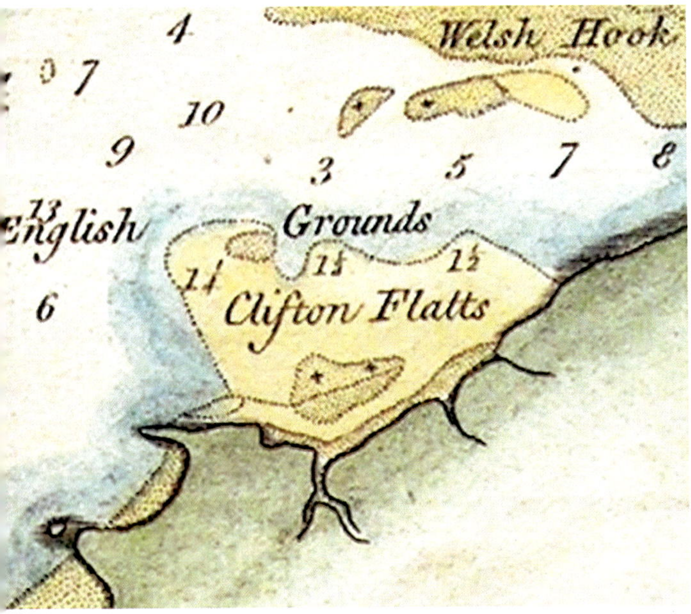

Illustration 2.16: Clevedon Flats as depicted by Murdoch Mackenzie senior in 1775[165] (Adrian Webb Collection)

Clevedon Pill

The combined estuary of the Blind Yeo and Land Yeo rivers. Mapped in 1539 as *Clevedonpyll* and as *Clyvedons pille* in *c.*1590.[166]

Clevedon Point

Mentioned in the early 1770s by Mackenzie junior in his sailing directions,[167] but the name does not appear on navigational charts before 1825.[168]

Cobbler Patch

Unexplained. Shown on the current Admiralty chart, number 1152, off the coast at Stogursey, offshore from Hinkley Point power station.

Cobb's Leaze Clyce (Pawlett)

Where Cobb's Leaze Rhyne exits into the River Parrett. Named after a local family + *leaze* 'pasture', + *clyce*. Mapped by the Ordnance Survey in 1886. [169]

Cockburn Bank

Thought to have been named after Admiral of the Fleet Sir George Cockburn, 10th Baronet, GCB (1772-1853), in the early nineteenth century. It is not named on a partial survey of the area by Richard Thomas in 1815;[170] however White's survey of the upper reaches of the Bristol Channel in 1825, which covers the area more thoroughly, does show it in some detail.[171]

Illustration 2.17: Cockburn Bank on White's survey of 1825 (U.K.H.O., H905)

Combwich Clyce, Combwich Pill and Combwich Reach

From the place-name *Combwich* + *clyce*, + *pill*, + *reach*. The place-name is recorded as *Comich, Co'miz* 1086, *Cumwiz* 1178, *Comb Wyche* 1421, *Comage* 1539, *Comwiche* 1592, *Combweeke* 1726.[172] It is from Old English *cumb* 'valley' + *wīc* 'specialized farm, dairy farm, trading station'; so probably 'trading station at the mouth of a (conspicuous) valley'. The valley must be the one descending from Fiddington. Combwich is known to have been a significant port in the Roman period,[173] and a small harbour remains. Combwich Pill and Combwich Reach are shown on a chart of 1728.[174]

Crockern Pill (Easton in Gordano)

The village is today called simply *Pill*; see *pill*. It was formerly *Crockern Pill*, strictly the name of the pill itself which was used as a base for the Severn pilots, hobblers, and rowers who formerly had the exclusive right to tow sailing ships up the Avon to Bristol docks.

The first part of the name is more difficult in detail than it might appear at first sight, and the evidence needs to be set out fully. Some forms show a first element apparently from Middle English *crokkere* 'potter', or a reduced form of **crok-ern* 'pot-house, pottery' (*Crokkerepill, Crokkerpill'* 1242-3 Somersetshire Pleas).[175] A second group shows a first element apparently from Middle English *crokkere* 'potter' in the genitive singular form with *-es* (*Crokerespull* 1268 Somersetshire Pleas,[176] *Crokkerespulle* 1303-4 Feet of Fines).[177] A third group shows a first element apparently from **crok-ern* 'pot-house, pottery' (*Crokkern Pyll* 1478,[178] *Crockern Pill* 1607).[179] This variant appears on navigational charts from 1693[180] through to the beginning of the nineteenth century. A separate group (or non-group) has a first element showing various signs of reduction or adaptation to other words (*Crokanpill* in the reign of Elizabeth I,[181] *Crockham Pill* 1599,[182] *Crocke and Pill* 1601,[183] *Crocrampill* 1654).[184] Another group omits the first element altogether, as in the modern place-name (*the Pill* 1651, Bristol Depositions).[185] Occasionally we find what looks like an effort to restore a supposed historically valid form of *Crockerne-Pill* in an 1841 *Parliamentary Gazetteer*,[186] whilst other sources show alternative names of *Pill or Crockern Pill* on the 1830 1" Ordnance Survey map. The spelling *Krapekijl* on Waghenaer's Dutch chart of 1589 appears to be a garbled form of *Crockernpill*.[187]

The adjacent Ham Green, a former detached tithing of Portbury but often now thought of together with Pill, is well known as the source of an easily recognized style of thirteenth-century glazed pottery, and the fuller older name may derive from this, if not from a pottery actually at Pill. The name is therefore 'potters' creek' or 'pottery creek', or some variation on these possibilities.[188]

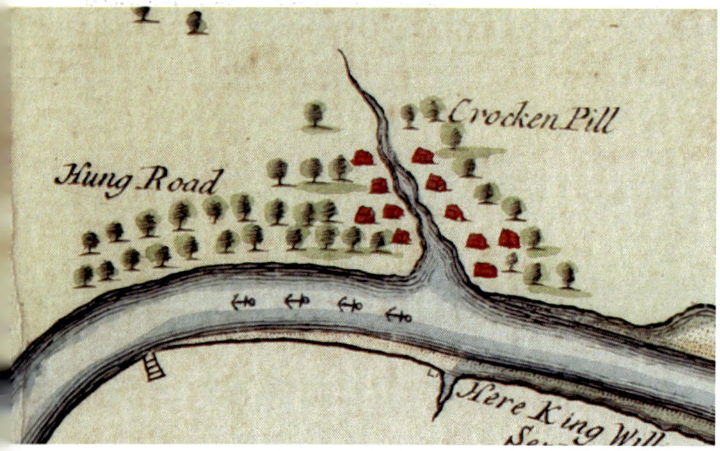

Illustration 2.18: Crockern Pill depicted by Captain Greenvile Collins in 1693[189] (Robin Bush Collection)

Crook Peak

Although a good distance away from the coast, this has been included in our study since it was mentioned in maritime works, apparently from the 1830s, by its local folklore name *See-me and see-me-not*.[190] It was mentioned by Mackenzie junior five times in his sailing directions from the early 1770s.[191] *Crooks Peak*, or *Crook Peak*, was a rare name on navigational charts until used by Denham and Robinson in their chart published in 1839.[192] One author thought *See-me and see-me-not* derived from the fact that it is often covered in low cloud, or mist, and cannot always be seen.[193] However, a chart of 1839 shows it with a leading line from the English Grounds, in line with a beacon on Worlebury Hill.[194] The accompanying sailing directions, published in 1839, including information from Captain F.W. Beechey who also made a sketch of the peak, state: 'See-me and See-me-not is an inland pointed hill, which, from the channel near the N.W. elbow of the English grounds, is seen just topping the ridge of Worle Hill'. Clearly See-me and see-me-not was an important landmark for navigating the upper part of the Bristol Channel and it was not always easy to see.[195] It was still being used as a navigational landmark in 1848.[196]

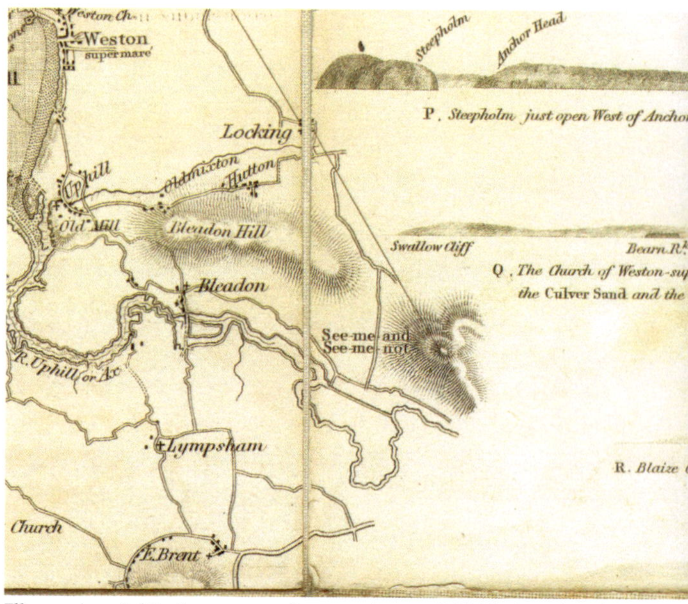

Illustration 2.19: An extract from a chart of 1839 showing See-me-and-See-me-not[197] (Adrian Webb Collection)

Crow Pill (Bridgwater)

Recorded as *Crowpille* in a charter of 1468.[198] It is shown on a chart of 1723 as *Crow Pill*[199] and on Ordnance Survey maps as *Crowpill* in 1887.[200] The name appears to be self-explanatory.

Culbone Rocks (Oare, but near Culbone)

From the place-name *Culbone* + *rock* (plural). Sometime before 1610 the parish name was changed from *Kitnor* to *Coulban*, a form of the sixth-century Irish saint's name *Columbanus* (though the two names interchanged for some time). The church's ancient dedication is uncertain, but there is no barrier to its having been the site of the cell of a 'Celtic saint'; there is a Dark Age stone with a cross incised in it on the footpath from the car-park on the A39.

Culver Cliff (Minehead and Walton in Gordano) and Culver Cliff Sand (Minehead)
From Old English *culfer* or *culfre* 'dove' + *clif*: a frequent coastal name. Culver Cliff Sand is shown on the Ordnance Survey mapping below Culver Cliff and not as an offshore hazard.

Culver Sand (*Columsonde,*[201] *Coluersonde*)
From Old English *culfer* or *culfre* 'dove' + *sand* in a spelling typical of western, especially midland, dialects *(sond)*. The first of the old spellings (in the fifteenth century) seems like an attempted translation of *culfer* into Latin *(columba)*.

Between 1461 and 1483 a text was compiled, possibly from a much earlier source, describing directions for sailing off the Somerset coast. In it the author warns mariners of the dangers of the tidal streams in the Bristol Channel, advising mariners 'not to goo for the stremes of brigge watir sette west northe west and be ware of coluersonde it floweth from londay to the holmes est and west'. Although there is no punctuation in the text, it is clear that mariners are warned of a significant feature named

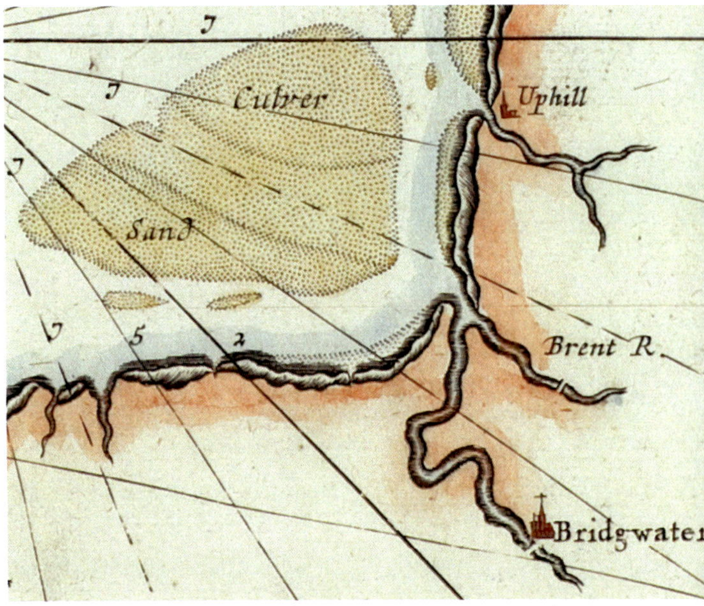

Illustration 2.20: Culver Sand, as depicted in 1693,[207] dominating the seabed from Watchet to Weston-super-Mare (Robin Bush Collection)

coluersonde.[202] Surprisingly, the feature is not shown on the early printed navigation charts, but Nash Sand is, which is also mentioned in the fifteenth century text.[203] The feature is not charted until 1693,[204] after which it appears on dozens of different charts, some of which show this feature in distinctly different locations.[205]

Illustration 2.21: Blaeu's chart of the Bristol Channel, published in 1625,[206] showing the 'Naes sandt' (Nash Sand) but not Culver Sand (Keith Needell Collection)

Cures Island (formerly in the River Parrett)
Known as *Dunball alias Cures Island* in the 1770s.[209] See **Dunball Island** in the River Parrett (below).

Cut, The (Chilton Trinity)
A sandbank which bisects the flow of the River Parrett in the parish of Chilton Trinity to the east of Chilton Trinity church. Shown on Ordnance Survey maps from 1887.[210] Since *cut* usually means 'canal', its use here is unexplained.

Cut Flood Way Reach
A stretch of the River Parrett in the parish of Chilton Trinity to the south of Dunball Wharf. Shown on Ordnance Survey maps from 1887.[211] The *cut* or artificial channel still shows as a straight channel on modern Ordnance Survey maps and carries the administrative boundary between Chilton Trinity on the west and Puriton and Bridgwater Without on the east. The *reach* is the whole stretch of the river including the cut.

Denny Island (Denny Rock)
Located opposite the mouth of the River Avon, but as far from King Road as it is from Portishead, this island in the Severn estuary is in historic Monmouthshire. The boundaries of the Bristol city parish of St Stephen, and the limits of the former Port of Bristol Authority, run up to its rocky foreshore. It appears in the historical record for the first time as *Dunye*, in the charter recording the creation of the county of Bristol in 1373.[212] This suggests that the name is from Old English *dūn* 'down' (*i.e.* 'hill with a rounded profile') + *ēg* 'island', so 'island shaped like a down or (rounded) hill'. The development to the modern pronunciation with /e/ in the first syllable is irregular and unexplained. + *island* or + *rock*.

It is an important navigational hazard and landmark charted since Waghenaer's time. In the late sixteenth century it was named *The Denne*.[213] Collins called it *Deny Rock* in 1693,[214] and Williams *ye Deny* around 1706.[215] Mackenzie junior noted that it was always above water except when there were high spring tides.[216]

Illustration 2.22: Although not named, the brown island can only be Denny Island, as depicted on Waghenaer's chart of 1589[217] (Robin Bush Collection)

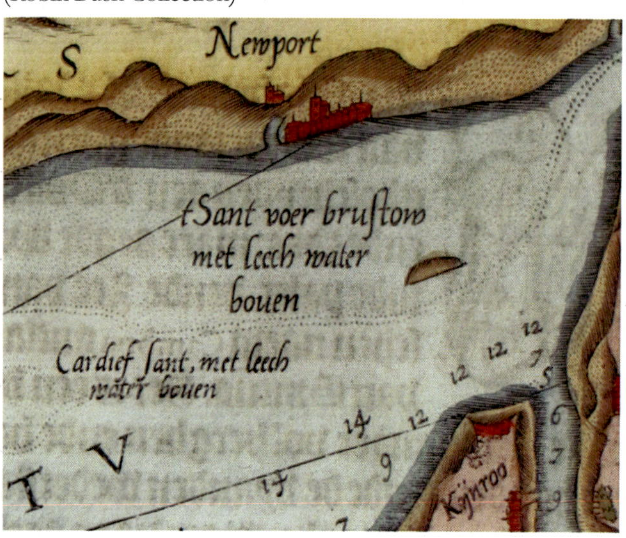

Denny Shoal (Denny Sands)
This shoal is situated in King Road. The names are from the place-name *Denny* (see above) + *shoal* and + *sand* (plural). In the late sixteenth century a bank between Denny Island ('The Denne') and the mouth of the River Avon was known to have existed. Both Williams (in *c.*1706) and Holliday (more clearly in 1712) used the description *New Bank* for the area of the present day Denny Shoal. This suggests that Williams may have been the first person to name and depict the New Bank, *i.e.* Denny Shoal, in the early eighteenth century.[218] However, the name *Denny Shoal* is not used in official Admiralty sailing directions until 1948. The 1933 Admiralty sailing directions refer to the *Newcombe Shoal* but not to the *Denny Shoal*,[219] whereas the 1948 edition states that the 'Denny (Newcombe) shoal, is an extension of Welsh Grounds'.[220] The name *Newcome Sands* thus fell out of use to be replaced with *Denny Shoal.* Today the Denny Shoal is still constantly moving.

Illustration 2.23: Holliday's survey of *c.*1712 showing New Bank about half way between Denny Island and Portishead Point 'Porshut Point'[221] (Adrian Webb Collection)

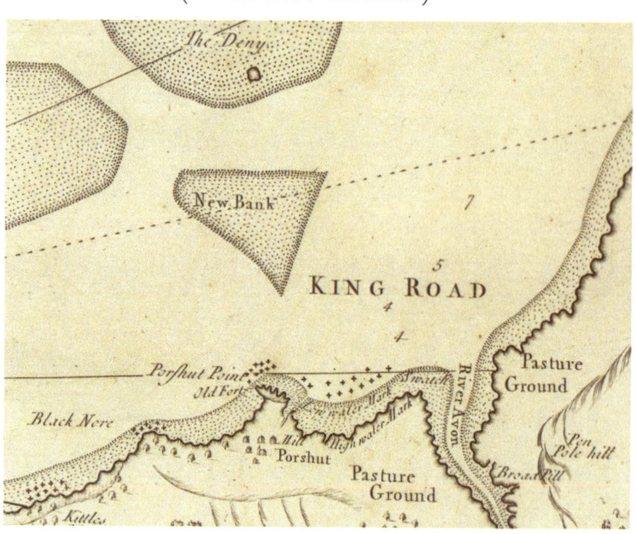

Dods Island

In 1700 Dods Island was described as 'lately thrown up by sea in Burnham or Huntspill', when a grant was made by Henry Dod to Henry Gatchell of North Petherton.[222] See **Batch** (above).

Down End Pill (Puriton)

In 1468, according to a charter recording the bounds of the borough of Bridgwater, there were pills at Pawlett, *Downendepille* (Down End), *Pagenspille* and *Crowpille* along the River Parrett.[223] When the River Parrett was altered in 1677, Down End lost its pill and a sluice was constructed which is now called *Dunball Clyce*.[224]

Dumball, Dunball

From a not widely recognized coastal dialect word (Glamorgan, Somerset, Gloucestershire) *dumble* 'pasture subject to occasional tidal flooding', *i.e.* something less integrally maritime than true saltmarsh. It appears to derive from Old Scandinavia *dunna* 'mallard' in the genitive case (*dunnu*) + *ból* 'lair, bed', so 'mallard's lair'.[225] Once there were also two islands with this word in their names, one in the River Avon and the other in the River Parrett.

(1) **Dunball Island, formerly in the parish of Easton in Gordano.**

In 1693 Collins showed an extended inter-tidal area jutting out from the north-west point of Easton in Gordano parish.[226] A chart, of *c*.1706, shows a spit at the mouth of the River Avon named *ye Point* the end of which was approximately in the location of Dunball Island.[227] In a chart of *c*.1712, neither the Point nor Dunball is shown, only the word *Swatch* on the Somerset side of the river.[228] Donn mapped the area in some detail in 1769 showing the Swash but no Dunball,[229] as did Day and Masters in 1782.[230] Mackenzie junior mentions Warth Point at the entrance to the River Avon, and the *swatchway* into the Avon, in the early 1770s, warning mariners that 'About midway between Warth point, and gibbet-post, the merged bank is so low, that at half flood, coasting vessels run across it into the Avon'.[231] According to one source, prior to 1760, Dumball Island was used for grazing sheep by a farmer from Easton in Gordano.[232] Neither Rack nor Collinson mention Dunball in their account of the parish written in the late 1780s.[233] Small-scale charts of 1798[234] and 1806[235] do not show any island. The Greenwoods, who could not have surveyed the area, also did not show Dunball in 1822.[236] However, Richard Thomas, in his survey of 1815, shows Dunball,[237] and it was substantial enough for White to land upon and use as an observation point for his survey undertaken in 1825.[238] In 1821 it was referred to as *the Dung-ball* that was 'formed by the Ship Channel, on the east side of the Swash-way, on the west side of it, both leading up to Bristol'.[239] Therefore Dunball was part of mainland Somerset until cut off, possibly in the 1800s or 1810s.

Ordnance Survey maps show it in 1830[240] as White depicted it, then document its decline from 1882 when the Swash Channel was to the south of it. It was absorbed and eliminated by the works for the developing Avonmouth Docks, the second phase of which opened in 1907. Until then, the area remained within the Parliamentary district of Somerset although it was on the Gloucestershire side of the river.

Illustration 2.24: An extract from a map of 1769 naming the Swatch (B. Donn, *Map of the country eleven miles around the city of Bristol* (Bristol, 1769))

(2) **Dunball Island (now part of Huntspill parish, formerly in the River Parrett) and Dunball Clyce**

Another Dunball, or *Dumbal Island*, appears to have been almost part of mainland Somerset when it was first mapped in detail in 1723.[243] Prior to 1739 Dunball Island, consisting of 80 acres, was described as 'having a large river on the west, and a small river on the east, in each of which the vessels passed and repassed'; it was also known in

1723 as a place near to where vessels could anchor. As a result of a hard frost of 1739 the small river was filled up with 'such vast quantities of ice that it turned the current into the large river' subsequently, before the ice melted, it was 'so much covered with slub and slime as to prevent the low water from passing'.[244] It was also known as *Cures Island*, and is shown on a map of 1776.[245] By 1789 the level of the land had risen to nearly the same height as the adjacent land.[246]

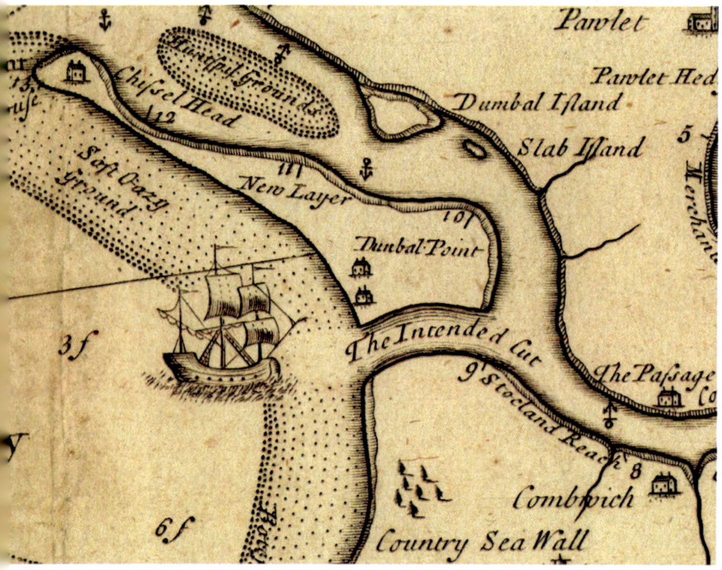

Illustration 2.25: Dunball Island and Dunball Point, as depicted in 1723 (S.H.C., D/RA 9/9)

Dunball Point (Otterhampton)

Not quite opposite the former Dunball Island (2) (see above), but probably named from it, this point was recorded in 1723[247] and copied by Strachey in 1736.[248] However, Day and Masters did not name it in 1782,[249] nor did the first edition of the Ordnance Survey,[250] or the Greenwoods in 1822.[251] It appears on Admiralty chart 1152 as *Lobspound Point.*

Dunball Wharf

Much further up the River Parrett than Dunball Island (2), and so possibly a third distinct instance of the name in question, rather than deriving from the one in Huntspill. This was formerly known as *Down End Pill* (see above). In the early eighteenth century there was a sluice or clyce here.[252] Today it is best known as *Dunball Wharf*, which is still used by commercial vessels; it is unclear whether this was originally named with *wharf* or *warth*.

Dunster Beach

From the place-name *Dunster* + *beach*. The place-name is 'Dunn's tor or crag' (*Dunestore* 1138, *Dunsterr* 1242),[253] *i.e.* the one on which the castle stands.

Embelle Wood Beach (Oare)

From the local name *Embelle Wood* + *beach*. *Embelle* duplicates the farm-name *Emble* in Stogumber (*Imele*, 1086 in Domesday Book), which is of unknown origin. The beach location in Oare is noted as the site of a seventeenth-century bark-drying house, converted in recent years into a home made largely out of driftwood.[254]

English Grounds (west of Clevedon; formerly known as English Hook)

These names are for features on the English side of the deepwater channel of the Bristol Channel; + *ground* (plural), + *hook*. They are paralleled by names formed with *Welsh* on the Welsh side. The English Grounds are named in Dutch by Blaeu as the *Engelsche gronden* in 1625,[255] as *English Ground* by Collins in 1693[256] and Williams in *c.*1706,[257] leading to the suspicion that the English name is an adaptation of one used by Dutch mariners (compare Dutch influence in the use of the name *Bristol Channel*). The name continues to be used in the plural form today.

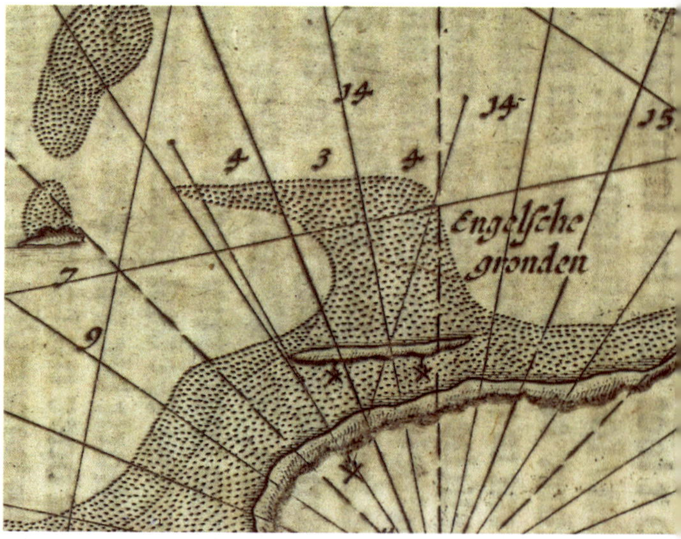

Illustration 2.26: An early Dutch depiction of the English Grounds on a chart published in 1625[258] (Keith Needell Collection)

English Hook

This appears to be the westernmost, hook-shaped, feature of the English Grounds and was first named *c.*1712 on a chart published in 1728.[259] It is a name which does not appear to have been popular or well documented.

Fenlyns Clyce (Cannington and Wembdon)

Unknown element + *clyce*. The first element appears to be a surname + *-s*, but no surname of this form has been traced, and the Irish *Fenlon* has not been discovered historically in Somerset. The feature is located on the parish boundary between Cannington and Wembdon on the south bank of the River Parrett. It is shown on Ordnance Survey maps from 1886.[260]

Fennings Island (Huntspill)

At the present northern tip of Stert Point, and as recently as the late nineteenth century a tidal island; perhaps a derivative of the word *fen* 'marsh', though it is worth recalling that the surname *Venning* is found in the Bridgwater area in the nineteenth century and the place-name has not been traced back any further. The apparently possessive *-s* may suggest such an origin.[261] The surname *Fenning* is also possible, but that surname is mainly East Anglian. If this is not correct, the name must be older than it appears from the documentary record, and be derived from Old English *fenn* 'fen, marsh', + the place-name forming element *-ing*. The *-s* would then be explained as a random accretion like the material which formed the island.

Like Dunball Island (1) formerly at the mouth of the River Avon, Fennings Island was formerly an area of inter-tidal mud. Over the years the build-up of marine deposits caused it to become an island. Payne on his map of 1723 shows this area as *Huntspil Grounds*.[262] Strachey, in 1736, shows a large unnamed bank in the River Parrett.[263] Significantly it was mapped as *North Slime Batch* and *Great Slime Batch* in 1776,[264] and then as an unnamed island by Day and Masters in 1782,[265] but as *Fennings Island* to the west of the main channel by the Ordnance surveyors in 1809 with an additional channel to the west again,[266] followed by Denham in 1832.[267] By 1886 there was only one channel to the east of it and by 1904 it was part of the mainland.[268] It is shown on Admiralty chart 1152 as the headland that is adjacent to Stert Point.

Illustration 2.27: North Slime Batch and Great Slime Batch (in the River Parrett) in 1776 (S.H.C., D/P/hun 23/6)

Fiddler's Point (Brean)
Probably from a surname + *point*; but the surname *Fiddler* or *Fidler* is very uncommon in Somerset.[270] Situated on the north side of Brean Down, it is mentioned on the 1884 six inch Ordnance map.

Firefly Rocks (off Portishead)
This feature was recorded as *Lucifer Rock* in 1847 but in that year it was also named *Firefly Rock*[271] and published as such on 10 May 1848.[272] Both the *Firefly* and the *Lucifer* were ships involved with famine relief work in Ireland in the autumn of 1846.[273] The former name, the one which stuck, commemorated a survey ship, commanded by Captain F.W. Beechey from 1844 to 1847, which was involved in numerous surveys at different places off the west coast of England and Wales.[274] Today the name is shown in the plural form on Admiralty chart 1176.[275]

First Rocks (Porlock)
Presumably the first rocks seen after clearing The Gore on leaving Porlock Bay, heading west.

Illustration 2.28: First Rocks at Porlock Weir, 2013 © Steve Daniels, and licensed for reuse under Creative Commons License Attribution-ShareAlike 2.0 Generic (CC BY-SA 2.0)

Flat Holm or Flatholm
From Old Scandinavian (Old Norse) *flatr* 'flat' or Old English *flot* 'deep water' + *holm*. Flat Holm, in St Mary's parish, Cardiff, Glamorgan, has been included in this study because of its relationship to Somerset's maritime place-names. Its name has been stated[276] to contain Scandinavian *floti* 'fleet' + *holm* 'small island' (on the basis of the spellings *Flotholm* recorded in 1375, *the Floteholmes* 1387); Charles took the view that it contains Old Norse *flatr* 'flat'.[277] Watts, following earlier scholarship, links the name with the incident reported in the *Anglo-Saxon chronicle*, when a Viking fleet was starved out of the island in 917, according to the A-version; the other versions of the *Chronicle* say this happened at Steep Holm, and Coates explains why this must be correct.[278] Flat Holm is actually quite flat, by marked contrast with its English neighbour Steep Holm. Coates (2014) suggests that Scandinavian names containing North Germanic */a/ with *u*-mutation (such as the word *flatr* would have) usually appear in England with /a/, so *flatr* is expected to yield *flat* in English names, rather than *flot*. But it is possible that this name originates later than the bulk of relevant names in England, that it was given by Dublin Vikings, and that it is from *u*-mutated *flot* 'piece of flat ground', and could therefore be rendered at a later date (post-eighth or -ninth century) with English or Welsh /o/. So if such a relatively late Scandinavian origin is accepted, there is no objection to its being 'flat island' rather than 'fleet island'. Alternatively, however, it may be from Old English *flot* 'deep water, sea', since it is the closer of the two islands to the (present-day) deepwater channel in the Severn Sea. Whichever explanation is preferred, the name does not have to allude to the tenth-century events which in any case probably took place on Steep Holm.

Flats Channel
From *flat* (plural) + *channel*. Mackenzie junior noted that this was 'between Langford Grounds and English Grounds' in the early 1770s.[279] He was referring to a channel over the Clevedon Flats, as can be clearly seen on a contemporary chart.[280] After this time the term is not used on printed charts, nor in sailing directions published before 1825.[281]

Fort Point (Portishead)
See **Portishead Point**.

Four Fathom Ledge (south-east of Flat Holm, north-east of Steep Holm)
Depth measurement + *ledge*. This was named by Denham in his survey published in 1839.[282] It should not be confused with the *Five feet Shoal* recorded by Mackenzie junior which was just to the south of Flat Holm and therefore close enough not to have been mistakenly placed in the wrong position.[283]

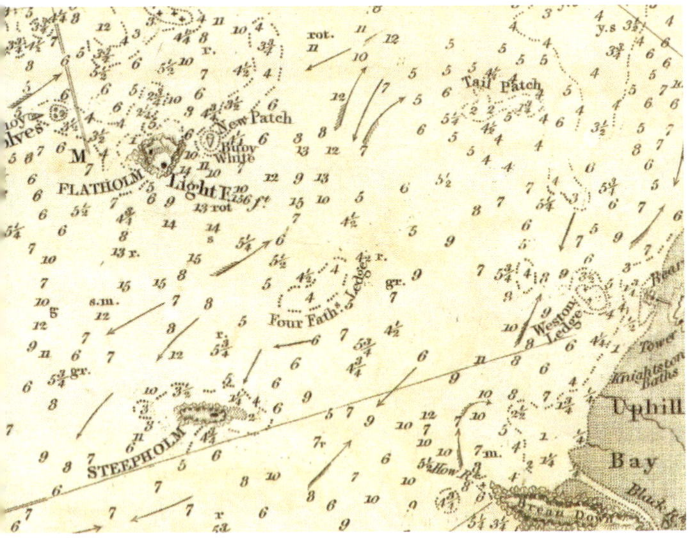

Illustration 2.29: Denham's depiction of the Four Fathom Ledge published in 1839 (Adrian Webb Collection)

Fresemare

This place was between Portishead Pill and Clevedon Pill, in an area possibly below Kettles Wood where ships used to moor. It is depicted in a map or view of the Somerset coast drawn in 1539, but not placed precisely enough to identify it with any modern feature.[284] The name, which is lost, appears to contain the words ancestral to *fresh* and *mere*, and in that case can be compared with the river *Cuckmere* in Sussex, from Old English *cwicu* 'live' + *mere* 'pool'.

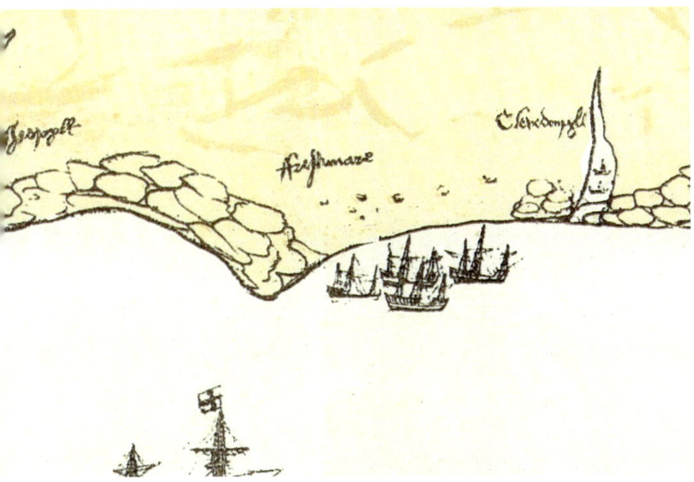

Illustration 2.30: *Fresemare* (centre) situated between Portishead and Clevedon, as depicted in 1539 (E. Green, *The preparations in Somerset against the Spanish Armada, A.D. 1558-1588* (London, 1888))

Gables, The (Minehead)

Currently shown on Admiralty chart 1152 near the low water mark off Minehead. The name presumably alludes to its shape.

Gaunt's Clyce (Pawlett)

To the south of Gaunt's Farm. From the surname *Gaunt*, rare in Somerset in recent centuries, + *clyce*. Mapped by the Ordnance Survey in 1886.[285]

Glenthorne Beach (Oare)

From the house-name *Glenthorne*, over the Devon county boundary in Countisbury, + *beach*. The Tudor Gothic house was built in 1829-30 by the Rev. Walter Halliday. The name is a fancy 'Romantic' invention hinting at his Scottish ancestry.

Glentworth Bay (Weston-super-Mare)

So called at least as early as 1887 (postcard evidence); named from a large house on the seafront, itself presumably named after the village in Lincolnshire. *Glentworth Terrace* is named in 1866.[286]

Gore Anchorage, Gore Bank and Gore Sand (Bridgwater Bay)

These three names contain the descendant either of Old English *gāra* 'gore, triangular feature' or of *gor* 'dirt'. + *anchorage*, + *bank*, + *sand*. The original triangular feature (if that is what is at stake) may be Gore Sand, recorded as such in 1809; of course sandbanks may change in shape and extent.

Payne, in his chart of 1723, shows an anchor symbol indicating a safe anchorage off Botestal Point.[287] Mackenzie junior, in the early 1770s, appears to have been the first to describe it in any detail as being 'between Gore Bank, and the drying muddy shore from off Bostol's point and Start point. Vessels that are going into Parret River, and are too early for the tide, anchor in the Gore; but other vessels, seldom come there'. He also notes: 'There is much more water, and room, in the western, than in the eastern part of the Gore anchorage' and it was 'more safe to anchor nearer to the muddy shore along the south side of the Gore anchorage, than it is to Gore Bank'.[288] This anchorage is still in use today.

A Spanish account of navigating the Bristol Channel, dated 1597, includes a brief description of navigating towards Bridgwater from the Holms. Although Gore Sand is not explicitly named, it is clear that between Steep Holm and the port of Bridgwater there were 'many sand bars which are ever changing'. It was also noted that at the mouth of the Parrett there were 'two fathoms at low water, large ships have to watch out for the currents. After entering within there is a depth of four or five fathoms'.[289] The depth of two fathoms corresponds with the depth on Waghenaer's chart that had been published in the previous decade.[290] The name did not change in the centuries that followed, with Payne's chart of 1723 being the first to depict the sand with any accuracy.[291] It is shown on Admiralty chart 1152 to the east and adjacent to Bridgwater Bar.

Illustration 2.31: The stippled area with the Dutch wording '*Met leech water twe fadem*', to warn mariners of a depth of only two fathoms at 'empty' (low) water; includes the area of the Gore Anchorage and Gore Sand in 1589[292] (Robin Bush Collection)

Gore Point (Porlock)

Shown on a plan of Porlock, at the western end of Porlock Bay, *c.*1714.[293] The name, of the same origin as the *Gore* names above, 'triangle', continues in use to this day.

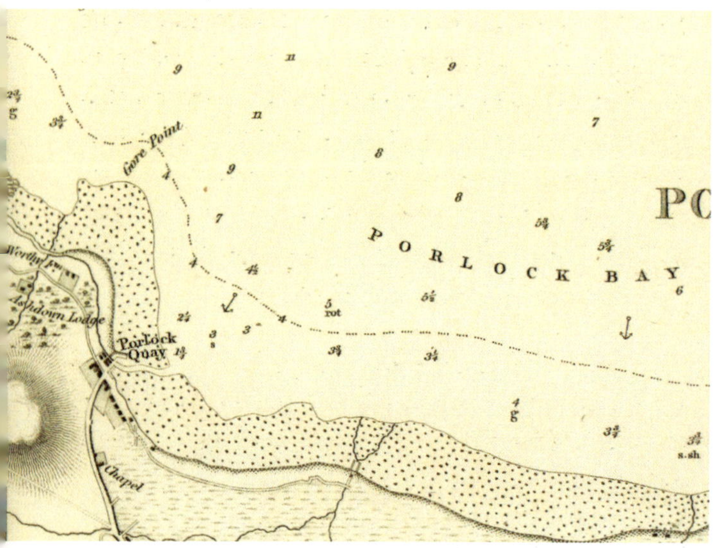

Illustration 2.32: Gore Point at Porlock from a survey of 1831 (U.K.H.O., OCB 1181 A1)

Graham Banks, Graham Shoal

Presumably named after Sir James Graham, who was First Lord of the Admiralty from 1830-4. It was initially named *Graham Shoal* in 1831 by Denham and Robinson,[295] but when their survey was published in 1839 it was changed to *Graham Banks*.[296] The latter name remains in use on Admiralty chart 1152.

Gray Rock (Old Cleeve)

Self-explanatory.

Greenaleigh Point and Greenaleigh Sand (Minehead)

From the place-name *Greenaleigh* + *point*, + *sand*. Greenaleigh is a farm towards the eastern end of North Hill above Minehead. Its name is of unknown age, but appears to be *green* with a retained inflectional vowel *-a* more typical of Devon names (compare *Greenawell* in North Bovey), but as also in *Smalla Combe* on Exmoor, + *leigh* descended from Old English *lēah* 'wood, clearing'. It is *Greenaley* in 1638,[298] *Green a Leigh* in 1684, and *Greenaleigh* in 1687.[299] From a charting perspective, this name is a late addition to charts of the Bristol Channel, only appearing in the 1770s.[300] Greenaleigh Sand is shown on the Ordnance Survey mapping below Greenaleigh Point and not as an offshore hazard.

Gullhouse Point (Clevedon)

On current Ordnance Survey maps. It is mentioned in 1864 that there is a cottage built against the sea wall.[301] The point is therefore named from a building, but nothing further is known about it.

Hang Rock (Portishead)

On current Ordnance Survey maps. Perhaps condensed from *Hanging Rock*, but evidence is lacking.

Hawn, The (Dunster)

A stretch of the River Avill. From *hawen*, a recorded variant of Middle English *hāven* 'harbour': it is the old harbour of Dunster, now just a water feature in the beach.

Helwell Bay (Watchet)

On current Ordnance Survey maps. Helwell is mentioned as a place on the land in 1870.[302] It appears in *Helwell Point* in 1876.[303] Helwell Bay is not shown on the 1887 Ordnance map[304] but appears on the 1904 edition.[305] The name is unexplained. If it is genuinely old, the first element may be Old English *hǣlu* 'health, cure', and the whole therefore 'healing spring' (Old English *wielle*) or similar.

Highbridge
A self-explanatory name on record since 1324, sometimes in its Latin translation, [*juxta* 'near'] *Altum Pontem*. The bridge was over the River Brue, and was the lowest crossing-point on that river.

Hinkley Point (Stogursey)
Shown on the first edition of the Ordnance Survey published in 1809 as *Inkley Point*.[306] It is mentioned in published sailing directions from 1839,[307] but otherwise remains an uncommon name on pre-1825 maritime publications.[308] No earlier record of this name has been discovered and its origin is unknown. It may be related to the equally elusive *Hankley Brake*,[309] adjacent in Stogursey parish, or it may be connected with the surname *Hinkley* (from Hinckley, Leicestershire) found in Middlezoy in 1781.[310] The feature was earlier known as **Botestal Point**.

Hole, The (off Portishead)
Shown on Admiralty chart 1859 since 1990.[311]

Hole's Mouth
The former mouth of the River Avon, or of what came to be called *the North Channel* when the new mouth opened up. This is a name appearing on Benjamin Donn's map of 11 miles around Bristol[312] but not mentioned in sailing directions published before 1825, possibly due to the greater importance of the adjacent anchorage King Road.[313] The name has not been fully explained. It is one of the places mentioned in the extent of the limits of the Port of Bristol in the seventeenth century.[314] It was stranded by the shift of the mouth of the Avon southwards in the mid-nineteenth century (see **Dumball (1)** and **Swash**), and today its site is within the Avonmouth dock complex, leaving its name on a railway junction at the northern end.

Holms, The
A collective name for Flat Holm and Steep Holm. A final *-s* also occurs from time to time in the names of the individual islands (*Floteholmes*, 1387;[315] *Stipehoames*, 1583;[316] the Islands *Flathomes*, and *Steepholmes*, between the shores of, the Channel, and the coast of Glamorgan, 1832;[317] Wenceslas Hollar's map of 1644 has *Flatholme Il.* but *Stepeholmes Il.*).[318] This curiosity, though striking and persistent, has not been explained.

Honeycombe Rock (Clevedon)
Presumably named from its pitted appearance. White included *The Honeycomb rock* on his chart of 1825 which appears never to have been published.[319] It is shown on the first edition Ordnance Survey of 1830 as *Spear Rock*,[320] but does not appear on modern published Admiralty charts. See under **Spear Rocks** (below) for an illustration.

Hope Sand (near Sand Point)
Probably from Old Scandinavian *hóp* 'small bay', which is appropriate here for the feature called *Middle Hope* (halfway between Sand Point and St Thomas' Head), though early spellings are lacking, + *sand*. Such a name may include the Scandinavian word borrowed as an English word; in any event, it would be expected to become *hoop* in Modern English, but it may have become associated with the common word *hope*, commonly found in maritime contexts in the expression *hope anchor*. The name does not appear on Day and Masters' map of 1782, but they distinctly show a cove or bay.[321] The names *Middle Hope Sand* and *Middle Hope* appear on the first edition Ordnance Survey of 1809.[322] It appears as *Hope-Sand* in a sailing direction published in 1821[323] and as *Hope Sand* on the Greenwoods' map of 1822.[324] A case might be made that the name includes Old English *hop* 'remote secluded valley' in the dative case, *hope*, which would give a better match phonologically; the existence of various *hope* names such as *Stanford le Hope* in non-Danelaw Essex appears to confirm the English word, but the sense there appears to be 'enclosure in marshland',[325] and cannot apply here near St Thomas' Head.

Horseshoe Bend (Abbots Leigh)
An accurate description of the shape of the most marked bend in the River Avon between Bristol and Pill.

Horseshoe Rock (Portishead)
Shown by Denham in 1839 on his chart[326] and

mentioned in his sailing directions of the same year. Shown by Beechey in his plan of 1847 to the north-west of Firefly Rock[327] and mentioned by J. S. Hobbs in 1854.[328] It is no longer marked on current Admiralty charts.

Horsey Pill (Bridgwater Without)

From a place-name meaning 'horse island' in Old English, + *pill.* The place in question is the lost village of Horsey in Bridgwater, at ST 3239, recoded as *Hursi* in Domesday Book (1086). The pill is shown on a chart of 1723.[329]

Howe Rock (off the end of Brean Down, Brean)

Shown on a nautical chart of *c.*1706[330] and named from 1723 as the *How Rock* or *How Rocks.*[331] It appears on today's Admiralty chart number 1152. The name is possibly from Old Scandinavian *haugr* 'mound, (hill shaped like a) burial mound' or *hǫfuð* 'head', with reference to the shape or the prominence of the adjacent Brean Down.[332]

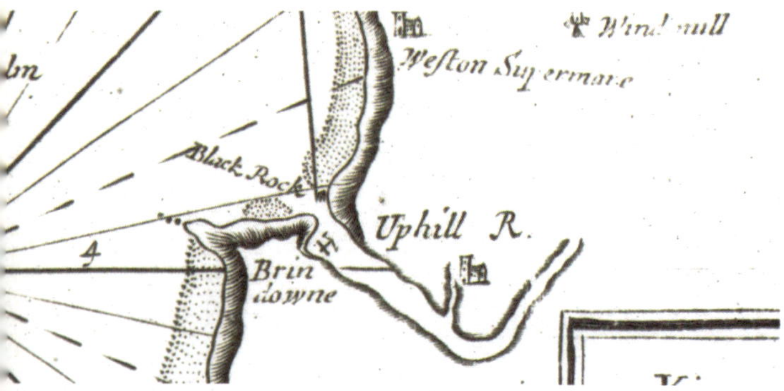

Illustration 2.33: Howe Rock shown as three rocks at the western end of Brean Down in *c.*1706[333] (Admiralty Library Collection)

Hung Road (reach of the River Avon between Pill and Shirehampton)

First mentioned in documents of the late fifteenth and early sixteenth centuries, as *Hongrod* in 1480[334] and *hungrode* also in 1480.[335] It was a *road*stead or sheltered anchorage. The huge tidal range here (some 43 feet) did not always permit sailing ships to depart for the historic port of Bristol. They frequently had to wait for the water to rise until there was enough clearance to make the journey, towed for centuries by the hobblers or teams of oarsmen from Pill. While waiting, they needed to be moored, and most local writers on the subject seem to think that that is how Hung Road got its name: as the tide fell, the ships were left suspended or hung and kept upright by ropes from their masts to bollards or rings above them on the riverbank. Others think they were simply left to rest as the tide fell, and were said to be hung as they hit bottom on the mud and maybe tilted over. The first idea sounds more plausible. The best interpretation is 'roadstead where ships need to be hung (*i.e.* rather than anchored)'.

Huntspill and Huntspill Grounds

The village takes its name from that of a creek, whose course is now impossible to trace with certainty because of drainage works, but which must have been interfered with by the engineering of the broad drain or river now called *Huntspill River.* The village is recorded as *Hunespulle* in the late eighth century (*Hunespille* 1084, *Honspil, Hvnespil* 1086, *Hunespil(le)* 1170, *Hunespulle c.*1250, *Honyspill* 1408, *Huntspill* 1610),[336] from the Anglo-Saxon personal name *Hūn* 'bear-cub' in the genitive case with *-es*, + *pill.*

Huntspill Grounds is from the place-name + *ground* (plural). See under **Fenning Island** (above).

Hurlstone Point (Bossington)

A prominent headland with a name of debatable origin + *point*, recorded in 1539 as *Hurston*[337] and in 1586 as *Horestone.*[338] The base place-name has been altered over the years from *Hoorston* or *Horestone*, to *Hurtstone*, and to modern *Hurlstone.* In 1558 it was mentioned in a local court record as *Horestone,*[339] and by a local man in the late Elizabethan period as *Hoorston.*[340] If these earliest records are reliable, it seems to be an instance of the common Old English *hār* 'grey, as if covered with lichen' + *stān* 'stone', probably used of, or compared with, a boundary marker or a standing stone.

The name is subsequently found in an unhelpful, and occasionally misleading, variety of spellings: as *Hurstone Point* on a chart of *c.*1706,[341] *Horsedon Poynt* on a map of 1735,[342] *Hurstone Point* in a sailing direction from the early 1770s,[343] and *Horestone Point* in 1791.[344] It has been variously named on charts published before 1830 as *Horsdown Point, Horsedown* or *Hurstone Point, Hulstone Point, Hurstone,*[345] *Hurtstone Point* and *Hustone Point.* The Ordnance Survey first edition of 1809 shows it as *Hurtstone, Hartland* (clearly an error for the well-known name on the north Devon coast) *or Bossington Point,*[346] and later editions of the Ordnance Survey continued to use *Hurtstone* until the spelling with <-l-> appeared in revisions of the 1970s.

Exactly when it became *Hurlstone* in nautical publications, and hence in general usage, can be pinned down accurately. It is due to what appears to be a typographical error in the 1813 edition of *Laurie and Whittle's new sailing directions to accompany the Channel pilot and their large general chart of the English Channel.*[347] In the previous edition, published in 1810, it appears as *Hurstone Point.*[348] In the 1813 edition it had been changed to *Hurlstone,*[349] perhaps by association with the idea of *hurl* + *stone*. Subsequently, in 1832, Denham incorrectly used the term *Hurlstone Point* on his survey published in 1839,[350] and the name has been in use in error on Admiralty charts ever since; see Admiralty chart 1152.

If, on the other hand, the <-l-> is authentic though ill-recorded, it is just about possible that this name may represent Old English *thyrel-stān* 'hole-stone', with the <th-> understood as the definite article *the* and removed. That would imply a rock-arch here. Compare *Thurlstone* in Devon, where there is a spectacular detached rock-arch on the beach, and the even better-known attached arch *Durdle Door* at West Lulworth in Dorset, where *Durdle* is from *thyrel* in a south-western dialect form. This is geologically possible in these parts, as witness the Giant's Rib natural arch on this stretch of coast, just over the county boundary in Countisbury (Devon). From the point of view of the spellings in the documentary record, this looks a fairly remote possibility, but, as Philip Ashford has noted, there is an arch of sorts here. Situated between Bossington Beach and Selworthy Sands, it is under an anticline of Hangman grit, and is little known, not being visible from any settlement or path and hence being unmapped. It is locally known as *Gull Hole*. It is only approachable by foot at low tide, and even then with extreme care. Ashford describes it as 'more a 40 metre long cave open at both ends than a conventional arch as at Thurlstone, Devon'.[351] Whilst this appears unlikely to provide the origin of the name as recorded, the possibility of its influence cannot be completely discounted.

Iron Grounds *(yren groundes, Iron Groundis)*

A name in use in the fifteenth century, but its exact location is not known;[352] it possibly refers to the southern shore of the Bristol Channel from Lundy to the Holms. It could well be below the Holms, but equally it could be above them. It is not an alternative name for Culver Sand, nor Nash Sands. Is there a clue on Blaeu's chart, published in 1625, that shows the English Grounds as the only significant danger to shipping?[353] With its numerous rocks and sand banks, at low tide it looks menacing enough perhaps to be thought of as iron-like.

Ivy Stone (Oare)

A narrow promontory on a coast with much slipped rock, the reason for whose name is not obvious, unless it was literally topped by an area covered with ivy, which cannot therefore have been directly in the way of salt spray. The surname *Ivey* is well represented in Somerset, but mainly in the east of the county (Wincanton, Evercreech). Mapped in 1887.[354]

Illustration 2.34: Ivy Stone, 2010 (© Tim Harrison, licensed for reuse under Creative Commons Licence Attribution-ShareAlike 2.0 Generic (CC BY-SA 2.0), https://creativecommons.org/licenses/by-sa/2.0/)

Kermoor Piling (Carhampton)

Named on Ordnance Survey maps since at least 1888. The *piling* is the remnant of an attempt to slow down coastal erosion. The place is on the edge of Ker Moor, whose name is of uncertain origin, but may include *curre*, a local word for various species of diving duck.[355]

Kilkenny Bay (off West Hill, Portishead)

The place in Portishead was recorded as such by the surveyor Richard Thomas on his chart of 1815.[356] The name must be directly or indirectly from the

Irish place-name *Kilkenny* (Irish *Cill-Chainnigh* 'church of [Saint] Cainneach)' + *bay*.

In England this is a fairly frequent minor name (*e.g.* for pubs, and there is a house of this name in Wraxall). Known connections between Somerset and Bristol with Kilkenny are numerous; for instance, in 1515[357] and the 1530s a man from Kilkenny was recorded in Bristol.[358] Kilkenny was granted city status by King James I in 1609, and figured in several important events of Anglo-Irish history. The present name must derive from one such event, perhaps the setting up there of a pro-Royalist government in Ireland in 1642, or its capture by Cromwell's forces in 1650, or the stay of the expelled King James II there in 1689-1690. Or perhaps the name alludes to brawling, and is due to the well-documented mutual hatred of the Irish and English inhabitants in earlier times which may also give rise to the famous rhyme about Kilkenny cats.[359] So in Portishead it is likely to be for a lost, almost certainly seventeenth-century, house or inn, and the bay must take its name from that.

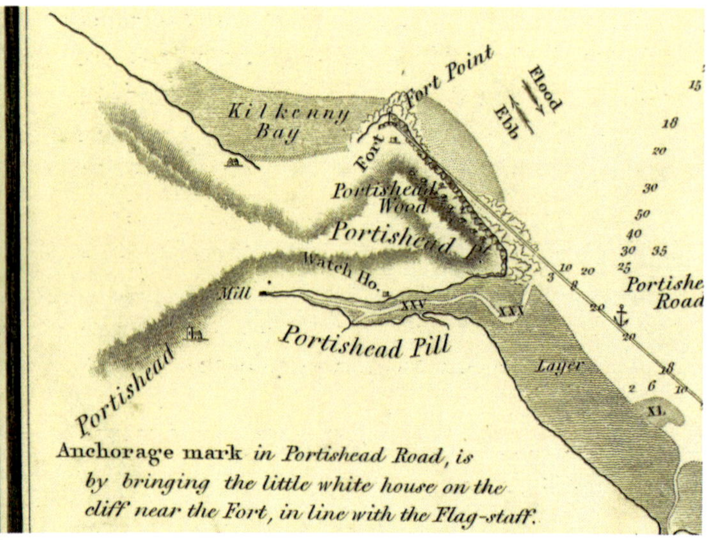

Illustration 2.35: An extract from a survey of the River Severn by Richard Thomas, 1815 (U.K.H.O., L3895)

Kilve Patch and Kilve Pill

From the place-name *Kilve* + *patch*, + *pill*. Kilve Patch does not appear to have been used on navigational charts until Denham recorded it in his survey of 1832, published in 1839.[360] According to Ekwall and Watts[361] the base place-name is from an unrecorded Old English **cylfe*, cognate with Old Scandinavian *kylfa* 'club', with reference to a hill of such a shape. No such hill is obvious there. An even riskier suggestion is that it might be an irregular derivative of British Celtic **gulbjo-* 'headland', which is in fact the regular cognate of the Old Scandinavian word. But initial <G-> would then be expected, rather than <K->. There is no significant headland either, but plenty of evidence at low tide for the erosion of a considerable amount of land, including the base of a possibly prominent headland evident in the map illustration: Stoke Spit, projecting from Little Stoke Point, and clearly visible from Kilve at low tide though actually in modern Stringston parish; an earlier one nearer to Kilve might be envisaged. The pill is now a freshwater stream which runs across the engineered pebbly beach.

Illustration 2.36: The remains of a formerly greater Stoke Spit?, 2016 (Richard Coates)

King Road

From Middle English *king* 'king' + *rōde* 'roadstead'. This is the sheltered roadstead in the Severn between Portishead Point and the mouth of the Avon. The reason for the royal designation of the roadstead, and its age, are not known, but it goes back to at least the fifteenth century. It appears as *Kynge Rode* in 1480,[363] *(le) Kingerode* in 1484,[364] and (frequently) *Kingsrode*, for ex. in 1577.[365] This is where ships waited for the tide before beginning the dangerous seven-mile journey up the Avon Gorge to Bristol. They would be escorted upriver by the traditional hobblers (rowers) from Pill.

Kingston Pill (Kingston Seymour)

From the place-name *Kingston* 'king's farm or village' + *pill*. Recorded as *Kingestones pille c.*1590.[366] Shown on Admiralty chart 1176 as a naturally shaped inlet.[367]

Knightstone (Weston-super-Mare)

Recorded as *Knyghston* in 1539.[368] This island at Weston is first mapped on the first series Ordnance Survey one-inch map of 1830.[369] Its origin is not firmly established. Perhaps it was 'the stone called The Knight', or the *nigh* or 'near' stone, being closer to the shore than its counterpart Birnbeck. Brian Austin notes that in early local deeds it is called *Nite Stone*, and we find also *Night Stone Rock* in 1813.[370] He interprets this older name as an allusion to black marble deposits. He attributes the <K-> to the discovery of a skeleton in a cave here in the 1820s, at the time locally dubbed a 'Roman knight'; but the <K-> predates this, and that particular wording for the discovery would hardly have been used if the place had not already been thought of as 'Knight Stone'.

In its modern spelling, it duplicates two Devon place-names, in Morchard Bishop and Ottery St Mary; it is not known whether it might incorporate a surname deriving from one of these places which has become extinct in modern times.

Illustration 2.37: Dr Fox's 'Knight stone', 20 August 1831 (S.A.N.H.S., A/DAS/1/439/4)

Ladye Bay and Ladye Point (Clevedon)

Unexplained. Mackenzie junior refers to *Ladie's Point* over twenty times in his sailing directions of the early 1770s.[371] This is shown as *Leedy Point* on a chart compiled in the 1820s[372] and on the first edition of the Ordnance Survey mapping in 1830, as well as *Leedy Bay*.[373] It is on the current Admiralty chart 1176 as *Ladye Point*, which has become the generally used spelling.[374] This present spelling curiously recalls that of Ladye Place, the house in Hurley, Berkshire, where the invasion of William, Prince of Orange, in 1688 was plotted.

Landrock (Weston-super-Mare)

In 1548 fish stalls are recorded as being in the sea on the *Owcerok* and the *Landrock*.[375] Perhaps the latter is to be interpreted as the rock nearer land, by comparison with the *Owcerok* [= *Outerock*?].

Langford Grounds and Langford Swatch

Apparently a place-name + *ground* (plural). A bank of mud and sand at the mouth of the river Yeo. No explanation has been offered. The surname *Langford*, from the Somerset place of that name (Old English *lang* 'long' + *ford* 'ford'), is well recorded in Somerset from at least the seventeenth century, but is not demonstrably relevant here. An early maritime text of 1461x1483 mentions sailing to Bristol through the *wasshe groundes and of langbord*, most likely the Welsh Grounds and Langford.[376] Langford Grounds was not named by Blaeu as he showed the area simply as the *Engelsche gronden* in 1625.[377] Neither was it named by Collins in 1693[378] or by Williams on his chart of *c.*1706.[379] Holliday delineated it in *c.*1712, but called it *Languerd*, possibly the 'long guard', possibly a reminiscence of *Landguard* (Shanklin, Isle of Wight) or more likely amounting to *Langverd* and if so just a spelling variant of *Langford* influenced by Somerset pronunciation.[380] Later chart makers also used a variant spelling *Longford*.[381] It continues to be known today as *Langford Grounds* on Admiralty chart 1176.[382]

Illustration 2.38: *Languerd Grounds* from Holliday's chart of the inner Bristol Channel, *c.*1712 (Adrian Webb Collection)

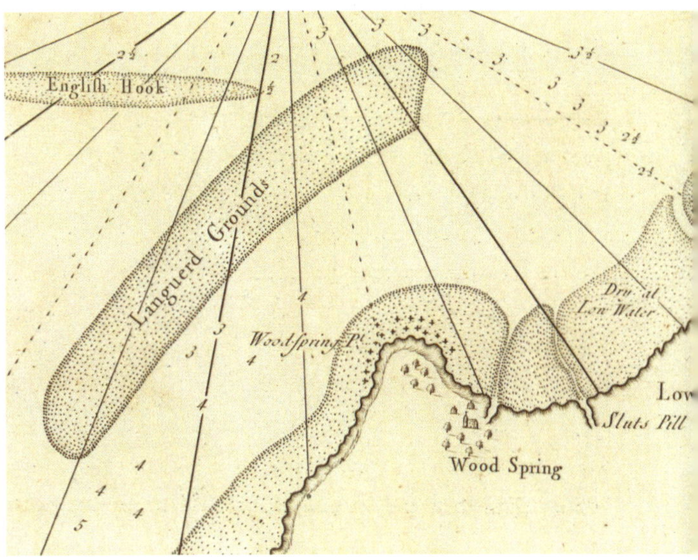

Langford Grounds gives its name to Langford Swatch. Although not named on charts in the early eighteenth century, a channel is depicted between Langford Grounds (see above) and the edge of the inter-tidal ground to the north of Woodspring.[383] It is shown on the current Admiralty chart, number 1176, as a channel running roughly north to south separating Langford Grounds from the coast.[384]

Lark Sand and Lark Spit

Spit in the sense 'long narrow feature like a roasting spit' is well established in maritime names. The spit is named from Lark Sand, a feature with a name of great antiquity appearing as *Laverkesond* (Middle English for 'lark sand', for no obvious reason) in a Patent Roll of 1310.[385]

Payne showed this as the Gore Sand in 1723,[386] whereas Denham recorded the feature as *Stert Spit or Lark Sand* in 1832.[387] Today only Lark Spit is shown on Admiralty chart 1152.

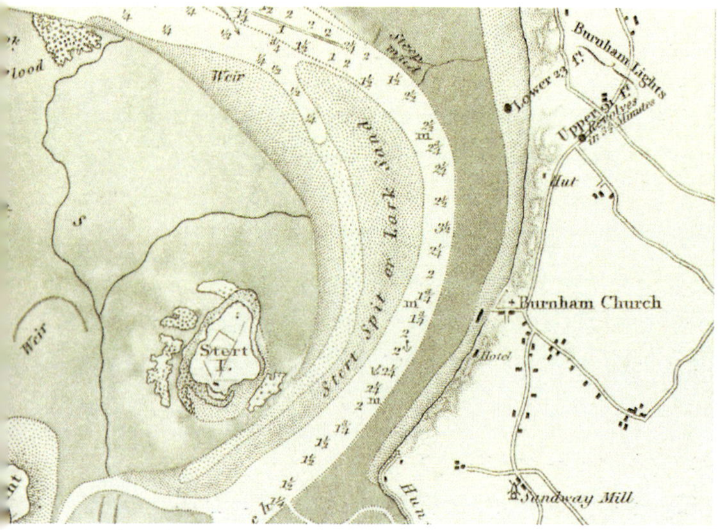

Illustration 2.39: Denham's 1832 survey of the River Parrett and surrounding area depicting the use of the dual name (chart published in 1839; U.K.H.O., OCB 1157 A1)

Lee Mouth (Porlock)

Mentioned in 1791 as a small village located where the River Lee exits into the Bristol Channel.[388] The name of the river is obscure, and further references to the 'village' are lacking.

Leedy Point

See **Ladye Point** above.

Lilstock Point (Lilstock)

From the place-name *Lilstock* + *point.* Shown by the Greenwoods in their county map of 1822.[389] The base place-name (*Lulestoch* 1086, *Lulinstoke* 1204, *Lillingstok* 1285, *Lillestoke* 1386, *Lylstok* 1532, *Lystoke* 1610) includes the Old English given name *Lilla* or *Lulla* + the connective *-ing-* + *stoc* 'secondary settlement of some kind'.[390] It appeared on a small scale navigational chart of the English Channel as *Lystock* in 1693,[391] which may be an engraver's error. It became corrupted to *Little Stoke Point* in the early nineteenth century thanks to its inclusion in that spelling on the first edition Ordnance Survey of 1809.[392] That name is extracted from *Little Stoke or Lilstock Point,* which appears in 1824.[393] Not shown on Ordnance Survey maps of 1887.[394]

Little Bay (Weston-super-Mare)

Shown on the 1888 Ordnance Survey map to the north of Knightstone Island. The site is that of Marine Lake and Glentworth Bay by the 1931 revision.

Little Stoke Point (Lilstock)

See **Lilstock Point** (above).

Littleharp Bay and Littleharp Point (Clevedon)

Shown on Ordnance Survey mapping close to the shoreline at Clevedon, but not shown on navigational charts before 1825.[395] These features take their names from the Little Harp pub, which is probably named after a sailing vessel, if the pub's sign is anything to go by. It has been suggested alternatively that the reference is to an item of salt-boiler's equipment. Such a sense is plausible – there is an Anglo-Saxon reference to a *sealtherpe* 'salt-harp' – but it is not recorded from England in Jennings' *Dialect of the West of England: particularly Somersetshire* (1869), Wright's *English Dialect Dictionary* (1898-1905) or the *Oxford English Dictionary.*

Lobspound Point (Otterhampton)

Formerly known as **Dunbal Point** (see above).[396] Its present name, shown on Admiralty chart 1152 to the north of Combwich on the banks of the River Parrett, is a modern one added before 1963.[397] Its origin is not established, but it may contain the surname *Lobb,* from Middle English *lobbe* 'pollack', well recorded in Somerset including at North Petherton in the early eighteenth century,[398] + *pound* 'enclosure of some type'.

Lucifer Rock (Portishead)

This is an offshore feature with possibly the shortest-lived name during the period of this study. When Denham's chart was published in 1839 it did not include this feature.[399] When the area was re-surveyed by Beechey in 1845 he also missed it,[400] but on his return in 1847 he recorded it and named it *Lucifer Rock*.[401] But it was named *Firefly Rock* in 1847 (see above).[402] It is likely it was named after the survey vessel of the same name that was commanded by Commander G.A. Frazer, working off the coast of Ireland from 1844 to 1847.[403]

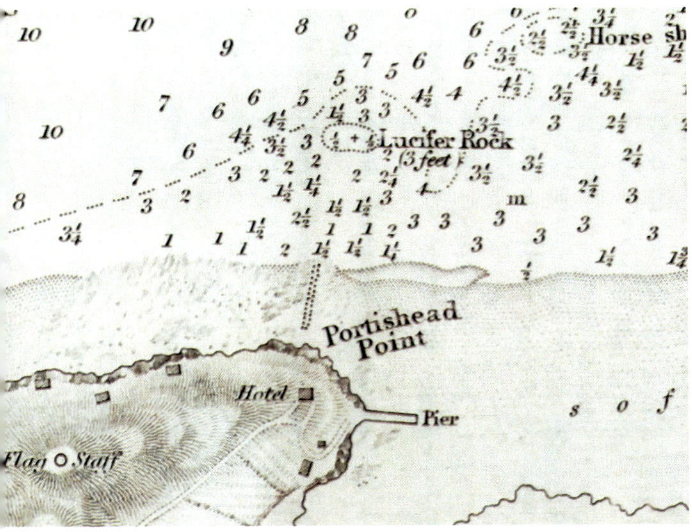

Illustration 2.40: Lucifer Rock off Portishead Point, as shown in the *Nautical Magazine* of 1847[404] (Admiralty Library)

Madbrain Sands (Dunster)

On current Ordnance Survey maps. It appeared on Admiralty chart 1160 from 1974.[405] It is the site of a shipwreck exposed at low tide, believed to be that of the Bristol Packet, lost in 1808.[406] No specific explanation of the name is known, but there are many possibly relevant reports posted on the Web of quicksand at Minehead.

Margaret's Bay (Walton in Gordano)

On current Ordnance Survey maps. From the given name + *bay*. The identity of Margaret has not been established. Not shown on current Admiralty charts.

Merchants Reach

A stretch of the River Parrett between Pawlett and Wembdon. Shown on a chart of 1723,[407] and recorded on the Ordnance Survey of 1886 as *Marchant's Reach* in 1886 on the Wembdon side of the River Parrett.[408] The surname *Marchant* is moderately frequent in Somerset in the eighteenth century, and may appear in this name.

Middle Grounds

Middle + *ground* (plural). This feature is in the geographical centre of the Severn estuary, but on the Welsh side of the deepwater channel. The area was depicted as part of the English Grounds by Denham in 1831.[409]

Middle Hope Cove and Middle Hope Sands (Kewstoke)

The names *Middle Hope Sand* and *Middle Hope* appear on the first edition Ordnance Survey of 1809.[410] Denham's survey published in 1839 shows *Middlehope Beach*.[411] Today it is shown on Admiralty chart 1152 on the north side of Middle Hope as *Middle Hope Sands*. See **Hope Sands** above.

Illustration 2.41: Middle Hope Beach as depicted by Denham and Robinson in the 1830s[412] (Adrian Webb Collection)

Miles Dock (Abbots Leigh)

Situated on the Somerset side of the River Avon near Leigh Woods, this was a small dock created in 1795 for the transportation of quarried stone, and later celestine and other materials, extracted on what became the Miles family estate of Leigh Court in the nineteenth century.[413]

Mine Head, Minehead; Minehead Bluff, Minehead Quay and Minehead Road (Minehead)

Mine Head is the ancient name of what is now called *North Hill*, the prominent mass overlooking Minehead town, + *head*. The town takes on the name of this headland. The ancient hill-name is *Myne Hill*, which is extracted from an unrecorded name deriving from Brittonic **mönïð* 'hill, mountain, (moorland) hill-pasture' + Old English *dūn* 'hill', according to Ekwall.[414] However, the earliest spellings, including the pre-Conquest *(æt) Mynheafdon*, point to **min-* or **myn-* + Old English *hēafod* 'head' or its plural form. Accordingly, Watts notes his and earlier scholars' reservations about Ekwall's solution.[415] The first element may instead be related to Welsh *min* 'edge, brink', referring to the precipitous cliffs on the higher north side of the hill, though this usually has the less specific meaning 'side' in more recent Welsh place-names such as *Minffordd* 'roadside'. In the sixteenth century it appeared on graphic depictions as *Mynyad* in 1539[416] and *Minhead* in 1589.[417]

Minehead Bluff (Minehead)
From the place-name + *bluff* (a term originally used in America for a cliff with a broad and steep face). Minehead Bluff is shown on Admiralty chart 1152 almost four nautical miles to the west of Minehead close to Hurlstone Point near Bossington. A relatively new name in nautical publications, first appearing in an Admiralty chart published in 1839.[418]

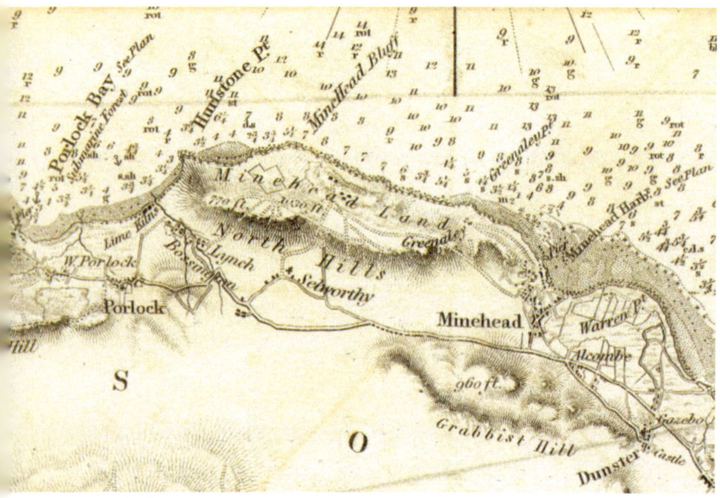

Illustration 2.42: 'MineHead' Bluff as it appeared in 1839, depicted by Denham and Robinson[419] (Adrian Webb Collection)

Minehead Quay (Minehead)
From the place-name + *quay*. In 1539 it appeared on a graphic depiction as *Mynyad Key*.[420]

Minehead Road (Minehead)
From the place-name + *road*. In the 1770s Mackenzie junior made a detailed written description of the area[421] and included an anchorage symbol on his survey,[422] being the first person to do this. An anchorage symbol had previously been used on a chart of *c.*1706 but no name was included to accompany it.[423] Minehead Road is not named on Admiralty chart 1152.

The headland with its lighthouse called *Mine Head* in County Waterford, Ireland, has a completely different origin, from Old Irish *mind*, *minn* 'badge of honour, crown' + *ard* 'high', or from later developments of these words.[424]

Morgan's Pill (Easton in Gordano)
From the surname *Morgan* in the possessive form + *pill*. Recorded on a chart published in 1693, this pill it is further down river than Crockern Pill,[425] and was to have served as a terminus for a canal from Taunton, planned in 1769.[426] The surname is that of a line of squires of Easton in Gordano descended from Sir Thomas Morgan, a Welshman appointed in the fifteenth century to guard the Pill-Shirehampton ferry across the Avon and to ensure that passengers paid their dues.[427]

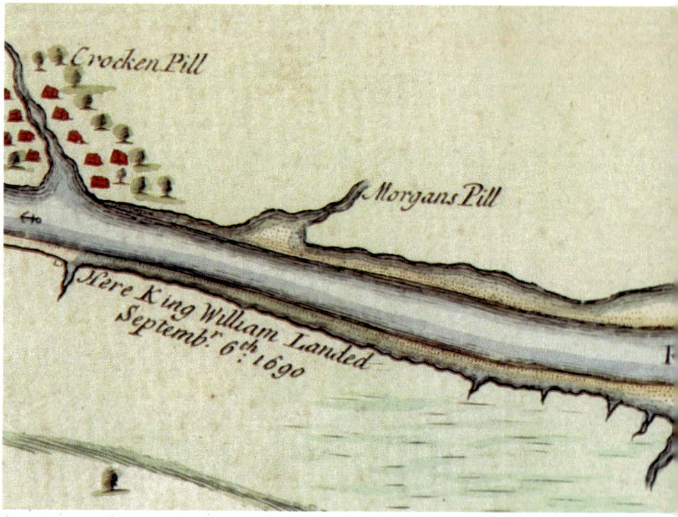

Illustration 2.43: An extract from a chart of the River Avon by Collins published in 1693 with north orientated to the south[428] (Robin Bush Collection)

Nap Lock and Nap Lock Ridge (Dunster)
This is mapped by the Ordnance Survey as a tidal pool on Dunster beach, though references to it are sometimes unclear about whether the name is really that of the ridge forming the pool's western bank (see next entry). This makes it uncertain whether the first word is from Old English *hnæpp* 'bowl' or *cnæpp* 'hillock'; the former appears more likely. The second word may be from Old English *loca* 'enclosure', or possibly 'lock' in the sense of 'river-barrier' – here, perhaps, on an old course of the Avill beyond the former Dunster harbour (see **The Hawn**), though

in medieval times this sense appears to be restricted to eastern England (see also **Porlock**). Alternatively, the Old English word may have been substituted for Brittonic Celtic or Proto-Welsh **luch* 'pool' because of the similarity in sound; in either case the name might be compared with *Porlock*. Uncertainty is compounded because of another place called *Naplock*, this time in the Hawkridge and Winsford area, mentioned several times in Charles Palk Collins' *Notes on the chase of the wild red deer in the counties of Devon and Somerset* (1862),[429] and a farm called *Knaplock* in Stockland Bristol. This recurrence suggests that *(k)naplock* was a meaningful expression in itself (though of uncertain meaning), and not just a name. *Knaplock* is also found as a surname in early-modern Devon and the London area.

Nap Lock gives its name to the adjacent *Nap Lock Ridge*, on current Ordnance Survey maps.

New Bank (between Denny Island and the mouth of the Avon, about a mile from the mouth of the Avon)

New + *bank*, testifying to seabed changes. In the late sixteenth century a bank between Denny Island and the mouth of the River Avon was known to have existed. Both Williams (in *c.*1706) and Holliday (in 1712) used the description *New Bank* for the area of the present day Denny Shoal. This suggests that Williams may have been the first person to name and depict the New Bank, *i.e.* Denny Shoal, in the early eighteenth century.[430] It was also charted in this position by Mackenzie junior in the early 1770s.[431] By the 1820s it was being charted, without a name, in the same position when Newcome Sands was shown between it and Denny Island, suggesting it was the same as what was later named *Cockburn Bank*.[432] In Denham's meticulous survey of 1832 no drying bank is depicted between 'Newcomes' and King Road, only Cockburn Rock and a drying line surrounding it are recorded,[433] as in White's survey of 1825.[434]

New Close Clyce (Pawlett)

Where New Close Rhyne (running to the east) exits into the River Parrett. Presumably from a field-name + *clyce*. Mapped by the Ordnance Survey in 1886.[435]

New Ground

New + *ground*, testifying to seabed changes. 1693 Collins shows this in the location of the Welch Grounds and not in the position of either the Newcome Sands or the Cockburn Bank as we know it today.[436] By *c.*1706 the banks were clearly defined as two areas, with that to the north called *The Welch grounds or whooks*.[437] By *c.*1712 the New Ground was not part of either of the banks depicted in *c.*1706 and it could have been either the Newcome Sands, or the Cockburn Bank.[438] Therefore it is safe to say that the New Ground became part, if not all, of the Welsh Grounds.

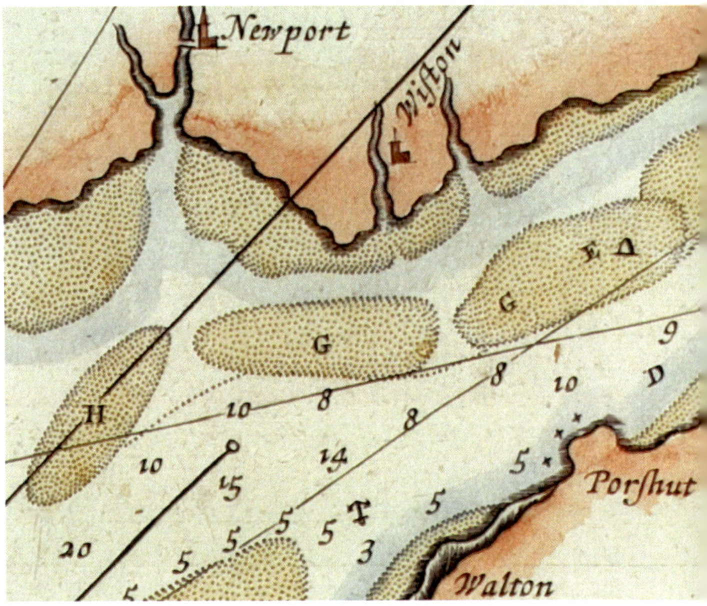

Illustration 2.44: Area 'G' is the 'New Ground' of 1693. Letter 'H' signifies Cardiff Ground[439] (Robin Bush Collection)

New Patch

New + *patch*. Shown on Admiralty chart 1152 very close to the east of Flat Holm.

Newcome Sands and Newcome Shoal

From *new come* 'newly arrived'[440] + *sands*, + *shoal*. Newcome Sands is depicted on a chart of 1815.[441] In 1884 it was noted that it was 'continually shifting'.[442] The 1933 Admiralty sailing directions refer to the Newcombe Shoal but not to the Denny Shoal (see above),[443] whereas the 1948 edition states that 'the Denny (Newcombe) shoal, is an extension of Welsh Grounds.'[444] The name *Newcome Sands* thus fell out of use to be replaced with *Denny Shoal*. Today the Denny Shoal is still constantly moving.

Nine Streams Reach

A stretch of the River Parrett between Chilton Trinity and Pawlett. Shown on a chart of 1723[445] and Ordnance Survey maps from 1887.[446] No reason for the name is obvious from the latter.

North Clyce (Otterhampton)
Where North Brook exits into the River Parrett. Mapped by the Ordnance Survey in 1886.[447]

Old Works Reach
A stretch of the River Parrett between Chilton Trinity and Pawlett, shown on Ordnance Survey maps from 1887[448] to the west of Dunball Wharf and the already disused Dunball Manure Works.

One Fathom Bank
Depth measure term + *bank*; from the reliable depth of water at low tide. Shown on Admiralty chart 1152 about four nautical miles west of Steep Holm.

***Owcerok* (Weston-super-Mare)**
In 1548 fish stalls were said to be in the sea on the *Owcerok* and the *Landrock* (see above).[449] *Owcerok* may really be for *Owterok*, *i.e.* the 'Out, Outer Rock', the *Landrock* being nearer the shore.

Owl Pool (Dunster)
A pool marked in the beach on current Ordnance Survey maps. Unexplained.

Oyster Bank (off Porlock)
From *oyster* + *bank*. Porlock was famous for its oysters until about 1900, and the beds have recently (2013) been reinstated.[450] It is shown on a plan of the area of *c.*1714 but its use in nautical publications is very uncommon after this.[451]

Pagenspille
See **Viking's Pill** (below).

Parrett
Before the Norman Conquest this river-name is recorded as *Pedredi(strem)* 725 (copy of about 1350), *Pedridan* 891, *Pedredan* 894; and after as *(la buche de) Pedredan* about 1140, *Peret* 1233 and frequently, *Paret* 1243, *Perret* 1253.[452]

The name dates back before the Anglo-Saxon period, and recurs in other names: one lost in Gloucestershire and Worcestershire, and at least two in Cornwall which are lost as river-names but have remained in use as place-names.[453] It is presumably from British Celtic. The fact that it recurs tells against a suggestion that it is from British **petwar* 'four' + **ritu* 'ford', in the compound form **petrurit-* 'four-forded', unless that had some now-obscure mystical significance. Such a form is remarkably similar to the Latin word *petorritum*, a word for a cart or carriage used by Celtic tribes, understood as being from British **petwar* 'four' + **roton* 'wheel(ed)'. But it is hard to see how that could be the origin of the river-name. The second element cannot be from a British ancestor of Brittonic **rēd* 'net' (modern Welsh *rhwyd*), since that is a borrowing from Latin. Formally it could be for Brittonic **red* 'running, course' (modern Welsh *rhed*). It is conceivable that the name could therefore be 'having four courses', but nothing about the modern, much engineered, hydrology of the Parrett suggests that this is appropriate. The most we can safely conclude is that the name probably derives from some ancient fixed traditional expression involving the British word for 'four', and that the last suggestion is more credible than the others.

Illustration 2.45: The River Parrett as depicted (including the name) by Christopher Saxton in 1575[454] (Robin Bush Collection)

Passage, The
A ferry formerly crossed the River Parrett between Combwich and Pawlett. It is documented from

medieval times until the twentieth century. The area where it landed on the Pawlett side is known as *The Passage*, *i.e.* the local word for 'ferry'.

Passage of St Catherine of Bristol

This is mentioned in an early navigation text from the fourteenth century, where it is said to be seven miles from the Holms.[455] The word *passage* locally means 'ferry crossing', and the ferrymen at Pill were known as *passers* during the sixteenth century, as they were also at Bristol (most likely working at Rownham). In 1312 there was a Richard *le Passour* in Bristol, and in 1327-8 a Hugh *le Passour* at Combwich.[456] The problem with the fourteenth-century text is the distance cited. It is really over 20 miles from the Holms to Pill, so this either refers to a different crossing, or illustrates a different measurement of a mile over 600 years ago. If this name does not refer to the St Catherine's Pill (otherwise *Chapel Pill*; see **Chapel Pill (2)** above) near Ham Green, which is perhaps the most likely, it must refer to some ferry associated with the medieval hospital of St Katherine Brightbow in Bedminster.

Pawlett Gore Sands (Pawlett), *Pawlett Pill* (Pawlett) and Pawlett Reach (in the River Parrett)

From the place-name *Pawlett* + *pill*, + *reach*. *Gore* and *sand* (here plural) as in **Gore Sand** (above). Ekwall suggests that the base name (*Pavelet*, *Paulet* 1086, *Poulet* 1186) is from Old English *pāl* 'pole' + *flēot* 'stream'.[457] The latter word, in eastern England, often has the sense 'creek'. This is linguistically acceptable, but saltwater creeks in Somerset are usually named with *pill*, not *fleet*, and there is no other *fleet* in Somerset. However, *flēot* also has the recorded sense 'estuary' and may refer here to what must have been the broad estuary of the Parrett whilst it remained unembanked. *Pill*s seem to be most frequently side-creeks of rivers, not arms of the sea, but occasionally run directly into the Bristol Channel.

Pawlett Gore Sands

A bank in the River Parrett depicted on the Ordnance map of 1886.[458]

Pawlett Pill

In 1468, according to a charter recording the bounds of the borough of Bridgwater, there was a pill at Pawlett, *Pauletpille*, to the north of Down End along the River Parrett.[459] The name has not survived on modern Ordnance Survey maps.

Pawlett Reach

Shown on current Ordnance Survey maps above Marchant's Reach but not included on Payne's 1723 chart.[460]

Penny Hook

An area to the south east of Chilton Trinity village clearly shows the horseshoe shape of a former meander of the River Parrett; this could possibly be the 'Newland' reclaimed by the late fourteenth century.[461] The area to the east of the loop is named *Penny Hook* on a mid-eighteenth century map.[462] Such a name may have to do with land-rents, or may enshrine the common Somerset surname *Penny*, which is however not noted in the Bridgwater area before 1800.

Pigeon House Bay (Walton in Gordano)

On current Ordnance Survey maps. Next to Culver Cliff, but the reference here is probably to birds reared for the lord of the manor's table.

Pill (Easton in Gordano)

See **Crockern Pill** above.

Pims Pill and Pims Pill Reach (Chilton Trinity)

Named after the Pim family who owned large tracts of land in this area from medieval times.[463] It is not shown on the Ordnance Survey map of 1887 but it was added when the sheet was revised in 1903; this must have been an oversight in 1887.[464] A *reach* (stretch) of the River Parrett in Chilton Trinity parish to the east of the church, is named from it, and is shown on Ordnance Survey maps from 1887.[465]

Pippin's Clyce (Wembdon)

Named after a local family recorded in Bridgwater in the 1870s and whose name appears in Pippin's Rhyne in the same parish. Mapped by the Ordnance Survey in 1886.[466]

Plotneys (Portishead and Portbury)

'Flat promontory', from Old Scandinavian *flatr* 'flat' + *nes* 'ness, land projecting into the sea', but with a modern form in <P-> probably due to a misreading of an early manuscript <F->, though it should be noted that surviving forms in <P-> are earlier than surviving forms in <F->. The misread manuscript in question must now be lost, or at least undiscovered. The charting history of the place is quite complex.

The first naming of this feature on a printed chart was made by Captain John Williams. He appears to have executed a survey around 1706. He referred to a small, but nevertheless noteworthy, area of rocks to the east of Portishead Point as *The Platness*; it was situated approximately halfway between Portishead Point and the entrance to the River Avon. As these rocks lay to the south of the important anchorage of King Road it is not surprising that this danger to navigation was shown, and more importantly named, by Williams.[467] What is surprising is that only a few years later, in *c.*1712, it was not named in a chart by Captain Holliday. The group of rocks is clearly shown in Holliday's chart.[468]

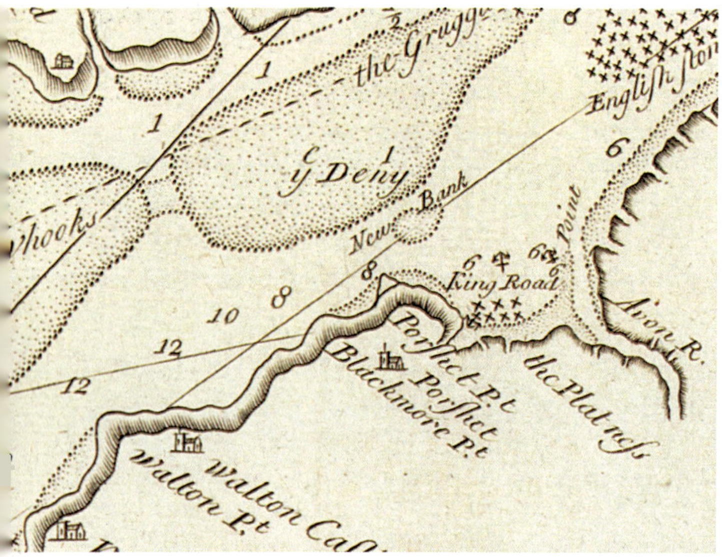

Illustration 2.46: An extract from a chart of the Bristol Channel by Captain Williams, surveyed *c.*1706, showing 'ye Platness' as a group of rocks at King Road[469] (Admiralty Library, Portsmouth)

Despite Williams' having marked and named the feature on his chart,[470] it was not universally copied by other hydrographic surveyors, cartographers or publishers.[471] Mackenzie senior and his nephew Mackenzie both show a feature on their published charts from the 1770s which appears to be a patch of drying ground, in the same area, but neither named it,[472] followed by Captain John Knight R.N. in his published chart of 1806.[473] However, Mackenzie junior appears to have been the first person to make a detailed, and what must be classed as accurate, description of the 'Flatness, or Platness Rock' in 1772.[474] His sailing directions for the Bristol Channel include the following description of Platness Rock as 'a rocky shoal that lies along the drying mud bank from the coast'.[475] From this time forwards the Platness Rock appears not to have been included in published sailing directions until 1821 (where it appears as *Plotness-rocks*).[476] In a manuscript description of 1815 it is described as 'a rocky shoal called the Flatness, to be avoided, which extends more than a Cable's length from the Shore, and is dry at low water'.[477] It did appear on numerous subsequent printed charts as *The Platness* in 1794,[478] *The Platnese* in 1800,[479] a *Rocky Bank* in 1803,[480] *the Flatness opposite Chapel Pill* in 1815,[481] and as an unnamed area of rocks in charts produced by different publishers in 1820[482] and 1829.[483]

Porlock Bay and Porlock Beach

On current Ordnance Survey maps. From the place-name *Porlock* + *bay*, + *beach*. The place-name is from Old English *port* 'port' + *loca* 'enclosure',[484] or possibly 'lock' in the sense of 'river-barrier', though in medieval times this sense appears to be restricted to eastern England. *Lock* might be an enclosure in a metaphorical sense; we find it as a local term specifically at Porlock for a man-made fish capturing construction,[485] though this sense may have emerged much later than the place-name forming period, and is not found in Wright's *English dialect dictionary*. Alternatively, the Old English word may have been substituted for Brittonic Celtic or Proto-Welsh **luch* 'pool' because of the similarity in sound, in which case the name might be compared with *Nap Lock*, a modern pool-name on the beach at Dunster.

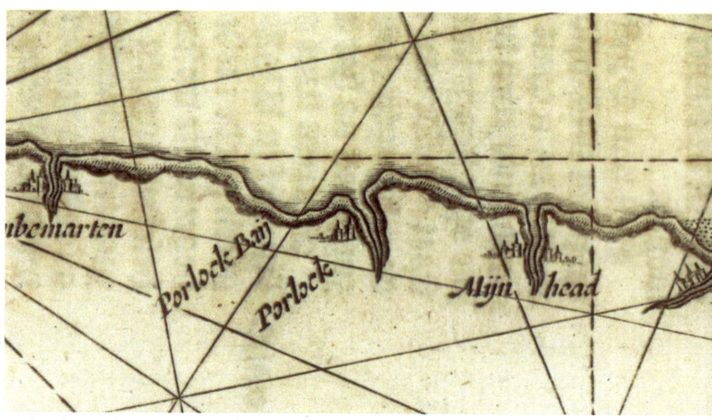

Illustration 2.47: Porlock Bay named with a Dutch spelling on a chart published in the Netherlands in 1625[486] (Keith Needell Collection)

Portbury Pill **(Portbury and Easton in Gordano)**
The parish boundary between Portbury and Easton in Gordano starts at the coastline at Chapel Pill. This was known as *Portebery pille* at the end of the sixteenth century.[487] However, this name does not then appear on any maritime charts examined from the period 1580 to 1830; this may have been due to its minor status compared to Portishead, King Road and Pill which were features that needed to be charted. At some unknown date the name was either replaced by, or in dual use with, Chapel Pill. It is recorded on maritime charts as **Chapel Pill** for the first time in 1815 by Richard Thomas.[488]

Portbury Point (Portbury)
From the place-name *Portbury* + *point*. The place-name is 'the stronghold or manor by the port', from Old English *port* 'port' + *burg* (dative case *byrig*) 'earthwork, fort'; later 'borough, manor'. The place-name is recorded as *Portbrig* between 899 and 925 and between 979 and 1016 (copied in the thirteenth century),[489] *Porberie*, *Porberia* [Latin form], *Porberiet* 1084 Exeter Geld Roll, *Porberie* 1086 Great Domesday Book, *Porberia* [Latin form] 1086 Exeter Domesday list of Somerset hundreds 2, *Portburi* 1196 Feet of Fines, *Porberi* 1205, *Porebur'* 1224 Close Rolls, *Portebury* 1358 Patent Rolls.[490]

The *port* was probably what came to be known as *Portishead Pill* or *Creek* (later *Harbour*, now *Marina*). Alternatively, the name may have denoted a locally suggested Roman dock or wharf at Sheepway. Significant Roman remains have been found in the parish, but the existence of such a dock is unproven. The *bury* may have been the small hillfort above the village, or a reference to the important manor house here.

Portishead Pill, Portishead Point and Portishead Road (Portishead)
From the place-name *Portishead* + *pill*, + *point*, + *road*. The base-name is 'headland of or by the port', from Old English *port* 'port' in the genitive case with *-es* + *hēafod* 'head', now used by metonymy as the name of the settlement that has grown into a town. The headland is the prominent ridge of Wood Hill, which tapers westward into Battery Point and provides a magnificent view over the Bristol Channel and King Road. *Port* is a word borrowed from Latin *portus* 'port', and that involves a clear suggestion that the port had existed in Roman times. Its most likely location was at Portishead Pill, west of the area now called *Portbury Wharf*; for this, see further under **Portbury** (above) and **Portishead Pill** (below).

The development of the name of Portishead is recorded as follows: *Porteshe'* 1086 Great Domesday Book,[491] *Portesheved* 1200 Curia Regis Rolls, 1324 as a surname,[492] *Porteseved* 1331 Patent Rolls, *Porteshede* 1490-1 Feet of Fines, *Porteshed(d)* 1616 contract and conveyance of a Portishead manor to city of Bristol, *Portyshed* 1544 will, *Portshead(e)* 1555 will, *Portishead* 1679 Bristol Survey of Country Estates,[493] *Portishead vulgo* [Latin for 'commonly'] *Possut* 1769.[494]

The documentary record clearly shows that by Tudor times the place was called 'Portshead', which was condensed and then in modern times re-lengthened to three syllables. The historian Collinson wrote in 1791 that '[t]he inhabitants corruptly call it *Possut*'.[495] Some variant spellings on navigational charts and pre-Ordnance Survey maps include *Passis of* [Dutch for 'or'] *Porshut point* in 1625,[496] *Portshead* in 1673,[497] *Portshut* in 1676[498] and *Posset Point* in 1808.[499]

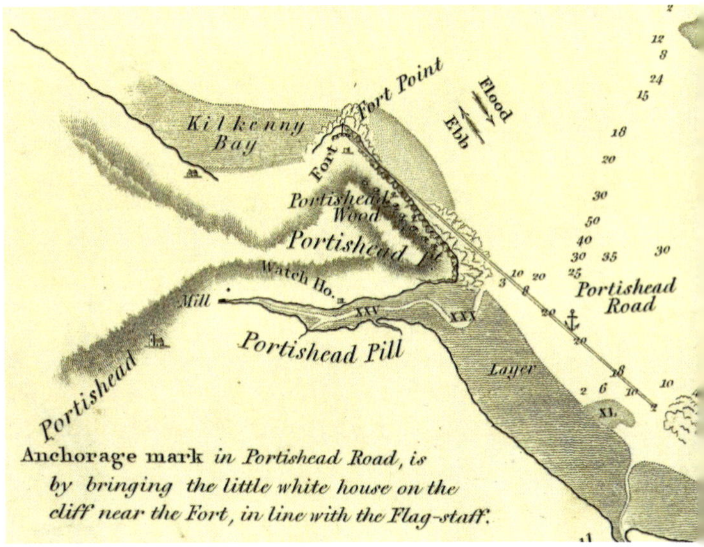

Illustration 2.48: An extract from a survey of the River Severn by Richard Thomas, published in 1815, showing the location of the Portishead features (U.K.H.O., L3895). The two appearances of *layer*, apparently perpetuating Old Scandinavian *leir(r)* 'mud', are noteworthy.[500]

Portishead Pill
A name used twice in maps and charts of the sixteenth century,[501] but not again until 1839 when it was referred to as *Posset Pill*.[502] In the twentieth century it was industrialized into *Portishead Harbour*, and more recently still the harbour was leisurized as *Portishead Quays Marina*.[503]

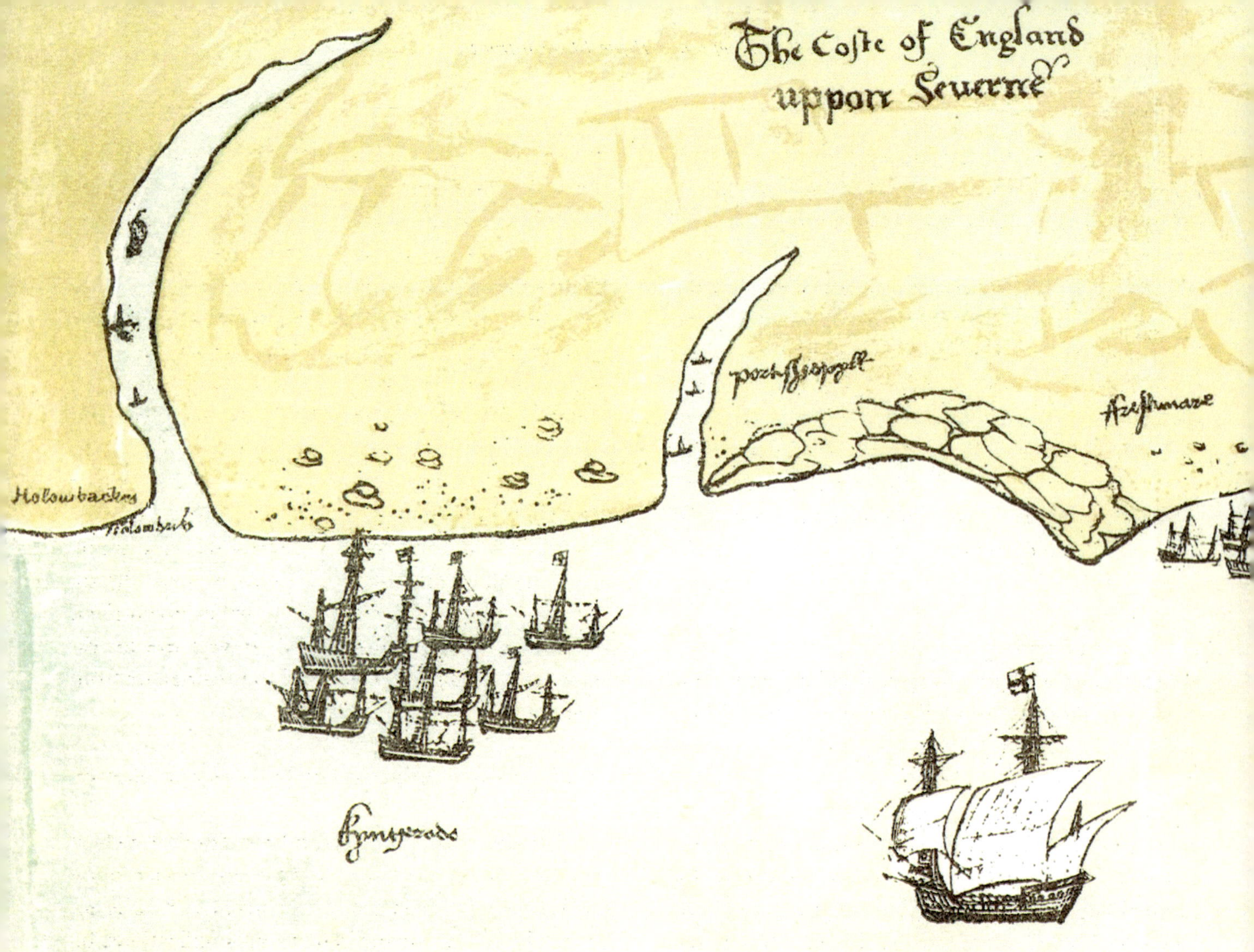

Illustration 2.49: Portishead's pill *(portshedpyll)* as depicted in 1539. Note the anchorage of *Kyngerode* is packed with ships; north is at the left of the map (E. Green, *The preparations in Somerset against the Spanish Armada, A.D. 1558-1588* (London, 1888))

Portishead Point

A headland marking the western extremity of Wood Hill, Portishead. The Point is an important place for navigating to and from Bristol. In the fifteenth century it was used as a notable landmark which navigators were advised to use when heading toward King Road: 'goo est and northe est with portis hed'. It was also close to Kettleswood (between Portishead Pill and Clevedon Pill) and the two places were also referred later in the same text as being together.[504] It is frequently named on navigational charts, appearing, with variants of the base place-name, interchangeably as *Passis* (possibly a misprint for **Passit?*) *Porshut*, *Portshead* or *Posset Point* since 1625.[505] *Portshead* and *Possett* are two variants which only start to be used on navigational charts during the early nineteenth century.[506]

Rutter noted that during the 1640s a fort had been erected on the site of an ancient fort, thought to have been a Roman guard station.[509] By *c*.1712 it was described as being the *Old Fort*.[510] Mackenzie junior called the headland *Fort Point* in the early 1770s, noting it as an important navigational mark.[511] During the Napoleonic Wars a small battery (artillery mount) was established here and the name *Battery Point* was also in use from then on.[512] By 1829 the battery had been dismantled.[513] Despite being called *Battery Point*, it was mapped as hosting *Portishead Point Battery* in 1830. This ambiguity is maintained in much

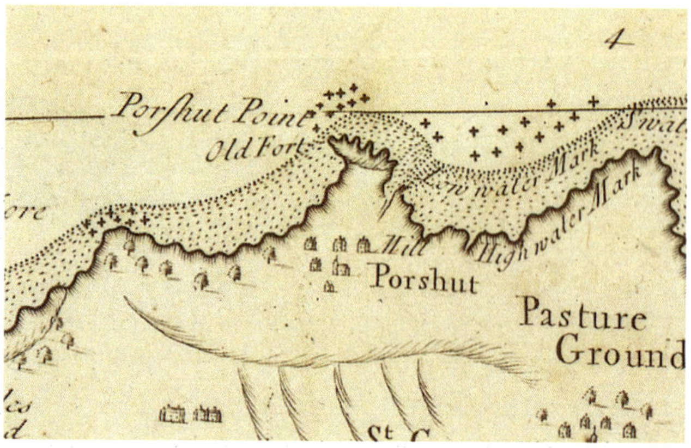

Illustration 2.50: Captain Holliday's chart, *c*.1712, showing the 'Old Fort'[508] (Adrian Webb Collection)

later mapping. The Ordnance Survey called it *Portishead Point* in 1884 and *Battery Point* in 1903. It reverted to being *Portishead Point* in 1931, and to *Battery Point* on an OS plan of the 1980s. The current consensus seems to be that *Portishead Point* is the official name and *Battery Point* the local one, hence both names appear as separate locations on the headland on the current 1:25,000 Ordnance Survey map.

Unusually, therefore, this feature of the Somerset coast has had three distinctly different names *i.e.* *Porshut* or *Portishead Point*, *Fort Point* and *Battery Point*, and two are still current. It was refortified during the Second World War.

Portishead Road

Shown on a navigational chart for the first time in 1815.[514] On today's Admiralty chart, number 1176, it is shown as *Portishead Pool*.[515]

Quantock's Head (East Quantoxhead)

The *head* or headland at the seaward end of the Quantocks, or strictly speaking, of *Quantock*, the original singular name of the range of hills (Old English *Cantuc*), with the Old English genitive singular suffix *-es*. It is recorded as *Cantokesheued* (Middle English *hēved* 'head') as early as 1185. It appeared as *Quantox Point* on a chart of 1808,[516] but its use in maritime publications before the 1770s when Mackenzie junior started referring to it as *Quantox Head* is unknown.[517]

Redcliff Bay (below Black Nore Point, Portishead)

From *red* + *cliff*, with reference to the cliffs of Old Red Sandstone here, + *bay*. Shown on the current Admiralty chart number 1176.[518]

Rownham (Long Ashton) and Rownham Ferry

'At the rough riverside pasture or watermeadow', from Old English *rūh* 'rough' in an inflected form with *-n* + *hamm* 'land hemmed in on three sides by water; riverside land, watermeadow', by the Avon. The base name is recorded as *Rowenham* 1322 (undated copy),[519] *Rownam* 1428,[520] *Rounham* and *Rownham* 1480,[521] and *Rownham* 1652.[522] The name is clearly ancient (because of the inflection *-n* of the first word, which is an Old English feature), but there is little early documentary evidence for it, and what there is is mainly in documents of Ashton Court in Long Ashton. There is evidence suggesting the place-name also had a home on the Clifton bank of the Avon: 'One other peice of meadow in Rowenham' (1625 survey of the smaller Clifton manor).

The ferry is generally *Rownham Passage*, from the place-name + *passage*, the usual local word for 'ferry'. It is *Rownam Ferry* in the reign of King Henry the Eighth,[523] *Rownham Passage* 1741.[524] This once well-known ferry crossed the Avon from Long Ashton to Hotwells, the duty being performed by a rowing boat at higher tides and a pontoon of boats at lower tides. It was moved from its ancient location as a result of new developments at the western end of Bristol harbour in 1873 to a site a little further down-river, and survived there until 1932. It was the lowest ancient and regular crossing of the river apart from the Pill to Shirehampton ferry.

Rudder Rock and Rudder Head (west side of Steep Holm)

Rudder Rock is shown on today's Admiralty chart number 1152. Holliday shows lots of rocks around Steep Holm in his survey of *c.*1712.[525] It is an exceptionally rare name in maritime publications. Its name is of uncertain age and origin; perhaps it simply derives from the rock's appearance, and from its being at the 'stern' of the island, going up-Channel. Steel's chart, published in 1820, and the same re-issued by Norie in 1822, names Rudder Head.[526] This was copied in 1831 by Denham.[527] In 1848 the area was just referred to as *Rudder*.[528] Rudder Head is named from the rock.

Illustration 2.51: The 'rudder' with its tall vertical stock can be seen on the left, 2016 (Richard Coates)

Saddle of Portishead,
In 1771 Mackenzie junior described the 'leading mark that leads in the gut or bed of the fairway channel, between English Grounds and New Spit, is, Blacknorth point; on with the concave gap or saddle-like appearance of the land, on the east side of the rising ground near Portshut point.[529] In 1825 it was drawn by White who actually named it as the *Saddle* of Portishead Point.[530]

Illustration 2.52: The 'saddle of Portishead' as drawn by Captain Martin White R.N. in 1825 (U.K.H.O., OD 190)

Saint Audrie's (or Saint Audries) Bay (West Quantoxhead)
From the place-name *Saint Audrie's* + *bay*. The bay is not named on the 1887 Ordnance Survey map but it does appear on the 1904 edition. Shown on Admiralty chart 1152. *Saint Audrie's* is the alternative name of the village of West Quantoxhead. The parish church is dedicated to the female Anglo-Saxon saint Æthelthryth, more generally known by the latinized form *Etheldreda*, but whose name appears here in its Norman French form, *Audrie*.

Saint Thomas's Head (Wick St Lawrence)
From the dedication of the nearby former Woodspring Priory to St Thomas à Becket. After it was named on Sayer and Bennett's chart of 1777,[531] the name regularly appeared on nautical charts. It is not used before 1810 in sailing directions,[532] although Woodspring Point is used from 1772.[533] It is shown on today's Admiralty chart number 1176.[534]

Salthouse Bay and Salthouse Point (Clevedon)
A Salt House, occupied by salt panners,[535] is mentioned at Clevedon in 1775.[536] This does not appear in early nautical publications, although it is shown on the first edition of the Ordnance Survey.[537] An Admiralty chart of 1839 shows the headland as *Salt Ho.*, *i.e.* Salt House, but shows no building.[538] However, the name testifies to industrial buildings for the extraction of salt from brine. The bay is named from the same feature. It does not appear in early nautical publications, although it is shown on today's Admiralty chart number 1176.[539]

Illustration 2.53: The Salt House in 2017. Today it is used as a public house frequented by local families[540] (Annabel Welsh)

Sand Bay (Kewstoke)
From *sand* + *bay*. A relatively late addition to maritime charts. The sand is referred to as *la Sande* as early as 1268.[541]

Sand Point (Kewstoke)
From *sand* + *point*, or more likely from the name of Sand Bay (above) + *point*, since Sand Point is a limestone feature rather than sandstone. Mentioned by Mackenzie junior 11 times in his sailing directions from the early 1770s.[542]

Sea Mills Reach
A stretch of the River Avon above Horseshoe Bend, named after a farm in Henbury parish, Gloucestershire, which has given its name to the modern Bristol suburb. The original mill appears to have been called *Seam Mill*, *i.e.* a mill named, for uncertain reasons, from a packhorse load.[543]

See-Me and See-Me-Not (Crook Peak)
See **Crook Peak** (above).

Selworthy Sand
From the place-name *Selworthy* + *sand*. The place-name is from Old English *sīele* 'sallow copse' + *worðig*, a word for an enclosure or smallholding.[544] The Ordnance Survey shows the sand on the coast in

Selworthy parish (the village itself is south of North Hill and not visible from the sea) above the low water mark, and not an offshore hazard. It is not shown on navigational charts published before 1825.[545]

Severn
See **Bristol Channel** (above).

Slab Batch (island in the River Parrett)
See under **Fenning Island** (above). In 1822 it was shown as *Slab Batch* on C. and J. Greenwood's map of Somerset.[546] The first word is more likely to be *slub*, a widespread dialect word for 'ooze, mud, slimy wash', recorded from Somerset, than the noun *slab* 'lump; flat stone' or the adjective 'thick and viscous', which are mainly northern and eastern words. *Slob*, recorded from Devon in the 'sea mud' sense, is a variant of the first word.[547]

Slab Island
In 1700, when a grant was made by Henry Dod to Henry Gatchell of North Petherton, Dods Island was described as 'lately thrown up by sea in Burnham or Huntspill';[548] there was also a Dods Paddock in Chilton Moor in 1710 part of the Corporation of Bridgwater's estate.[549] It is not known where this island was exactly situated. However, the wording 'in Burnham or Huntspill' must mean that it was on the east bank of the Parrett. No such feature is named on the 1723 map, but it may be Slab Island.[550] A detailed map of 1776 was drawn by local man William Locke. It is likely that Slab Island is shown on this map to the south of Cures Island, which is separated from the mainland by an area called *Huntspill Warth*.[551] It is not shown on later mapping, but Slab Island had become part of the mainland by 1782, just to the south of Dunball in Huntspill.[552] For *slab*, see **Slab Batch** (above).

Slut's Pill (Wick St Lawrence)
From *slud* 'mud', a dialect word usually of eastern England, sometimes appearing as *slut*, + *pill*. Once *slut* has been mistaken for the word for 'slatternly woman', it can sprout the genitive *-'s* appropriate to possession. Although shown in some detail in 1539 as *sattpyll*,[553] Saxton clearly recorded it as *Sutte pill* in his 1575 map of the county.[554] It did not appear again on charts until *c.*1712 when it had its modern name *Sluts Pill*,[555] after which it was charted infrequently.

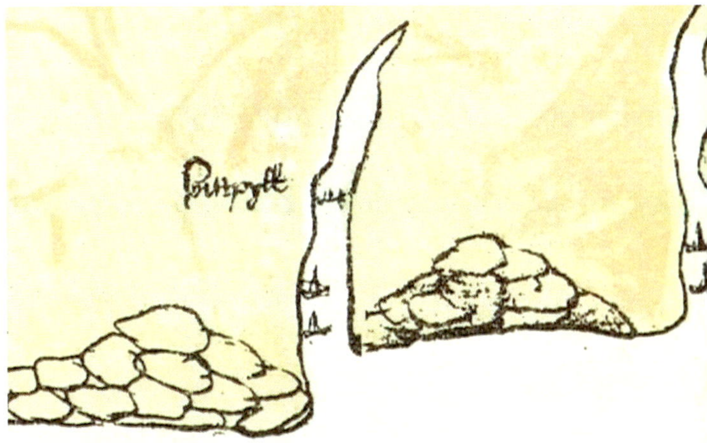

Illustration 2.54: Between Clevedon and Woodspring as depicted in 1539 (E. Green, *The preparations in Somerset against the Spanish Armada, A.D. 1558-1588* (London, 1888))

South Patches (between Steep Holm and Weston-super-Mare)
A relatively new feature shown on Admiralty chart 2682 in 1888.[556] It shown on today's Admiralty chart number 1152.

Spear Rocks (Clevedon)
White included this feature on his hydrographic survey of 1825, which appears never to have been published.[557] Shown on the first edition Ordnance Survey map of 1830 as *Spear Rock*.[558] Shown on Admiralty chart 1176 as *Spear Rocks* close to the shoreline at Clevedon.[559] No particular reason for the name is known. *Spear-wigeon* is a regional name for the goosander and red-breasted merganser in England, but it is not known whether that could be relevant here; they are not usually maritime birds. *Spear* is also a regional word for 'reeds', which cannot be relevant.[560] An allusion to shape seems the most likely, on balance.

Split Rock (Steep Holm)
Self-explanatory; shown on the 1886 Ordnance Survey map.[561]

Sprat Beach (north side of Brean Down)
On current Ordnance Survey maps. Presumably from the fish-name *sprat* + *beach*.

Spring Cove (close to the end of Worlebury Hill)
From *spring* + *cove*; on current Ordnance Survey maps

at the foot of Worlebury Hillfort. Jackson refers to *Spring Cove* in 1874.[562] A Site of Special Scientific Interest because of the volcanic rocks (basalts and tuffs) exposed on the shoreline. Phil Quinn stated 'The hillside hid a mysterious cave that was only accessible at low tides, and inside lay the Dripping Well: 'a solemn place, high vaulted, with water pure and cold dripping from the roof into a crystal pool.".[563] This accessible pure water source accounts for the *spring* in the name.

Illustration 2.55: Spring Cove at low tide in 2012 (© Jaggery and licensed for reuse under this Creative Commons Licence)

Stallington's Clyce (Cannington)
From a surname + *clyce*. A woman named Frances *Stalington* is recorded in 1662, rather far away in Hemington near Radstock.[564] The feature is shown on Ordnance Survey maps from 1886.[565]

Starslands Clyce (Chilton Trinity)
Where Chinehorne Rhyne exits into the River Parrett. From a surname + *land*, + *clyce*; *Starr* is the name of a local family during the seventeenth century. Mapped by the Ordnance Survey in 1886.[566]

Steep Holm or Steepholm
From Old English *stēap* 'steep' + *holm* 'small island', the latter word a borrowing from Old Scandinavian (see also **Flat Holm**). It is recorded in several manuscripts of the *Anglo-Saxon chronicle* in the phrase *æt Steapan Reolice*, in which the last word is the Old Irish word *reilic* 'graveyard' (itself copied from Latin *reliquiae* 'relics, remains') borrowed as part of the Old English name. One manuscript has instead *æt Bradan Relice* ('at (the) large graveyard'). Coates has shown that this must also mean Steep Holm, rather than Flat Holm, as had previously been assumed.[567] The island is 4½ nautical miles from Wales and about 2½ from Brean Down. Both the Holms are shown on the earliest maps of the region, including the famous Gough map on which the word *holm* is written on each island.[568] Two variants of note are *The stype Holmes* (*c.*1590),[569] and on a Dutch chart (published in Calais, 1601) *Stopel holm.*[570] The latter may be an attempt to write *stepel*, for English *steeple*, because no relevant Dutch word exists; Steep Holm was called *Stepelholme* in an English record of 1331.[571] Otherwise maritime charts show the name as one or two words.[572] For final *-s* in the island name, see **The Holms** (above). Steep Holm marks the southern limit of the Port of Bristol.[573]

Illustration 2.56: Steep Holm from Captain F.W. Beechey's survey of 1848 (U.K.H.O., L7313/2 4e)

Stert Flats, Stert Island, Stert Point and Stert Reach (Otterhampton)
The base-name is from Old English *steort* 'tail', used also in the topographical sense of *point* before that word, of French origin, replaced it in place-name usage. *Point* has been added, presumably when *stert* was no longer understood as a word and was taken simply to be a name, as has also happened in the case of *Start Point* (Stokenham, Devon). Stert Point is a very long peninsula forming the western bank of the lower Parrett. Over the centuries, two different places have borne this name. It appears on Payne's chart of 1723[574] and was in the position he records, at the north-eastern end of Stert Island, until 1795.[575] After this date, when Stert Island was created, the name was used for its present-day location at the new end of the truncated peninsula.

Stert Flats and *Stert Island* are from the place-name + *flat* (in the plural), + *island*. Stert Flats was not recorded on maritime charts[576] until Denham included it on his manuscript chart of the southern part of the Bristol Channel in 1831.[577] It is shown on Admiralty chart 1152. In 1791 there was a high spring tide which flooded over the then Stert Point (see below), and as a result of this and subsequent inundations Stert Island was created in 1795.[578] *Stert Reach* is also from the place-name, + *reach*. It is shown on Ordnance Survey maps from 1886 in the parish of Huntspill above Stockland Reach; the River Parrett runs closer to the shore here.[579]

Stockland Reach (in the River Parrett)
On current Ordnance Survey maps. From the place-name *Stockland* + *reach*. The base name (*Stocheland*, *Stochelande*, 1086) is from Old English *stoc* 'dependent farm' + *land* 'agricultural land',[580] probably implying 'newly taken-in ploughland at the dependent farm', with allusion to land reclamation. Shown on Ordnance Survey maps from 1886 in the parish of Huntspill below Stert Reach; the River Parrett runs closer to the shore here.[581]

Stoke Bluff and Stoke Spit (Stogursey)
From the place-name *Stogursey*, earlier *Stoke Courcy*, + *bluff* (a term originally used in America for a cliff with a broad and steep face), + *spit*. The base name *Stoke* is from Old English *stoc* 'secondary, dependent farm'. The spit appears on a chart published in 1839.[582] Stoke Bluff, shown on Admiralty chart 1152 on the coast near Lilstock, is more commonly known as *Lilstock Point*; Stoke Spit runs in a north-west direction from Stoke Bluff.

Strand, The (Minehead)
A survival of the traditional word for 'beach'. The sandy Strand at Minehead was used as a racecourse at least in the late nineteenth century.[583]

Sugar Loaf Beach (Portishead)
From *sugar loaf* + *beach*, presumably from some distinctive land feature shaped like an old-fashioned sugar loaf, *i.e.* a 'moulded conical mass of hard refined sugar'.[584] On current Ordnance Survey maps. This name is often applied from about 1700 onwards to high conical hills such as that on Tenerife and one near Abergavenny. There is also one of this name in Oare. It is not clear to what this name refers in Portishead unless there was a pub of this name nearby (nothing was found in the S.H.C. catalogue), or unless you can see the prominent Abergavenny Sugar Loaf Mountain from here through a gap in the Welsh hills; the Bristol Channel can reportedly be seen from the mountain-top on a clear day.

Swallow Cliff, Swallow Point and Swallow Rocks (Kewstoke)
The first edition Ordnance Survey of 1809 shows *Swallow Cliff* but names no rocks in the vicinity.[585] The Rocks are shown on Admiralty chart 1152 at Sand Point. In coastal place-names, *swallow* may refer to sand martins. *Swallow Point* shares this origin; see also under **Woodspring Hillock** (below).

Swatch (Easton in Gordano)
A *swatch* or waterway navigable at certain times of the tide. Situated at the mouth of the River Avon, it was named and shown as an area of inter-tidal mud by Holliday *c.*1712.[586] It developed to be the name of a navigable channel that White noted on his survey undertaken in 1825.[587] This channel developed, in the 1860s, into the modern mouth of the Avon. See also **Dumball** (above).

Illustration 2.57: Captain Holliday's chart, *c.*1712, showing the Swatch[588] (Adrian Webb Collection)

Swill Point (Williton)
Uncertain element + *point*. The feature is not shown on the first edition Ordnance Survey of 1809. [589] It appeared on Admiralty chart 1160 in 1974 to the west of Saint Audrie's Bay,[590] and appears on the current Admiralty chart number 1152. Its name is taken from a stream that falls into the sea at Doniford. It seems to be obscurely related to *swall*, an obsolete English word corresponding to Middle Low German *swal(l)* 'whirlpool, swollen mass of water', but it also

suggests the modern verb *swill* 'to swish (water) back and forth'.

Tail Patch (between Flat Holm and Sand Point)
In 1625 a Dutch sailing direction referred to a great tail stretching to the west of the English Grounds.[591] It is possible that this could be the origin of the Tail Patch and was referred to as such in sailing directions until the early nineteenth century.[592] It was named by Denham as 'The Tail End Patch' in his survey of 1831.[593] Shown on the current Admiralty chart number 1152.

Three Elms Reach
Self-explanatory name for a stretch of the River Parrett near Sydenham House, Bridgwater. Shown on a chart of 1723 as *3 Elms*,[594] and on the Ordnance Survey first edition of 1809 but not on later editions.[595]

Three Feet Shoal (between King Road and the mouth of the River Avon)
This name indicates a submerged feature (*shoal*, *bank*) with a predictable minimum clearance at low or neap tide. *Three Feet Shoal* is mentioned by Mackenzie junior in his sailing directions of the early 1770s.[596] He also referred to it on one occasion as *the Three Feet Bank*.[597]

Tower Rock (Steep Holm)
A prominent feature shown on the 1886 Ordnance Survey map as *Castle Rock*;[598] changed to *Tower Rock* on the 1904 edition.[599]

Tuckett's Clyce (Cannington)
Situated to the south of Combwich. Named after a local family recorded in Bridgwater in the 1860s. Mapped by the Ordnance Survey in 1886. [600]

Uphill Bay
From the place-name *Uphill* + *bay*. Uphill village stands beside a striking hill (unnamed on current Ordnance Survey maps) close to the coastline at the southern end of Weston Bay. However, older spellings of the place-name reveal that this is irrelevant, and that it is from Old English *uppan pylle* 'up the pill, higher along the pill' (*Opopille* 1086, *Uppepull* 1197), with reference to the long creek discharging into the estuary of the Axe to the south of the present village. It was understood very early in its history in the way indicated by the modern spelling (*Uppehill* 1176).[601] The name of the bay is found in the early nineteenth century, but not before then on navigational charts.

Uphill Harbour, Uphill Haven
The harbour at Uphill is called *Uphilhaven* in a Dutch chart of 1625 and copied into the 1680s. On the 1625 chart it was the only place name mentioned between Huntspill and Portishead.[602] *Uphill Harbour* is referred to by Payne in his chart of 1723,[603] but on no navigational charts after this occurrence.

Illustration 2.58: Blaeu's chart of the Bristol Channel, published in 1625, showing *Uphilhaven*[604] (Keith Needell Collection)

Uphill Sands (Uphill)
From the place-name *Uphill* (see above) + *sand* in the plural. In 1657 Joseph Moxon's chart covering the Somerset coast includes this name,[605] which was not used by other cartographers, surveyors or publishers before 1825.[606]

Viking's Pill (Chilton Trinity)
Presumably the *Pagenspille* mentioned in a charter recording the bounds of the borough of Bridgwater drawn up in 1468,[607] last mentioned in a maritime sense in the 1670s. When a large meander of the River Parrett was cut off in 1677, the pill effectively was lost, since the river, over a period of years, was replaced by exceptionally fertile dry land.[608] The origin of the current name is mysterious. It is certainly not old.

Wain's Hill (Clevedon)
On current Ordnance Survey maps. A prominent coastal hill and viewpoint, the site of an Iron Age hillfort. Probably a late name from surname *Wain*, known in Easton in Gordano in the early eighteenth century.

Walpole Clyce (Pawlett)
A *clyce* named after the local hamlet of Walpole, whose name is recorded in *c.*1250 as *Wallepulle*, in 1598 as *Waple* and in 1698 as *Warpill*.[609] The name is formed with Old or Middle English *w(e)all* 'wall', presumably with reference to a seabank, + *pill* or *pull* 'pool, creek', and possibly influenced by the prominent surname of the long-serving eighteenth-century prime minister. The clyce was mapped in 1886 by the Ordnance Survey.[610]

Walton Bay (Walton in Gordano)
From the place-name *Walton* + *bay*. The place-name is probably from Old English *weald* 'high woodland' + *tūn* 'farm, village',[611] but *weall* 'wall' is another possibility for the first element. The bay is not shown on the first edition Ordnance Survey map of 1830,[612] but is shown on the current Admiralty chart 1176.[613]

Warren Bay (Watchet) and Warren Point (Dunster)
From *warren* 'rabbitat' in sandy soil + *bay*, + *point*. Mackenzie junior refers to the Minehead feature in his sailing directions from the early 1770s,[614] after which it became a regular feature on navigational charts. Shown on Admiralty chart 1152.

Watchet (St Decumans)
This place-name is generally analysed as an anglicized form of a Brittonic Celtic name deriving from **wo-* a prefix meaning 'below, lower' + **kēd* 'trees, wood'. It is not clear whether reference might be to some former wood on the hill behind the harbour, or rather more diffusely to the Brendon Hills. The name is recorded in the *Anglo-Saxon Chronicle*, various manuscripts, as *[to] weced* 914x919 [copied centuries later], *Weced* 915 [copied twelth century], *Wæced* 918, *Wecedport* about 1121 for annal 987, and in other texts as *Wacet* 1086, *Wechet* 1243.[615] Early maps and charts include *Wachatt* in 1539[616] and *Watchet* in 1589.[617] The prominent hilltop church of St Decuman, which supplies an occasional alternative name for the place, is dedicated to a Welsh saint with a range of legendary deeds to his credit, including arriving in Somerset on a raft with a cow.

West Clyce (Pawlett)
Where New Close Rhyne (running to the west) exits into the River Parrett. This is called *West Clyce* because New Close Rhyne also exits into the Parrett at New Close Clyce. Mapped by the Ordnance Survey in 1886.[618]

Weston Bay
From the place-name *Weston (super Mare)* (see below) + *bay*; formerly known as *Uphill Bay* before the modern expansion of Weston to a major town and the eclipse of Uphill. Shown on Admiralty chart 1152.

Weston Head (Weston-super-Mare)
From the place-name *Weston* + *head*. See **Anchor Head** (above).

Weston Ledge (Weston-super-Mare)
From the place-name *Weston* + *ledge*. It was named by Denham in his survey of 1831[619] and shown on Admiralty chart 1152 just off Birnbeck.

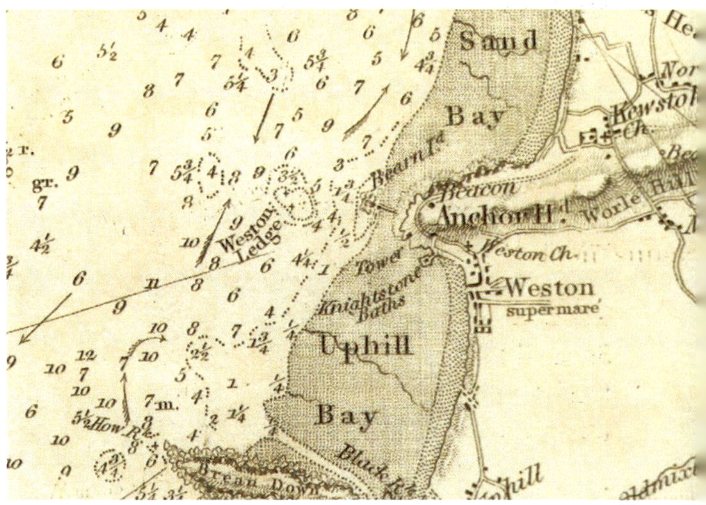

Illustration 2.59: Weston Ledge as depicted by Denham and Robinson in their published chart of 1839 (Adrian Webb Collection)

Weston-super-Mare
'Weston on sea', with the distinguishing phrase in bureaucratic Latin first recorded in 1349;[620] this was to distinguish it from other Somerset *Weston*s such as Weston Bampfylde, Weston Zoyland, Weston in Gordano, Kingweston, and so on. *Weston* is 'west

farm', *i.e.* originally the western farm within Worle parish. This Weston was also known as *West Weston* for the same reason. It first appeared on a navigational chart in *c.*1712[621] after which time it appeared far more frequently as the resort began to develop. *Mare* in the name was formerly pronounced like *Mary*, but the obvious English pronunciation of the spelling has won out. The name is now often pronounced with stress on the *super* rather than the *Mare*, rather as in *Aston Subedge*, pronounced 'súbbidge', in Gloucestershire. The place-name has recently spawned the Super Mare pub near junction 21 of the M5, run by the Hungry Horse chain.

Wharf Point (Easton in Gordano)
Probably from Old English *waroð* 'shore', *i.e.* the local word *warth* 'shore' seen in many Severnside minor place-names, which has here, as in other cases, been confused with *wharf*. The name still appears on today's Admiralty charts.

White Rocks (Stogursey)
On the coast to the west of Hinkley Point, as depicted on the first edition of the Ordnance Survey in 1809.[622] The self-explanatory name rarely appears on navigational charts.

Wick Rocks (Stogursey)
Named from the hamlet of Wick in Stogursey + *rock* in the plural. *Wick* is from a form of Old English *wīc* 'specialized farm, dependent farm'.[623] The rocks are on the coast to the west of Hinkley Point, as depicted on the first edition of the Ordnance Survey in 1809.[624] They were included by Denham in his hydrographic survey of 1831.[625]

Woodhill Bay (Portishead)
From the self-explanatory mainland place-name + *bay*. Shown on the current Admiralty chart 1176 to the north of Kilkenny Bay (see above) but below Portishead Point.[626]

Woodspring (Kewstoke), Woodspring Bay (Wick St Lawrence), Woodspring Pill (Kewstoke), Woodspring Point (Kewstoke) and West Woodspring Point (Kewstoke)
From the place-name *Woodspring*, + *bay*, + *pill* and + *point*. The place-name appears as *Worsprinc* in Domesday Book (1086) and *Worspring(e)* in thirteenth-century records, indicating derivation from Old English *wōr* a word for some gamebird + *spring* 'copse'.[627] The copse must have been on the rising ground north of the present farm bearing this name. Its continued existence must have encouraged the change of the name from *Wor-* to *Wood-*. On land, the name was best known as that of a medieval priory here. It was still *Worspryng* in 1536, and the change to the modern form is not permanently effective until the nineteenth century. However, the name in the form *Woodspring* has appeared on navigational charts since 1693.[628] See further under **Worle** (below).

Woodspring Point appeared for the first time on a navigational chart published in 1728[629] and was used infrequently until used on Admiralty charts. Only Woodspring Point is shown on the current Admiralty chart, number 1176, covering this whole area.[630]

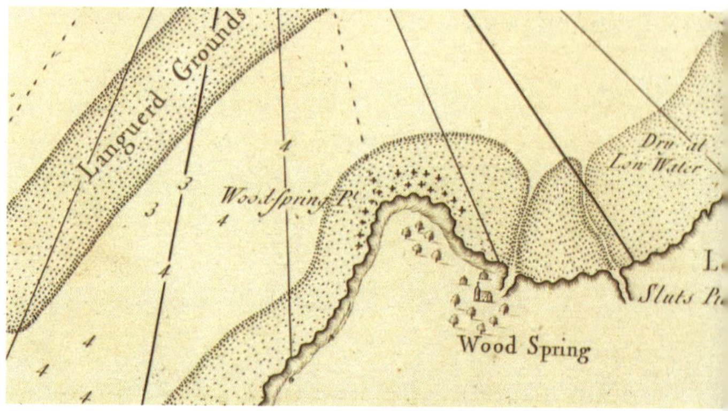

Illustration 2.60: Captain Holliday's chart, *c.*1712, showing *Woodspring Point* and *Wood Spring*[631] (Adrian Webb Collection)

Woodspring Hillock or Swallow Point (Kewstoke)
Named in 1838.[632] *Woodspring Point* (see above) has superseded both of these names on Admiralty charts.

Worle Bay (formerly also World Bay)
From the place-name *Worle* + *bay*. The place-name appears to be a reduced form of Old English *wōr* a word for some gamebird + *lēah* 'clearing, glade; wood' (compare nearby Woodspring),[633] and to have been reinterpreted occasionally as the more familiar *world*. The appearance of a rare Old English word for a gamebird on two adjacent headlands, and perhaps in no other English place-names, is worth dwelling on. The black grouse (if that is what the word really denotes) is extinct in Somerset but was formerly found on the heaths of the Quantocks, the Brendon

Hills and Exmoor; note that *Heath Poult Cross* on the Brendons contains a local name for the grouse, and *poult* is 'the only name for black-game'.[634] Habitat of the heathland type must once have been found at the two promontories of Worle and Woodspring. *World Bay* was in the 1770s the name for the bay that is known today as *Sand Bay*.[635] It is a name that does not appear on navigational charts before 1825.[636]

Illustration 2.61: Captain William's survey of *c.*1708, showing *Worlehill* and *Weston Supermare*[637] (Admiralty Library)

Worlebury

The once conspicuous, but now wooded, hillfort (Old English *byrig*, the dative case form of *burg* 'massive earthwork, hillfort') on the promontory north of Weston-super-Mare, taking its name from Worle (see previous entry). The hill, now known as *Worlebury Hill*, appears as *Worle Hill* on charts from 1728[638] until the 1830s, and the hillfort only once as *Worle Berry*.[639]

Yellow Rocks, Yellow Stone (Oare)

On current Ordnance Survey maps. Self-explanatory; compare also *Yellow Hammer Rock*, just across the Devon county boundary in Countisbury. But yellow is not the typical colour of the Hangman grits or Lynton beds exposed along this coast.

Yeo

In northern Somerset there are four rivers called *Yeo*: the Blind Yeo, the Land Yeo, the Lox Yeo and the plain Yeo, and these are only the most conspicuous of a larger number in Somerset and Devon. In Somerset they name the network of rivers which took a sluggish and variable course through the Levels before drainage. The name is simply from Old English *ēa* 'river' via a dialect development to **eā*, **yā*, in some cases displacing an earlier British Celtic name.[640] The Land Yeo flows from Dundry Hill past Nailsea into the Bristol Channel through a common mouth with the Blind Yeo at Clevedon. The plain Yeo or Congresbury Yeo enters the Bristol Channel at Wick St Lawrence. The Lox Yeo flows into the Axe and does not reach the Bristol Channel.

The Yeo river flowing into the sea south of Clevedon is named by White on his survey of 1825.[641]

Illustration 2.62: The River Yeo, starting next to Kingstone Seymour church, as depicted on Strachey's survey of the 1730s (S.A.N.H.S.)

Acknowledgements

Our thanks go to Philip Ashford, Brian Austin, Dr R.W. Dunning, Jennifer Scherr and Christopher Whittick for discussion of individual names and documentation, and to Ian Coleby for designing our map showing the locations of names of Scandinavian origin.

Abbreviations

B.A.	Bristol Archives, B Bond, Bristol
B.L.	British Library, St Pancras, London
B.R.S.	Bristol Record Society
C.D.E.P.N.	*Cambridge dictionary of English place-names*
D.E.P.N.	*Concise Oxford dictionary of English place-names*, 4th edn
O.S.	Ordnance Survey
S.D.N.Q.	*Somerset and Dorset Notes and Queries*
S.R.S.	Somerset Record Society
S.A.N.H.S.	Somerset Archaeological and Natural History Society
S.H.C.	Somerset Heritage Centre, Norton Fitzwarren, Taunton
T.B.G.A.S.	*Transactions of the Bristol and Gloucestershire Archaeological Society*
T.N.A.	The National Archives [of England and Wales], Kew
U.K.H.O.	United Kingdom Hydrographic Office, Taunton

References

1 Quoted in A.H. Powell, *The ancient borough of Bridgwater in the county of Somerset* (Bridgwater, 1907), 192-3.

2 The National Archives (T.N.A.), SC 8/156/7761 petition, *c.*1320.

3 Quoted in Powell, *Bridgwater*, 192-3.

4 A.J. Webb, *Charts and surveys of the Somerset coast, c.1350-1824*, Somerset Record Society 97 (2014), facsimile 9.

5 U.K.H.O., 790 Dd 'A Mercator's Chart. Projected, and Drawn, from M: Mackenzie Junrs. Surveys of England, and Wales [1770-1773]; and from G: Spence's Survey of the Scilly Isles: by Græme Spence, 1808'; U.K.H.O., E143/1-3 Dc Hydrographic Department office chart compilation based on various sources, *c.*1824; U.K.H.O., H732 15b Lieutenants H.M. Denham and C.G. Robinson ms survey of the southern shores of the Bristol Channel, 1831; Lieutenants H.M. Denham and C.G. Robinson, *England west coast sheet IV Bristol Channel inner part* (London, 1839).

6 Information kindly supplied by Brian Austin, Weston-super-Mare, 2016.

7 Webb, *Charts*, 39.

8 R. Laurie and J. Whittle, *Laurie and Whittle's new sailing directions to accompany the Channel pilot and their large general chart of the English Channel* (London, 1810), 80; R. Laurie and J. Whittle, *Laurie and Whittle's new sailing directions to accompany the Channel pilot and their large general chart of the English Channel* (London, 1813), 82.

9 Scandinavian words are given in their Old Norse form.

10 Archaeological investigation in Womanby Street, Cardiff, has revealed nothing (G. O. Pierce, *Place-names in Glamorgan* (Cardiff, 2002), 183).

11 R. Coates, 'South-West English *dumball, dumble, dunball* 'pasture subject to (occasional) tidal flooding" in *Journal of the English Place-Name Society* 39 (2007), 59-72.

12 A.H. Smith, *English place-name elements*, vol. I (Cambridge, 1956), 19; D.N. Parsons and T. Styles, with C. Hough, *The vocabulary of English place-names*, vol. I (Nottingham, 1997), 47.

13 U.K.H.O., *The mariner's handbook* (Taunton, 2009), 355.

14 Smith, *Elements*, vol. I, 258-9.

15 Smith, *Elements*, vol. II, 74.

16 *Oxford English dictionary*, sense II, 19 (b).

17 *Oxford English dictionary*, sense I, 1 (a).

18 B. Waters, *Severn tide* (London, 1947); S. Crowther and A. Dickson, with K. Truscoe, *Severn Estuary rapid coastal zone assessment survey, National Mapping Programme* 68 (2008), SDV351398; M. Jecock, *Introductions to heritage assets: river fisheries and coastal fish weirs* (English Heritage, 2011).

19 U.K.H.O., 790 Dd survey, 1771 corrected 1808.

20 Bristol Archives (B.A.), AC/D/11/29 lease, 1480; reading uncertain.

21 Information kindly supplied by Brian Austin, Weston-super-Mare, 2016.

22 British Library (B.L.), Cotton MSS, Aug 1 volume 1, survey, 1539.

23 Information kindly supplied by Brian Austin, Weston-super-Mare, 2016.

24 Information kindly supplied by Dr R.W. Dunning from a deed of 1496 in private hands.

25 E. Ekwall, *English river-names* (Oxford, 1928), 20.

26 A.L.F. Rivet and C. Smith, *The place-names of Roman Britain* (London, 1979), 240.

27 Ekwall, *River-names*, 152, 154-5; Ekwall, *Concise Oxford dictionary of English place-names*, 4th edn (Oxford, 1960), 20.

28 M. Förster, *Der Flussname Themse und seine Sippe* (Munich, 1942), 822; K.H. Jackson, *Language and history in early Britain* (Edinburgh, 1953) 259; W.F.H. Nicolaisen, 'Die alteuropäischen Gewässernamen der britischen Hauptinsel' in *Beiträge zur Namenforschung* 8 (1957), 241-2; A.L.F. Rivet and K.H. Jackson, 'The British section of the Antonine Itinerary' in *Britannia* 1 (1970) 74-5; Rivet and Smith, *The place-names of Roman Britain*, 376-8.

29 V. Watts, *Cambridge dictionary of English place-names* (Cambridge, 2004), 28.

30 S.H.C., DD/DP 64/3 grant, 1700.

31 S.H.C., DD/BW 461 survey, 1710.

32 Webb, *Charts*, facsimile 9.

33 Actually, no such surname is known, locally or nationally. It is probably an error for *Sheldon*, found for example at Dunster in 1620.

34 S.H.C., D/P/hun 23/6 A plan of the parish of Huntspill in the county of Somerset divided into tythings by William Locke, 1776.

35 Webb, *Charts*, facsimile 9.

36 Ordnance Survey, Sheet 20 (London, 1809).

37 C. and J. Greenwood, *Map of the county of Somerset, from actual survey made in the years 1820 & 1821* (London, 1822).

38 Webb, *Charts*.

39 Ordnance Survey, Sheet 20 (London, 1809).

40 Greenwood, *Map of Somerset* (1822).

41 Webb, *Charts*.

42 U.K.H.O., OCB 1157 A1 *The Parrett or Bridgewater River and the Bar* (London, 1839).

43 R. Locke, 'On the improvement of meadow land' in *Letters and Papers on Agriculture, Planting, &c.* . . . vol. 5 (London, 1790), 205.

44 R. Locke, *A letter to George Templer, Esq. on the propriety of imposing a new tax on eighteen parishes in the county of Somerset, (under the denomination of Huntspill Level,) for repairing a certain extent of sea wall in the parish of Huntspill, which was beaten down by the sea about a year since* (Taunton, 1800), 23.

45 Greenwood, *Map of Somerset* (1822).

46 U.K.H.O., OCB 1157 A1 *The Parrett or Bridgewater River and the Bar* (London, 1839).

47 Webb, *Charts*, 66.

48 U.K.H.O., 790 Dd survey, 1771 corrected 1808.

49 U.K.H.O., E143/1-3 Dc compilation, *c.*1824.

50 U.K.H.O., H732 15b Denham and Robinson ms survey, 1831.

51 Denham and Robinson, *England west coast sheet IV*.

52 S.H.C., DD\BK/3/17 lease, 1790.

53 *Gentleman's magazine*, 75:2 (London, 1805), 1097.

54 *Bristol Mirror*, 7 December 1811.

55 Webb, *Charts*, 111.

56 S.H.C., A/DAS/1/439/4 print of Bearn Backs by W. Day, published by R. Hill, Weston Library, August 1825.

57 H.M. Denham, *Sailing directions for the Bristol Channel* (London, 1839), 120.

58 *The Builder*, volume 3 (London, 1845), 262.

59 J. Murray, *A Handbook for travellers in Wiltshire, Dorsetshire, and Somersetshire* (London, 1856), 164.

60 J. Whereat, *New hand-book to Weston-super-Mare and its neighbourhood, etc* (Weston-super-Mare, 1855), 18.

61 S. Robinson, *Somerset place names* (Wimborne, 1992), 29.

62 R. Coates, with J. Scherr, 'Some local names in medieval and early-modern Bristol' in *T.B.G.A.S.* 129 (2011), 155-96, at 156-161.

63 Ekwall, *D.E.P.N.*, 33.

64 Webb, *Charts*, facsimile 6; J. Strachey, *Somersetshire survey'd and protracted by Mr. Strachy* (London, 1736).

65 Webb, *Charts*, 67.

66 Webb, *Charts*, 87.

67 Webb, *Charts*, facsimile 7.

68 Webb, *Charts*, facsimile 6.

69 J.W. Gough, *Mendip mining laws and forest bounds*, S.R.S. 45 (1931), 167.

70 S.H.C., DD/X/BRC/9 conveyance, 1797.

71 Ordnance Survey, Sheet 35 (London, 1830).

72 U.K.H.O., 1176 *Bristol Channel, Severn Estuary, Steep Holm to Avonmouth* (Taunton, 2015).

73 B. Cox, *English inn and tavern names* (Nottingham, 1994), 89.

74 J. Larwood and J.C. Hotten, *English inn signs* (London, 1907, reprinted 1985), 26.

75 Larwood and Hotten, *Inn signs*, 202.

76 S.H.C., DD/WY/64/10 lease, 1674.

77 S.H.C., DD/SAS C 77/27 Old Cleeve leases.

78 S.H.C., DD/L 2/11/63 Old Cleeve leases 1693-1794, 2/12/65–6 Old Cleeve leases, 1801-1893; *Post Office Directory of Somerset* (London, 1861), *Post Office Directory of Somerset* (London, 1866).

79 Strachey, *Somersetshire.*

80 U.K.H.O., 640 13k Murdoch Mackenzie junior, Part of Bristol Channel from Lundy Isle and Worms Head; to Watchet and Barry Isle, manuscript, 1771.

81 R. Warner's, *Walk thro' Western counties* (London, 1800), 79.

82 Webb, *Charts*, passim.

83 The story can be read for example in A. Barrie, *Sutton companion to the folklore, myths and customs of Britain* (Stroud, 2005) and S. Jacksties, *Somerset folk tales* (Stroud, 2011).

84 Wright, *English dialect dictionary, s.v.*

85 U.K.H.O., H367/2, H367/6 A. Nimmo, To the Corporation for improving the Port of Dublin this chart of the coasts of Ireland and St. Georges Channel, exhibiting the sea and harbour lights under their management drawn chiefly from original surveys, is respectfully dedicated by Alexander Nimmo civil engineer and hydrographer (London, 1830).

86 U.K.H.O., z101/1-3 J.W. Norie, *To the Right Honorable the Master Wardens and Elder Bretheren of the Trinity House, this chart of the English Channel, is by permission most respectfully dedicated by their obliged and grateful servant JW Norie, hydrographer* (London, 1839 corr. 1842).

87 Webb, *Charts*, passim.

88 Admiralty Library, Vn24 A correct chart of the Channel between England and France (London, 1721).

89 H. Kurath and S. M. Kuhn, eds, *Middle English dictionary* (Ann Arbor, 1954-2001), online at http://quod.lib.umich.edu/m/med/, accessed frequently.

90 J. Speed, Bathe, panel from Speed's original map of Somerset-Shire, in *The Theatre of the Empire of Great Britain*, atlas (London, 1610).

91 C. Saxton, *Somersetensem comitat[um] ... ponit tabula* (London, 1575).

92 G. Collins, *Great Britain's coasting pilot* (London, 1693).

93 Webb, *Charts*, facsimile 9.

94 Ekwall, *D.E.P.N.*, 62; Watts, *C.D.E.P.N.*, 82.

95 Webb, *Charts*, facsimile 9.

96 U.K.H.O., 790 Dd survey, 1771 corrected 1808.

97 Webb, *Charts*, facsimile 9.

98 Webb, *Charts.*

99 Webb, *Charts*, 90.

100 U.K.H.O., OCB 1157 A1 *The Parrett or Bridgewater River and the Bar* (London, 1839).

101 Collins, *Pilot.*

102 Webb, *Charts.*

103 National Library of Ireland MS 700, Giraldus Cambrensis, Latin transcripts of 'The Topography of Ireland' and 'The Conquest of Ireland'. Including map of Europe and a number of marginal illustrations including that of the Norman leader, Hugh de Lacy, late twelfth century.

104 Hereford Cathedral Library, Hereford *Mappa Mundi.*

105 R. Higden, *The description of England*... (Westminster, 1480), un-numbered page.

106 B.L., K Top V 2: G. Lily, *Britanniae insulae quae nunc Angliae et Scotia regna continent cum Hibernia adiacente nova descriptio* (1546).

107 Webb, *Charts*, facsimile 1.

108 Rivet and Smith, *Place-names of Roman Britain*, 450-1.

109 Webb, *Charts*, facsimile 1.

110 Webb, *Charts*, 24.

111 B.L., Cotton Augustus I.i f.8.

112 M. Drayton, *Poly-Olbion* (London, 1612).

113 Webb, *Charts*, 119.

114 W. Camden, *Britain, or a chorographicall description of the most flourishing kingdomes, England, Scotland, and Ireland, and the ilands adjoyning, out of the depth of antiquitie beautified vvith mappes of the severall shires of England: vvritten first in Latine by William Camden Clarenceux K. of A. Translated newly into English by Philemon Holland Doctour in Physick: finally, revised, amended, and enlarged with sundry additions by the said author* (London, 1637).

115 Webb, *Charts*, 48.

116 Webb, *Charts*, facsimile 6.

117 Webb, *Charts*, facsimile 4.

118 Webb, *Charts*, 134.

119 Webb, *Charts*, 91.

120 Webb, *Charts*, 38.

121 Webb, *Charts*, facsimile 1.

122 Webb, *Charts*, facsimile 7.

123 Ekwall, *D.E.P.N.*, 66; A. H. Smith, *The place-names of Gloucestershire* (Cambridge, 1964), vol. III, 83-4; Watts, *C.D.E.P.N.*, 88.

124 D.H. Higgins, *Saint Jordan of Bristol: from the catacombs of Rome to College Green at Bristol* (Bristol Branch of the Historical Association pamphlet 120, 2007).

125 U.K.H.O., NP 37 *Admiralty Sailing directions west coasts of England and Wales pilot* (Taunton, 2011), 139.

126 Webb, *Charts*, facsimile 2.

127 U.K.H.O., 1152 *Bristol Channel, Watchet to Weston-super-Mare*

and Newport to Barry (Taunton, 1977); U.K.H.O., NP 37 *West coasts of England and Wales pilot* (Taunton, 1974).

128 Ekwall, *River-names*, 55-6.

129 S.H.C., DD/WHh 581 grant, *c.*1270.

130 M. Williams, *Draining of Somerset Levels* (1970), 70 n.

131 Collins, *Pilot.*

132 W. Day and C.H. Masters, *County of Somerset* (Blagdon, 1782).

133 Webb, *Charts*, facsimile 4.

134 Ekwall, *D.E.P.N.*, 76; Watts, *C.D.E.P.N.*, 102.

135 Ordnance Survey, Somerset XV.NE (London, 1886).

136 Ekwall, *D.E.P.N.*, 85; Watts, *C.D.E.P.N.*, 113.

137 Webb, *Charts*, facsimile 9.

138 Ordnance Survey, Somerset L.NW (London, 1886).

139 Ordnance Survey, Somerset XV.NE (London, 1886).

140 Ordnance Survey, Somerset XV.NE (London, 1904).

141 J. Rich, *A treatise on the Bristol pilots from their origination, to their amalgamation. Including a list of pilots' names, dates and some of the boats, for almost 500 years* (Pill, 1996), 29.

142 Webb, *Charts*, facsimile 5.

143 S. Lewis (London, 1840).

144 J. Rutter, *Delineations of north western division of the county of Somerset and the Mendip caverns* (Shaftesbury, 1829), 248.

145 Webb, *Charts*, facsimile 5.

146 Webb, *Charts*, facsimile 2.

147 U.K.H.O., L3895 R. Thomas, *Survey of the River Severn* (London, 1815).

148 U.K.H.O., H905 13k Captain Martin White, Plan of the triangle's (*sic*) for the Bristol Channel, manuscript, 1825.

149 J. Rutter, *Delineations of north western division of the county of Somerset and the Mendip caverns* (Shaftesbury, 1829), 248; see also E. Wigan, *The tale of Gordano ...*, 1st ed. (Taunton, *c.*1950), 70.

150 U.K.H.O., OCB 1859 A1 *King Road* (London, 1848).

151 Ordnance Survey, Somerset II.NW (London, 1884).

152 *The London Gazette*, part 2 (London, 1840), 2883.

153 U.K.H.O., 1176 *Bristol Channel, Severn Estuary, Steep Holm to Avonmouth* (Taunton, 2015).

154 Ekwall, *D.E.P.N.*, 95; Watts, *C.D.E.P.N.*, 125.

155 Webb, *Charts*, facsimile 9.

156 Webb, *Charts*, facsimile 10, 13-14.

157 U.K.H.O., OCB 1157 A1 *The Parrett or Bridgewater River and the Bar* (London, 1839).

158 Webb, *Charts*, facsimile 9.

159 Webb, *Charts.*

160 Ekwall, *D.E.P.N.*, 111; Watts, *C.D.E.P.N.*, 143; with elaboration here by R. Coates.

161 U.K.H.O., 1176 *Bristol Channel, Severn Estuary, Steep Holm to Avonmouth* (Taunton, 2015).

162 Webb, *Charts*, 145.

163 U.K.H.O., H905 13k Captain Martin White, Plan of the triangle's (*sic*) for the Bristol Channel, manuscript, 1825.

164 U.K.H.O., 1176 *Bristol Channel, Severn Estuary, Steep Holm to Avonmouth* (Taunton, 2015).

165 Webb, *Charts*, 145.

166 Webb, *Charts*, facsimile 2.

167 Webb, *Charts*, 72.

168 Webb, *Charts.*

169 Ordnance Survey, Somerset XXXVIII.SW (London, 1886).

170 U.K.H.O., L3895/1 Thomas, *Chart.*

171 U.K.H.O., H905 13k White, Bristol Channel, 1825.

172 Ekwall, *D.E.P.N.*, 119; Watts, *C.D.E.P.N.*, 153. Comage appears in B.L., Cotton MSS, Aug 1 volume 1, survey, 1539.

173 Somerset Historic Environment Record, record number 10658, at http://www.somersetheritage.org.uk/record/10658#, accessed December 2016.

174 Webb, *Charts*, facsimile 9.

175 L. Landon, *Somersetshire pleas from the rolls of the itinerant justices (41 Henry III to the end of his reign)*, S.R.S. 36 (1923).

176 Landon, *Somersetshire pleas.*

177 E. Green, ed., *Pedes Finium, commonly called Feet of Fines, for the county of Somerset, A.D. 1196 to A.D. 1307*, S.R.S. 6 (1892), 330.

178 S.H.C., DD\SPY/16/21, Newton family deed.

179 S.H.C., Q/SR/2/38, settlement examination, 1607.

180 Collins, *Pilot.*

181 *Calendars of proceedings in Chancery* (London, 1827-1832).

182 S. Smith, comp., and E.A. Fry, ed., *Index of wills proved in the Prerogative Court of Canterbury: and now preserved in the principal Probate registry, Somerset House, London*, British Record Society vol. 25 (London, 1893), 113.

183 Smith and Fry, *Wills*, 101.

184 H. E. Nott and E. Ralph, eds, *The deposition books of Bristol, vol. II, 1650-1654*, B.R.S. 13 (1948), 177.

185 Nott and Ralph, *Deposition books of Bristol, vol. II*, 55.

186 *Parliamentary gazetteer of England and Wales* (1841).

187 Webb, *Charts*, facsimile 1.

188 K.J. Barton, 'A medieval pottery kiln at Ham Green, Bristol' in *T.B.G.A.S.* 82 (1963), 95-126.

189 Collins, *Pilot.*

190 Denham and Robinson, *England west coast sheet IV.*

191 Webb, *Charts*, 67, 72, 76.

192 Denham and Robinson, *England west coast sheet IV.*

193 *Taunton Courier, and Western Advertiser*, 4 March 1939.

194 Denham and Robinson, *England west coast sheet IV.*

195 H.M. Denham, *Sailing directions for the Bristol Channel, by Henry Mangles Denham, Lieutenant, R.N., F.R.S. Being the result of a survey made by order of the Lords Commissioners of the Admiralty* (London, 1839), 116-18; see also a note in *S.D.N.Q.* 33 (1893), 76.

196 *Public Ledger and Daily Advertiser, 4 September 1848.*

197 Denham and Robinson, *England west coast sheet IV.*

198 Powell, *Bridgwater*, 192-3.

199 Webb, *Charts*, facsimile 9.

200 Ordnance Survey, Somerset L.SE (London, 1887).

201 Webb, *Charts*, 39, quoting from B.L., Lansdowne MSS 285 printed in D.W. Waters, *The rutters of the sea: the sailing directions of Pierre Garcie. A study of the first English and French printed sailing directions with facsimile reproductions* (New Haven, CT, 1967), 192.

202 Webb, *Charts*, 39.

203 Webb, *Charts*, 123.

204 Collins, *Pilot.*

205 Webb, *Charts*, 6-7.

206 Webb, *Charts*, 123.

207 Collins, *Pilot.*

208 Webb, *Charts*, 150.

209 S.H.C., DD/RG/30 Jones family of Huntspill deeds, 1747-

1788.

210 Ordnance Survey, Somerset L.NE (London, 1887).

211 Ordnance Survey, Somerset L.NE (London, 1887).

212 N.D. Harding, ed., *Bristol charters 1155-1373*, B.R.S. 1 (1930), 155.

213 Webb, *Charts*, facsimile 2.

214 Webb, *Charts*, facsimile 4.

215 Webb, *Charts*, facsimile 6.

216 Webb, *Charts*, 72.

217 Webb, *Charts*, facsimile 1.

218 Webb, *Charts*, 8.

219 Hydrographic Department, *West coast of England pilot comprising the coast of Great Britain from the Scilly Isles to the Mull of Galloway, including the Isle of Man*, 9th ed. (London, 1933), 206.

220 Hydrographic Department, *West coast of England pilot comprising the coast of Great Britain from the Scilly Isles to the Mull of Galloway, including the Isle of Man*, 9th ed. (London, 1948), 208.

221 Webb, *Charts*, facsimile 7.

222 S.H.C., DD/DP 64/3 grant, 1700.

223 Quoted in Powell, *Bridgwater*, 192-3.

224 Williams, *Draining*, 93, 113.

225 Coates, '*Dumball*'.

226 Webb, *Charts*, facsimile 5.

227 Webb, *Charts*, facsimile 6.

228 Webb, *Charts*, facsimile 7.

229 B. Donn, *Map of the country eleven miles around the city of Bristol* (Bristol, 1769).

230 Day and Masters, *Somerset.*

231 Webb, *Charts*, 65, 67, 78.

232 E. Thomas, *Down the 'Mouth: a history of Avonmouth*, private publication (1981), 31.

233 Rev. J. Collinson, *History and antiquities of the county of Somerset*, 3 volumes (Bath, 1791).

234 U.K.H.O., B259/2 shelf Dc W. Heather, *To the Right Honorable The Master, Wardens and Elder Bretheren of the Trinity House, this chart of St. George's Channel is most humbly dedicated by their obedient servant, William Heather* (London, 1798).

235 Knight (London, 1806).

236 Greenwood, *Map of Somerset* (1822).

237 U.K.H.O., L3895/1 Thomas, *Chart.*

238 U.K.H.O., H905 13k White, Bristol Channel, 1825.

239 Webb, *Charts*, 111.

240 Ordnance Survey, Sheet 35 (London, 1830).

241 Webb, *Charts*, facsimile 5.

242 Based upon a rough sketch that appeared in the *Western Daily Press*, 6 February 1950.

243 Webb, *Charts*, facsimile 9.

244 Webb, *Charts*, 17.

245 S.H.C., D/P/hun 23/6 A plan of the parish of Huntspill in the county of Somerset divided into tythings by William Locke, 1776.

246 Webb, *Charts*, 17.

247 Webb, *Charts*, facsimile 9.

248 Strachey, *Somersetshire.*

249 Day and Masters, *Somerset.*

250 Ordnance Survey, Sheet 20 (London, 1809).

251 Greenwood, *Map of Somerset* (1822).

252 A.J. Webb, 'The building of the Dunball Clyce' in *S.D.N.Q.* 36 (2007), 157-61.

253 Ekwall, *D.E.P.N.*, 154; Watts, *C.D.E.P.N.*, 199.

254 *Telegraph*, 16 June 2011, http://www.telegraph.co.uk/news/picturegalleries/howaboutthat/8579413/Beachcomber-told-to-leave-driftwood-home.html, accessed January 2017.

255 Webb, *Charts*, facsimile 3.

256 Webb, *Charts*, facsimile 4.

257 Webb, *Charts*, facsimile 6.

258 Webb, *Charts*, facsimile 3.

259 Webb, *Charts*, facsimile 7.

260 Ordnance Survey, Somerset L.NW (London, 1886).

261 Information available to the Family Names of the United Kingdom project, University of the West of England (2010-2016).

262 Webb, *Charts*, facsimile 9.

263 Strachey, *Somersetshire.*

264 S.H.C., D/P/hun 23/6 A plan of the parish of Huntspill in the county of Somerset divided into tythings by William Locke, 1776.

265 Day and Masters, *Somerset.*

266 Ordnance Survey, Sheet 20 (London, 1809).

267 U.K.H.O., OCB 1157 A1 *The Parrett or Bridgewater River and the Bar* (London, 1839).

268 Ordnance Survey, Somerset XXXVIII.NW.

269 Strachey, *Somersetshire.*

270 The name is almost totally absent from any coastal parish in the nineteenth century census returns. There was a Charles *Fidler* in Bridgwater in 1859.

271 U.K.H.O., L6241 Captain F.W. Beechey, Plan of King Road in the Bristol Channel, manuscript, 1847.

272 U.K.H.O., OCB 1859 A1 *King Road* (London, 1848).

273 L.S. Dawson, *Memoirs of hydrography*, volume II (Eastbourne, 1885), 10.

274 Captain T.H. Tizard, *List of British discovery and survey vessels from the earliest time to 1900* (London, 1900), 20.

275 U.K.H.O., 1176 *Bristol Channel, Severn Estuary, Steep Holm to Avonmouth* (Taunton, 2015).

276 For example by Watts, *C.D.E.P.N.*, 232.

277 B.G. Charles, *Non-Celtic place-names in Wales* (London, 1938), 163.

278 R. Coates, 'The Severn Sea islands in the Anglo-Saxon Chronicle,' in *Notes and Queries* 259 [61.1] (2014), 1-3.

279 Webb, *Charts*, 69.

280 Webb, *Charts*, facsimile 10.

281 Webb, *Charts.*

282 Denham and Robinson, *England west coast sheet IV.*

283 Webb, *Charts*, facsimile 13.

284 B.L., Cotton Augustus I.i f.8.

285 Ordnance Survey, Somerset XXXVIII.SW (London, 1886).

286 S.H.C., D\B\wsm/24/4/236 plan, 1866.

287 Webb, *Charts*, facsimile 8.

288 Webb, *Charts*, 62.

289 Webb, *Charts*, 42.

290 Webb, *Charts*, facsimile 1.

291 Webb, *Charts*, facsimile 9.

292 Webb, *Charts*, facsimile 1.

293 Webb, *Charts*, facsimile 8.

294 Webb, *Charts*, facsimile 8.

295 U.K.H.O., H732 15b Denham and Robinson ms survey, 1831.
296 Denham and Robinson, *England west coast sheet IV.*
297 Denham and Robinson, *England west coast sheet IV.*
298 S.H.C., DD\L/P30/86 Luttrell to Knolles, 1638.
299 S.H.C., DD\L/1/44/5/15 lease, 1684, DD\L/1/53/35/1 lease, 1687.
300 Webb, *Charts*, facsimile 10.
301 Anon, *The new handbook to Clevedon and the neighbourhood* (Clevedon, 1864), 99.
302 *Taunton Courier, and Western Advertiser*, 31 August 1870.
303 *North Devon Journal*, 27 July 1876.
304 Ordnance Survey, Somerset XXXVI.SW (London, 1887).
305 Ordnance Survey, Somerset XXXVI.SW (London, 1904).
306 Greenwood, *Map of Somerset* (1822).
307 J.W. Norie, *The new British Channel pilot . . .* (London, 1839), 86.
308 Webb, *Charts*, passim.
309 Ordnance Survey, Somerset XXXVII.NE (London, 1886).
310 Information available to the Family Names of the United Kingdom project, University of the West of England (2010-2016).
311 U.K.H.O., OCB 1859 I1 chart published 1990.
312 B. Donn, *Map of the country eleven miles around the city of Bristol* (Bristol, 1769).
313 Webb, *Charts*, passim.
314 H.D. Barton, *The Law Journal Reports, volume 11* (London, 1839), 106.
315 Patent Rolls, cited in *D.E.P.N.*, 181.
316 Letter of Christopher Kenn to Sir John Thynne, 26 March 1583, Longleat House MS., TH/VOL/V, known through T.N.A. Discovery online catalogue.
317 C.T. Moore, *Country houses*, vol. II (London, 1832), 339.
318 E. Down and A.J. Webb, *Somerset mapped* (Wellington, 2016), ix.
319 U.K.H.O., H905 13k White, Bristol Channel, 1825.
320 Ordnance Survey, Sheet 35 (London, 1830).
321 Day and Masters, *Somerset.*
322 Ordnance Survey, Sheet 20 (London, 1809).
323 Webb, *Charts*, 111.
324 Greenwood, *Map of Somerset* (1822).
325 P.H. Reaney, *The place-names of Essex* (Cambridge, 1935), 170; Smith, *English place-name elements*, vol. I, 259-60.
326 Denham and Robinson, *England west coast sheet IV.*
327 Captain F. Beechey, *Portishead Point*, 1847, un-numbered plate in the *Nautical Magazine* (London, 1847).
328 J.S. Hobbs, *New and complete sailing directions for the Bristol and St. Georges Channel . . .* (London, 1854), 21.
329 Webb, *Charts*, facsimile 9.
330 Webb, *Charts*, facsimile 6.
331 Webb, *Charts*, facsimile 9.
332 Coates, *Dumball*, 64, image 72.
333 Webb, *Charts*, facsimile 6.
334 B.A., photocopy of 'The accounts of John Balsall, purser of the Trinity of Bristol', 1480.
335 J.H. Harvey, ed., *William Worcestre intineraries* (Oxford, 1969); F. Neale, ed., *William Worcestre: the topography of medieval Bristol*, B.R.S. 51 (2000), 30, 48.
336 Ekwall, *D.E.P.N.*, 258; Watts, *C.D.E.P.N.*, 324. The mid-thirteenth century form is from S.H.C., DD/CN/5/10 Pawlett deed of *c.*1250.
337 Down and Webb, *Somerset mapped*, 39.
338 F. Hancock, *Minehead in the county of Somerset: a history of the parish, the manor, and the port* (Taunton, 1903), 35.
339 Hancock, *Minehead*, 35.
340 S.H.C., DD/L/P29/41/2 deposition, temp Eliz. I.
341 Webb, *Charts*, facsimile 6.
342 Strachey, *Somersetshire.*
343 Webb, *Charts*, 60.
344 Collinson, *History*, vol. 1, xi.
345 T.N.A., ADM 344/115 coastal view, second half of the nineteenth century.
346 Ordnance Survey, Sheet 20 (London, 1809).
347 Laurie and Whittle, *Channel pilot* (1813), 82.
348 Laurie and Whittle, *Channel pilot* (1810), 80.
349 Laurie and Whittle, *Channel pilot* (1813), 82.
350 Denham and Robinson, *England west coast sheet IV.*
351 We are grateful to Philip Ashford for this information.
352 Webb, *Charts*, 39.
353 Webb, *Charts*, facsimile 3.
354 Ordnance Survey, Somerset XXII.SE (London, 1887).
355 W.B. Lockwood, *The Oxford book of British bird names* (Oxford, 1984), 51.
356 U.K.H.O., L3895 Thomas, *Chart.*
357 M. Vanes, ed., *The overseas trade of Bristol in the sixteenth century*, B.R.S. 31 (1979), 61.
358 T.N.A., C 1/860/34 Murfyne v The Mayor of Bristol, 1533-1538.
359 "There once were two cats of Kilkenny; / Each thought there was one cat too many. / So they fought and they fit / And they scratched and they bit / Till (excepting their nails / And the tips of their tails) / Instead of two cats there weren't any." The history of the rhyme can be read at https://en.wikipedia.org/wiki/Kilkenny_cat, accessed January 2017.
360 Denham and Robinson, *England west coast sheet IV.*
361 Ekwall, *D.E.P.N.*, 276; Watts, *C.D.E.P.N.*, 345.
362 Denham and Robinson, *England west coast sheet IV.*
363 B.A., photocopy of 'The accounts of John Balsall, purser of the Trinity of Bristol', 1480.
364 B.A., CC/2/7, Ricart's Kalendar, *c.* 1480.
365 Saxton, *Somersetensem.*
366 Webb, *Charts*, facsimile 2.
367 U.K.H.O., 1176 *Bristol Channel, Severn Estuary, Steep Holm to Avonmouth* (Taunton, 2015).
368 B.L., Cotton MSS, Aug 1 volume 1, survey, 1539.
369 Ordnance Survey, Sheet 35 (London, 1830).
370 *Journal of the House of Commons*, 19 November 1813.
371 Webb, *Charts*, 66-7, 69, 73-6.
372 Webb, *Charts*, facsimile 13.
373 Ordnance Survey, Sheet 35 (London, 1830).
374 U.K.H.O., 1176 *Bristol Channel, Severn Estuary, Steep Holm to Avonmouth* (Taunton, 2015).
375 S.H.C., DD/CTP/2/1/140 Oldmixon to Stokwud, 1548.
376 Webb, *Charts*, 39.
377 Webb, *Charts*, facsimile 3.
378 Webb, *Charts*, facsimile 4.
379 Webb, *Charts*, facsimile 6.

380 Webb, *Charts*, facsimile 7.
381 Webb, *Charts*, 150, 156.
382 U.K.H.O., 1176 *Bristol Channel, Severn Estuary, Steep Holm to Avonmouth* (Taunton, 2015).
383 Webb, *Charts*, facsimile 6 and 7.
384 U.K.H.O., 1176 *Bristol Channel, Severn Estuary, Steep Holm to Avonmouth* (Taunton, 2015).
385 *Calendar of the patent rolls preserved in the Public Record Office: Edward II, A.D. 1307-[1327]* (London, 1894), 254.
386 Webb, *Charts*, facsimile 9.
387 U.K.H.O., OCB 1157 A1 *The Parrett or Bridgewater River and the Bar* (London, 1839).
388 Webb, *Charts*, 93.
389 Greenwood, *Map of Somerset* (1822).
390 Ekwall, *D.E.P.N.*, 298; Watts, *C.D.E.P.N.*, 373.
391 Collins, *Pilot.*
392 Ordnance Survey, Sheet 20 (London, 1809).
393 T. Telford and Captain G. Nicholls, *Ship Canal for the junction of the English and Bristol Channels* (London, 1824), 23.
394 Ordnance Survey, Somerset XXXVI.SE (London, 1887).
395 Webb, *Charts*, passim.
396 Webb, *Charts*, facsimile 9.
397 United States Defense Mapping Agency, *List of lights, radio aids, and fog signals: British Isles, English Channel, and North Sea*, Issue 20 (1963), 99.
398 Information available to the Family Names of the United Kingdom project, University of the West of England (2010-2016).
399 Denham and Robinson, *England west coast sheet IV.*
400 U.K.H.O., L4505.
401 Captain F. Beechey, *Portishead Point*, 1847, un-numbered plate in the *Nautical Magazine* (London, 1847).
402 U.K.H.O., L6241 Beechey, King Road, 1847.
403 Captain T.H. Tizard, *List of British Discovery and Survey Vessels from the Earliest time to 1900* (London, 1900), 20.
404 Beechey, *Portishead Point.*
405 U.K.H.O., OCB 1160 D1, *Harbours in Somerset and North Devon* (Taunton, 1974).
406 Historic England, https://historicengland.org.uk/listing/the-list/list-entry/1437202, accessed January 2017.
407 Webb, *Charts*, facsimile 9.
408 Ordnance Survey, Somerset XXVIII.SW (London, 1886).
409 U.K.H.O., H732 15b Denham and Robinson ms survey, 1831.
410 Ordnance Survey, Sheet 20 (London, 1809).
411 Denham and Robinson, *England west coast sheet IV.*
412 Denham and Robinson, *England west coast sheet IV.*
413 Industrial Railway Society, http://www.irsociety.co.uk/Archives/22/Paradise.htm, accessed January 2017.
414 Ekwall, *D.E.P.N.*, 327.
415 Watts, *C.D.E.P.N.*, 416.
416 Down and Webb, *Somerset mapped*, 39.
417 Webb, *Charts*, facsimile 1.
418 Denham and Robinson, *England west coast sheet IV.*
419 Denham and Robinson, *England west coast sheet IV.*
420 Down and Webb, *Somerset mapped*, 39.
421 Webb, *Charts*, 61.
422 U.K.H.O., 640 13k Mackenzie junior, Part of Bristol Channel, 1771.
423 Webb, *Charts*, 6.
424 D. Flanagan and L. Flanagan, *Irish place-names* (Goldenbridge, Dublin, 1994), 239.
425 Webb, *Charts*, facsimile 5.
426 Down and Webb, *Somerset mapped*, xviii; Canal Routes, http://www.canalroutes.net/Bridgwater-and-Taunton-Canal.html, accessed January 2017.
427 E. Wigan, *The tale of Gordano . . .* (Taunton, *c.*1950); M. Bunce, *Pill Ferry and it's* [sic] *environs* (Pill, 1993), at https://pillvillage.com/pill-ferry-and-its-environs/, accessed September 2016.
428 Webb, *Charts*, facsimile 5.
429 C.P. Collins, *Notes on the chase of the wild red deer in the counties of Devon and Somerset* (London, 1862), 197, 199, 224, 231, 268.
430 Webb, *Charts*, 8.
431 Webb, *Charts*, facsimile 10.
432 Webb, *Charts*, facsimile 12.
433 Denham and Robinson, *England west coast sheet IV.*
434 U.K.H.O., H905 13k White, Bristol Channel, 1825.
435 Ordnance Survey, Somerset XXXVIII.SW (London, 1886).
436 Webb, *Charts*, facsimile 4.
437 Webb, *Charts*, facsimile 6.
438 Webb, *Charts*, facsimiles 6 and 7.
439 Webb, *Charts*, facsimile 4.
440 The surname *Newcombe* might be considered instead, but this has the same origin: 'newly arrived'.
441 Webb, *Charts*, 155.
442 Captain E.J. Bedford, *Sailing directions for the Bristol Channel*, 4th ed. (London, 1884), 145.
443 Hydrographic Department, *West coast of England pilot*, 9th ed., 206.
444 Hydrographic Department, *West coast of England pilot*, 9th ed., 208.
445 Webb, *Charts*, facsimile 9.
446 Ordnance Survey, Somerset L.NE (London, 1887).
447 Ordnance Survey, Somerset XXXVIII.SW (London, 1886).
448 Ordnance Survey, Somerset L.NE (London, 1887).
449 S.H.C., DD/CTP/2/1/140 Oldmixon to Stokwud, 1548.
450 *Daily Mail*, http://www.dailymail.co.uk/news/article-3006585/Oysters-grown-Cornwall-s-Porlock-Bay-time-120-years-good-eaten-straight-sea.html (accessed June 2016).
451 Webb, *Charts*, facsimile 8.
452 These and other recorded spellings may be found in Ekwall, *River-names*, 320.
453 Ekwall, *River-names*, 320-2.
454 Saxton, *Somersetensem.*
455 Webb, *Charts*, 38.
456 A.J. Webb, ed., *A maritime history of Somerset, volume two* (Taunton, 2015), 127, 140.
457 Ekwall, *D.E.P.N.*, 359.
458 Ordnance Survey, Somerset XXXVIII.SW (London, 1886).
459 Quoted in Powell, *Bridgwater*, 192-3.
460 Webb, *Charts*, facsimile 9.
461 *VCH Somerset* VI, 252.
462 S.H.C., DD/SAS C212/Map 17.
463 S.H.C., DD/BR/ely/2 and DD/BW/1 for collections of original documents relating to the Pym family.

464 Ordnance Survey, Somerset L.NE (London, 1887) and Somerset L.NE (London, 1904).
465 Ordnance Survey, Somerset L.NE (London, 1887).
466 Ordnance Survey, Somerset L.NW (London, 1886).
467 Copies of this are held at the B.L., Maps MAR III.79.1; Admiralty Library (A.L.), Vf2/33; National Library of Wales, 6013; Newberry Library, Ayer 135.E55 1766 between pages 42-43 (PrCt).
468 N. Cutler, *A general coasting pilot; containing directions for sailing into, and out of, the principal ports and harbours thro'out the known World, with a set of sea-charts, some laid down after Mercator, . . .* (London, 1728).
469 Webb, *Charts*, facsimile 6.
470 Webb, *Charts*, facsimile 6.
471 Webb, *Charts*, passim.
472 For details of the Mackenzie's see A.C.F. David, 'Collins, Mackenzie and the hydrographic surveys of the Somerset coast' in A.J. Webb, ed., *A maritime history of Somerset volume one: trade and commerce* (Taunton, 2010), 93-106.
473 B.L., Maps1068(24); AL, Vu8/1; B.L., Maps1068(27).
474 David, 'Collins, Mackenzie . . .', 100.
475 Corporation of Trinity House, 1314 D5 f.59.
476 J. Barlow, *The coasting pilot for the Bristol Channel and The Scilly Islands, from Scilly Islands and The Longships to Saint Ann's Light, Milford, and King-Road* (Ilfracombe, 1821), 84-5.
477 U.K.H.O., MP92 remark book of H.M.S. *Myrtle*, 1815.
478 B.L., Maps 1103(2) Laurie and Whittle's chart of the Bristol Channel, 1794.
479 United Kingdom Hydrographic Office (U.K.H.O.), B265/3 Steel's chart of the Irish Sea or St Georges Channel (London, 1800).
480 National Maritime Museum, Greenwich, D8824 *W. Heather's new chart of the Bristol Channel* (London, 1803).
481 B.L., Maps 1244(1) *Thomas junior's chart of the lower reaches of the River Severn* (London, 1815).
482 B.L., Maps 1103.11 *Steel's new chart of the Bristol Channel* (London, 1820).
483 B.L., Maps 1068(29) *Laurie's Chart of the English Channel* (London, 1829).
484 Ekwall, *D.E.P.N.*, 371; Watts, *C.D.E.P.N.*, 478.
485 Webb, *Charts*, 93, quoting Revd J. Malham, *The naval gazetteer* ... vol. II (London, 1795), 287.
486 Webb, *Charts*, facsimile 3.
487 Webb, *Charts*, facsimile 2.
488 U.K.H.O., L3895 R. Thomas, *Survey of the River Severn* (London, 1815).
489 H.P.R. Finberg, *Early charters of Wessex* (Leicester, 1964), 128 and 148.
490 Ekwall, *D.E.P.N.*, 371; Watts, *C.D.E.P.N.*, 479.
491 The final <v> in the Great Domesday Book form is written small, raised and faint.
492 B.A., 00460/3, grant, 1324.
493 Spellings of this name from some local documents are taken from E. Wigan, *Portishead parish history* (Taunton, 1932), as well as the national ones from Ekwall, *D.E.P.N.*, 371; Watts, *C.D.E.P.N.*, 479.
494 B. Donn, *Map of the country eleven miles around the city of Bristol* (Bristol, 1769).
495 Collinson, *History*, volume 3, 144.
496 Webb, *Charts*, facsimile 3.
497 J. Millerd, *An exact delineation of the famous citty of Bristoll and suburbs* (Bristol, 1673).
498 J. Speed, *Somersetshire* (London, 1610).
499 U.K.H.O., 790 Dd survey, 1771 corrected 1808.
500 J. Wright, *English dialect dictionary* (Oxford, 1898-1905), has an entry for *lair*, sb.2, meaning 'mud', but only as a Scots and North Country word.
501 B.L., Cotton MSS, Aug 1 vol 1, survey, 1539; Webb, *Charts*, facsimile 2.
502 Denham and Robinson, *England west coast sheet IV*.
503 Portishead Quays Marina website http://www.quaymarinas.com/our-marinas/portishead-quays/overview/ accessed 1 January 2017.
504 Webb, *Charts*, 39.
505 The 1625 version can be found on Blaeu's chart of the Bristol Channel (Webb, *Charts*, facsimile 3).
506 For the 1804 use see Admiralty Library, Vl 8; for 1808 use see U.K.H.O., 790 Dd survey, 1771 corrected 1808; for 1809 use see Admiralty Library, Vv6.
507 Webb, *Charts*, facsimile 3.
508 Webb, *Charts*, facsimile 7.
509 Rutter, *Delineations*, 246.
510 Webb, *Charts*, facsimile 7.
511 Webb, *Charts*, 67.
512 Rutter, *Delineations*, 246.
513 Rutter, *Delineations*, 246.
514 Webb, *Charts*, 164.
515 U.K.H.O., 1176 *Bristol Channel, Severn Estuary, Steep Holm to Avonmouth* (Taunton, 2015).
516 U.K.H.O., 790 Dd survey, 1771 corrected 1808.
517 Webb, *Charts*, passim.
518 U.K.H.O., 1176 *Bristol Channel, Severn Estuary, Steep Holm to Avonmouth* (Taunton, 2015).
519 B.A., AC/36074/12, undated translation by John Hugh Smyth of part of deed of confirmation, 1322.
520 B.A., AC/D/1/58, charter of feoffment, 1428.
521 Neale, *William Worcestre*, 30, 32, 252.
522 S.H.C., DD\MGR/1/2, grant, 1652.
523 T.N.A., STAC 2/25/315, Proceedings of the Court of Star Chamber, Right to a ferry over the Avon called Rownam Ferry (not precisely dated).
524 B.A., 8930/7, conveyance, 1741.
525 Webb, *Charts*, facsimile 7.
526 Webb, *Charts*, facsimile 12.
527 U.K.H.O., H732 15b Denham and Robinson ms survey, 1831.
528 U.K.H.O., L7313 4e Captain F.W. Beechey, Survey of the Bristol Channel, 1848.
529 Webb, *Charts*, 74.
530 U.K.H.O., OD 190 manuscript sailing directions for the Bristol Channel, 1825.
531 For the reprint of this work see Webb, *Charts*, facsimile 10.
532 Webb, *Charts*, 81.
533 Webb, *Charts*, 66.
534 U.K.H.O., 1176 *Bristol Channel, Severn Estuary, Steep Holm to Avonmouth* (Taunton, 2015).
535 S.H.C., A\DIQ/79/145 photograph, 1995-1998.
536 S.H.C., DD\EN/88 mortgage, 1775.

537 Ordnance Survey, Sheet 35 (London, 1830).
538 Denham and Robinson, *England west coast sheet IV*.
539 U.K.H.O., 1176 *Bristol Channel, Severn Estuary, Steep Holm to Avonmouth* (Taunton, 2015).
540 For its depction on a maritime chart see Denham and Robinson, *England west coast sheet IV*.
541 Landon, *Somersetshire pleas*, 36-7.
542 Webb, *Charts*, 60, 66, 69, 71-2, 75, 77.
543 R. Coates, *Your city's place-names: Bristol* [provisional title] (Nottingham, forthcoming 2017).
544 Ekwall, *D.E.P.N.*, 412; Watts, *C.D.E.P.N.*, 536.
545 Webb, *Charts*, passim.
546 Greenwood, *Map of Somerset* (1822).
547 Wright, *English dialect dictionary*, *s.v.*
548 S.H.C., DD/DP 64/3 grant, 1700.
549 S.H.C. DD/BW 461 survey, 1710.
550 Webb, *Charts*, facsimile 9.
551 S.H.C., D/P/hun 23/6 A plan of the parish of Huntspill in the county of Somerset divided into tythings by William Locke, 1776. Cures Island is shown on the map as being owned by 'Sheldom' (see under **Batch** and note 33) and was also known as Dunball alias Cures Island in this period (S.H.C., DD/RG/30 Jones family of Huntspill deeds, 1747-1788).
552 Day and Masters, *Somerset*.
553 E. Green, *The preparations in Somerset against the Spanish Armada, A.D. 1558-1588* (London, 1888).
554 Saxton, *Somersetensem*.
555 Webb, Charts, facsimile 7.
556 U.K.H.O., OCB 2682 B1, chart published 1888.
557 U.K.H.O., H905 13k White, Bristol Channel, 1825.
558 Ordnance Survey, Sheet 35 (London, 1830).
559 U.K.H.O., 1176 *Bristol Channel, Severn Estuary, Steep Holm to Avonmouth* (Taunton, 2015).
560 Wright, *English dialect dictionary*, *s.v.*
561 Ordnance Survey, Somerset XV.NE (London, 1886).
562 Rev. W. Jackson, ed., *A brief account of Worlebury, Weston-super-Mare* (Weston-super-Mare, 1874).
563 P. Quinn, *Holy wells of the Bath and Bristol region* (Herefordshire, 1999).
564 Information available to the Family Names of the United Kingdom project, University of the West of England (2010-16).
565 Ordnance Survey, Somerset L.NW (London, 1886).
566 Ordnance Survey, Somerset L.NE (London, 1886).
567 Coates, 'Severn Sea islands …'.
568 Down and Webb, *Somerset mapped*, 24-5.
569 Webb, Charts, facsimile 2.
570 L. Waghenaer, *Thresorie ou Cabinet de la Route Marinesque* (Calais, 1601), unnumbered chart of the south west of England.
571 Watts, *C.D.E.P.N.*, 573.
572 Webb, *Charts*, passim.
573 B.A., 04482 (2)b the port of Bristol delineating its limits prescribed by Exchequer writ, n.d.
574 Webb, *Charts*, facsimile 9.
575 Locke, *A letter*, 9-10.
576 Webb, *Charts*, passim.
577 U.K.H.O., H732 15b Denham and Robinson ms survey, 1831.
578 Locke, *A letter*, 9-10.
579 Ordnance Survey, Somerset XXXVIII.NW and Somerset XXXVIII.NE (London, 1886).
580 Ekwall, *D.E.P.N.*, 444; Watts, *C.D.E.P.N.*, 576. *Bristol* in the name of the village of Stockland Bristol arises from the possession of the estate in medieval times by Gaunt's Hospital in Bristol, and after the Dissolution by the Mayor and Corporation.
581 Ordnance Survey, Somerset XXXVIII.NW (London, 1886).
582 Denham and Robinson, *England west coast sheet IV*.
583 Ordnance Survey, Somerset XXXV.NW & NE (London, 1888).
584 *Oxford English dictionary*.
585 Ordnance Survey, Sheet 20 (London, 1809).
586 Webb, *Charts*, facsimile 7.
587 U.K.H.O., H905 13k White, Bristol Channel, 1825.
588 Webb, *Charts*, facsimile 7.
589 Ordnance Survey, Sheet 20 (London, 1809).
590 U.K.H.O., OCB 1160 D1, *Harbours in Somerset and North Devon* (Taunton, 1974).
591 Webb, *Charts*, 44.
592 Webb, *Charts*, 102.
593 U.K.H.O., H732 15b Denham and Robinson ms survey, 1831.
594 Webb, *Charts*, facsimile 9.
595 Ordnance Survey, Sheet 20 (London, 1809).
596 Webb, *Charts*, 70.
597 Webb, *Charts*, 71.
598 Ordnance Survey, Somerset XV.NE (London, 1886).
599 Ordnance Survey, Somerset XV.NE (London, 1904).
600 Ordnance Survey, Somerset XXXVIII.SW (London, 1886).
601 Watts, *C.D.E.P.N.*, 637.
602 Webb, *Charts*, facsimile 3.
603 Webb, *Charts*, facsimile 7.
604 Webb, *Charts*, facsimile 3.
605 J. Moxon, *A book of sea plates containing the scituation of all the ports, havens, creeks, capes, rocks, sands and schoalds in all Europe . . . newly corrected* (London, 1657).
606 Webb, *Charts*, passim.
607 Quoted in Powell, *Bridgwater*, 192-3.
608 Williams, *Draining*, 93, 113.
609 S.H.C., DD\CN/5/10, Pawlett deed, *c.*1250; DD\SF/2/45/10 lease, 7 March 1598; DD\BW/2/845 lease, 2 December 1698.
610 Ordnance Survey, Somerset XCCVIII.SE (London, 1886).
611 Ekwall, *D.E.P.N.*, 495; Watts, *C.D.E.P.N.*, 649.
612 Ordnance Survey, Sheet 35 (London, 1830).
613 U.K.H.O., 1176 *Bristol Channel, Severn Estuary, Steep Holm to Avonmouth* (Taunton, 2015).
614 Webb, *Charts*, 60-1.
615 Ekwall, *D.E.P.N.*, 500; Watts, *C.D.E.P.N.*, 654.
616 Down and Webb, *Somerset mapped*, 39.
617 Webb, *Charts*, facsimile 1.
618 Ordnance Survey, Somerset XXXVIII.SW (London, 1886).
619 U.K.H.O., H732 15b Denham and Robinson ms survey, 1831.
620 Ekwall, *D.E.P.N.*, 509; Watts, *C.D.E.P.N.*, 666.
621 Webb, *Charts*, facsimile 7.

622 Ordnance Survey, Sheet 20 (London, 1809).

623 R. Coates, 'New light from old wicks: the progeny of Latin *vicus*', *Nomina* 22 (1999), 75-116.

624 Ordnance Survey, Sheet 20 (London, 1809).

625 U.K.H.O., H732 15b Denham and Robinson ms survey, 1831.

626 U.K.H.O., 1176 *Bristol Channel, Severn Estuary, Steep Holm to Avonmouth* (Taunton, 2015).

627 Ekwall, *D.E.P.N.*, 532.

628 Webb, *Charts*, facsimile 4.

629 Webb, *Charts*, facsimile 7.

630 U.K.H.O., 1176 *Bristol Channel, Severn Estuary, Steep Holm to Avonmouth* (Taunton, 2015).

631 Webb, *Charts*, facsimile 7.

632 U.K.H.O., B1404 Captain F.W. Beechey, manuscript 'Plan Shewing the Alterations in the Bristol Channel. Between Flatholm Island & Kings Road Since the Surveys made in 1827 and 1831'.

633 Ekwall, *D.E.P.N.*, 534; Watts, *C.D.E.P.N.*, 700.

634 Wright, *English dialect dictionary*, *s.v.*

635 Webb, *Charts*, 60, 66.

636 Webb, *Charts*, passim.

637 Webb, *Charts*, facsimile 6.

638 Webb, *Charts*, facsimile 7.

639 U.K.H.O., E143/1-3 Dc compilation, *c.*1824.

640 Ekwall, *River-names*, 480-1.

641 U.K.H.O., H905 13k White, Bristol Channel, 1825.

Chapter Three

A Somerset Mercantile Community: The Customs District of Bridgwater, 1320-1500

Philip Ashford

Introduction

WHILST ASPECTS OF Bridgwater's trade in the later medieval period, alongside that of other ports in their wider contexts, have been investigated by local and national historians,[1] there is ample justification for a reconsideration of the port of Bridgwater in the later medieval period. The 'customs district', when it was formed at the end of the fourteenth century, of Bridgwater covered the coast from the Devon/Somerset border in the west to the River Axe, north of Brean Down. Therefore a comparison of the maritime communities and their trading activities at Minehead, Dunster, Watchet, Bridgwater, Combwich and Axewater has been undertaken. This has been made possible thanks to greatly improved access to customs accounts, or port books from the districts of Bridgwater and Bristol, as well as records of the Court of Common Pleas. Similarly the increasing availability of obscure sources (made digitally available) has provided surprising details towards this new analysis of maritime mercantile activity and trade from 1320 to 1500 along this section of the Somerset coast.

Political, economic, social and maritime facilities contexts

The political context of this study is dominated by the 'Hundred Years War', between 1337 and 1453, which had a significant impact on Somerset's maritime trade and affairs in at least three ways. First, the Somerset ports were not attacked, burned or pillaged by the French and their allies for the whole duration of the war. Even Minehead, exposed on the coast, and the first main port of call in the county, escaped harm. It would have taken a far less determined enemy to attack maritime facilities there than it would for the French to navigate several miles up the tidal Parrett to attack the town of Bridgwater protected by its castle. Elsewhere, Southampton was first to be burned by the French and their allies in 1337 subsequently taking decades to recover, there were 11 raids on Plymouth between 1337 and 1404, Salcombe was attacked in 1403 and Dartmouth repulsed an attack in 1404. In Dorset, Lyme Regis, Poole and Melcombe Regis (Weymouth) were 'wasted and burned by reason of the war' in 1376-1378 and had not recovered a generation later. Melcombe was further attacked in the 1430s causing the loss of much valuable merchandise and the subsequent loss of its staple port status to the more easily defended Poole.

The absence of attacks in the Bristol Channel meant users of those ports did not suffer the disruption and loss by war that the southern ports experienced, thus allowing trade to prosper. However, attacks on Melcombe and Lyme Regis were said to have prejudiced Somerset, as well as Dorset and Wiltshire, since Somerset was 'victualed' by the Dorset ports.[2] It is shown later in this chapter how Somerset's trade increased at the expense of the southern ports because of their vulnerability. Having said this, a recent study of Somerset's mercantile debt in the fifteenth century has shown the recovery of the southern ports because Somerset merchants were trading with Dartmouth, Plymouth and Exeter merchants from the early 1400s, followed by trading in Poole from the 1440s, Melcombe Regis from the 1470s and Lyme Regis from the 1480s.[3] The loss of Gascony in 1453 at the end of the Hundred Years War may well have disrupted Somerset's overseas trade for a time.

During the period of the Hundred Years War a Welsh revolt of the early fifteenth century did have an impact on the Somerset coast. Owen Glendower's revolt against King Henry the Fourth began in September 1400. His revolt gained strength and by 1402 he was leading the fight against Henry by winning battles in England. In 1403 a number of people from the Minehead area were keeping or sheltering movable goods belonging to Welsh rebels;

moving their goods out of the principality was a wise move, unless they were found out. An inquisition, held at Minehead, found that John Usher was storing a bundle of Welsh cloth that had been brought to Minehead, John Robard had half a boat worth 30s, John Franklyn had a quarter share in a boat worth 10s, John Clerk had 6 tons of coal worth 23 shillings and John Hort, the forester of Exmoor, had two cows worth 50s. At Dunster the inquisition found that Richard Harton had a chest belonging to a Welsh rebel in the town and William Scolemaister had a parcel of wool and some wool yarn. These rebel stocks seem less significant that the hundreds of Welsh sheep and tens of cattle that had been moved to Uphill, as an inquisition at Banwell had found. Furthermore, a boat of an unknown Welsh rebel worth 53s 4d lay at Clevedon.[4]

To counter those Welsh sympathisers in 1403, Somerset and Dorset officials were ordered to supply 20 men at arms and 50 archers to be mustered at Dunster by late October. The men were destined to serve in Carmarthen for three months. Ships and boats were to be arranged for them at Dunster ready for their transportation. Arrest and imprisonment was threatened for anyone who refused to take orders and sail to Wales.[5] 1403 was also the year when Cardiff Castle was being threatened by Glendower's forces. Bristol officials were charged with shipping archers to Cardiff from Uphill to meet the threat.[6] In the same year Somerset officials were ordered to buy and gather 119 quarters of wheat, 620 quarters of oats, 14 tuns of wine, 46 tuns of ale and 2,700 Hake and transport the provisions to Carmarthen, Swansea and Kilkenny Castle in Ireland.[7] No doubt the wine was gathered at Bridgwater and the grain transported from other ports which may have included Minehead, Dunster and Axbridge. The Hake was probably sourced at Minehead. A couple of years later, in 1405, when the tide was turning against Glendower, the Luttrell's household accounts show on 11 September that 2s was paid for the delivery of six standards of Sir Hugh Luttrell's (*c.*1364-1428) arms, which were used as colours on 'divers ships of Minehead carrying vitals to my Lord in the ports of Wales'.[8] Later, beer and loaves were bought on more than one occasion and sent to Wales for the 'master' who was 'in the retinue of the King'. On another occasion there seems to have been a Welsh vessel involved belonging to 'Howell'.[9] Sir

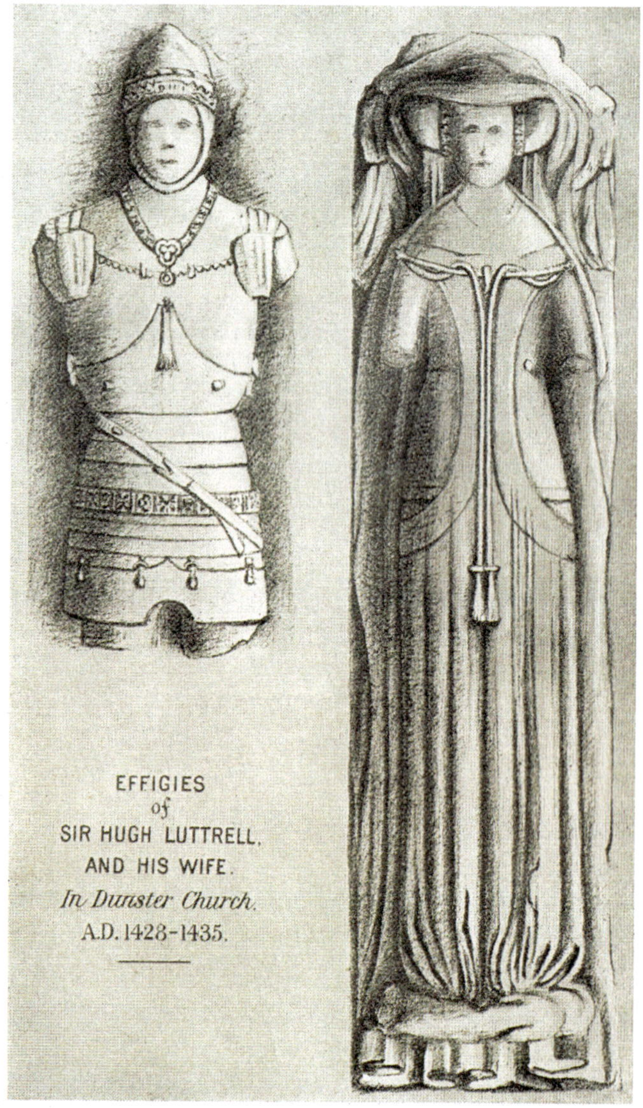

Illustration 3.1 (above) and 3.2 (below): A drawing of Alabaster effigies in Dunster church thought to represent Sir Hugh Luttrell (*c.*1364-1428) and his wife, Catherine Beaumont (d.1435). A Tudor version of the Luttrell coat of arms is found in St George's church, Dunster with black birds on a yellow background, which were flown on 'divers ships' carrying supplies from Somerset to Wales in 1405, similar to those used by the standard bearer in the Luttrell psalter. (H. Maxwell-Lyte, *A history of Dunster* (London, 1909), 104, 128)

Hugh Luttrell, the first Luttrell to take up residence in Dunster, was playing his part in putting down the rebellion. After a battle near Worcester in 1405, Glendower retreated back into Wales with his supporters and by 1406 the tide was turning against the revolt.

A second manner in which the Hundred Years War had a significant impact on Somerset's maritime affairs is the fact that Somerset vessels and mariners were often called up to serve the King in France, as shown in Appendix 2. This also meant that the knowledge of navigation and opportunities along the French coast increased amongst Somerset mariners and trades people. Trade between Gascony, Spain, and to a lesser extent Portugal continued throughout the period studied here. Thirdly, occasional maritime losses of Minehead and Bridgwater vessels and cargos to 'enemies', due to the war, must have significantly affected particular merchants at particular times. However, those occasions appear to have been relatively few. Gaining foreign cargos through acts of war, or piracy, may have more than compensated Somerset maritime communities for their losses. Some of the losses and gains are detailed below.

The Wars of the Roses, 1455-1485, that followed the Hundred Years War had little impact on Somerset's maritime affairs. Essentially, the conflict was a land-based war and no major actions took place in Somerset. However, in 1461 mariners from Bridgwater and Bristol were press-ganged to help Yorkist King Edward the Fourth suppress resistance to his reign in Wales; a ship, *Trinity* of Minehead, was also requisitioned.[10] Then, in 1469, Yorkist supporter, Humphrey Stafford, the Earl of Devon was caught and lynched by a mob in Bridgwater, then executed, all a few weeks after the Battle of Edgecote in Oxfordshire.[11] The Luttrells of Dunster, who were closely connected with Somerset maritime affairs in the fifteenth century, supported the House of Lancaster and thus between 1461 and 1485 forfeited their lands when Yorkist interests were in the ascendency.[12] They may also have owned and forfeited the *Trinity* of Minehead.

Natural phenomena also affected Somerset's maritime trade. The 'ravages' of the sea claimed Minehead's jetty prior to 1407 and Watchet's facilities, whatever they were, and possibly some houses, were destroyed by storm in 1458.[13] Furthermore, a storm event, in 1485, saw the River Axe overflow in Bleadon parish because of the 'ferocity of the sea' and a few ships were damaged or sunk in King Road at the mouth of the Avon.[14] However, these setbacks seem small compared to the experience of Lyme Regis on the south coast, which was a significant point of trade for many Somerset merchants. A storm in 1341 destroyed a great part of the town; a further storm in 1377 destroyed at least 70 houses and ruined 35 vessels; other storms destroyed facilities prior to 1481 that took inhabitants at least a generation to recover.[15] Some of the people and materials affected would have been involved directly with Somerset. Thus, despite the strong tides in the Bristol Channel, the dangers of the north-west winds and the treacherous shoals in Bridgwater Bay, which caused the destruction of ships off Dunster, Lilstock, Brean Uphill and Pill in the fourteenth century, Minehead in the early fifteenth and King Road in the late fifteenth century, it seems that the Somerset coast was a comparatively safe place to trade compared to Lyme Bay and other areas along the English Channel.[16] Whilst there were tidal floods in Bridgwater and district, along the Parrett, no event was significant enough to leave documentary evidence of damaged ships or facilities at Bridgwater for this period. Arguably, therefore, unlike Lyme Regis, trade to and from the Somerset coast was not significantly affected by storm events.

A final catastrophe that affected Somerset coastal trade in the fourteenth century was the Black Death of 1348-9. Studies of court rolls show that a significant number of deaths took place in the settlement of Chedzoy, just east of Bridgwater. The frequency of death was at its highest between December 1348 and March 1349 and this had a notable effect on landholding in the manor. Whole families were wiped out.[17] Further inland, at Curry Rivel, court rolls reveal the death of over 60 of the 150 or so tenants, again with evidence of entire families being taken.[18] Apparently the Black Death reached Bridgwater before November 1348, but the published Bridgwater borough archives, whilst making no direct reference to the plague, reveal an interesting perspective on the tragedy. All five signatories on a quitclam of a property in St Mary's Street, in September 1348, who were active in town affairs in previous years all disappear from the record. However, four signatories of a conveyance of a

Friarn Street property from September 1347 all survive into the 1350s, as do at least four of the five signatories on a South Street conveyance from September 1348.[19]

With respect to a possible impact on trade, such signatories tended to be the men of mercantile standing in the town. It is clear, therefore, that many of these people survived, and in so far as there was enough labour to man local ships, there may not have been a long term impact on trade.[20] There is also specific evidence that two grain exporters, David le Palmer and Hugh le Marys, survived the illness.[21] Given that Bridgwater was the largest settlement with maritime activity in Somerset in the fourteenth century, it is argued here that the effect of the Black Death on Somerset maritime trade might not have been as significant as could have been imagined. Furthermore, records of foreign merchants importing into Bridgwater do not appear to demonstrate a change in their activity from 1333 to 1348, a period where continuous data indicates that on average two cargos of their goods arrived in the town annually without a break in 1349 or 1350.[22] Unhelpfully, there is a gap in information regarding grain exports from Bridgwater for most of the 1340s and 1350s, which may in itself be significant.

In west Somerset it was Dunster, not Minehead, was the earliest documented location where maritime facilities of this period are first mentioned. A harbour is mentioned 1321 when there was a conduit at the port.[23] Also, 'diverse weirs on the sea' were recorded at Dunster in 1331.[24] The building and maintenance of an early fifteenth-century weir occurred at Porlock and a Porlock trader selling fish in Dunster market in 1486 hints at the type maritime economic activity engaged in at the time.[25] Very little data on Porlock's fourteenth and fifteenth-century maritime trade has been found but there is a possibility that John Pypere of 'Doverey', accused of taking a boat in 1396, came from Doverhay, the part of Porlock in the parish of Luccombe. The fact there were three persons who brought the action, William Muskham, John Feyrher and John Webb is indicative that they were joint boat owners.[26] Were they also residents of Porlock? If they were, there is a possibility that Porlock had some maritime facilities in the late fourteenth century.

At Minehead, maritime facilities included fish weirs, boat houses and a jetty. The jetty (jutte) was probably present in the fourteenth century, as there was a pier at Minehead in 1381,[27] but by 1407 it was utterly destroyed and nothing remained. Investment in Minehead's pier facilities by the Luttrells may well be linked to the silting of Dunster harbour in the fourteenth century.[28] Minehead's pier was rebuilt in 1420 when Margaret Lutterell gave £10 towards the project. It is quite likely, of course, that the wooden structure needed continual maintenance, being exposed to the ravages of the sea and the weather. Dating of wooden piles, found at the position of the jetty in the 1990s, show the timber had been felled in 1466.[29] Boathouses at Minehead are mentioned in 1421, six 'botehouses' in 1428, whilst in 1454 Stephen and

Illustration 3.3: Postcard of a mural at Townsend House, Minehead. This image is a reconstruction of the fifteenth-century jetty at Minehead looking east towards Warren Point. (Ted Borrett, late twentieth century)

Margaret Dyke leased a 22 foot boathouse (amongst other property) and in 1492 Joan Wyke, widow of Stephen, rented one at Minehead's weir as part of a larger holding.[30]

In the early fifteenth century fish weirs in west Somerset were let with small amounts of agricultural land. For example, in 1403 a weir in the parish of Carhampton, rented by Richard Prus and his wife, Christine, came with about three acres of land. When Stephen Corier rented a fish weir at Minehead, in 1405, he also took on three acres of arable land, an acre of salt marsh and an area of foreshore.[31] At Minehead in 1428 there were 'seven fishtraps next to the tideway'[32] and in 1456 Thomas Chapman leased a tenement and stakes in the sea.[33] Thus, in the fifteenth century, Minehead had a number of coastal net, weir and other inshore fishermen who were likely to have used open boats up to twenty feet long.

Bridgwater's port facilities were more developed than those at Minehead by the late fourteenth century. The corporation's income from charges for the use of its moorings, quays, crane, measures, and planks was on average between £5 and £6 per annum in the 1420s, but had dropped considerably to £2 10*s* in the 1460s.[34]

The crane was mounted on the west quay. According to Somerset historian Robert Dunning, two quays were built on the west and eastern sides of the river in 1424 where sea-going ships could dock.[35] The crane was predominantly wooden construction and continual lubrication was required. The crane man in the 1430s, John Keysham, was responsible for collecting and presenting the income from the use of the crane. The crane man also had the unenviably dirty job of clearing the estuarine silt from the quay wall. Income from the use of the crane appears to have been reasonably consistent with one year, 1461, seeing much reduced activity. Seven years of accounts have income broken down by quarter. In five of those years the most remunerative period was the Christmas quarter, whilst the Easter quarter was the busiest quarter in the remaining two years. This analysis ties in with the arrival of fish boats from Ireland and the exportation of beans (discussed later). In six of the seven years with quarterly accounts, the Michlemas quarter was the least busy. An account remains from 1455 as to the cost of

Illustration 3.5: The nineteenth-century crane at west quay, Bridgwater. Perhaps the medieval wooden cranes were at a similar position to this crane, its later replacement. (Elliot Lowe, 2014)

Illustration 3.4: Stake and net fishermen to the east of Minehead harbour, *circa* 1800. Detail from an unsigned watercolour (S.A.N.H.S.)

hiring porters and the crane to lift 30 cwt of lead from a vessel at the quay, for which the fee was 4d. It had cost 2s 8d to bring the lead from Bristol and a further 4d to take to lead from the quay to the church.[36] In 1488, a quay was built upstream of the bridge, known as the Langport quay which was a location for the management of river transport.[37]

The West Somerset fish trade and the Irish connection, 1317-1500

Fishing boats were in operation at Dunster in 1317.[38] That there were also fishermen in Minehead in 1380 indicated by the fact that Ralph Cooke and others were forbidden to sell their fish outside the immediate vicinity of the parish. A few years later, in 1383, Minehead fish were exported to Beaumaris on Anglesey.[39] From the fifteenth century, beach net fishermen, inshore fishers and larger Minehead vessels operating near the Irish coast brought a wealth of fish back to Minehead, which went on sale to the local population and fish traders. Dunster Castle household and other accounts record the types of fish bought at Minehead and Porlock for consumption by the household and sometimes for transportation elsewhere. In June 1405, twelve Milwells (Cod) were bought, in August two Rays and in January 1406 it was Herring and salt fish that were purchased. The household accounts for 1405 also show Hake and pipes of other fish were bought in Bristol and transported to Minehead for the household; presumably they were shipped down the Bristol Channel rather than taken overland. In 1419, Luttrell was serving his King in France and 100 Congers and one pipe of Salmon were forwarded to Harfleur. In 1420 another twelve dozen Milwells and Ling were bought from Minehead and forwarded via Poole and Southampton through the services of Roger King, a Minehead shipman. Twelve Salmon were bought from Watchet in 1423 for a total of 8s 2d, whilst in 1432 a more expensive Salmon at 1s 6d was sourced from Bridgwater. During 1429 Sir John Luterell bought 677 Millwell and Ling and 53 Congers at Minehead, four of which were given to the reeve at Woolavington and 24 in his sister's dowery. The following year other salt Millwell were given to the reeve of Woolavington. In 1435 Minehead tenants sold Herrings to the Lutterells, whilst the Reeve of Minehead presented the Luttrells with another barrel of Herrings; Red Herring costing 6s a mease at the time.[40]

Prior to 1440, Minehead's maritime community was augmented by at least 34 overseas people, probably mainly Irish migrant families and servants with maritime interests of their own. All Somerset's towns had small numbers of aliens at this point in time except Minehead, Bridgwater and Taunton; only Taunton had slightly more than Minehead. Some of the migrants that had settled in Minehead were fishermen, or had surnames based on fish, such as Cod and Herring, indicative of the fishing trade. Others were undoubtedly the ancestors of namesakes who helped run the Irish-Bristol fish trade from Minehead in the later fifteenth century. Immigrant John Passelowe was a fisher, a likely relation, Thomas Passelowe (deceased by 1440), had an immigrant servant. William Codd had an immigrant servant who was an immigrant himself and was a Minehead ship master involved in the Ireland-Bristol fish trade in the 1460s. Donnel and Mabilla Heyring, were also immigrants; an undoubted relation, John Heryng, had an immigrant servant. Either Donnel or John were the likely male ancestor of Richard Herying master of a Minehead ship involved in the Ireland-Bristol fish trade in the 1470s.[41] This significant group of immigrants are bound to have had an influence on the cultural identity and feel of Minehead in the early fifteenth century.

Throughout the fifteenth century Minehead operated a fishing fleet of larger vessels capable of operating in St George's and Bristol Channels, and the Irish Sea. They caught fish in Irish waters and then transported and sold them to merchants in Bristol. It is possible of course that some of the fish were bought from Irish fishermen whilst offshire, or onshore in Ireland before the final journey back to Bristol. Political instability and perhaps baronial or other petty squabbles meant that men from Minehead were sometimes captured and needed to be ransomed or otherwise released from captivity. In 1404 for example, Minehead fishermen, John Bray, David Neethe, John Lacy, William Touky, Maurice Spencer and David Walter had just dropped their anchors in order to commence fishing off Carlingford, north of Dublin, when they were captured by a Spanish ship. They were taken to Scotland where they were incarcerated for at least four months by William Carneys at Bothwell. Henry the Fourth wrote to the Scottish King asking him to exert influence to have the fishermen released.[42] There is a possibility that the fisherman returned, as two John Bray's (senior and junior) are mentioned in a Minehead rental of 1407.[43] Perhaps relating to fishermen, in 1409, Minehead people were trying to raise 26s 8d to ransom John Stones from Ireland and, in 1415, 25s for William Prenere from Brittany.[44] Towards the end of the century, in 1497, Robert Basher of Minehead leased a decked Swansea vessel, a pykard, for fishing off the Irish coast but he was taken by the Scots. Seizure of Basher's ship and goods in Minehead meant that he was unable to raise the capital to pay his ransom, but it seems that Basher and the leased ship were back in Minehead in 1498.[45]

Bristol port books survive for a number of years between 1461 and 1485 showing the passage of many of the Minehead vessels into Bristol from Irish waters. In some years up to six or seven Minehead vessels made a total of twelve visits to Bristol to offload salted fish, Hake, barrels of Red or White Herring, pipes of Salmon and occasionally Pollock. On the shaky but unavoidable assumption that there was only ever one vessel of a particular name, it is clear that there were 15 Minehead vessels operating in this trade between 1461 and 1485. The number of Minehead vessels involved in the trade increases to 20 if the 1503-4 data is included; this picks up five more vessels that may have operated in the 1490s.[46] Some, like the *Christopher* and the *Maudelyn*, are only heard of during the early 1470s. Other vessels, such as the *George*, operated in the Bristol fish trade from 1465 to 1475 and again in 1503, and it is heard of for other reasons in 1480 and 1540. Equally, the *Marie* is recorded in the trade from 1461, at other times through to 1480s and again in 1504. The *Trinity* had an even greater longevity. It was involved in the Irish fish trade to Bristol in 1437; it is mentioned in the 1460s, 1470s and 1480s and again in 1504. Table 3.1 below gives a fuller picture of the details of Minehead Irish fish trade at the time.

The 15 Minehead vessels involved in the Bristol

Table 3.1: Minehead vessels operating in the Irish waters and taking Irish fish to Bristol, 1438-1500

Vessel	Dates when known to sail to Bristol	Number of years with sailings to Bristol	Comments and other information regarding the vessel
Christopher	1470-1472	3	
George	1465-1474	7	1480 made a sailing to France. 1485 brought Irish Herring to Minehead.[47]
James	1465-1480	7	In the 1440s she was used for troop movements, 30 tons.[48]
John	1465-1479	2	
Katherine	1438	1	Made three sailings into Bristol with fish from Ireland in 1438.[49] 1434 took 40 pilgrims to Spain.[50] 1440s used for troop movements, 80 tons.[51]
Catherine	1465-1479	5	1480 made a sailing to France.[52]
Marie (Mary)	1461-1485	10	
Maudelyn	1473-1474	2	1485 brought Irish fish to Minehead and Bridgwater and returned to Ireland in 1486 with beans.[53]
Michel	1465-1472	3	1482 took beans from Bridgwater to Ireland and 1485 Irish White Herring from Ireland to Minehead.[54]
Nicholas	1438, 1461-1480	5	1482 took beans from Bridgwater to Ireland and 1485 brought beans back from Ireland into Minehead.[55]
Patrick	1461-1500	4	1485 brought Herring and Hake to Minehead. From Ireland.[56]
Peter	1461-1475	4	
Sonday	1461- 1480	6	1486 brought Irish fish into Minehead and Bridgwater from Ireland.[57] 1496 owned by Maurice Quilain, Maurice Quirke, John Philip and George Donnell, 40 tons.[58]
Trynyte	1437 1465-1485	6	In 1461 and perhaps the years following this vessel acted against Edward IV's enemies off the Somerset coast.[59] 1486 brought salt fish and hides to Minehead from Ireland.
Welfare	1437	1	

Sources: T.N.A., E 122/18/39, 19/1, 19/3-4, 19/6-12, 20/4-5, 174/3, 176/27. These are the customs books or part customs books for the port of Bristol for 1461, 1465, 1466, 1469, 1470, 1471, 1472, 1473, 1474, 1475, 1476, 1483, 1485 and 1486. The latter two books have no references to Minehead or the port of Bridgwater. I am grateful to Dr Evan Jones of Bristol University for access to transcripts of these sources. For 1437 and 1479 see E. Carus Wilson (ed.), *The overseas trade of Bristol in the later Middle Ages* (New York, 1967), 204-89. For the *Welfare* and the *Nicholas*, 1438 see H. Bush, *Bristol town duties* (Bristol, 1828), 18-24).

fish trade were commanded by over 50 masters. Whilst the vessels may have had considerable longevity 37 of the masters are only recorded in the customs accounts for one year only. Some of the Masters had Irish surnames such as Brenan, and Corke and were either Anglo-Irish living in Minehead, or Irish men who leased Minehead vessels. Irish crew were on Minehead vessels in 1411 and 1412 for example and in 1496 two owners of Minehead's *Sonday* were named Donnell and Quilayn, hardly traditional Somerset names.[60] Some of the surnames appear again and again, such as Thomas Philip in 1461, Robert Philip in 1471 and John Philip in 1473; these people may well have been related, as might have Richard Blake from 1471 to 1474, John and Roger Blake in 1473. Masters with longer service include William Childe, John Curslade, Richard Halton and Maurice Tye who all sailed into Bristol from Ireland in the 1460s and 1470s. Germaine Berebrewer or Beremaker was an experienced master operating on this route throughout the 1470s; in the mid-1470s, also described as a ship's master from Minehead, he was involved in transporting Herring and Hake to Bridgwater.[61]

The well-known Minehead maritime family of Basher, or Bosher, were also familiar visitors to Bristol and involved themselves in the Irish fish trade. Henry and Agnes Basher were recorded as immigrants at Minehead in 1440 whilst, at the same time, Thomas Basher, a probable relation, resided in Porlock and was quite possibly involved in the fish trade.[62] Other occurences of the name include Henry Basher of Minehead, fisher, in 1475,[63] Richard Bosher a Minehead shipmaster during the 1460s, Robert Basher in the 1470s and Oliver Bosher in the 1480s who were involved in the Irish fish trade into Bridgwater.[64] There were a large number of merchants who traded the fish carried in Minehead vessels. Whilst it is clear that some of Minehead's ship masters were also merchants for a proportion of the cargo they were transporting, it is likely that other merchants, of whom there were many, were Irish exporters or Bristol importers, or possibly both.

During the fourteen years of extant customs accounts between 1461 and 1486, it is clear that Minehead vessels reached Bristol with Irish fish in every month of the year, with August being the most frequent month of arrival. Most of the salt fish was taken to Bristol between April and October and most of the Herring and Hake between August and April. Salmon arrived between January and August and a consignment of Pollock in August. Such considerable trading between Minehead mariners and Bristol merchants inevitably led to some debts not being honoured on time, such as the debt owed by John Hargate of Minehead to Bristol merchant Richard Roberdys in 1484.[65] All this implies that during the fifteenth century, Minehead fishermen had strong relationships with Bristol merchants and fish markets, and, for the most part, were able to make money in the fish trade throughout the year.

Though all these vessels arrived in Bristol with fish from Irish waters, a few arrived in the metropolis of Bristol with fish from the Somerset coast. For example, the *Trynyte* took salt fish from Minehead to Bristol in 1466, as did the *Mary* and the *George* in 1474, and the *Peter* in 1475. Additional comments made in Table 9 in Appendix 2 shows that Minehead vessels, during the period 1461-1500 were not used solely for fish transportation. Bristol port books point to a more efficient use of Minehead shipping resources. On one occasion, in 1466, the *Trynyte*, having offloaded salt fish from Minehead, Philip Burnhan master, sailed back from Bristol to Minehead with salt, which no doubt was used to cure more fish from Somerset's or Irish waters. It is interesting to note that another master, William Nichol, was master of the *Trynyte* when it arrived in Bristol with Minehead fish two weeks earlier.

Sometimes cloth was loaded onto Minehead ships that had delivered fish and taken it either to Minehead or back to Ireland. For example The *Kateryn* took cloth from Bristol to Minehead in 1465 as did the *George* in 1472. Minehead vessels taking cloth back to Ireland on a return trip included the *George* in 1473 and 1474 and the *Trynyte* in 1485. A question that needs to be asked is why Minehead vessels were used to supply Bristol's demand for fish and not Bristol fisherman. Supply and demand would be one explanation, but, perhaps the location of Minehead is part of the answer, as it is further to the west of the Bristol Channel and had the fishing expertise. In addition, Minehead shipping could more easily arrive in Irish waters when difficult winds trapped Bristol shipping in the upper part of the Bristol Channel. In this way Minehad vessels could more efficiently serve the market with less days spent wind bound. When margins were tight this fact was,

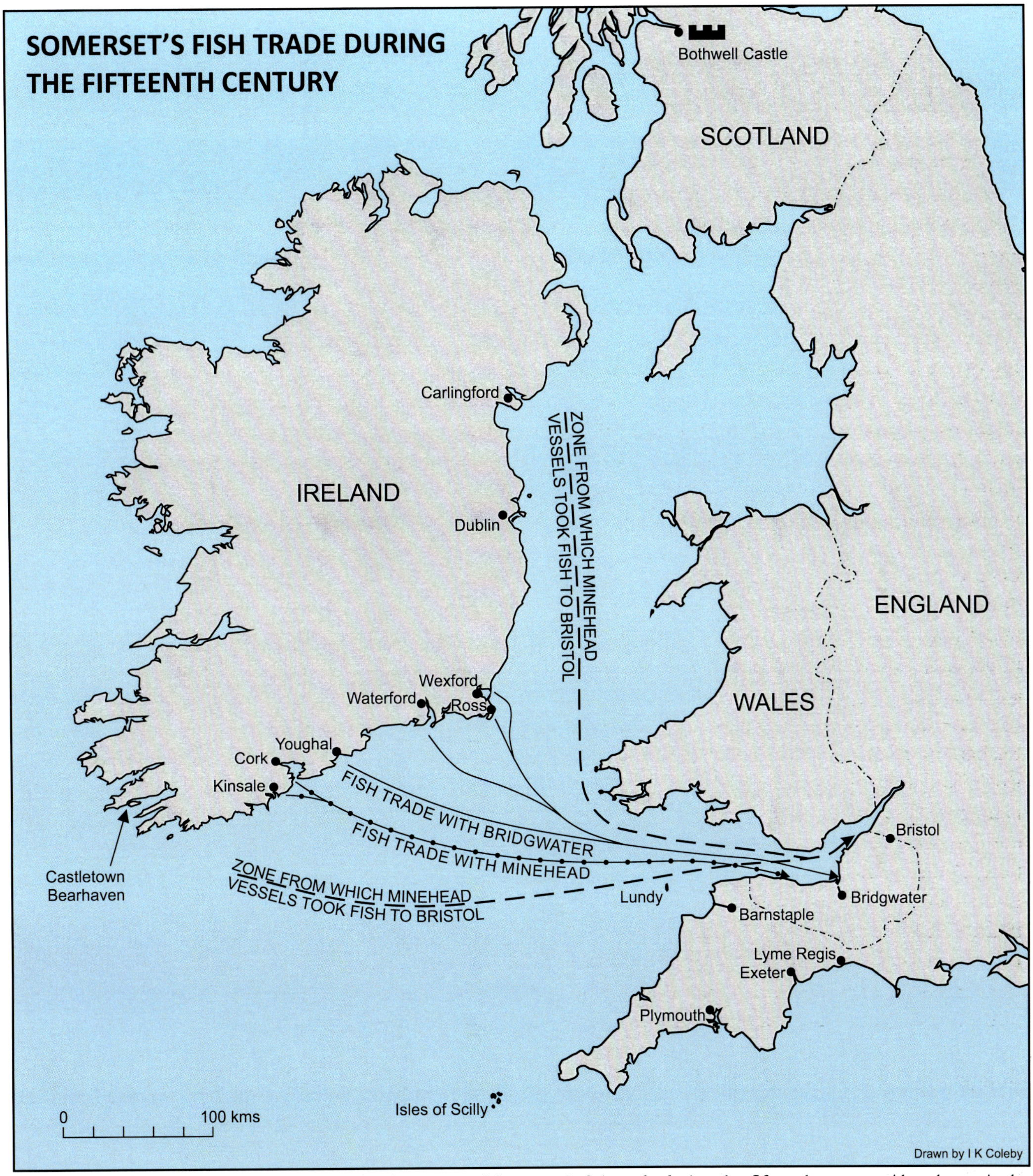

Illustration 3.6: A map showing the imports and exports of Somerset's fish trade during the fifteenth century. Also shown is the approximate limits of the zone from which Minehead vessels took fish to Bristol during this period. Note the locations of Bothwell Castle, Castletown and Bearhaven as mentioned in the text. (Reg Highnam, 2017)

no doubt, important.

With respect to vessels, including Minehead ones, bringing Irish fish to Minehead itself, evidence from the 1480s exists which helps build up an understanding of the trade. In May 1482 two Kinsale and two Cork vessels brought salt fish and pipes of Salmon to Minehead, as did two Minehead vessels in April and July 1486. However, six vessels, mainly from Minehead, brought Red and White Herring consignments back to the town from Ireland in December 1485 and January 1486 along with a small amount of Salmon and Hake.[66] It is possible to surmise, even from this limited amount of information that Minehead vessels were busy transporting Herring during the winter 'Herring season', whilst in the Summer they delivered preserved fish that had been caught at other times of the year.

Kowaleski states that a multitude of small vessels left Minehead each year with salt and returned to Bristol, or Bridgwater, with salted catches. An Exchequer investigation of 1476 seems to point to the ease in which local ships evaded custom duty when carrying salt and landing fish at Bridgwater and Bristol, thus the remaining customs records would not be a true representation of trade. It is observed that in 1490, the relative value of the fish trade was more important to Minehead than any other south-western port, which is indicative of the port's specialism at the time. Finally, in 1494, the Carlingford area was a significant location for Minehead fishermen, as it had been in 1404, given the 'enormous catches' of White Herring brought back to the town in that year.[67]

West Somerset maritime affairs and trade other than in fish, 1336-1495

West Somerset merchants and mariners caught up in legal affairs indicates the nature and extent of west Somerset trade in the fourteenth and fifteenth centuries. For example, it seems that just prior to 1418 Leonard, Abbot of Cleeve Abbey, had his boat stolen by the Nicholas, Abbot of Newnham, Devon.[68] Newnham is up-river of Plymouth, so there is a possibility that the Abbot of Cleeve's vessel was large enough and capable of rounding Cornwall. In 1443 Devon and Cornwall pirates sold goods, tuns of wine and quarters of salt evidently brought in by sea, to a number of Minehead people including Thomas Chapman, John Philip and to Richard God, rector of Oare. There may have been some holding to account as careful enquiries were made all along the coast.[69] In 1461 two Minehead men, John Castell, yeoman and Thomas Gurley, master of the carvel *David* of Minehead, became involved with many others in unlawfully taking over two French ships. This is unusual as England was not at war with France at the time.[70] Simon White (or Wight), a Minehead mariner, mastered vessels carrying Irish fish into Bristol during the 1460s and the 1480s. White was clearly a man to be reckoned with. At some point between 1475 and 1485 he was in legal dispute with a Bristol merchant, John Porter. Porter claimed that he was so afraid of physical hurt threatened by White, or perhaps White's associates, that Porter was afraid to appear in court.[71]

In December 1477, Maurice Thye, who between 1461 and 1475 had been involved in sailing a number of Minehead vessels into Bristol with Irish fish, had a significant accusation made against him regarding his conduct in Irish waters. Thye was master of *Le Pykard* of Minehead of which he and John Curtslade were owners; Curtslade had also sailed into Bristol with Irish fish in 1465 and 1473. Thye allegedly boarded a ship off Beere (Castletown-Bearhaven), Ireland, sailed the vessel into Youghal and ruined the cargo worth £60. Apparently Thomas Fitzjohn and Thomas Walshe were kept prisoner for nine days and sent ashore naked at Kinsale.[72] Adversarial behaviour seems to have run in the Thye/Thyne family, since a John Thyne brought Irish vagabonds into Minehead in 1495 against the orders of the local court. The use of Minehead's *Sonday* in attempting to gain restitution over Youghal mariners and shipping was authorised in 1496 after difficulties between Somerset and Irish mariners had occured.[73]

The misdemeanours of Nicholas Hatton and Maurice Quylayn (or Quailin), both described as mariners and merchants of Minehead, caused them, in 1487, to need the receipt of a general pardon and restitution of possessions.[74] It is not unlikely that they were involved in acts of near piracy relating to Irish vessels.[75] Whatever the cause, they were both at liberty in Minehead in the 1490s.

One impact of trading in Irish waters was the concerns in Minehead of the effects of Irish vagabonds, as well as prostitution. Such concerns were brought before the manor court in 1495 when the tenants of Alice Blake were presented as whores, Juliana Spencer was presented as acting as a procuress (or in modern terms a madam) and 'nourishing suspect persons'. Thomas Power received vagabonds in his house against the order of the court, John Thye was presented for transporting vagabonds from Ireland and Thomas Whyte for not transporting Irish vagabonds back to their home country. Other people allowed tenants to be 'night-walkers' and gave bad governance to people who lived in their houses.[76] Whilst the economy of Minehead depended on the Irish fish trade and many benefitted financially, there was clearly a social cost to pay.

It is clear that fishing was not the only maritime trade at Dunster. Corn was purchased in the Dunster area in 1336, as well as around Wells and Taunton to be shipped to Scotland for a military campaign;[77] it is not unlikely that the west Somerset grain was shipped from Dunster haven. In 1338 it was proclaimed that Dunster and Bridgwater were locations where Spanish, Italian and Gascon merchants could safely trade, but how often such traders took advantage of Dunster's facilities is not known.[78] During the 1370s and early 1380s, for certain, Thomas Carter(e) was one of Dunster's boat-owning merchants. He had business contacts along the coast at Ilfracombe, and Parrett at Cannington and Combwich, the latter location being the home of John Ryche who allegedly took some of Carter's goods.[79] Little other information remains from the fourteenth and early the fifteenth century regarding Minehead's trade other than fishing and fish transportation. That there was a trade coal with Wales is clear, but in 1381 there was mention of 'a decay' or a decrease in the daily passage from various parts of Glamorgan to the pier at Minehead.[80] During the early years of the fifteenth century an investigation into woollen and corn trading indicated that John Usser had goods at Minehead, as did Richard Horton at Dunster.[81] Then, in November 1405, Sir Hugh Luttrell bought live cattle in Wales and had them sent across to Somerset, presumably to Dunster, where he had them salted down for winter provisions. More cattle were shipped over in the spring of 1406 in anticipation of the conclusion of Lent and the Easter celebrations.[82]

In the Luttrell's household accounts it appears that 22 Welsh sheep were bought, but it is not clear whether they were brought back to Somerset or consumed by Luttrell and his entourage in Wales. However, 400 Welsh sheep were brought back to west Somerset from Wales in 1416, customs free, for 'Est Kantok', *i.e.* East Quantoxshead, where the Luttrells had land.[83] It has been noted that Sir Hugh was involved in the suppression of Owen Glendower's revolt during the early years of the fifteenth century. Being in Wales may have enhanced his knowledge of local cattle and sheep prices, and he could have taken advantage of cheaper animals than were available in Somerset. However, it is also possible that some of the cattle shipped over to Dunster were spoils of war.

Goods arriving by sea from Bristol at Dunster for the Luttrell household in the early years of the fifteenth century included 15 flaggons of olive oil in 1405 for which 'stowage and carriage' was paid. Ten years later a number of books bought in Bristol came 'by sea to Dunster'.[84] No doubt these valuable hand written articles were for the Castle library, the clerics in the town or even the school if the above-mentioned presence of William Scolemaister is of significance .

In 1419, Roger King, shipman of Minehead, whilst shipping goods including live oxen, meat, fish, candles and coal to Sir Hugh Luttrell campaigning in France took the opportunity to bring wine back to Minehead on at least one return journey. At about the same time King owed 40s to Philip Batt, probably in association with maritime trade.[85] Accounts of the *Leonard* of Dunster, including repairs, which sailed from Minehead probably to Bordeaux, also remain; it is not unlikely that wine was brought back to Somerset on that voyage.[86] Also in 1419, Sir Hugh embarked on the construction of some new buildings at Dunster Castle. Sandstone and possibly Dundry Stone for window and door frames, was sourced in Bristol and then delivered to Watchet. Smaller boats then conveyed it to Dunster where it was off-loaded and dragged by oxen and horse sledge up to the castle.[87] Ten thousand stone slates from Cornwall were landed in 1426, presumably for the same building programme. Construction of strong buildings needed lime mortar. There was a working lime kiln at Dunster in 1427 when coal, which would have been sourced in Wales, was landed for use in it.[88]

After Sir Hugh Luttrell died in 1428 he was succeeded briefly by Sir John Luttrell who within a few weeks had bought a barge, paid in instalments, from an Irishman named Foughler.[89] Interestingly, this man, or his son, may have been mentioned again in the Dunster household accounts of 1466. Great efforts were made to bring Thomas Fouler (Foughler again?) of Youghal to court to answer debt, hinting at an Irish trade, and in the same paragraph of the accounts 'George' of Lisbon is mentioned, as is the master of the *None* of Portyngale (Portugal). This may well be evidence of a Portuguese wine trade with Dunster.[90] Minehead and Dunster tradespeople had links with Bristol in the late 1430s and early 1440s.

Illustration 3.7: A smooth-grained Red Sandstone doorway, possibly from Redcliffe, Bristol, surrounding a small door on the inside of Dunster Castle's main gatehouse (Philip Ashford, 2016)

In 1438 it was alleged that William Hygyns of Dunster, dyer owed a Bristol tradesperson £10 due to the taking out of four bonds in 1438 and in 1440 it was alleged that Minehead merchant, Thomas Fysscher, owed 53s 4d to a Bristol merchant.[91] It is quite possible that the debts were to do with Minehead's maritime trade with Bristol.

A further hint of a wine trade between Bristol and Minehead remains from 1473 when an Ilfracombe vessel sailed from Minehead to Bristol with a tun of wine and lamb skins.[92] Perhaps the wine had been offloaded from a vessel from Spain or Portugal, but presumably the lamb skins were from western Exmoor. Minehead vessels also carried French or Iberian wine in 1480. At the behest of a group of Bristol merchants whose large vessel had gone aground in a French estuary, Minehead vessels *le Floure*, James Quirke master, *le Katheryn*, Reginald Nichol master and *le George* with Oliver Batchelor as master, were dispatched to fetch the cargo of wine and woad to Bristol.[93] The former two vessels (at least) were well known visitors to Bristol with their cargos of Irish fish. Presumably the vessels were shallow drafted enough to come near enough to the wreck without grounding themselves, or the cargo was offloaded into the ships' boats.

Some Minehead vessels that carried fish to Bristol returned to Minehead with small amounts of salt and cloth. Some other goods must also have been taken to Bristol in Somerset vessels, such as in July 1480 when Bridgwater/Combwich's *Anne*, William Fairyman master, took hides and salted fish from Minehead to Bristol.[94] Also in the 1480s, Minehead had a trade in beans with Ireland, but, unusually, in 1482, a Kinsale boat brought three wey of beans into Minehead, as did the *Nicholas* of Minehead in December 1485. More typically, in 1485 three Minehead vessels the *Nicholas*, the *Maudelyn/Magdelene* (twice) and the *Gabriel* left Minehead with between three and ten wey of beans during each sailing. In 1486, the *Mari Basher* of Minehead left the town with five wey of wheat and eleven cloths for Ireland. Other goods brought to Minehead included Irish mantles and shipboards shipped on Irish vessels from Cork and Kinsale in May 1482. With so many vessels operating out of Minehead at the time, it is not surprising materials that could have been used in ship maintenance, or ship building in the town were being imported. In July 1486, three dickers of salted Irish hides were landed at Minehead, no doubt for the local tanning industry.[95]

Larger ships from Bristol may well have commonly anchored off Minehead, sending small boats in for supplies as they waited to embark on longer voyages, providing additional impetus to the local economy. Such an event occured in October 1480 when the 300 ton Bristol *Trinity* with 28 mariners and boys aboard, about to sail to Spain to sell cloth, sent in to Minehead for supplies. The fortunate survival of the purser's accounts for this voyage show that twists and hasps for ships doors, bolts, a gun and a mantle were bought in the town.[96]

Watchet to Stogursey

Watchet had business links with Cowbridge, Glamorganshire during the fourteenth century.[97] There was also a fishery at Watchet called *la iveres* for which accounts remain from 1385 and 1388.[98] Perhaps this was the fishery which supplied Dunster Castle with Salmon in 1423 (mentioned above).[99] Mention has also been made of stone destined for Dunster Castle being offloaded at Watchet in 1419 so that smaller local vessels could transport it for the final leg of the journey. In 1429 two Watchet business people, John Anylde, husbandman and John Camberleyn, tyler, each owed Thomas Erle of Bristol, merchant £20; it is very likely that these debts were as a result of some aspect of maritime trading.[100] Perhaps the ruination of Watchet's port facilities in a storm in 1458 is the reason why vessels from the port do not figure in any Bristol customs books from 1465 to 1485, which do provide evidence for Minehead's maritime activities for the same period.[101]

Echoes of maritime affairs at Donniford remain from the late fourteenth century. In 1392 it was stated that a fish weir had been present at Donniford since before the memory of man. It was on the foreshore 'where salt water ebbs and flows on the bank of the Severn'.[102] Whether this weir was the same one which was allegedly dismantled in the early fifteenth century is not known.[103] Also at Doniford, a ship was beached there in 1379 that belonged to the 'chief enemies' of King Richard the Second, who was still in his minority. Whether the vessel was present for trade or carrying people is not known. The outcome, however, was that persons loyal to the Crown broke the ship's 'oar' (or possibly its rudder) so it could not sail away. Goods from the ship were stored in the houses of loyal subjects including that of John Melow at Dunster.[104]

In terms of the fishery along the coast between Donniford and Steart, in 1455 the vicar of Stogursey received 10s a year for tithes of all fish caught.[105] It is clear that the fishery was in thc ownership of Joan Sydenham, widow, prior to 1492 and then was bought by John Seytaben along with other property in the Quantock area.[106] Small vessels could beach along the section of the coast near Stogursey and in 1446, Stoford was a location used for the importation of stones used in the district.[107]

Bridgwater and Combwich: the hub of maritime and river trade in late medieval Somerset

It is not clear where exactly the largest vessels, perhaps ships of 80-120 tons, that used the Parrett 'docked' during the fourteenth and fifteenth centuries. The fifteenth century topographer, William of Worcester, claimed in the 1470s that Combwich was 'Bridgwater's port for ships'.[108] This meant ships lying on the mud banks at Combwich would have their cargoes lightered up to the quay at Bridgwater, which was outside the castle.[109] This arrangement of offloading at or near the mouth of the river for transportation to a larger port was also practised in the River Avon. As well as goods arriving at Combwich, or Bridgwater, via the Bristol Channel in sea-going vessels, there was an active riverine trade along the Parrett and its tributaries. For example, from 1371 to 1400 the vicar of Meare, near Glastonbury, received his dues of corn from lands at Huntspill by boat.[110]

Before 1400, possibly as early as the 1360s, an inquisition found that all manner of goods were taken up to Taunton from Bridgwater on boats and trows 'by force of the water', that is, taken up by the tide. Goods included wood for fuel and construction, coal, pitch, salt, iron, lime, grain, malt, wine and other victuals. All was fine until the construction of a mill which impeded the passage of boats.[111] However, in 1382 the Abbott of Glastonbury, stated that within living memory boats had not risen as far as Taunton but had unloaded their merchandise at Bathpool, a mile or so from the town.[112] Nevertheless, the list of goods transported gives a fine indication of fourteenth-century commodities offloaded and loaded at Combwich or Bridgwater, then passing from Bridgwater upriver on the rising tide. In 1381 there was an incident when a whole group of men including two from Bridgwater and one from Hamp were accused of taking a river boat, no doubt from along the Parrett.[113]

It is probable that woollen cloth from the Taunton area was transported downstream to Bridgwater when Bridgwater merchants desired to trade the commodity. Two Taunton merchants, Robert Coullying, portreeve for Taunton three times between 1386 and 1414 (who was assessed for 205 cloths sold in Somerset between 1395 and 1397) and Robert Eysel, portreeve of Taunton in 1390 (who was assessed for 283 cloths sold in Somerset between

1395 and 1397) were both members of separate inquiries into the alleged navigation of the Tone being damaged by the activities of the Abbott of Glastonbury; Coulling in 1382 and Eysel in 1414. No doubt they were interested in ensuring a route for transporting cloth was kept open.[114] It is also likely that fourteenth-century pottery from Donyatt, found in sherds at the site of Bridgwater's Franciscan Friary, were shipped down the Parrett.[115]

Bridgwater trade may have declined during the fourteenth century if town tolls are a measure of the volume of trade as some historians assert. However, at the beginning of the fourteenth century the market tolls collected in the town of Bridgwater created a greater income than port tolls.[116] In 1348, over 16s of port tolls were collected, whilst in 1359 the amount collected decreased to under 13s. In nearly every year between 1381 and 1401 the tolls were less than half of this latter amount.[117] Arguably, since most merchants would have tried to evade tolls and customs in order to reduce their costs, these figures are a very unreliable measure of trade trends. For example, in 1347, as the King was losing considerable customs duty on wool, woolfells and skins, a Government order came to the officials of Bridgwater that ships should, henceforth, lade and unlade at the town quay and not along the Parrett at other locations.[118] Then, in 1348, it was alleged, presumably by customs officials with few local connections, that merchants and others were landing wine, at night as much as by day, along the Somerset coast between Bridgwater and Bristol in order to evade customs duty.[119]

It was not just customs officials who were concerned about the loss of revenue, but Bridgwater borough officials as well. In the 1360s, Bridgwater town worthies, including provost Thomas Spicer and bailiffs William Topet and Robert Wake, complained that vessels now off-loaded at Highbridge and not in the town, therefore defrauding the Crown of duties;[120] this would have also had a knock-on effect in the reduction of the amount of town dues that were collected. Later in the fourteenth century, possible after 1380, various Bridgwater merchants and others, including the vicar of Otterhampton, were accused of causing vessels to offload goods at Combwich, again causing the loss of custom income to the Crown and other dues to local lords. A ship laden with salt, an Ilfracombe crayer laden with Herring, a Cornish pykard with a cargo of fish, the *Holke* of Tenby and a barge laden with salt on one occasion and corn on another, were all detailed as having offloaded downstream at Combwich and did not take their goods by water to Bridgwater, hence avoiding paying any dues.[121]

Bridgwater's maritime trade in the fourteenth century

During the fourteenth century the port of Bridgwater was a notable English point of departure for cereals and pulses, probably grown in the Bridgwater hinterland. In 1307 the bailiffs of Bridgwater were urged not to allow corn or animals to be exported to any destination save Gascony.[122] This would have been to ensure that useful materials did not end up in the hands of its enemies. It seems that some Bridgwater traders took this seriously for many years. Richard Crych and John Spencer,

Illustration 3.8: In the foreground are cereals in fields next to Bridgwater Bay. A coastal trading vessel lies at anchor in the Bay awaiting the tide. This type of scene, with differing types of vessels, would have been a familiar sight to those people living on the coast for hundreds of years (Elliot Lowe, 2014)

Bridgwater merchants, became involved in 1369 whilst at sea, presumably in their ship, in an action whereby a vessel was arrested and taken into Falmouth on suspicion of illegally trying to transport wheat to the French enemies of the King.[123]

In 1321 the Sheriff of Somerset and Dorset, Nicholas de Cheynne, gathered corn from land around Taunton and Glastonbury and stored it in rented buildings at Bridgwater. Presumably this was grain to be used in support of a military campaign and may well have been shipped out of the port in 1332 (see table 3.1). Also in 1322, John, son of Philip Boye, merchant of Bridgwater, 'bought' a considerable amount of grain, valued at £33, from Walter de Enmore but defaulted on paying for it.[124] This grain may also have been bought to support the military campaign that Bridgwater vessels were involved in (see Appendix 2).

Bridgwater's John Cole may well have been the most significant trader in agricultural products in west and central Somerset during the fourteenth century. He operated during the 1360s and 1370s. The British and Biscayan destinations of his exports are listed in table 3.3. Cole had a long trading and merchant career, lasting from 1364 to 1409. Cole bought up land, including 400 acres of pasture in North Petherton in 1370, as well as the lease of a water mill and other property in Cannington and Wembdon. One of his licences for the export of cereals in 1375 stated that he had grown 200 quarters of wheat and 200 quarters of beans himself. It is not known whether the crops were grown on the land purchased in North Petherton, but wheat yields were about one quarter per acre at the time, which adds up to 400 acres worth. He was a frequent witness to local deeds and was issued with trading licences for 3,200 quarters of cereals and pulses. However, in 1380 it was alleged he had traded at least 10,000 quarters and evaded customs on a considerable quantity, as well as dealt in uncustomed fish, salt and wine, suggesting a wide interest in the Biscayan trade. Apparently Cole shrugged off these accusations, as well as others in Bridgwater alleging illegal wine measures, as well as leaving millstones and timber in thoroughfares and watercourses around the town.

Illustration 3.9: Steep Holm across Bridgwater Bay with bales of straw, remaining from harvested grain, in the foreground. John Cole's grain exports from Bridgwater in the fourteenth century would have passed in full view from this position. (Elliot Lowe, 2014)

As a prosperous local merchant he became a target for rebels caught up in the Peasant's Revolt at Bridgwater in 1381. He did not suffer any bodily harm, but many of his court rolls and leases were destroyed. He went on to represent the borough of Bridgwater as its M.P. in 1394. Between 1395 and 1397 it is clear that he also had an interest exporting cloth through the port as he was assessed for 32 'dozens' produced in the town.[125] Cole's scale of smuggling adds further questions to the accuracy of the measures of trade passing through Bridgwater in the fourteenth century. If the accusations were true then perhaps only a quarter of exports of grain were being recorded.

Biographical details of many fourteenth-century exporters of cereals and pulses from Bridgwater can be found in Appendix 4. However, as yet, little more is known about Walter Blaunkpayn, John Gardener, Thomas Bush of Cannington and Roger at Mille and their export licences of 1371, except that Blaunkpayn was Cole's brother-in-law and a guarantor of one of Coles's licences to ship beans from Bridgwater.[126]

Table 3.2 shows that in 1364 corn was being exported illegally from Bridgwater. On two occasions John Godesland, who does not appear to have played a significant role in Bridgwater's mercantile community, illegally took corn to Ireland in his ship despite a royal embargo and efforts by the town's bailiffs. Then, on a third occasion, Godesland's corn and malt was put aboard an Irish vessel and, once more, despite the efforts of bailiffs swimming (or rowing perhaps) on the flowing tide to the ship anchored at 'Brodeshyn' (presumably a position on the Parrett), to try to detain it, they were seen off by the Irish master and crew. The ship then departed on the tide.[127]

From about 1375, licences ceased to be granted to Bridgwater and other Somerset merchants. Instead they were granted to Gascon merchants, possibly due to the uneasy truce that had been negotiated with

Table 3.2: Exports of grain and pulses by English merchants from the port of Bridgwater, 1331-1375

Merchant	Residence	Date of licence	No. of licences granted	Average volume and cargo	Destination and/or comments
[Name not given]		1330	[?]	wheat	Bordeaux. Destined for Plymouth but was ordered to Bridgwater.
David le Palmer, Hugh le Marys	Bridgwater	1331	1	500 quarters of corn	Wales as there was a shortage.
John Wroxhale, Sheriff of Somerset		1333	[?]	Corn and beans	Skinburness on the Solway Firth, military use, in the *Nicholas* of Southampton.
[Name not given]		1336	[?]	Cereals from around Taunton, Dunster and Wells	Military purposes.
[Name not given]		1340s	0	Cereals	From Combwich to Ireland to avoid obtaining a licence.
Richard de Stowey		1361	1	300 quarters of corn	Bordeaux from Bridgwater or Combwich.
The Rector	Huntspill	1361	1	[blank]	Wales by river and sea.
Hugh le Marys, John Sopham		1362	1	200 quarters of corn	Gascony from Bridgwater or Combwich.
Walter de Aldebury (King's clerk)		1364-1365	2	400 quarters of beans and peas from Bridgwater and around	Military purposes.
John Michel	Sydenham	1364	1	300 quarters beans	Devon and Cornwall.
John de Godesland	Combwich	1364	None	160 quarters of corn	Ireland, illegal shipment.
John Michel, John Bythesea, Walter Dodde, Robert Plumpton	[blank]	1365	1	300 quarters of beans and peas	Ireland and Bayonne.
William Cannynges	Bristol	1367	1	150 quarters of beans and 50 quarters oats	Gascony.
John Cole	Bridgwater	1367-1377	10	320 quarters of mainly beans, some peas oats and wheat	A little to the South West of England, Wales and Ireland but most to Bayonne and Bordeaux.
Robert Plumpton	Bridgwater	1367-1371	3	230 quarters of mainly beans but some wheat	Devon and Cornwall but mainly Gascony.
William Criche	Bridgwater	1367-1371	3	200 quarters of wheat and 100 of beans and peas	Gascony.
Walter Blaunkpayn		1371	1	300 quarters beans	Wales.
William Holwaye, Roger ate Mille	Wellington Bridgwater	1371	1	500 quarters of wheat and 500 of beans	Cardiff, Carmarthen, Cork and Waterford.
John Gardener	Bridgwater	1371	1	200 quarters of beans	Bordeaux.
John Gardener, Robert Plumpton	Bridgwater	1371	1	200 quarters of beans	Bordeaux.
Thomas Ingleby	Bridgwater	1374-1377	2	550 quarters of wheat, oats beans and peas	Bordeaux and Bayonne.
Thomas Bush	Cannington	1375	1	400 quarters of beans and peas	Bayonne or Bordeaux.

Sources: A. Powell, *The ancient borough of Bridgwater* (Bridgwater, 1907), 191; *C.P.R. Edward III* vol. 11, 554, vol. 13, 44, 61, vol. 14, 109, 467, vol. 15, 52, 94; www.gasconrolls.org/en/ 61/74, 61/80, 61/84, 61/85, 61/86, 61/87, 61/88, 61/90; R.W. Dunning, *Bridgwater: history and guide* (Stroud, 1992), 19.

Illustration 3.10: The medieval water gate on Bridgwater quay, part of Bridgwater Castle. In the bottom right of the image is perhaps the only remaining visible part of Bridgwater that John Cole would have recognised. Some goods offloaded from ships would have been taken through the gate and placed in the castle for safe keeping. (Elliot Lowe, 2014)

France and Castile. During the truce, Castilian galleys took an unprecedented 37 English ships in the Bay of Bourgneuf, including two Somerset vessels.[128] It is quite likely that in the aftermath English ship owners were less keen to risk their own vessels in the Biscay trade and, thus, were more willing to load their cargoes on vessels from Gascony that arrived to collect Somerset corn.

It is clear that William Criche, Robert Plumpton, Hugh le Marys and John Bythesea were important individuals concerned with maritime trade along the Somerset coast in 1365 as they, along with Matthew Michel and Thomas Large were charged by the Crown to monitor the movements of people and money from the coast. Security measures at the time dictated that, apart from known merchants, no-one and no money was allowed to leave the country by ship from Bridgwater, Minehead, Dunster, Axewater, Uphill, Rooks Mill and Combwich.[130]

Bridgwater vessels that sailed to Gascony with cereals returned with wine to their home port. The *Grand coutume* records of Bordeaux which remain from 1303 to 1309, detail Bridgwater ships that departed with wine from that port.[131] At some point prior to 1305, William de Saut, a merchant from Bayonne was in Bridgwater, perhaps negotiating wine sales.[132] Other evidence for this trade remains from 1317 when a vessel belonging to a Bridgwater merchant, Richard Godwyne, arrived in Bordeaux for wine but was hired by merchants of Rouen to take wine and other goods back to their home port.[133] In 1326, Roger Odgy, merchant and burgess of Bridgwater, bought wine from Roger Tertle, merchant and burgess of Bristol; allegedly, 60s of the debt was still owing and was sought through the courts in 1327, 1328 and 1329.[134] In 1352 two tuns of wine belonging to Bridgwater's David Palmere and two belonging to John atte More were stolen at Bridgwater by Sir Thomas Fichet, an official of the King.[135] Later, in 1360, wine was imported in a

Table 3.3: Exports of cereals and pulses by foreign merchants from the port of Bridgwater, 1375-1405[129]

Merchant	Residence	Dates of licence	No. of licences granted	Average volume	Destination and/or comments
John Dore, Laurens Durcos, Pey Lovayn	Bayonne	1375	1	600 quarters of beans and 200 of wheat	Bayonne
Johan de Lagua, Pey Guirant, Pernaut Laporte	Bayonne	1375	1	900 quarters of beans	Bayonne from the ports of Bristol and Bridgwater
John Parlebien	[blank]	1375	1	400 quarters of rye, beans and peas	Bordeaux
[blank]	[blank]	1378	2	corn	Two barges of Bordeaux licenced to take corn to Gascony
Arnald de Bernatet	Bayonne	1400	1	Beans and peas and other merchandise	In the *Margarete* of Bayonne of 50 tons of which Arnald was the master
Miguel de St Jean, Guilhem Arnaut	Bayonne	1405	1	300 quarters of wheat and 300 of broad beans from Somerset	Bayonne in the *St John* barge and Arnaut's ballinger from Bristol or Bridgwater

Sources: W. Bird, *Calendar Close Rolls Henry IV 1399-1402* (London, 1927), 44; www.gasconrolls.org/en/ 61/74, 61/88. The 1378 shipments are referenced in J. Sherborne, *War politics and culture in fourteenth-century England* (London, 1994), 76. In 1381 there were discussions in Bridgwater regarding the ship of a Bayonne merchant, John Carsett (T. Dilks (ed.), *Bridgwater Borough archives 1377-1399*, S.R.S. 53 (1938), 242).

Combwich vessel belonging to Robert Plumpton; it appears that at least two tuns of wine belonged to Plumpton and two to Bridgwater merchant Adam Best.[136] In 1366 a significant amount of wine, some 40 gallons belonging to Plumpton was siphoned off in a Bridgwater store or cellar and stolen. The remaining wine was 'adulterated' *i.e.* spoiled.[137] More evidence of the trade survives by inference when, in 1377, Thomas Ingleby was licenced to trade with Bordueaux for goods 'to bring back to England', which meant that tuns of wine arrived on the return voyage.[138] In 1394, Bridgwater merchant William Criche was selling wine to town worthies, no doubt wine he had imported.[139] Then, in 1396 and 1397, Bridgwater's borough accounts show income from hiring skids used to drag tuns of wine from the quay to cellars, as well as expenditure in making a wooden gangway for landing stone and wine. In 1399 and 1400 the town made charges for moving 101 tuns of wine.[140]

A small amount of statistical data on the number of tuns of wine imported by aliens into Bridgwater exists for the fourteenth century. However, for many years (when data is available), Bridgwater's figures are subsumed into the Dorset ports, sometimes the Devon ports but not with Bristol. The following dates are for the accounting year running for 12 months from Michaelmas. Thus for the accounting year starting in Michaelmas 1331, 44 tuns were landed, as were 38 tuns during the following twelve months and 26 tuns in 1334. 31 tuns were landed in 1340 and 34 tuns in 1352. Notably the records show no alien imports of wine for 1336, 1338 to 1339, for the two years 1341 to 1342, the three years 1349 to 1351 and the 17 years from 1355 to 1372.[141] Given alien merchants did not land wine every year at Bridgwater before 1338, and local merchants also imported wine, this data is no evidence for the effect of the Black Death. The data suggests a local demand for wine and a lack of capacity amongst Bridgwater ships because alien importers with their vessels were needed to make up the shortfall.

With regard to fifteenth-century trade other than cereals and wine, in 1375 coal (no doubt from Wales), was imported for the maintenance of the church, perhaps as a fuel for forging ironwork.[142] Also from Wales came millstones; in the 1290s Tintern millstones were obtainable at 6 or 8 shillings, twice that of their price if bought where they were quarried. There are records of 12 millstones arriving in the town between 1300 and 1350 and 48 from between 1351 and 1400. This may not sound significant, but in terms of remaining evidence from other ports, the figures make Bridgwater the second most important town in the country for importing millstones, behind Southampton which imported French stones.[143] Stone exports through Bridgwater in the fourteenth century included Ham Hill Stone, from near Montacute, which would have been brought down the Parrett in river craft. Evidence for its exportation through Bridgwater can be seen in fourteenth-century churches around the south-west peninsula. At Ilfracombe, Newton Tracey (accessed via Bideford or Barnstaple), Tavistock and Ermington (accessed from near Plymouth), Exeter, Cullompton (accessed from Exeter) and Axminster (possibly via Lyme Regis if the stone was not transported overland).[144] More specifically Ham Hill Stone was used in Exeter Cathedral, as 'great stones' and stone for bosses were bought in 1301.[145]

Evidence from 1382 suggests that Herring was brought to Bridgwater in the *Cog John,* part owned by a Bridgwater merchant William Thomer.[146] Mention has already been made of Devon and Cornish vessels bringing Herring and other fish into Combwich in the later fourteenth century. Table 3.6 shows that a Dunster and a Bridgwater vessel were taken in the Bay of Bourgneuf, Brittany in 1375. They were part of a convoy loading salt, no doubt for the Bristol Channel fishing industry.[147] In 1384 a Bridgwater merchant, John Henton, bought salt and Herring from John Gernesey whilst at sea off Lowaris (Looe in Cornwall?). Presumably the goods were to be brought back to Bridgwater. Henton allegedly did not pay for the goods, or their freighting and other unidentified expenditure, which meant that a long series of court cases ensued into the 1390s. At some point in the late 1380s John Kedwelly, a Bridgwater lawyer and merchant, under the authority of William Thomer, Bridgwater's M.P. and deputy to the 'Admiral in Bridgwater', broke into Henton's house and detained property worth £287 in order to extract payment for the alleged debts.[148]

Other exports from Bridgwater include wool and woollen cloth. During the 1340s, a time when a considerable tonnage of wool was exported from England, before the development of the home woollen industry the Bardi, Florentine merchants, used Bridgwater as a collecting point for wool exports.[149] This was a direct result of the French destruction of Southampton in 1338 and the subsequent decisions of the Florentine merchants to move the centre of operations for their wool collection in England to Bristol.[150] Presumably, wool collected at Bridgwater was first shipped to Bristol before exportation. A Bridgwater ship, the *Blome*, was involved in the export of 23 woollen cloths from Dartmouth in 1349 and Somerset merchants were involved in exporting cloth in Bristol ships from 1348 to 1350.[151] However, evidence that local cloth left Bridgwater for export during this period is still to be found. As the English cloth industry developed, detailed Government advice was sent to emerging cloth producing districts regarding standards of fulling and duties payable, amongst other edicts. In 1357 such advice was sent to Bath, Wells and Bridgwater, indicating the growing importance of these towns in the county for woollen cloth production.[152]

In 1358 investigations relating to the 'statute of labourers', including information from Bridgwater and Wells, showed that women were amongst spinners and weavers employed in the industry.[153] In 1381, Ralph Fishpond otherwise Taylor, merchant of Bridgwater, had three cloths of various colours and worth 40s in the town. In 1367, Fishpond owed a Bath merchant for merchandise and in 1381 he owed money to at least two Bristol merchants totalling £48.[154] Perhaps he bought cloth from Bath and Bristol for sale at Bridgwater. The exact date when cloth exports began from Bridgwater in significant amounts is not known, but the town was one of Somerset's most significant woollen producing towns by 1390; the aulnage accounts also show that Somerset had become the most important woollen cloth producing county in England.[155] Not all Somerset cloth was exported through Bridgwater. For example, in 1397, '19 dozens of Tauntons', narrow cloth, were aboard a ship in Plymouth ready for exportation.[156]

Appendix 2 shows how during the medieval period merchant vessels doubled up as warships and/or troop carriers. As Bridgwater was a river port, on a relatively small tidal river, it could only accommodate vessels under 175 tons. Some ships and masters may have been in operation for over twenty years. The masters were familiar with the waters of the Bristol Channel, St George's Channel, the English Channel and the Bay of Biscay though, no doubt, there were specialisms. As for the types of vessels, some of them were described as cogs, an image of which appears in illustration 3.11.

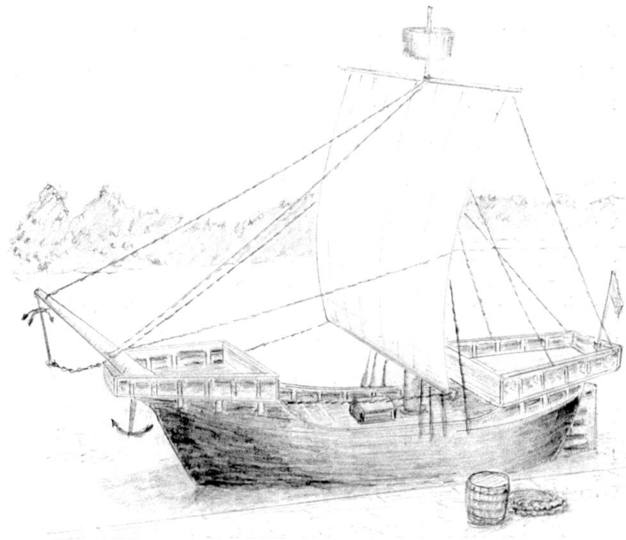

Illustration 3.11: An image of a medieval cog, *c.*1320 (Reginald Highnam, 2017)

Bridgwater and Combwich imports during the fifteenth century

Very early in the fifteenth century, in 1401 or 1402, *Le Marie,* a large vessel from Bilbao, was detained at Combwich in retaliation for a Bristol ship that had been taken by Castillians. The cargo, worth £400, was impounded by Bristol merchants dubbed 'the conspiracy and confederation at Combwich'. The vessel carried over 62 tons of iron and later, 28 tons were found to be in the keeping of John Gardiner and Nicholas Neeth (or Neth) of Combwich; Neeth served as Bridgwater's reeve in 1407, as a burgess and operated as a merchant of Bridgwater, who made his will in 1410.[157] Neeth along with a fellow Bridgwater maritime entrepreneur John Warde, were named in another dubious action that took place within the port of Milford prior to 1410, when a number of mariners from various ships took cargo from a carrack belonging to Genoese merchants.[158] It is not unlikely that other Spanish vessels arriving at Bridgwater had quantities of iron aboard, since Spain was one of the most significant sources of iron for England in the fifteenth century. During the mid-fifteenth century it was not uncommon for 20-30 tons of Spanish Iron to be delivered to the port of

Bridgwater, often in Spanish ships.[159] In his will of 1481, John Hill(e), merchant of Bridgwater, bequeathed a ton of iron to be left to his brother Stephen.[160] In 1486, one ton of iron left Bridgwater in a Wexford vessel, undoubtedly for Wexford itself, as part of its cargo.[161] Whether or not it came from Spain, it most probably arrived in Bridgwater by ship prior to its re-export.

A boat load of stone was brought to the town quay from Pibsbury (in the parish of Huish Episcopi), upriver from Langport, in 1415 for use in the church, costing 2d to unload, 2d to load into waggons and 2s 3d to transport nine loads by cart from the quay to the church.[162] In 1431, someone named Wolmer had a vessel that brought stone to Bridgwater. This vessel may have been a 'crayer' of Barnstaple which is known to have brought stone for use in public works in Bridgwater at the time.[163] In 1455 John Bythesea was involved in bringing a cargo of lead from Bristol for use on the church.[164] From Wales, 57 millstones have been identified as being imported between 1400 and 1454. In 1453 the Bishopric of Winchester made a bulk purchase of 10 millstones for its Taunton estate paying £10 for the stones, 6s for cranage at Bridgwater and 20s for carting the stones to the relevant mills.[165]

Small amounts if coal were bought in Bridgwater on seven occasions in 1415 when there appeared to be considerable restoration taking place of St Mary's church. The coal was used to melt lead for roofing and plumbing, heat solder and melt brass for a large bell. In 1455, 4s worth of coal was bought of John Braus, a man involved in town affairs and likely to have been a coal merchant, again for use with regard to lead on the church.[166] No doubt the coal had arrived from Wales by boat.

Salt was traded through Bridgwater, most likely sea salt from France, Spain or Portugal. No cargos of salt have been found arriving in the borough, but arrived they must have, since 34 wey of salt was stored in the town in 1445.[167] In May 1482 and February 1486, salt was dispatched from Bridgwater as small parts of larger cargos.[168] No doubt it was used for salting fish that were brought back to Bridgwater and Bristol. It has already been stated that during the 1470s salt duties were commonly and easily evaded at Bridgwater. The paucity of information on the fifteenth century salt trade at Bridgwater should not be taken as an indication that it was a rarely traded commodity. However, was the 35 wey of salt in 1445 brought by land in order to avoid customs duty? If so where had it been imported?

There are several references to details of wine imports through Bridgwater in the fifteenth century, as well as records of cargos of wine that may have never made it back to Somerset. In 1403 six tuns of wine from Bordeaux, bought of Oliver Mawliverer, appear to have been traded in the *Marie* of Bridgwater by the master, Nicholas Somering. On the way back to Bridgwater the vessel ran aground, as salvage and re-rigging expenses needed paying.[169] Whether the early fifteenth-century wine trade between Bordeaux and Bridgwater was enhanced by the fact that Sir Hugh Luttrell of Dunster was made mayor of Bordeaux in 1404 is not known.[170] Then, in 1410, a vessel belonging to a prosperous Bridgwater clerk and merchant, John Kedwelly, borough M.P. seven times between 1395 and 1417, was on its way to Rochelle to pick up wine in the *Cog John*. It was captured by men of Harfleur and held ransom, despite France being at peace with England at the time.[171] This shows that not all the wine imported into Bridgwater was from Gascony.

Sometime before 1420 a Bridgwater carvel was used by Spanish merchants to take Gascon wines to London.[172] In 1427, Philip and William Bokeland, of Bridgwater, were standing surety for the import of Spanish goods; no doubt some of these imports were wine.[173] In 1443, Spanish wine, as well as some iron

Illustration 3.12: The *George* of Bridgwater would have sailed long the Parrett in the 1480s. Its crew would have seen the tower of Cannington church, one of several aids to navigation, which is visible to the right in this image (Elliot Lowe, 2014)

and salt destined for Ireland, was stolen by pirates and offered for sale in Bridgwater. The chief perpetrator of the crime, John Colville, who does not seem to have had other documented connections with the town, was ordered to be arrested and imprisoned.[174] A further loss of wine by Bridgwater merchants William Founs and John Hill, occurred in the 1450s when Breton pirates seized a cargo of 9 tuns worth £2 per tun. The wine had been bought off John de Vesy of Bilbao; in 1456 William Founs (Founce) had bonds relating to trade with Julius Redrugis, merchant of Lisbon,[175] which may also have been to do with wine. John Croppe seems to have owned and traded Spanish red wine in Bridgwater in 1463.[176]

George Cuper of Bridgwater, merchant of the 1480s, was licenced to trade in wine at 'Burdewes' (corruption of Bordeaux) in Gascony in the *George* of Bridgwater. On one occasion '100 fothers' of tin to trade was taken out to trade for wine by Cuper.[177] Presumably the cargo of tin was picked up in Devon or Cornwall on the outward journey, rather than loading it in Bridgwater itself. At some point between 1475 and 1485, Spanish merchant Roderigo de Samodio was in dispute with John Pellycorn of Combwich regarding alleged disobedience over instructions concerning the disposal of a cargo of Gascon wines.[178] Yet more wine that may have failed to reach Bridgwater was sequestrated by British pirates off Ilfracombe in 1483. Allegedly, the *Julyan* of Brittany, Henry Mathewe master and part owner, which had been freighted by Bridgwater merchants 'with diverse goods' in Lisbon, was at anchor when Matthew Craddock of Swansea, 'captain of a ship of war of the realm' committed a piratical act against the vessel at the instigation of some Ilfracombe men.[179] In the 1490s, Bordeaux wine was imported by a Bridgwater and Irish merchant, Denis Dywin, in his vessel the *Gabriel* of Bridgwater.[180] Such was the value of wine that Adam Hamelyn, merchant of Bridgwater, left a pipe of wine to his brother, John, in his will of 1493.[181]

The recorded quantities of wine brought into Bridgwater, according to one source, were non-existant in 1470, but in 1475, 366 tuns were imported and in 1505, 285 tuns were unloaded, including small amounts of sweet wine from Breton and Gascon ships.[182] Information from 1476 does not tie in with the information from other sources. Detailed customs accounts of tuns of wine imported through Bridgwater survive for most years from 1403 to 1500. Table 3.4 details the decadal averages from this source. No record seems to be available for the years 1422 to 1425.

The data shows a clear pattern of significant imports between 1403 and 1422, a decline during mid-century with trade picking up again from the 1460s. The decline in imports had set in well before the loss of Gascony in 1453, but it is perhaps significant that a decade of low imports occurred from 1455 to 1465, indicating that political turmoil did affect Bridgwater's trade before its recovery later in the century. Though these wine imports were significant, a tun being 252 gallons of wine, the trade is dwarfed by the significance of Bristol. For example in 1441, 166 tuns arrived in Bridgwater, whilst Bristol imported about 3,000 tuns. On the other hand, when Bridgwater imported 344 tuns in 1466, Bristol imported around 1,000 tuns. As a 'rule of thumb', throughout the century, Bridgwater imports of wine were often about a tenth of Bristol's imports, not an insignificant figure considering the size of their populations.

The maritime nature of Bridgwater's economy is the reason why, apart from Taunton and Minehead, that Bridgwater had significantly more resident immigrants than any other Somerset town in 1440,

Table 3.4. Wine imports into Bridgwater, 1403-1500

Years	Tuns imported (decadal average)	Comments Note: The annual average is 122 tuns for years with data.
1403-1413	104	No imports 1409.
1413-1422	200	Nine years only. 380 tuns imported 1414 and 396 tuns in 1415.
1425-1435	88	No imports 1425-1427.
1435-1445	82	Only 5 tuns imported 1436.
1445-1455	65	No imports 1447.
1455-1465	46	No data for 1459-60 and 1462-1465.
1465-1475	114	No data for 1468-71. 344 tuns imported 1465.
1475-1485	144	330 tuns imported 1484.
1485-1495	136	Only 16 and 18 tuns imported in 1485 and 1486 respectively.
1495-1500	237	Five years. 330 tuns imported 1498.

Source: M. James and E. Veale, *Studies in the medieval wine trade* (Oxford, 1971), 108-16.

some of whom would have been involved in maritime trade. Bridgwater included two of Somerset's five Gascons, two of Somerset's three Bretons and a Portuguese immigrant, Domingus Fons. Fons may well have been the father of William Founs, a Bridgwater merchant who traded with a Lisbon merchant in 1456. Immigrant servants, in 1440, worked for members of Bridgwater's maritime community. For example, 'Michael' was servant to Richard Gosse, collector of customs in the 1430s and steward of the merchant guild. 'John' was servant to ship-master Thomas Cradock.[183] No doubt the servants were an asset to their merchant masters when communicating with European ship-masters and merchants arriving in the port when they traded in wine and other goods. Furthermore, along with other Flemish, Irish, French and Dutch residents, all the immigrants would have contributed to a cosmopolitan feel in fifteenth-century maritime Bridgwater. In 1477 Bridgwater was also the place of residence for a merchant '*de la Farga*' probably from the Iberian peninsula.[184]

As the significance of the Bridgwater district as a hub of Somerset's woollen industry expanded in the fifteenth century, and woollen cloth exports from the town increased, it is not surprising to find that it was also a centre where dyes were imported. However, the presence of woad, a plant used to produce a blue dye, in the town does not mean it was brought in by ship and unloaded at the quay. It is known that Somerset was also supplied with woad through Southampton in the fifteenth century, including direct carting to Bridgwater merchants.[185] Nevertheless, woad came into Bridgwater on vessels from Iberia and Gascony. Woad and seam oil stolen from a property at Bridgwater in 1467 and John Galsere's promise to fellow Bridgwater merchant, John Kendall, for two pipes of woad by Christmas 1477, possibly involved shipping.[186] At some point between 1475 and 1485, John Howell of Bridgwater purchased woad in Morliax, France, but in transit he alleged that French pirates took the cargo.[187] Whether the woad was due to be carried to Bridgwater by ship, or landed at a southern port such as Lyme Regis, which had a trade with Morlaix, is not known. Furthermore, woad owned by Bridgwater merchants and their widows, mentioned as gifts in the wills of John Hill in 1481, Thomasine Hill in 1483 and Adam Hamelyn in 1491, may point to imports through Bridgwater itself.[188] During the 1490s Denis Dywin imported woad in his vessel the *Gabriel*.

Despite some fish, for example, Conger Eels, Dogfish and Herring being caught locally, there was a demand for fish imports. Their sale at Bridgwater was controlled by the corporation. Breaking those controls and regulations in September 1445, Nicholas Deveras of Waterford sold salt fish and 'other merchandise' in Bridgwater without a licence, a misdemeanour for which he was fined 3s 4d.[189] Those who stayed on the right side of the law included Robert Brydde of Minehead who *c.*1450 had eight barrels of Herring in Bridgwater which, no doubt, he had imported. The town of Bridgwater rented out fish market stalls to Thomas Acton and Thomas Lacombe from 1449 to 1455.[190] No doubt they sold fish imported into the town. During the winter months, at the same time Minehead vessels were taking Irish fish to Bristol, vessels were arriving in Bridgwater with Irish fish. In 1470, a picard from Wexford arrived with Red Herring, Salmon, Conger and Eels.[191] In May 1482 a larger vessel, the carvel *Rascada* from Opporto, arrived in Bridgwater. The ship had clearly visited Cork on its way to Bridgwater. It brought 26 hundredweight of Cork Herrings on behalf of an Irish merchant and another 250 quintals (a quintal may be a weight of 100 pounds) of Cork Herring which belonged to Adam Hameleyn of Bridgwater, merchant. The *Mary* of Youghal also arrived at Bridgwater in May 1482 with a small amount of salt white fish. Then, in December 1485 the *John* of Bridgwater, a larger vessel than the usual fish and bean carrying vessels that used the port at the time, arrived with White and Red Herring, Hake and Salmon for at least five Bridgwater merchants: John Hoell, William Selwood, Nicholas Jobe (Jobe was appointed guager, a customs post, in the town in 1485),[192] William Gardiner and William Clifford. Then, in January 1486, the *Marie* of Combwich departed Bridgwater with beans for Ireland and returned within two weeks with Hake and salt fish for William Power.[193] In February 1486, four or five smaller vessels from Wexford and other Irish ports arrived in Bridgwater with Salmon, Hake, salt fish, White and Red herring. The vessels left around two weeks later with beans aboard.[194] Kowaleski has observed, just a little inaccurately, that Bridgwater had no vessels of its own involved in the fish trade with Ireland, but did point to Irish vessels involved in the trade as evidenced by references in the Bridgwater water bailiff's accounts in 1473, 1494 and 1503 to 1505.[195] It is clear that some of the large quantities of Herring and Hake that arrived at Bridgwater, mainly from Ireland were re-exported to Spain, sometimes in Spanish ships.[196]

Other imports were traded through Bridgwater. Spanish merchant, Martin Geldo, commanding the *San Juan de Pasagas,* from Pasages in northern Spain arrived at Bridgwater in 1466 with unidentified 'goods'. Geldo traded with Bridgwater on several occasions between 1478 and 1491, as well as at other south-western ports.[197] In May 1482, a Portuguese vessel entering Bridgwater, the *Rescada*, brought goods that were clearly from Iberia. It offloaded several hundredweight of wax and two hundredweight of sugar.[198] Gascon, Spanish and Italian ceramics are also very likely to have arrived at Bridgwater on these or other ships from Iberia. Sherds of medieval French pottery have been excavated from Bridgwater's Castle moat and also from trenches in George Street.[199] Similarly dated French ware has been found at Cheddar;[200] the import route for this pottery may well have been along the Axe and not the Parrett. A fourteenth century Saintonge polychrome jug from western France has been found at Glastonbury Abbey, thought to have come to Somerset on a ship carrying Gascon wine.[201] Further Saintonge ware from the thirteenth century or later has been found at Burrow Mump,[202] as well as on Steep Holm, on or near the site of the Augustinian Priory.[203] Spanish Lustreware was purchased for Glastonbury Abbey in the fifteenth century[204] and late medieval finds of Spanish origin include pottery from Malaga, Valencia and Seville. Material from Tuscany has also been found there.[205]

Other imported commodities include Welsh boards that were traded in the town in 1454 which would have come by sea.[206] Furthermore, in May 1482, 50 boards arrived in the town from Ireland, as did a small number of Irish mantles in May 1482 and March 1486.[207] A dearth of corn in the country in 1482 meant 126 quarters of corn were imported into Bridgwater in 1482, a consignment that probably came in from Europe.[208] Records between 1459 and 1497 do not indicate that other consignments of grain were imported into Bridgwater.

Exports from Bridgwater during the fifteenth century

During the fifteenth century it seems that the most common commodity exported from Bridgwater, normally used to trade for wine, was woollen cloth. In 1410, at the same time as one of Kedwelly's vessels was attempting to sail to Bridgwater with wine, another of his vessels, two of his men and 60 pieces of cloth were held at Cherbourg.[209] The sale of cloth was used to buy Foun's wine in the 1450s. In 1446, it was clear that cloths 'of Bridgwater making' were white in colour. At some time during the 1470s, John Hemering of Bridgwater was involved in trading 12 'Bridgwater cloths'. Hemering's merchant's mark is still clear in the record. In some way the trade at the time may have involved the *Trinity* of 'Fountainbry' (this could be Fontainblue a little upriver from Bordeaux) and the *Mighell* of Bridgwater trading between Bridgwater and Bayonne.[210]

The *Patrick* of Youghal departed Bridgwater for Ireland in May 1482 with six cloths as part of the cargo, as did the *Tullock* of Wexford with 12 narrow cloths in February 1486. A larger consignment of six dozen narrow cloths and 12 cloths (presumably of full width), left in the *Saviour* (possibly a Minehead vessel) in March 1486. Small amounts of cloth left Bridgwater in at least two other vessels for Ireland in February and March 1486.[211]

Local merchants who owned locally manufactured cloth did not always use Bridgwater to export their goods. There appears to have been no localised monopoly. For example, in 1443, Bridgwater's William Clever (Clewer) was able to send two dozen straights to Southampton, presumably to be exported.[212] However, Bridgwater was a collection point for woollen cloth produced elsewhere, some of which was re-exported. For example, in 1461 and 1479 the vessel *Marie Tintern* brought cloth, including Welsh cloth, from Chepstow and Bristol to Bridgwater. In 1480, William de la Fount of Bristol brought cloth overland to Bridgwater, probably from north Somerset, and then shipped it in the *Margrit* to an unrecorded destination. In 1482, Barnstaple whites were stolen from a property in the borough.[213] However, before the end of the fifteenth century Taunton and Bridgwater 'straits', 'osetts' and 'dozens' were being regularly taken to Bordeaux, Bayonne, San Sebastian, Bilbao and Fuenterrabia in northern Spain.[214] Around 1490 a Bridgwater vessel arrived at

Table 3.5: Amount of woollen cloth exported from Bridgwater, 1410-1530

Decade	No. of woollen cloths	Decade	No. of woollen cloths
1410-1420	921	1470-1480	2435
1420-1430	775	1480-1490	4690
1430-1440	746	1490-1500	4958
1440-1450	873	1510-1520	2603
1450-1460	304*	1520-1530	2067

*Some accounts missing. Source: Dunning, *Bridgwater*, 24.

Genoa with a cargo of woollen cloth.[215] Whether it departed from Bridgwater itself is not known.

According to one historian, the exportation of broadcloth from Bridgwater fell dramatically after the invasion of France in 1413, recovered after the Hundred Years War ended in 1453, slumped again in the 1460s, sustained recovery from 1472 and a record number of 494 pieces were exported in 1476 only to be surpassed in 1481 when 964 left the port.[216] However, after the loss of Gascony in 1453, which was one of the main destinations of Bridgwater cloth, the town's economy must have declined. Then, as other markets were established, including those in Spain, cloth exports increased from the 1470s from which the local economy must have benefitted enormously.[217] From 1402 to 1506 the average number of cloths exported from Bridgwater was just over 200 per year.[218] Placing this amount in context, the Somerset aulnage records for 1395-1397 show that three Taunton and nine Wells clothiers were assessed for a total of just over 2,000 cloths, 'dozens', in total for that period and eight Wells clothiers were assessed for 355 broadcloths in 1402.[219] If these figures are relatively representative of reality at the time, they show that export of cloth from Bridgwater was relatively insignificant in relation to the total amount of cloth manufactured in Somerset. Overland trade in Somerset cloth is indicated by the fact that 'Briggewaters' were sold in London in the late 1480s or early 1490s, the same merchant shipping other 'Briggewates' to Portugal a few years later.[220]

In the plethora of records remaining from the fourteenth century, there is not much evidence of the Bridgwater cereal and pulse trade until the late 1450s. One reason for this may have been shortages of cereals at various times in Somerset, which caused authorities to stop exports of grain. For example, in the late 1420s there was such a shortage of grain in Somerset that the Cathedral authorities, at Wells, disbursed a considerable amount for bread for the poor.[221] However, in 1436 there must have been an excess of cereals as John Hawe of Bridgwater was given leave to purchase 100 quarters of wheat, 200 quarters of Barley and 200 quarters of beans export to sell in Cornwall or the Welsh Marches.[222] In any event these cereals are likely to have left through the port.

Information relating to the volumes of corn exports from 'Bridgwater and its members', which included Minehead, Watchet and Axewater survive for many years between 1459 and 1497. Table 3.6 (below) shows the quantities varied considerably due to periods for which the data is available as well as, presumably, the weather conditions in the particular year. Thus, it is difficult to see any definite trends and it is also unclear how a national proclamation banning exports of corn in 1482, and one made in Wells in 1492, because of 'the dearth of corn' had any impact on grain movements through the port.[223] Notably there were zero exports from 9 April to 26 June 1483. However, in years where the remaining data is relatively complete, it is clear that the number of quarters of grain exported can be measured in thousands rather than hundreds. This made Bridgwater a more important grain exporting port than Exeter. It was also on a par with Bristol for corn exports in the second half of the fifteenth century, perhaps reflecting the fertility of Bridgwater's hinterland and cereals exported from the vale of Taunton Deane.[224]

Pulses were also exported from Bridgwater. In 1470, a picard from Wexford took beans from Bridgwater and returned with Red Herring, Salmon, Conger and Eels.[225] This event typifies Bridgwater's Irish trade in the later fifteenth century in that the majority of the goods were shipped in Irish vessels, the main export from Bridgwater was cereals and pulses, and the main import was fish. In April 1482, two Minehead vessels, the *Michael* and the *Nicholas* left Bridgwater with eight wey and 13 wey of beans respectively. No Bridgwater or Combwich ships were involved in this trade in 1482 during the period for which records remain. However, from January to March 1486/7 there were eight sailings from Bridgwater to Ireland with beans contained in Somerset vessels carrying, on average, nearly seven wey of beans each. Two of the vessels also had a

Table 3.6: Corn exports from 'Bridgwater and its members', 1459-1497

Dates	Quarters exported	Dates	Quarters exported
27 December 1459 – Michaelmas 1461	246	5 April - 22 August 1485	486
23 July 1470 - 24 October 1470	0	26 September 1485 – Michaelmas 1486	3,554
5 May 1472 - 10 October 1472	0	16 November 1486 – Michaelmas 1487	992
28 July 1475 - 4 March 1475/6	402	9 October 1489 - 18 February 1489/90	309
8 April 1482 - 20 May 1483	2,241	18 February 1489/90 – Michaelmas 1490	1,427
9 April 1483 - 26 June 1483	0	Easter 1496 – Michaelmas 1497	4,622
Michaelmas 1484 - 6 April 1485	156		

Source: N. Gras, *The early English customs system* (London, 1918), 283-6.

small amount of malt aboard. The value of the beans and the malt was the same, 13s 4d per wey. The vessels involved were the *Mary* or *Marie*, *Mighell* and *Christopher* all of Combwich, and the *Mighell* of Bridgwater; the latter may well have been the same vessel as its Combwich namesake since the master for both vessels was Thomas Dowding. Also involved were the *Sonday* and *Mighell* of Minehead, as well as the *Saviour* which may also have been a Minehead vessel.[226]

In April and May 1482, 210 wey of beans, valued at £210, left Bridgwater on 21 occasions in 19 separate Irish vessels from Cork, Youghal, Waterford and Wexford, carrying on average 10 wey per voyage. Most of these vessels did not arrive from Ireland with customable goods during this period, but they may have arrived a month or so earlier with fish. Most of the vessels departed within a few days of each other in early May, so many craft may have been sailing on the Parrett for a brief period. The customs records survive for February and March of 1485/6, which show three Irish vessels arriving in February in Bridgwater with fish and departing in late February and early March with beans; this time an average of 5 wey per vessel with the beans valued at 12s per wey, similar to the value of the beans that left Bridgwater in the Somerset vessels at the same time. An Ilfracombe vessel also left Bridgwater with six wey of beans aboard in February 1485/6. Given that beans were sold at £1 a wey at Bridgwater in 1482 and as low as 12s a wey in 1486, it can only be assumed there was a relative shortage in 1482 or a glut in 1486.[227] The importance of Bridgwater's bean exports during the last decade of the fifteenth century is evident when it is seen in a wider context. Bean exports from Bristol to Ireland in the 1490s were valued from £50 to £160 per year, whilst the exports from Bridgwater were valued at £100 to £200, reaching a peak of £300 in 1496.[228]

Since pottery was a non-customable good, there is no documentary record of its export from Bridgwater during the period under consideration here. However, the distribution of sherds of medieval Somerset pottery found outside the county show that the pottery was transported by sea, most likely from Bridgwater. Archaeologists recognise particular medieval pottery types made in specific kilns in the county during the fourteenth and fifteenth centuries. Medieval kilns of this period operated at Nether Stowey, Crowcombe[229] and Bridgwater; material used in the latter kiln possibly derived from Puriton.[230] However, a very productive kiln near Chard produced 'South Somerset Ware' otherwise known as 'Donyatt Ware'.[231] Ceramics from this kiln would probably have been shipped down the Parrett to Bridgwater to ships that worked the Bristol Channel, or sailed to locations further afield.

Nether Stowey Ware dating from medieval times has been found in the Newport area, south Wales, and in Bristol.[232] Donyatt Ware dating from the fourteenth and fifteenth centuries has been found at Porthskewett, Monmouthshire.[233] Recent research and evaluation of ceramic finds in south Glamorganshire has shown that a reliance on Welsh-made ceramics declined in the fourteenth century to be replaced, in the fifteenth century, by imported Devon and Somerset wares including Somerset 'redwares'. According to one pottery expert, this indicates an 'increase in connectivity' between both sides of the Bristol Channel.[234]

Further afield, later medieval Somerset wares have been found on Lundy Island[235] and discarded shards of medieval Somerset wares have been discovered by divers working with archaeologists in the channel/road between Bryher and Tresco in the

Isles of Scilly.[236] The interpretation is that cargos were trans-shipped at this point with broken items being thrown overboard. Were the main cargos on their way to France or Spain? Perhaps unsurprisingly, given the context of this chapter, remains of a Bridgwater cooking pot has been found in Cork, southern Ireland, dating from the thirteenth or fourteenth century, along with large quantities of Somerset ware from the late fifteenth century.[237] In addition, a small amount of medieval Donyatt Ware has been found 30 miles inland from Waterford in Kilkenny City.[238]

Bridgwater and the Irish trade in the fifteenth century

It is clear that, like Minehead, there were strong trading links between Ireland and Bridgwater in the fifteenth century. In 1402, John Kedwelly, merchant of Bridgwater was empowered, with others, to collect a debt from Walter Baker of Ross in Ireland.[239] Irish merchants were well known to Bridgwater merchants and officials, thus it is not surprising that Bridgwater tradespeople took on apprentices from Ireland. For example, in 1424, John Davey of Bridgwater, tanner took on Michael Layleye of Ireland as his apprentice. Later, in 1443, a John Davey of Bridgwater, merchant, had a trading bond with Thomas Caldy of Wexford, merchant.[240] Also in 1443, Robert Jerveyse, fuller, of Bridgwater took on William Gose of Galway, Ireland as his apprentice.[241] At some point in the late 1440s, or early 1450s, Nicholas Morthy, a Youghal merchant was in Bridgwater and was known to John Mey, a local merchant; Morthy probably traded with Mey as well as with a Bristol merchant.[242]

This close link between Bridgwater and Ireland meant that of the 18 resident Irish aliens in Somerset in 1440, half resided in Bridgwater and nearby villages such as Cannington and Combwich. They may well have arrived in Bridgwater on trading vessels.[243] The Irish connection continued in 1473 when the *Trinity* of Waterford and the *George* of Wexford were in the port, probably at the quay.[244] The Roche family were also heavily involved in the 'Irewater' connection. William Roche commanded a Cork ship calling at Bristol and Bridgwater from 1480 to 1486, as did Edmund Roche from 1480 to 1497.[245] Table 3.7 indicates that between 1460 and 1497 the four Irish towns with the most considerable trade with Bridgwater were Waterford and Ross on the

Table 3.7: Recorded shipments of customable goods relating to Bridgwater and Ireland, 1460-1497

Port	Goods 'out'	Goods 'in'
Waterford	26	12
Ross	27	22
Wexford	27	22
Youghal	26	13
Cork	6	8
Kinsale	6	6
Dingle	2	1
Other	1	1
Total	121	85

Source: W. Childs, 'Irish merchants and seamen in Late Medieval England' in *Irish Historical Studies* 32 (2000-1), 25.

Barrow estuary, Wexford and Youghal. However, relationships between Munster and Somerset were not always cordial. Problematic events between merchants and mariners of Youghal, Bridgwater and Minehead between 1475 and 1496, and the possible effects of these difficulties on trade, are discussed elsewhere.[246]

The Bristol customs port books occasionally make reference to Bridgwater and Combwich vessels shipping goods from and to various regional ports. In 1469 for example, a small vessel, the *Katerine* of Combwich, with Thomas Mech as master, set out from Bristol with 118 cloths bound for Padstow. This was an unusual sailing in its own right, let alone a Combwich vessel being chartered for such an event. Another small vessel, the *Mighel* of Bridgwater with Richard Dodying as master, took a tun of wine from Tenby to Bristol in 1471 and, in 1472, the *Katerine* of Bridgwater (possibly a Combwich vessel) with John Robyns master, sailed into Bristol with Irish salted fish.

Larger Somerset vessels sailed to destinations further afield during this period. The *Christopher* of Bridgwater sailed from Bristol to Bordeaux with cloth in 1470 and, in 1472, the *Mary* of Taunton sailed into Bristol with iron, honey and rosin. The cargo suggests that the vessel had sailed from Spain.[247] This is the only time a vessel has been found being 'of Taunton'. Since it was a large enough vessel for European trade it could not have sailed up the Parrett further than Bridgwater Bridge, so it is most likely have been owned by Taunton traders and moored elsewhere. It is clear that prior to 1493 Henry Bishop, merchant of Taunton, owned at least a quarter of a ship that was capable of trading with

Illustration 3.13: Medieval seal of the community of Bridgwater showing the castle, bridge and River Parrett. (T.B. Dilks, *Bridgwater Borough archives 1200-1377*, S.R.S. 48 (1933), frontis)

Spain and may well have brought back woad to England.[248]

The hazards of maritime life during the fifteenth century

Unusual events, the type that would make the press today, not only gives more flavour to a relatively dry analysis of trade but also indicates the geographical extent of Bridgwater's maritime trade. For example, in 1406, men from Somerset, Devon and Cornwall were taken at sea by men from Brittany, Normandy and Picardy and taken to Harfletem (possibly Harfleur). Thomas Codeworth, of Bridgwater, had diligently sued for the release of the prisoners in the Court of Chancery. Given that Somerset seamen had been taken, it is likely that some were from Bridgwater and they may have been encouraged by news that a local man was working for their release.[249] The activities of Nicholas Neth of Bridgwater, during the first decade of the fifteenth century, have already been summarised. A few years later, in 1414, prisoners and goods were taken from English ships, including ones from Exeter and Bristol, by the French. The English ambassador and the Duke of Brittany drew up a document in order to help resolve the problem. One of the vessels, the *Isabel* of Bridgwater, was owned by Richard Gardiner, Phelip Vaugre and Guillem Coque. Provisions of lemon or lime juice, eighteen large loaves, barrels of butter and flour, presumably the supplies of food for the crew, were taken.[250] What is of interest here is that the Gardiners, a well-known Combwich/Bridgwater trading family of the fifteenth century, owned part of a vessel with Gascon merchants. Both these incidents are likely to have occurred as English ships were on their way to Gascony or Spain. At about the same time Richard Gardiner had further troubles with Walter Cley of Combwich, shipman, who was accused by Gardiner of 'trespass and taking', a matter that was taken to the Court of Common Pleas in 1418.[251]

In 1422, the ship *Ballinger of Clarence*, whilst operating in the English Channel with others from Southampton, was allegedly involved in piracy; Richard Gardment, captain and victualler, Willy Sallez and John Crepy, all of Bridgwater took a ship of Lisbon loaded with raisins and other goods.[252] Thomas Cradok of Bridgwater also seems to have been involved in a number of piratical acts in the 1440s. First, in November 1441, according to Bertram Godet, a merchant of Brittany, Cradok (with others) was in Barnstaple, after he imprisoned Godet on a false pretext, he made off with 20 tuns of wine.[253] Then, probably in 1443, Fernandus Dalyys, master of the *St Anthony* of Biscay, sailed to Ireland and sold much of his merchandise to Dublin merchants. He alleged that John Colwell, master of a ship whose owner was Thomas Cradok of Bridgwater, along with people from another vessel, attacked the ship and took the remaining cargo. Some 40 tuns of wine and 800 quarters of salt were shipped back to Bridgwater and sold. A commission of Somerset Justices of the Peace was set up to investigate the claims.[254] In the 1450s Bridgwater merchants, William Founs and Richard Botkyn, may well have spent time in a Bilbao goal over trading debts, but this is unclear as the information is an unsubstantiated allegation in a legal case.[255]

Trouble of another type came to the owners of a vessel, the *Mighell* of Bridgwater, probably in the late 1470s. After the vessel was wrecked off Guernsey a lawsuit was brought between two Bristol fishmongers whose goods were lost in the vessel.[256] It is not unlikely that they had commissioned the vessel to bring back fish from Ireland to Bristol when a storm blew the vessel off course. On the other hand, also in the 1470s, a *Mighell* of Bridgwater had been involved in the cloth trade between Bridgwater and Bayonne and it might have been returning to Bristol with fish from France. Rioting Bridgwater mariners caused trouble in Youghal sometime before 1475.[257] Then, in about 1494, John Palgo(o)se, mayor of Bristol, was taken to the Court of Chancery over the delivery of goods brought into Bridgwater in the *Trinity*. This vessel was owned by Thomas Fissher and others. Fissher appears to have been a Taunton merchant and was particularly litigious during the 1490s concerning a whole range of matters often involving Taunton properties.[258]

Trade in the River Axe basin, 1320-1499

Axewater, lying to the north of Brean Down, marked the northern boundary of the customs port of Bridgwater. The anchorage at the mouth of the Axe, near Black Rock, was the area of the 'harbour' of Uphill. Presumably ships sailed up the Axe on the rising tide in order to be close to the thriving town of Axbridge where Mendip lead,[259] Mendip cloth and animal skins were traded, amongst other goods. About eight miles up-river from Uphill and three miles downriver from Axbridge, was the medieval port of 'Radclyf', now the tiny settlement of Rackley in the parish of Compton Bishop.

In medieval times, as the parish name suggests, trade here was under the control of the bishops of Bath and Wells. In 1347 the sheriff of Somerset was ordered to cause vessels which been trading in wool, hides and other merchandise along the river at 'Radecliff', to cease doing so as the Exchequer had allegedly been losing customs duties. However, at some point, this order was either ignored or rescinded, because, in 1390, ships from as far away as Dartmouth and Brittany were trading in salt, iron and fish at Rackley.[260] The crown continued to be concerned about its loss of revenue, and the fact that the Abbot of Glastonbury was charging dues for the landing of salt and other merchandise along the banks of the Axe; the Abbott had bought salt from merchant, Roger Brymore, which arrived in the *Mary* of Dartmouth to be offloaded in Axewater. In 1401 a commission met in Combwich to inquire into the 'irregularities' but the custom of the Abbot of Glastonbury was not the interests of the Crown.[261]

Pulses and corn were exported from the Axe in the fourteenth century and in 1369 it was alleged that 80 quarters of beans and peas worth 40 marks were stored at Oldmixon (near Weston-super-Mare) ready for shipping from the Axe to Cardiff. For some reason the stores were ruined, or stolen, so the shipment failed and a court case ensued.[262] It has been recorded, and often re-quoted, that Thomas Tanner of Wells, clothier, exported cloth and corn to Portugal from Rackley in the 1380s receiving iron and salt in exchange. Tanner was Somerset's leading clothier at the time who also had links with Bristol merchants.[263] It is likely that he did used Rackley as a point of departure for his cloth but may have exported much of his cloth through Bristol. In 1396, Thomas Austin of 'Redeclyf' and John Haynes of Axbridge, tanner, were indebted to John Galeway.[264] An interpretation of this event is that Austyn and others were importing hides from Ireland and

Illustration 3.14: An anchorage on the River Axe, just inland of the mouth of Axewater at Uphill, taken from Brean Down looking north-east. However, the marshy land between the farm buildings and pleasure boats appears to be the location of the main anchorage used in earlier centuries. (Elliot Lowe, 2014)

bringing them up the Axe to Rackley, then on to Axbridge for tanning.

During the fifteenth century, there were more tanners and leather workers in Axbridge who were plaintiffs in the Court of Common Pleas than for any other town in Somerset indicating that it was a significant centre for Somerset's leather trade.[265] Such was the demand for leather and hides that the town attracted traders and people from far and wide. For example, John Hayne, tucker, of Axbridge, prior to 1449, took on an apprentice from Youghal.[266] In 1474 the *Peter* of Axewater sailed into Bristol from Axewater with sheep skins, wine and mantles, and in 1475 with ship boards and oars.[267] The most likely scenario is that Irish vessels had called into Axewater for cloth or beans and deposited their cargoes that originated in Spain or Ireland; this allowed a local vessel to take the customable goods up to Bristol. Similar transhipment took place in 1471, when the *Elianor* of Portbury arrived in Bristol from Tenby with cork, grain, olive oil and wine probably originally imported from the Iberian Peninsula.[268] In May 1482, there was one inward sailing to 'Radclyf' from Ireland and two return voyages with customable goods. One of the vessels was from Waterford. In came five hundredweight of the dye mordent, alum (used in dyeing and medicine) and out went several weys of beans, wheat, barley and malt.[269] The remaining customs record from 1486 does not mention 'Radclyf' but instead uses 'Axewater', which may or may not mean the same position on the Axe. Thomas Gylys of Axbridge, merchant, owned the *Trinity* of Axbridge in 1485, but it was taken by the *Castillan* of 'St Mary Castell'.[270]

Between January and June 1486 there were at least 22 sailings in and out of Axewater connected to the Irish trade. Most of the vessels were Irish; four from Waterford, another from Cork and others from unspecified ports. The trade also involved one vessel from Bristol, Ilfracombe and Milford Haven and two vessels of Combwich, the *Anne* and the *Mary*, the former having John Dowding as master and John Kendall of Bridgwater as merchant and owner of the exported goods. Some vessels must have arrived at Axewater in ballast, since of the 22 sailings only four were inward. These vessels carried Salmon, Hake, Red and White Herring mantles and Irish linen. Interestingly, amongst one of the inward cargos were 300 untanned sheepskin pelts, likely to have been destined to Axbridge's many tanners. All the 18 outward sailings carried beans, at an average of 12.5 wey per cargo. In addition, six cargos also contained cloth, 211 of regular and 72 of narrow width. These were likely to have been brought from Wells, Croscombe or Axbridge itself. Two outward cargoes contained rotten wine and 100 dyed and plucked pelts; this may indicate that the Axbridge tanners were skilled at colouring leather for various purposes.[271]

Another location on a tributary of the Axe where sea-going shipping arrived was near the present-day Rooks Bridge, or Rooks Mill. In 1400, Edmund Whittock of Cheddar was in possession of armour obtained from a sea-going vessel that had arrived at 'Rokysmylle'. The vessel belonged to the former Duke of Surrey, a significant supporter of King Richard the Second, just deposed by the future King Henry the Fourth. The ship had sailed, in 1399, fully freighted, from Ireland and the armour was part of the cargo. Other cargo, including cartloads of plate and cloth, was taken by the Abbott of Glastonbury for storage, initially at the Abbey.[272] One hundred years later, in 1500, wooden seating for the church of St John's, Glastonbury was loaded onto 'two great boats' in Temple Back, Bristol and brought to Rooks Mill. Thirteen river boats were then used as lighters to transport the seating closer to Glastonbury, the last leg of the journey to the church being in carts.[273] An alternative route to this location would have been via the Brue, a few miles shorter but this would have involved navigating the mouth of the Parrett with its attendant dangers.

A further landing place along the Axe was in the parish of Lympsham at the site of an ancient ferry near the present day Hobbs Boat Inn. In the early 1840s the names of the fields by the earthen embankments taken to be wharves were 'warf' and 'south warf' and another local Inn is named the 'Ship and Castle'.[274] Sadly no specific ship arrivals or cargoes loaded or unloaded have been linked with this particular location, but, undoubtedly, beans and cereals could have been loaded here for exporting. Given that most vessels leaving Axewater had not arrived with a customable cargo, it seems clear that the majority would have called into Bristol from Ireland with salt fish, Salmon, Herring and Hake and then dropped down to Axewater to pick up beans which had a ready market in Ireland.

Fifteenth-century Bridgwater customs officials

Seventy one men have been identified as having been appointed to, or having operated in, official customs positions within the port of Bridgwater during the fifteenth century. Eleven of the 14 searchers do not appear to have had any local connection with Bridgwater and may never have actually been in the town. They held the position in Bristol and may have been fully employed there. Similarly five of the six deputy butlers, a position relating to customs duty on wine imports, also do not seem to have lived or functioned locally. This strongly suggests that they may have sub-contracted some, or all of their day-to-day duties for others to perform. 67% of the 12 controllers and 67% of the 39 collectors had strong links with Bridgwater during and after their appointments. A third of the collectors were described as Bridgwater merchants prior to their appointment. Many also operated as merchants throughout their official duties and continued to do so once others had been appointed in their place. Ten collectors represented the borough as its M.P. prior to, during and after their appointments. The split loyalties between their own interests and those of the Crown must have meant that smuggling was rife throughout the medieval period, as has been shown earlier in this chapter.

A review of Bridgwater's customs officials and other merchant's trading activity has thrown more light upon Bridgwater's sphere of influence within the counties of Somerset and Devon, Bristol, South Wales, Ireland, Gascony and Iberia. Several customs officials and merchants also had land and dealings in west Somerset; this may well have been connected with wool production and trade. The frequent use of the Court of Common Pleas by so many people connected with the port reveals different and more complex patterns of trade.

Since the appointment of customs officials was often political, it is not surprising that there were changes to those appointments as allegiances lurched between the Houses of Lancaster and York. Early in the fifteenth century, one of the first Lancastrian appointments to the position of collector was Richard Boyton, who was a strong ally of King Henry the Fourth and had served with him in Gascony. The changes in Lancastrian kingship during the reigns of Kings Henry the Fourth, Fifth and Sixth did not cause customers to lose their appointments; there were overlaps of officials across the reigns, with Boyton continuing to serve into the reign of King Henry the Fifth. Similarly, John Gunne served under King Henry the Fifth and Sixth. However, when the Yorkist King Edward the Fourth was enthroned in 1461 there seems to have been a total clear-out of officials, when new ones including Bridgwater's James Fitzjames received preferment. In 1471, when Edward the Fourth was back on the throne for the second time, two of Bridgwater's most notable merchants, John Hill and John Kendale both rose to prominence in the roles of controller. When the first Tudor king, Henry the Seventh, arrived on the throne in 1485 there was no overall purge and Kendale continued in his role in the 1490s.

Potted biographies of those men appointed to undertake customs duties who were involved in maritime trade are included in Appendix 3.

Conclusion

This chapter has shown that as far as Somerset's fourteenth century trade is concerned, in the west of the county Dunster appears to have had a significant maritime trade. Minehead, Watchet and Dunster's importance compared to Bridgwater can be seen as relatively small when compared to the significantly fuller range of maritime activities along the Parrett. Plenty of evidence of trade from Axewater remains from the fourteenth century but the records have not survived for the west Somerset anchorages. It is clear that fourteenth-century Bridgwater merchants, and probably ships, exported cereals and pulses, and imported wine, salt, millstones and fish. The Gascony trade appeared to be based on grain exports and wine imports. There is evidence that lead and cloth and Spanish Iron were also traded.

As the woollen trade grew in Somerset during the late fourteenth and early fifteenth centuries, it produced a higher value export, cloth, with which to trade with the Gascons and the Iberians. It is clear that Bridgwater merchants were often indebted to Bristol merchants, 'for merchandise', indicating that there was a coastal redistribution of goods that had entered Bristol. Bridgwater merchants were in debt to Bristol merchants in the 1330s and 1380s.[275] Sadly, there is little evidence of the type of goods that came coastwise from Bristol, but it may have included fruit, wine and cloth. Some Bridgwater merchants survived the Black Death, but the overall effect of the disease on Bridgwater trade is debatable. The port of Bridgwater became a distinct customs area from Bristol in 1402.[276]

It would be a mistake to think that Bridgwater was the gateway for all Somerset's imports during the fourteenth century. Whilst Taunton merchants may well have used the port for imports and exports, it is also clear towards the end of the fourteenth century that they often used the port of Exeter. Between 1381 and 1391 Somerset merchants accounted for 10% of the iron imports through Exeter, as well as 75% of alum, 18% of madder and 10% of woad imports. Taunton merchants figured significantly in those imports, accounting for 189 tuns of wine, 22.5 tons of iron and 126 quarters of salt. Two of the most prominent Taunton merchants were John Cullyng and William Marchaunt, clothiers, who also exported cloth through Exeter and another, Alexander Walys, had trading partners in Bishops Lydeard and Wellington, most probably also connected with cloth making. Exeter, at this time, had customary provision [what does this term mean?] for carts travelling to Porlock, Stogumber and Taunton, indicating that some of the Somerset ports did not have the monopoly in provisioning all of west Somerset.[277] Clearly the cost of overland traffic from Exeter, though more expensive than water-borne traffic to the Somerset coast, and onwards via river up the Parrett and Tone towards Taunton, was not, in comparison, prohibitively expensive. Thus, it may have been the preferred method of transport as it was less risky, and more direct, than sending ships around Cornwall and up the Bristol Channel.

The role of Uphill and Axewater in the fourteenth century is a little clearer than that of the western anchorages; evidently there was a link with the Cardiff area, on a route that would have passed the Holm islands. It was a location for the exportation of beans and cereals that would have been drawn from a significant hinterland. Furthermore, it was a location where Iberian goods could be off-loaded to try to avoid customs duty.

During the fifteenth century, the role of Minehead became relatively more important, especially as the Luttrell's landing place at Dunster receded in importance. Early in the fifteenth century, the Somerset coast was a strategic location with regard to the English Crown's handling of Owen Glendower's revolt. Maritime activity relating to this revolt occurred at places along the Somerset coast from Minehead to Clevedon. A coastal and inshore fishing industry thrived and developed at Minehead during the fifteenth century and by mid-century had also built up a very significant trade shipping fish from Ireland to Bristol. By the end of the century Bristol ships were re-provisioned at Minehead and West Somerset's largest coastal port had developed a small Iberian trade of its own.

Trade along the west Somerset coast tripled between 1460 and 1490, part of a general expansion of trade in the region. Minehead. In 1495 Minehead had 55 shipping movements of customable goods during one year. Minehead vessels were not the only Somerset vessels to use the facilities at their home port. 26 movements by other vessels included, one Welsh, five Irish, one Breton and eight Iberian.[278] Clearly such information, derived from customs accounts, disregards those who evaded taxation and the movement of un-customable goods, such as stone, wood and animals. Since many of Bridgwater's fifteenth century customs officials were also merchants, conflicts of interest were inevitable and trade in customable goods was probably significantly under-recorded.

As there is no example of customs books for both Bristol and Bridgwater in the fifteenth century for the same complete year, a complete pattern of trade in Minehead vessels is unobtainable. Parts of customs books survive for both ports for 1486. These reveal a Minehead vessel, the *Sonday* visited Bristol, Bridgwater and Minehead carrying fish from Ireland, and beans from Bridgwater to Ireland. From 1461 to 1486, the dominant trade for a large number of Minehead vessels involved fetching fish from Ireland to Bristol, Bridgwater or Minehead, a trade that might have been remunerative for merchants without involvement any other incidental trade that could be found. However, it seems that, wherever possible, salt, cloth, beans and other un-customable goods, such as stone, were looked for in order to make the return trip and the whole enterprise more economic. If no such goods were available in Bristol, boats might slip down to Bridgwater to look for a cargo there. Whilst this might have been the dominant pattern of trade there were exceptions. This conclusion concurs with research by mercantile and fishing industry historians writing of the 1470s and 1480 with regard to the Bristol Channel from the

Irish perspective. For example, Wendy Childs stated that between 1475 and 1487 Thomas Steward sailed the *Trinity* of Waterford in and out of Bristol, Bridgwater and Minehead.[279] Marianne Kowaleski has noted that vessels left Minehead and Ilfracombe with salt and returned to Bristol and Bridgwater with Irish Herring in 1479.[280]

The safety of the Somerset coast from wars with France, which affected shipping in the English Channel, meant Bridgwater's international trade with Gascony and Iberia flourished; a trade that was not extinguished with the loss of Gascony to the English Crown in 1453. Spanish and Portuguese ships and merchants were regular visitors to Bridgwater throughout the century. Bridgwater's cloth exports, mainly to Gascony and Iberia, were significant and cloth making became important in the borough. Wine, fish, salt, iron and dyestuffs were the most significant imports and cloth, cereals and beans were the most significant exports. Un-customable goods that arrived in river boats, such as pottery, were also shipped from the town. Bridgwater merchants did not just rely on trading in vessels that came in and out of Bridgwater itself for their income. For example, in 1496, the *Mary Undercroft* of Dartmouth carried goods for Bridgwater merchants between La Rochelle and Ireland.[281] The role of Combwich, its ships and mariners was significant in all of this trade. Small Irish ships bringing fish to Bridgwater and leaving with beans and corn would have been a familiar sight on the Parrett. Bridgwater merchants developed trading contacts throughout south-west England, as well as having contacts in Gascony, Iberia, Ireland and Wales.

Alongside these trades at Bridgwater in the fifteenth century was the Irish trade. Fish arrived, mainly in Irish vessels that were unloaded and filled with beans and cereals for the return journey. Somerset vessels, especially from Minehead after having deposited Irish fish at Bristol, arrived at Bridgwater in ballast, and did not necessarily find a cargo to ship. The business of sailing south to Bridgwater, maybe with small amounts of un-customable goods, to pick up beans for the return journey made this process more economically viable.

Towards the end of the fifteenth century, in 1494, of 101 recorded arrivals in Bridgwater with customable goods (some visited several times). The dominant home ports of those vessels were located in Ireland, on 41 occasions. Minehead was second with 19 occasions, Iberia 14, Combwich 10, Dartmouth, Wales and Bridgwater itself three visits each, Barnstaple one visit and 5 visits from vessels of unknown or uncertain origin made up the remainder.[282] The small number of entries of Bridgwater vessels, owned by Bridgwater merchants, is probably accounted for by the fact that most of the Combwich vessels would have been Bridgwater owned. Furthermore, local merchants were able to lade and sail a higher proportion of vessels without reference to the customs authorities. This was the case since a high proportion of the customs officials were Bridgwater merchants. Apart from one or two mentions of coal, it appears that the Welsh trade with Bridgwater at this time may have been relatively insignificant.

During the fifteenth century, Uphill and Axewater thrived as a location for the exportation of beans and tanned leather to Ireland; these were shipped in Irish and Bridgwater vessels. Occasionally, Irish fish and European goods came into Axewater, perhaps some of these cargos made an overland trip to Bristol for sale.

The area north of the Mendips undoubtedly came within the influence of Bristol's maritime trade, as did Minehead due to its triangular fish trade with Ireland and Bristol. The rest of Somerset was certainly no economic backwater. The information in this chapter relating to Bridgwater merchants shows that they not only had a sphere of influence within the county, but traded with merchants throughout the south-west of England, in south Wales, Ireland, western France and the Iberian peninsula.[283] They exported agricultural products, manufactured items (such as woollen cloth) and pottery. In return they imported wine, dyestuffs, salt, iron and other products from Gascony and coastal Iberia, but at a much smaller tonnage than that off-loaded at the quays at Bristol. Bridgwater ships and men were also conscripted for Government service, mainly in Ireland and France. Therefore, the Somerset coast, which gave the county access to international markets, helped enable Somerset to become a significant economic centre during England's late medieval period.[284]

Acknowledgments

This Minehead section of this study would have been

so much thinner if Professor Evan Jones of University of Bristol had not granted me access to the spreadsheets of Bristol's fifteenth-century port books transcribed for the John Cabot Project. Grateful thanks goes to Steve Popham for help with French translations, to Julia McDonald and staff at the Somerset Heritage Centre for help with Latin translations, to Eliot Lowe and Garry Holden for professional support with photographs. Special thanks go to Dr Adrian Webb for guiding me to various sources including the database on Medieval migrants, and for all the time and energy he gives to editing my work to bring it to print.

Appendix 1. Bridgwater's town crane and quay, 1424-1467

Date	Crane income	Crane expenditure and comments	Quay expenditure and comments
1424	£5 2s 6d	Grease bought for lubrication.	4s for digging the quay
1428	£3 18s 7d	Grease, bolts, planks, a pair of slings at 5s 2d and a lock required. Labour for mending the crane, 2s 6d.	4s for digging the quay
1431	£3 1s 7d	Income paid by John Keysham. Expenditure for grease, slings, bolts, nails, spikes and a hawser.	7s for digging the quay
1438	£2 13s 2d	Income paid by John Keysham. 1s 3d required for grease.	7s to John Keysham for digging the quay
1440	£4 5s 3d	Tallow for lubrication. Nails, 22 boards and timber required for considerable repair.	6s 8d to craneman for throwing silt from the quay
1441	£3 18s 9d	Tallow for lubrication 10d.	6s 8d to W.C. and R.S. for digging the silt this year
1443	£3 2s 2d	10 lb swine grease for lubrication 10d.	Scouring silt under quay for one day by two men 4d. 2 men to dig silt from quay 8s
1445	£3 16s 10d	10 lb of tallow for lubrication.	8s for digging away silt from quay
1449	£4 4s 4d	Income for hauling wine and other merchandise to the quay.	8s to crane porters for clearing the silt from the quay
1453	£3 12s 0d	Grease and a pulley required. Two slings for the crane from Taunton, 5s 10d.	8s for clearing silt under quay
1454	£3 16s 7d	Grease for lubrication 1s 6d.	5s 8d for crane porters to clear silt from quay
1455	£3 18s 8d	Grease for lubrication 1s 6d.	5s for clearing silt from quay
1456	£2 2s 6d	Grease for lubrication 1s 2d.	5s for crane porters to clear silt from quay
1458	£2 14s 0d	Grease for lubrication 1s 3d.	5s for crane porters to clear silt from quay
1461	£0 17s 6d	Grease, tar and cables required.	5s for clearing silt from quay
1467	£3 5s 3d	Grease 1s. Pulleys bought and made for the crane 5s.	4s for clearing silt from quay

Sources: Dilks, *Bridgwater 1400-1445*, 78-9, 91-3, 105-110, 123-4, 132-3, 140 1, 149-50; Dilks, *Bridgwater 1445-1468*, 2-3, 54-5, 62-3, 69-70, 82-3, 92-3, 103-4, 116-18, 136-37. There is no income recorded for 1431-2 but close by in the original documents there is an undated set on incomes. This has been assigned to the year 1431-2.

Appendix 2. Somerset vessels, 1320-1500

Table 3.8: Bridgwater, Combwich, Dunster, Minehead and Axewater vessels used for military service, 1297-1467

Date	Origin of vessels	No. Ships	Details and or purpose
1322	Bridgwater vessel owners	[blank]	In 1322, 1326 and 1328 the Close Rolls reveal orders to vessel owners in relation to Ulster, Scotland and French matters.
1326	Bridgwater vessel owners	[blank]	In 1322, 1326 and 1328 the Close Rolls reveal orders to vessel owners in relation to Ulster, Scotland and French matters.
1328	Bridgwater vessel owners	[blank]	In 1322, 1326 and 1328 the Close Rolls reveal orders to vessel owners in relation to Ulster, Scotland and French matters.
1342	Bridgwater and Combwich	4	Sent four ships and a barge to Brittany.
1347	Bridgwater	1	Vessel for a campaign.
1363	Bridgwater	[blank]	Small ships of up to 20 tons, except fishing vessels were ordered to Bristol by mid-Lent to take soldiers to Ireland.
1372	Bridgwater	1	Vessel for a military expedition.
1374	Bridgwater	1	February. Orders to arrest a crew for the *Saint Mary* cog for military service.
1386	Bridgwater and Axewater	[blank]	Order given on 14 April to provide ships and mariners for Robert de Veer, Marquess of Dublin.
1396	Bridgwater	1	A 160 ton ship was involved in the transit of King Richard the Second and his forces to Ireland including one of his justices William Hankford. John Welch of Bridgwater was given protection for six months to accompany Hankford.
1401	Bridgwater and Dunster	[blank]	Locations where ships of 30 tons or more could be stayed to await orders for the King's service.
1415	Bridgwater	1	Grant to John Gilhampton, master of the barge, *Mary* to whom £10 15s 3d was due for wages for him and his mariners lately sailing in the King's service for a voyage to foreign parts for six weeks after 1 August.
1417	Bridgwater	1	One of the many ships that conveyed King Henry the Fifth and his army to Normandy, in July 1417, was the 'bargee' *Marie* of Bridgwater.
1424	Bridgwater	[blank]	Amongst ships of Bristol and Liverpool for the conveyance of Edmund, Lord of the March and his retinue to be conveyed to Ireland on the 4 February.
1439	Bridgwater	[blank]	Any ships in 'arrested' with their mariners and sent to Plymouth so John, Earl of Huntingdon could sail to Aquitaine on the King's service.
1439-1452	Minehead and Bridgwater	3	Ships used for troop movements included the *Katharine* 80 tons and the *James* 30 tons, both of Minehead and the *Marie* of Bridgwater, 80 tons.
1449	Bridgwater	[blank]	April, ships arrested to transfer Richard, Duke of York, his wife and 600 troops to Ireland.
1461	Minehead	1	The *David* commandeered by the King for military service.
1461-1467	Minehead	1	The *Trinity* of Minehead, crewed from Somerset acted against King Edward the Fourth's enemies, probably outlawed Lancastrians off the Somerset coast. It is possible that the vessel had been confiscated from the Luttrells for supporting the Lancastrians.

Sources : N. Rodger, *The safeguard of the sea: a Naval history of Britain 660-1649* (London, 2004), 496; *Calendar of Rotuli Normanniae*, 1 (London, 1835), 326; T. Kaye, *The stranger in Liverpool: a historical and descriptive view of Liverpool* (Liverpool, 1833), appendix lvi; *C.P.R. Henry VI*, 3, 273; *C.P.R. Henry VI*, 5, 238; F. Hancock, *Minehead*, 236; T. Dilks (ed.), *Bridgwater Borough archives 1400-1445*, S.R.S. 58 (1943), 169-71; S. Rose, 'Maritime logistics and Edward I's military campaigns' in *The Mariner's Mirror*, 99 (2013), 388-97; C. Knighton, *C.I.M.* 8 (2003), 163, I am indebted to Mary Siraut for this last reference. J. Black, *C.P.R., Edward I*, 4, 61,75; A. Powell, *The ancient borough of Bridgwater* (Bridgwater, 1907), 190; *V.C.H. Somerset* 6, 213-23; R. Isaacson, *C.P.R. Edward III 1363*, 317; G. Morris, *C.P.R. Richard II*, 3 ,131; G. Morris, *C.P.R. Richard II*, 5, 514; T. Rymer, *Rymer's Foedera* 1 (London, 1869), 467; Oppenheim, *V.C.H. Somerset* 2, 247; R. Fowler, *C.P.R. Henry IV*, 1, 487; R. Fowler, *C.P.R. Henry V*, 1, 370.

Table 3.9: Port of Bridgwater trading vessels, 1326-1394

Vessel	Date	Tonnage	Comments
Michel	1326	-	Richard Gode master, in London with wine from Rochelle
Michel	1327	-	In the port of Bristol
-	1346	15	At the siege of Calais
Blome	1349	-	Loading cloth at Dartmouth
St Marie	1375	175	A cog, destroyed in the bay of Bourneuf. In 1374 it was ordered that 54 seamen be impressed at Bridgwater for the *St Marie* to join the Royal fleet in Plymouth
Marie	1381	-	Nicholas Someryng master, who was involved in an insurrection at Bridgwater
Cog John	1382	-	Owners, John Bursy and William Thomer of Bridgwater
-	1385	120	Irish military action under the Duke of Lancaster
-	1394	160	Four Bridgwater ships arrested for King Richard the Second's passage to Ireland in October, one of 160 tons

Sources: J. Edwards, *Book of prests of the King's wardrobe 1294-5* (Oxford, 1962), 66; G. Farr, *Somerset harbours* (London, 1954), 104; *Calendar of Plea and Memoranda Rolls 1323-1364* 1 (Cambridge, 1926), 25; E. Carus-Wilson (ed.), *The overseas trade of Bristol in the later Middle Ages* (New York, 1967), 177; M. Oppenheim, 'Maritime history' in W. Page (ed.), *V.C.H. Somerset* 2 (1906), 249; T. Dilks, 'Bridgwater and the insurrection of 1381' in *P.S.A.N.H.S.* 73 (1927), 57-69; Dilks, *Bridgwater 1377-1399*, 139; Dilks, *Bridgwater 1400-1445*, 16; J. Chapman, *C.I.M. 1399-1422* (1968), 141.

Table 3.10: Bridgwater/Combwich vessels operating in the fifteenth century

Vessel	Date	Master/owner	Comments
Marie	1403	Nicholas Somering master	Gascon trade
John	1410	John Kedwelly owner	Gascon trade
Isabel	1414	Richard Gardiner, Philip Vaugre, Guillem Coque owners	Gascon trade
Mary	1415	John Gilhampton	Barge in King's service
?	1431	Woolmer	Carrying stone
Marie	1439-1452	?	80 tons, troop movements
?	1443?	John Colwell master, Thomas Cradok owner	Piracy off Ireland
George	1454	John Cupar?	Gascon trade
?	1455	John Bythesea	Carried lead from Bristol
Mighell	1433-1443 or 1467-1477	?	Wrecked off Guernsey. There were two ships of this name.
Christopher sometimes of Bridgwater or Combwich	1470, 1476, 1485, 1486	Richard Fans, John Kenet and John Wilkins masters	Gascon and Irish trade
Mighell sometimes of Bridgwater or Combwich	1470s, 1486	John Hemerying master and part owner, Nicholas Mackrell, Thomas Dowding masters	Gascon trade, Spanish trade, Irish trade
Kateryn	1472	Germain Berebrewer master	Irish trade
Anne sometimes of Bridgwater, sometimes of Combwich	1480, 1486	William Fairyman, John Dowding masters	Bristol Channel trade, Irish trade
Margaret	1481	John Hill and Henry Burnham part owners	Hill's portion was left to his wife.
Nicholas	1481	John Hill part owner	Left to his wife
John	1481, 1482	John Hill part owner, Edmund Gibbs master	Left to John Hill's wife Irish trade
Marie of Combwich	1486	Evan Ap Owen	Irish trade
Gabriel	1490s	Denis Dywyn	Gascon trade

Sources: F. Weaver (ed.), *Somerset medieval wills, 1500-1530*, S.R.S. 19, 64-8; Dilks, *Bridgwater 1400-1445*, 16, 105; T. Dilks (ed.), *Bridgwater borough archives 1445-1468*, S.R.S. 60 (1948), 87; Dunning, *Bridgwater borough archives 1468-1485*, S.R.S. 70 (1971), 22, 28, 43; Fowler, *C.P.R. Henry V 1413-1416*, 370; Bland, *C.P.R. Henry VI 1441-1446,* 247; Harleian manuscripts 433, 12 (1980), 209; Rymer, *Rymer's Foedera*, 9, 164; T.N.A., E 122/19/7, 20/5, 174/3, customs accounts and legers 1470, 1485-1487; Dunning, *Bridgwater*, 38; Carus Wilson, *Overseas trade*, 289; Dryburgh and Smith, *Handbook* (London, 2005), 282-9; T.N.A., C 1/45/41, Chancery proceedings regarding the *Mighell* of Bridgwater, 1433-1472.

Appendix 3. Some Somerset people with maritime occupations, 1415-1500

Name	Occupation	Year(s)
Bridgwater		
[blank] Gilhampton	ship's master	1415
Robert Gardour	shipman	1418
John Crepy	mariner	1422
Richard Gardour	shipman	1422
William Sallez	mariner	1422
John Alleward	shipman	1430
David Curtis	shipman, mariner	1430, 1440
John Benne	shipman	1437
John Smyth	mariner	1440
John Gardner	mariner	1440, 1444
William Gardner	mariner	1440
Richard Botkin	mariner	1457
Thomas Anable	mariner	1484
Thomas Smyth	mariner	1489
Henry Burnham	mariner	1486, 1492
Combwich		
Walter Cley	shipman	1418
Henry Burnham	mariner	1470
John Paynter Snr	mariner	1490
John Paynter Jnr	mariner	1490, 1492
[blank] Allewyll	mariner	1492
Kingston Seymour		
Roger Ram	mariner	1470
John Toky	mariner	1470
Minehead		
Roger Kyng	shipman	1422
David Nete	mariner	1442
Matthew Lumbrey	mariner	1458
John Hargate	mariner	1484
Maurice Collyn/Quailin	part ship-owner	1496
George Donell	part ship-owner	1496
John Philip	part ship-owner	1496
Maurice Quirke	part ship-owner	1496
Robert Bassher	master	1497
John Botston/Buston	master/part ship-owner	1497
Thomas Boteston	mariner/master	1497
Robert Broke	mariner/master	1497
William Culleren	mariner/master	1497
Thomas Donell	mariner/master	1497
Richard Grant	mariner/master	1497
Nicholas Hatton	mariner/master	1497
Henry Laughwyll	mariner/master	1497
John Lymryk	mariner/master	1497
John Thye	mariner/master	1498
William Rosell	mariner	1500
Portishead		
John Raulyn	mariner	1458, 1460
Stockland Gaunt		
Richard Dodyng	mariner	1464
Stogursey		
William Pruette	mariner	1465
Uphill		
William Batyn	mariner	1455
Winscombe		
John Beksy	mariner	1470

Source: T.N.A., CP 40 Court of Common Pleas.

Appendix 4. Biographies of some Bridgwater's customs officials and merchants

The biographies below are included in order to present a fuller picture of Bridgwater's mercantile and maritime community. Considerable reference has been made to actions brought in the Court of Common Pleas which often give a clear indication of the merchant's trading area, in Somerset, south-west England and sometimes Wales or Ireland. By implication this can imply water-borne trade. Furthermore, when the occupation of the debtor or creditor is known, which is often the case, this can suggest the type of goods that were traded. For example, if a dyer is involved in the action, the trade might have been dyestuffs, woad or madder.

Richard Boyton (fl.1389-d.1422)[285] benefitted from service under the Lancastrians. He was retained by John of Gaunt, King Henry the Fourth's father, in Bayonne in 1389 to serve him in times of peace and war; this retention being later confirmed by Gaunt's son, Henry Bolingbroke, before becoming King Henry the Fourth. After Henry's grasped the throne, Boyton became a figure of some importance in the Bridgwater port and locality, as well as in the county of Somerset and south-west region. He married, before 1402, to Margery, daughter of Sir Matthew Stawell of Cothelstone and owned land in Charlinch and Currypool. The Currypool land probably derived from Margery's prior marriage to Richard Lylle of Currypool. Boyton held the manor of Currypool until 1412.[286] In 1420 he was granted an interest in a whole range of other manors in the Bridgwater area.[287] His first appointment at Bridgwater in 1398 was as collector of customs and subsidies for Bridgwater, Combwich, Dunster and Axewater. Boyton's appointment was reconfirmed on many occasions from 1398 to 1413.[288] In 1399 he was made deputy butler for the same area.[289]

1400 must have been a significant year for Boyton as in January he was granted a ship, a crayer, the *George*, valued at 30 marks, one of the forfeited possessions of Thomas Holland, second Earl of Kent and was described as 'the King's esquire'. It is not known where the *George* operated, or whether it was used to bring wine from Gascony to Bridgwater, though this is not unlikely given Boyton's connections with both locations. Within months he had been elevated to the position of Constable of Taunton Castle by appointment of Bishop Wykeham of Winchester, an office which he held until 1406. Also in 1400 he was granted two tuns of Gascon wine out of the 'prise of Bridgwater' for life.[290] Later appointments included deputy butler for the ports of Weymouth from 1404 to 1418, Melcombe from 1407 to 1413 and for Topsham from 1408 until his death.[291] Boyton also served four terms as Sheriff of Somerset and Dorset from 1400 to 1417. He was M.P. for Bridgwater in 1416. How much time Boyton spent in and around Bridgwater is not known but he did travel to Calais in 1409.

After Boyton died his executor, Thomas Stawell, in 1430 tried to extract debts from the executors of Robert Crook of Taunton and Richard Cheddar esquire of Thornfalcon.[292] Whether the debts were trading debts is unknown.

John Broke (*c.*1380-fl.1417) was appointed collector in 1404 and again in 1405. He seems to have been busy in town affairs in the 1380s and 1390s, being involved in leases and legal affairs connected with bridge building at Bridgwater in 1395. He was involved in the conveyance of rents from a corner shop in the town twice in the first decade of the fifteenth century and was last heard of in 1417.[293]

Thomas Cave (fl.1406-d.bef.1438) was portreeve for Bridgwater in 1406, constable in 1417 and M.P. in 1414, 1426 and 1432.[294] He was engaged in the manufacture of cloth.[295] In 1420 he came into possession of half a burgage in Bridgwater and made a quitclaim to Robert Beste of Bridgwater of half a burgage in 'Frerenstrete' Bridgwater in the same year.[296]

William Criche (fl.1341-fl.1394) was a cereal exporter who signed Bridgwater documents from 1341 to 1394. In 1361 he was left a third of a ship by a fellow Bridgwater merchant, Roger S(w)opham, who was also active in the town in the 1350s. Criche was licenced several times to export cereals and pulses to Gascony between 1367 and 1371. He also traded within the borough, being owed money by William Loue in 1378. Criche seems to have been a bailiff in Bridgwater in 1381 and had a debtor.[297] He also had wider trade links as he was owed £4 by Robert Cran of Somerton in 1393. Criche's other responsibilities included representing the borough in parliament in 1362, 1363, 1366 and 1368.[298]

John Dav(e)y (fl.1424-d.bef.1461) is first recorded at Bridgwater in 1424 when he took on an Irish apprentice. Subsequently he was responsible for a number of other more local apprentices. He began his trading life as a tanner. Whilst he remained in the tanning business until his death he was also described as a merchant in the latter years of his life. In 1436 he was appointed constable of the borough and was steward of the merchant guild in 1441. By 1447 he had married a rich widow from Woolavington who inherited considerable lands from her husband. He was important enough during the Wars of the Roses to be granted by three earls the safe and unmolested movement for him and his servants for the purposes of trade.

Davey had trading links in Bridgwater itself, throughout Somerset, Devon, in south Wales, western Ireland and the Iberian Peninsula. He traded in white cloth of 'Bridgwater making' in 1446 and entered into bonds with local merchants in 1447, 1448, 1452 and two local saddlers in 1459. He was owed money by a Bridgwater husbandman in 1450 and his estate was indebted to a Bridgwater yeoman in 1465. Elsewhere in Somerset, Davey was chasing debts of a Bruton merchant, a North Cadbury drover and a Taunton tailor in 1450, whist in 1465 his executors chased debts owed by a North Newton husbandman, yeomen from Minehead, Old Cleeve and Chard, a butcher from Pitney, a merchant and one other person from Dunster

It is likely that a Bridgwater merchant's trading bond with an Exmouth mariner in 1438 related to John Davey since he had many trading contacts with Devonians.[299] From 1441 to 1443 he had links with Barnstaple merchants; in 1450 he was creditor to a Cullumpton smith and in 1452 he had dealings with a Plymouth plumber. Davey died in 1461, but in 1465 his executors were chasing an Ilfracombe merchant for debt. Davey's other commercial links included a Neath merchant in 1438, a Bristol merchant in 1442 and in 1465 his executors were chasing debts from a Dorsetshire barber, a merchant from Sherborne and a yeoman from Dorchester. International links included a Wexford merchant in 1443 and John Redguges (probably a spelling of Rodrigues) of Lisbon in 1456. He also had dealings with Richard Botkin, mariner of Bridgwater in 1457 who went on to trade in Bilbao, Spain in 1458.[300]

James Fitzjames (fl.1459-fl.1467) was appointed controller of customs in 1464[301] but did not appear to hold the position for long. Fitzjames was described as 'merchant of Bridgwater' in 1463 and 1468.[302] He appears to have been active in town affairs from 1459 to 1466.[303] He married Alice, widow of John Salmon, by 1463. He suffered trespass by a Huntspill husbandman and Richard Dodyng, a Stockland Gaunt mariner, in 1465. In the same year he was owed money by merchants from Exeter and Hereford.[304] Fitzjames represented Bridgwater at a parliament in 1467.[305]

William Gascoigne (fl.1402-d.1423) was appointed collector of customs in 1408,[306] retaining the position for four years. In 1402, as custodian of the merchant guild, he received a general pardon from King Henry the Fourth for any offences committed before 8 December 1400.[307] He was very much a prominent local man engaged in business. As a burgess of the town he served as guild steward from 1411 to 1423. He acquired property within Bridgwater from 1405 to 1417.[308] In 1418 he chased debts from fellow Bridgwater merchants, John Henton and Henry Taillor, as well as a merchant from Taunton, a skinner from Exeter, a Bridgwater tailor and two or three husbandmen from the Bridgwater district.[309] This indicates he had a wide trading sphere in the west of England. He accrued a substantial amount of land during his lifetime, owning 360 acres at his death. The largest portion, 200 acres at Exton, was purchased for £300 in 1416. His Exmoor interests also included the advowson of Hawkridge.[310] Wool from Exmoor sheep grazed on his lands could well have been taken to Bridgwater for making cloth.

As well as being prominent in Bridgwater's trade and local civic affairs, Gascoigne served as an M.P. on twelve occasions between 1406 and 1422, on the last occasion he represented the burgesses of Bridgwater in the 'upper exchequer'.[311] His widow, Matilda, divested some of her Bridgwater property in 1423,[312] presumably after William's death.

Richard Gosse (fl.1433-fl.1453) served as collector of customs from 1433 to 1440.[313] He was son of William Gosse.[314] One of his accounts remains from 1438.[315] Richard leased property in Dampier Street in 1438[316] and was steward of the merchant guild at Bridgwater in 1441.[317] In 1444 Gosse was owed money by a Bridgwater cordwainer and a local yeoman. Furthermore, in the same year, he accused a number of Bridgwater mercers, yeoman and an apothecary of trespass and assault.[318] In 1446 he was described as being a 'gentleman of Wemdon' when he should have been travelling to Picardy to serve his King but 'was tarrying in Westminster'.[319] It was alleged in 1453 that Richard Gosse of Bridgwater, gent, was indebted to Walter Portman.[320]

William Gosse (fl.1401-d.bef.1461) was appointed collector of customs in 1419, a position which he held until 1422.[321] He held official positions in the town before the end of the fourteenth century. In 1401 he was involved in a commission of enquiry over the cargo of a Bilbao vessel at Bridgwater which had been sequestrated by Bristol merchants.[322] Like William Gascoigne, Gosse, as custodian of the merchant guild, had received a general pardon from King Henry the Fourth in 1402 for any offences committed before December 1400.[323] Gosse traded in cloth and victuals and was steward of the merchant guild from 1406 sometime after 1416. He owned property in the town, as well as at Stogursey and in south Somerset. He was elected M.P. for Bridgwater in 1413 and was involved in election procedures elsewhere in the county from 1410 to 1421.[324] In 1450 his wife, Margery, sought to claim back land that had somehow come into the hands of Walter Portman.[325] Posthumously, in 1461, William and Margery, now both dead, were granted a pardon for all 'trespasses, offences, arrears and forfeitures'[326] which applied to them.

John Gunne (Gonne) (fl.1420-d.1440) was appointed collector of customs in 1421, a position he held for two years.[327] He was involved in electoral returns for Somerset between 1420 and 1435 and was M.P. for Bridgwater in 1422 and 1437.[328] By 1419 he was clearly a prominent Bridgwater merchant. Described as a mercer in 1420,[329] he was granted (by John Beste) three and a half market stalls in the town. In September 1424 he was steward of the merchant guild.[330] Gunne had properties in a number of Bridgwater streets from 1423 to 1429.[331] He witnessed an agreement in Bridgwater in 1433 whereby John Beste took over two tenements in St Mary Street from John Avyle of Watchet.[332] By 1422, he was trading throughout Somerset and was owed debts by a Langport dyer, a Taunton chapman and a Bridgwater 'shipman' John Aylleward.[333] After his death, in 1440, his executors, Joan and Robert Grene were trying to claw back debts owed to his estate from Porlock and Shepton Beauchamp mercers, as well as a pewterer and a bowyer, both from Wells.[334]

Adam Hamelyn (fl.1460-d.*c.*1493) came to prominence at Bridgwater in the 1460s as merchant, mayor and notary public. In terms of his property interests in the town, he leased a burgage in St Mary Street in 1464 and passed on half a burgage in Friarn Street in 1480.[335] He was involved in church, borough and legal matters from 1469 until 1482.[336] He was mayor in 1480 and it seems he might have also been mayor in 1487.[337] Hamelyn was styled as merchant and tucker in 1475. He was owed money by a Cannington merchant, a chapman and a glover, both of Langport.[338] He imported Herring from Cork on a Portuguese ship, the *Rescarda* carvel of Opporto, which had evidently called at an Irish port prior to arriving at Bridgwater in 1482. The cargo also included wax and sugar.[339] Other evidence that Hamelyn was a fish trader dates from 1484 when he was in debt for £6 13s 4d to John Assheley, a Worcester fishmonger. It is highly likely that other fish bought by Hamelyn were brought down the Severn to Bridgwater. Hamelyn's will of 1493 shows he owned wine and woad which he probably traded. In 1484, connections with Glastonbury included a debt owed by a clerk but Hamelyn was allegedly indebted to William Lancokes of Glastonbury. In 1486, Glastonbury clothier, John Mudeford was owed money by Hamelyn, which may indicate that he bought and traded cloth from central Somerset.[340]

Hamelyn seemed to have no male heir at the time of writing his will in 1493, so he left much of his estate to his brother John. He was referred to as one-time mayor and notary public in the will. Prior to his death he sold off land in and around Bridgwater. One example of this took place in 1490, but the process continued after his death in 1495 when his estate was divested of 'Shovel' in North Petherton.[341] Hamelyn's wife died before 1500 when her executor from Taunton was chasing a debt on behalf of her estate.[342]

Alexander Hamelyn (fl.1489-fl.1506) was collector of customs in the port of Bridgwater in 1489 and 1490.[343] He may have been a relation of Adam Hamelyn (see above). In 1496 Alexander, described as a gentleman of Bridgwater, was granted a general pardon and release arising from his office as collector of customs.[344] Also in 1496, with William Harding (below) he received payment from King Henry the Seventh for organising the 'shipping and passage' of a Royal messenger, John hon, to Ireland, presumably from Bridgwater. In 1506 he was in dispute over access through 40 acres of land he held at Luxborough, as well as the removal of hedge timber.[345]

William Harding (fl.1489-fl.1496) was collector of customs between 1489 and 1491.[346] He witnessed a deed relating to land in Huntspill and North Petherton in 1487.[347] In 1496, described as a 'Bridgwater merchant', he was granted a pardon except for debts to the Exchequer by reason of his office.[348]

William Hastyngs (fl.1409-fl.1428) was appointed collector of customs in 1413 with further confirmations at least until 1418.[349] His accounts for the port remain from 1413 to 1420.[350] Hastyngs was involved in a grant of property at Woolavington in 1409[351] and served as a bailiff at Bridgwater in 1416.[352] In 1418 he was owed money by a Taunton vintner and a Highbridge husbandman, whilst also having trouble with some Shepton Beauchamp husbandmen over trespass and taking. In 1422 he suffered 'trespass and taking' by a Middlezoy woman and in 1440 he was owed money by Thomas Kingston of Bishops Lydeard, gentleman.[353] Other evidence that Hastyngs was well respected include his involvement with land deals between 1405 and 1425,[354] receiving a bequest of £5 by Bridgwater churchman, Sir Leonard Hakelyut, in 1413[355] and being involved in civic matters in 1428.[356]

John Henton (fl.1373-fl.1418) was a rich, powerful and litigious Bridgwater merchant. In 1374, he was owed nearly £100 by a Bristol merchant, John Babcary.[357] Henton had personally imprisoned him for debt.[358] In 1383, he was ordered by the King to release Babcary, who was by then in dire circumstances. He owed Bridgwater merchant Robert Plumpton (deceased by 1391 when the case came before the High Court of Chancery) £60 since 1373.[359] In 1381 he was indebted to William Taillour.[360] In 1382, Henton, as a burgess of Bridgwater, represented the town in parliament. Mention has already been made of his debts for Herring and salt, in 1384, which resulted in well over a decade of litigation and £287 of Henton's Bridgwater assets being sequestrated in about 1390. He was being chased for debt by Sir Thomas Mortimer and William Ford, clerk in 1396 and by William Gascoigne of Bridgwater in 1418.[361]

John Hill (fl.1423-d.bef.1461) was appointed customer in 1455.[362] It is not impossible that this John was a relation of a man of the same name who was one of Bridgwater's most prominent merchants during the 1470s (see below). From 1423 to 1426 it seems that Hill served as a reeve of the borough, whilst in 1436 he was termed a mercer and in 1438 was bailiff of the community. He appears in the community accounts at various times in 1445 and 1453.[363] He was also involved in chantry affairs in 1445 and 1455, and was a substantial donor towards the repair of the church in 1445.[364] Hill's reputation was strong enough to have been appointed as an arbiter in a dispute between significant Bridgwater citizens in 1446 and was elected to Parliament in 1450.[365] He was involved in borough affairs between 1455 and 1459 being named on a number of conveyances. He traded in wine in 1458 but seems to have died by 1461.[366]

John Hill (fl.1463-d.1481), merchant, and Thomasine (d. *c.*1485) his wife. John had a number of debts in Somerset in 1463.[367] Along with John Kendale, he was collector of customs and subsidies for the port and presented accounts for 1470.[368] In 1470 he imported wine, canvas, barley and pepper through the port of Southampton, though the destination of those goods in unknown. In 1472, he was recorded as being a constable in the borough.[369] In 1474, with Kendale again, he entered an agreement to supply Nicholas Palmer of Bristol, merchant, with five pipes of woad and William Shore of London, mercer with 33 'Bridgwaters' of which Kendale was to supply 34.[370] In the late 1470s he was also dealing with Arnold Delestale, a Bordeaux merchant, regarding woad.[371] In 1477 and

1479, he acquired land in the Bridgwater area and, also in 1479, a butcher's stall in the shambles was conveyed to him.[372] Hill was mayor in 1478 and 1479, which indicates that he was one of the foremost and respected merchants in the borough.[373]

Hill's will, dated 18 May 1481, in which he left a pipe of woad and a ton of iron to pay his administrators, one of whom was Kendale, indicates his trading interests towards the end of his life.[374] Hill's wife, Thomasine, was his executrix who, in June 1482, quickly set about trying to sell the quarter interest in John's ships that had been passed on to her; the armed vessels were the *John*, the *Margaret* and the *Nicholas*.[375] John's business partner, Kendale, shipped goods in the *Margaret* in 1481, so it is likely he owned a further portion of the vessel.[376] The *John* was possibly the same vessel in 1486 that entered the port carrying Irish White and Red Herring.[377] In 1483, his executor, Thomas Hill, was pursued in the Court of Common Pleas for one of John Hill's debts.[378] Thomasine's will was written in 1485 where it is recorded that she gave four pipes of woad to named people, including Nicholas Jobe, John and Margaret Stallinch.[379] This either indicates that stores of John's goods were still considerable, or that Thomasine continued to trade after John's death. Intriguingly, the first names of these individuals are the names of Hill's ships, so they may also have been part owners of the vessels. Further evidence of Thomasine's trading activity comes from the Court of Common Pleas from 1490. Thomas Phillip, an executor of Thomasine, who had received two pipes of woad in her will, was chasing a debt owed to Thomasine from William Brown a dyer of Uffculme, Devon, no doubt for woad.[380]

Robert Hochyns (fl.1460-1467) was appointed customer in 1460,[381] but he did not appear to hold the position for long. Described as 'of Bridgwater' in 1463, his alleged debts included money owed to a London tailor and doublet maker, as well as a Norfolk merchant.[382] In 1465, he was described as a merchant. He seems to have had a wide sphere of connections and debts in south-west England, Wales and Ireland. In Somerset he was owed money by a South Petherton 'scoser', an Ilchester baker and a Milverton tailor. There were also debts due from two Plymouth mercers, a gentleman of Swansea, as well as Wexford and Dublin merchants.[383] Hochyns is mentioned in 1467.[384]

Thomas Ingleby (or Engleby) (fl.1367-fl.1387) was granted licences to export cereals in 1374 and 1377. He served the borough as M.P. in 1368. He was a signatory of a Bridgwater town document in 1367, involved in Chantry affairs between 1370 and 1372 and the borough court during the late 1370s and into the 1380s. Ingleby may have been involved in customs matters; in 1380 he resorted to a higher authority when James Douding (probably of Minehead or Dunster) and John Barlabyn of Dunster did not render accounts to him.[385] However, he became infamous for helping to lead an insurrection in the town in 1381[386] but continued to be involved in town affairs until 1387.[387]

Gilbert Joce (or Joos) (fl.1406) was appointed collector of customs for the ports of Bridgwater, Dunster and Minehead in 1406,[388] having been nominated by Bristol merchants; he held this position for about a year. Joce was himself a Bristol merchant who had interests in one or more ships, including perhaps the *Welfare* of Bristol. He traded with Ireland and Spain at the end of the fourteenth and beginning of the fifteenth centuries, exporting cloth and importing wine. He served as M.P. for Bristol in 1406.[389] There does not appear to be any evidence of strong links with Bridgwater. There is a possibility that the *Welfare* of Minehead of the 1430s (See table 3.1) could have been Joce's ship as it certainly traded with Bristol.

John Kendale (or Kendall) (fl.1468-fl.1489) was one of Bridgwater's most prominent merchants of the late fifteenth century. He served as M.P. for the borough in 1467[390] and as Mayor of Bridgwater in 1472.[391] He was appointed deputy butler in 1478 and was collector of customs in 1481, 1484 and 1489.[392] Kendale had mercantile dealings locally with Henry Brenham of Combwich, mariner, and further afield in Dorset, Bristol, Gloucestershire and Southampton, as well as Bordeaux.[393] In addition he was allegedly owed money in 1468 by a skinner and a Combwich 'stainer'.[394] He was also indebted to a Devon man, Philip Ralegh, in 1486 and to Exeter and London mercers in 1489. In this latter year he was also a creditor of a Banwell dyer and a group of Huntspill husbandmen[395]

Hugh le Mary(e)s (fl.1324-fl.1376) was at Bridgwater in 1324 when a burgage by the River Parrett was conveyed to him. The location of the property may well have helped him organise his maritime affairs including his part in exporting corn in 1331 and 1372. He was very active in town affairs between 1327 and 1376 and represented the borough in parliament in 1372.[396] If all these comments relate to the same Hugh le Marys, he survived the Black Death.

Richard Mayne (fl.1413-fl.1440) served as collector of customs from 1413 to 1420 and as the town's M.P. in 1419. He was sometimes known as 'of Wiltshire' since he had many dealings in that county.[397] It was from Mayne that William Gascoigne obtained land at Exton in 1416. He was a lawyer and became an important associate of John Stafford, Bishop of Bath and Wells from 1425. He became M.P. for Wells in 1433 and chased debts from a Wells merchant and a Wells brass worker in 1440.[398]

John Michel (fl.1335-fl.1372) of Sydenham, who exported beans from Bridgwater in 1364 and 1365. He is mentioned in town affairs between 1367 and 1372.[399] Michel, with John Bythesea and others exported beans and peas in 1365. John Michel's father, William, made his will in 1336 and an inventory of his goods was taken in September of that year which showed he had 19 acres of beans growing, as well as six quarters of grain and other beans in store.[400] This was significant commercial farming by any measure, so it is likely that John's part in the exports of 1365 came from the same land whether he was managing it or not. Another co-exporter of the 1365 consignment was Walter Dodde, a Bridgwater merchant who gave up a property by the South Gate in that year. In the late 1360s and in early 1370 Michel had much to do with the administration of a chantry in the town.[401]

Roger Moore (fl.1439-d.1454) and John Salle were both appointed searchers in the port of Bridgwater in 1439.[402] Nothing is heard of the two in the town before their appointment. In 1441 Salle paid into the Bridgwater community account for a tenement and Moore is mentioned in the same document. Moore then became more involved in the workings of the borough's legal affairs, being associated with a conveyance in 1441, community income in 1443 and with community affairs in 1445. He served as reeve in 1453 a year before his death in 1454, and was buried inside the church so a note from 1455 records.[403]

Nicholas Neth (or Neeth) (fl.1379-d.1410) is one of the few Bridgwater merchants known to have owned a ship, a crayer called the *Nicholas*, in the very early fifteenth century.[404] He is perhaps first heard of in April 1379 when he was the principal merchant shipping pipes of honey into Bristol.[405] He was involved in at least two, and possible three incidents in the first decade of the fifteenth century when goods from captured ships were brought back to Bridgwater, including iron and oil. There were several inquiries as to whether these actions were legal. An inquiry in 1410 alleged that he and John Warde 'carried off and concealed' goods.[406] In 1409 he witnessed the signing of a Bridgwater lease.[407] In his will of 1410 he is referred to as burgess and merchant of Bridgwater, but sadly no hint of his mercantile activities is given in this document. He appointed his wife, Constance, to be his executrix to whom he left his tenements and lands in Bridgwater, as well as the residue of his estate.[408] In 1411 Constance transferred ownership of some of that property to Thomas Ermyte and Philip Clopton of Bridgwater.[409]

David le Palmer(e) (fl.1299-fl.1353) was licensed to export corn to Wales in 1331. He was active in borough affairs and was a signatory on numerous legal documents from 1299 and 1345.[410] It might have been the same David le Palmere, or perhaps his son, that had two tons of wine taken by Sir Thomas Fichet in 1353.[411] As with Hugh le Marys above, if all the comments refer to the same David le Palmer, he survived the Black Death.

Thomas Philip (fl.1475-*c.*1485) was appointed controller in 1473.[412] Whether he was related to the person of that name who lived in the borough in the 1450s is not known. It is likely, though not certain, that this Thomas Philip was the same man as 'Sir Thomas Philip' who was involved in mercantile and maritime affairs in Bridgwater in the early 1480s. He witnessed bonds relating to John Kendale, a well-known Bridgwater merchant and appears to have bought shares in John Hill's ships after Hill's death.[413] Philip was one of five Bridgwater merchants being pursued for a debt of £19 relating to wine imports by Rodrigo de Samodio at some time between 1475 and 1485.[414]

Robert Plumpton (fl.1320-d.bef.1378) was a significant exporter of cereals and pulses from Bridgwater during the 1360s and 1370s to Biscay and elsewhere in Britain. As a prominent Bridgwater citizen he witnessed a number of legal documents in the town from 1363 to 1374.[415] He represented the town in parliament in 1354, 1362 and 1366 but had died by 1378.[416] Unless he had a relative of the same name in the 1320s, he was also one of the provosts of the borough of Bridgwater. He had rights to five acres of arable land at Dunwear in 1373, so, like John Cole, he may have grown some of his own cereal exports.[417] This view is supported by a record from 1371 that he was licenced to sell 200 quarters of beans 'of his own growing' to agents of castles in the Welsh Marches, or Pembrokeshire.[418] Plumpton traded with other Bridgwater merchants and was owed the considerable sum of £80 by Adam Best. In 1391 John Henton still owed Plumpton's estate £60.[419]

John Pytt(e) (fl.1387-fl.1441) was made collector of customs in 1421; this appointment was renewed in 1433, 1437 and 1439. He was made controller in 1426 a position held for several years and was described as customer in 1439.[420] Customs and tunnage accounts of his remain for 1430 and customs accounts for 1438.[421] A John Pitt owned property in Bridgwater in 1387, who was probably John's father. John Pytt leased a cottage in Friarn Street in 1410, a garden in the town in 1423 and other property in 1428.[422] Pytt was bailiff of Bridgwater in 1410, constable in 1423 and steward of the merchant guild in 1431. He was elected M.P. for the town eight times between 1421 and 1435 and was responsible for the requisition of ships for the King in March 1436 and May 1439. In terms of business in 1413 and 1414 he was engaged in the export of various types of cloth. He accused a Bristol jeweller and a Bristol merchant of trespass and assault in 1418. He was described as a merchant in 1422, when, along with other Bridgwater merchants, he allegedly owed money to Eleanor May.[423] Pytt the collector was husband to Alice. His son, Richard, sold family property in St Mary's Street and elsewhere in the town in 1455.[424]

John Salle, see Roger Moore.

John Sopham (fl.1342-fl.1379) was granted an export licence with Le Mary(e)s in 1362. He may well have been a relation of Roger Sopham who left part of a ship to William Criche in 1361. John Sopham was active in borough affairs from 1342 to the 1370s. He had interests in wine imports as he was found to have used false wine measures in 1379.[425]

John Sprott(e) (fl.1466/7-d.bef.1472) was collector of customs at Bridgwater in 1466/7.[426] He does not appear to have held the position for long and in 1470 he was quitting property in the town including property on the quay.[427] In the same year he chased a debt from John Crosse a Dunster dyer, a Long Load merchant and the estate of a Taunton man.[428] Thus it seems that Sprott was a local merchant who possibly traded in woad amongst other goods. In 1472 his wife and executrix, Joan, was being chased for debt by a clerk and Thomas Baker of Langport.[429]

William Thomer (fl.1377-fl.1406) made 13 appearances in Parliament for Bridgwater from 1377 until 1406. In the summer of 1380, when portreeve of Bridgwater, Thomer took part in a night-time attack on the Hospital of St John the Baptist in the town, in which doors and windows of the church were broken down, and certain papal bulls relating to the appropriation of the vicarage were stolen. This was a prelude to the disturbances in the following year during the Peasants' Revolt, in which he was involved. Subsequently a crayer called *Le Cog John* and three lasts of Herrings worth £15, which he owned jointly with one John Bursy, were confiscated by the sheriff; Bursy is known to have taken part in the most violent of the local riots. The vessel and fish were returned to Thomer in March 1382/3. In 1381 Thomer took legal action against a former servant, William Betyvylle, regarding improper accounting.[430] In later years he became a substantial property owner, not only at Bridgwater, but also at Chedzoy, Langport, Weston Bampfylde and Gothelney in Charlinch. Thomer's position as Lieutenant to the Admiral of the West must also have considerably increased his influence in Bridgwater. In 1388 he heard the opening stages of the prolonged Guernsey-Henton dispute. He stood as pledge for John Kedwelly when the latter became embroiled in a dispute after acting as his deputy for the seizure of Henton's goods. Thomer's standing in the locality can be seen when, in 1392, stewards of the merchant guild sought his assent before leasing a tenement; he was a trustee for the rebuilding of the town bridge in 1395. Thomer was steward of Bridgwater's merchant guild in 1391 and 1402. Merchant, burgess, rabble rouser and justice, Thomer appeared as plaintiff or defendant in several cases of debt brought in the Borough and Admiralty courts, including an action in 1396 against him for an unpaid debt by a fellow Bridgwater citizen Richard Wely.[431]

Richard Trenode (fl.1414-fl.1440) was appointed searcher for the Somerset coast in 1414.[432] This gave him authority to search any ship, in person or through a deputy, entering or leaving the customs district of Bridgwater for uncocketed and uncustomed wool, skins and other goods. He returned accounts from 1414 to 1418.[433] There is no evidence of his activity in the port of Bridgwater in his capacity as searcher, or as a merchant in Bristol where he traded in cloth and salt in the 1420s. In 1416, Trenode's salt, shipped to Bristol, originated from Le Croissic, Brittany. In 1430, Trenode bought 50 casks of beans in Somerset and obtained a licence to ship them to Bayonne early the next year. He owned a vessel, the *George*, in which he transported 30 pilgrims to the shrine of St James of Compostella in 1434.[434] There is a possibility that the *George* had previously belonged to Richard Boyton (see above). In 1440, Minehead merchant Thomas Fyssher was indebted to Richard Trenode of Bristol, merchant.[435]

Richard Ward (fl. 1388-1414). From humble and discreditable beginnings as an innkeeper, who sold bread at short weight, unsealed wine, and was a persistent debtor, Ward rose to the highest office in Bridgwater. He was a frequent witness to local deeds from 1388 to 1414. In 1395 he served a term as bailiff but and represented the community in their financial manoeuvres concerning a new bridge. He was elected to Parliament in 1407. By 1414, at the end of his career, he had become a wealthy merchant by trading in cloth, foodstuffs and wine. He had occupied the stewardship of the merchant guild for more than a decade. In an Exchequer case, in 1401, Ward asked John Kedwelly and John Henton to stand surety for him. Presumably he was exonerated since his trading and public career blossomed. Ward's son is also known to have been formally exonerated in 1403. Ward junior was the owner of one of the vessels in the fleet commanded by John Hawley, of Dartmouth, and Thomas Norton, of Bristol, which seized foreign ships in the English Channel in 1403. Subsequent inquiries established that Ward's father had possession of 20 quintals of iron, perhaps at Bridgwater, from the cargoes taken in a naval action.[436] The 'men' of Bridgwater took back 13 tuns and one pipe of oil to the town from this action.[437]

References

1 J.F. and J.C. Lawrence, *A history of Bridgwater* (Chichester, 2008) chapter 7; R.W. Dunning (ed.), *Victoria County History of Somerset* 6 (1992), 213-23; W. Childs, *Anglo-Castilian trade in the later Middle Ages* (Manchester, 1978), 79; W. Childs, 'Ireland's trade with England in the later middle ages' in *Irish Economic and Social History* 9 (1982), 5-33; W. Childs, 'Irish merchants and seamen in Late Medieval England' in *Irish Historical Studies* 32 (2000), 22-43.

2 M. Kowaleski, *Local markets and regional trade in medieval Exeter* (Cambridge, 2003), 35-6; P. Lacey, *Ebb and flow: the story of maritime Lyme Regis* (Wimborne, 2011), 33-4; M. Hughes, 'The fourteenth century French raids in Hampshire and the Isle of Wight' in A. Curry *et al* (eds.), *Arms, armies and fortifications in the hundred years war* (Woodbridge, 1999), 121, 131. Anon, A selection of primary documents, in modern English translation, illustrating aspects of urban society, http://users.trytel.com/~tristan/towns/florilegium/government/gvdef14.html , accessed January 2015; this academic site uses parliamentary rolls and inquisitions as its sources. Sections used include 'Investigation of complaints from Lyme Regis, 1405', and 'Melcombe Regis, 1408'.

3 P. Ashford, 'Mercantile debt patterns in Somerset in the fifteenth century', in *P.S.A.N.H.S.* 159 (2016), 140-57.

4 J. Chapman (ed.), *C.I.M. 1399-1422* (London, 1966), 143.

5 R. Fowler (ed.), *C.P.R. Henry IV 1401-1405* (London, 1905), 439.

6 Fowler, *C.P.R. 1401-1405*, 439.

7 Fowler, *C.P.R. 1401-1405*, 296.

8 H. Maxwell Lyte, 'Dunster and its Lords' in *The Archaeological Journal* 38 (1881), 74.

9 Maxwell Lyte, *Dunster*, 72.

10 D. Bret, *The Yorkist kings and the Wars of the Roses; part 1 Edward IV* (London, 2013), 107; H. Evans, *Wales and the Wars of the Roses* (Cambridge, 1915), 140-1.

11 P. Fleming, *Time, space and power in later medieval Bristol* (2013), 213 found at http://eprints.uwe.ac.uk/22171/2/TimeSpacePowerFinalVersion%20%283%29.pdf accessed January 2015.

12 Obituary of Colonel Sir Walter Luttrell in *The Telegraph*, 5 June 2007.

13 J. Betty, 'The church in the landscape: From the Norman Conquest to the Reformation' in M. Aston (ed.), *Aspects of the Medieval landscape of Somerset* (Taunton, 1988), 64.

14 M. Williams, *The draining of the Somerset Levels* (Cambridge, 1970), 83.

15 Lacey, *Ebb and flow*, 48-9, 60.

16 Records of fourteenth and fifteenth century shipwrecks or ship wreckage along the Somerset coast are as follows: Dunster 1310 and 1380 (G. Handcock (ed.), *C.P.R. Edward II 1307-1313* (London, 1894), 311 and D. Richardson, *Plantagenet ancestry* (Utah, 2011), 432); Stogursey 1310 (Handcock, *C.P.R. 1307-1313*, 254); Uphill 1358 (R. Isaacson (ed.), *C.P.R. Edward III 1358-1361* (London, 1911), 75); Pill 1362 (W. Bird, *C.C.R. Edward III 1360-1364* (London, 1909), 344); near Bristol, possibly King Road 1375 (M. Davies (ed.), *C.P.R. Edward III 1374-1377* (London, 1916), 63-4); Brean *c.*1390 (P. Helm, 'The Somerset levels in the Middle Ages' in *Journal of the British Archaeological Association* 12 (1949), 46); Minehead 1417 (F. Hancock, *Minehead in the county of Somerset* (Taunton, 1903), 37); King Road 1484 (S. Seyer, *Memoirs historical and topographical of Bristol and its neighbourhood*, 2 (Bristol, 1823), 202).

17 F. Gasquet, *The Black Death of 1348 and 1349* (London, 1908), 195-6.

18 S. Pettitt, 'Somerset manorial document project update', May 2014 found at www1.somerset.gov.uk/archives/ accessed January 2015.

19 Gasquet, *Black Death*, 195; T. Dilks (ed.), *Bridgwater Borough archives 1200-1377,* S.R.S. 48 (1933), 102-20.

20 There were labour shortages in 1354 at Witham and in 1355 at Hinton (probably Charterhouse) in north-east Somerset. In the latter case local people ceased to make woollen cloth for the Carthusian brethren. Presumably there were not enough available people to spend time on the job that had been completed prior to the Black Death (Gasquet, *Black Death,* 198-9). Personnel shortage in Bridgwater may be indicated by a Devonian, Nicholas Lyver taking on a burgage plot in Bridgwater in late 1349 and the appearance, of John Combmartin in 1351, perhaps also from Devon (Dilks, *Bridgwater borough 1200-1377*, 110-14).

21 See the biographical section of this chapter and appendix

two.

22 M. James and E. Veale, *Studies in the medieval wine trade* (Oxford, 1971), 100-3.

23 R. Bush, *Somerset stories* (Wimborne, 1994), 17-8. D. Stevens, 'A Somerset coroner's roll 1315-1321' in *S.D.N.Q.* XXXI (1985), 460, 467, 470.

24 H. Maxwell-Lyte, *Calendar of inquisitions post mortem* 7 (London, 1909), 218.

25 *M.H.S.* 1, 46.

26 T.N.A., CP 40/541/f552 Muskham v Pypere, 1396.

27 M. Williams, 'A contribution to the commercial history of Glamorgan' in *The National Library of Wales Journal*, 9 (1956), 192.

28 C. Gathercole, 'Somerset urban archaeological surveys: Minehead', at www1.somerset.gov.uk/archives/hes/eus/minehead_eus.htm acessed January 2015 accessed January 2015.

29 M. Freeman-Archer, 'Minehead Harbour' in *S.A.N.H.S. Newsletter* 35 (1987), 5. However, in a report a few months later stating that a significant number of timber piles relating to the structure had been further investigated, doubt was cast on whether this was part of Minehead's medieval quay or a significant fish weir (M. Freeman-Archer, 'Minehead' *S.A.N.H.S. Newsletter* 36 (1987), 5).

30 S.H.C., DD\L/P26/7/2, P27/12/6 and P28/20/1, Luttrell papers, rentals and deeds, 1421, 1454 and 1492; C. Noble (ed.), *Calendar of inquisitions post mortem 6-10 Henry VI*, 23 (2004), 22. Quoting other Luttrell papers, court rolls, S.H.C. DD\L/P11/1, P28/13 and P29/9, Maryann Kowaleski states that the proliferation of sea weirs and boathouses in Minehead and Dunster during the fifteenth century, as well as the 'lively demand' for them when they came up for rent, indicates a growth in the inshore fishery at Minehead during the fifteenth century (M. Kowaleski, 'The expansion of the south-western fisheries in late medieval England' in *Economic History Review*, 53, (2000), 440-1).

31 S.H.C., DD\L/P17/1/75, Luttrell papers, lease, 1403; M. McIntosh, *Working women in English society 1300-1620* (Cambridge, 2005), 143.

32 Noble, *Inquisitions*, 22.

33 S.H.C., DD\L/P27/12/7, Luttrell papers, lease, 1456.

34 E. Odgers, 'A short report on some of the ms. accounts of the commonality of Bridgwater' SANHS Proceedings 23 (1878), 41-2. This source reveals that Bridgwater's crane was in action in 1397 and 1399. Its hemp sling, made in Taunton is mentioned, as are its pullies, its iron clamping and the porters who worked with it. Furthermore a plank-way which was used to draw wine barrels and stone from boats and pikards was also in use.

35 Dilks, *Bridgwater 1377-1399*, nos. 613, 641, 686, 703, 711, 718; Dilks, *Bridgwater 1445-1468*, nos. 728, 757, 768, 774, 785, 793, 824, 830, 850. Bridgwater's crane operation in the 1430s is significant since the firs reference to a crane at Bristol quays is 1475. (J. Macmillan, The port of Bristol in the second part of the eighteenth century 2 (University of Exeter Phd thesis 2015), 32). Dunning, *Bridgwater*, 193.

36 Dilks, *Bridgwater 1445-1468*, 87-8.

37 Dunning, *Bridgwater*, 193.

38 Bush, *Somerset stories*, 17-8; Stevens, 'Coroner's roll', 460, 467, 470.

39 F. Hancock, *Minehead in the county of Somerset* (Taunton, 1903), 37, 167.

40 Hancock, *Minehead*, 232-36; H. Maxwell Lyte, 'Dunster and its Lord's' in *The Archaeological Journal*, 38 (1881), 72; C. Woolgar *et al*, *Food in Medieval England* (Oxford, 2006), 121-2; M. Rubin, *The hollow crown: a history of Britain in the Middle Ages* (London, 2005), chapter 4. Not all fish consumed in west Somerset was sourced in Minehead and Porlock. The household at Dunster Castle sourced fish from the Exeter fish market in 1429 and as did the household at Porlock manor house in 1469 (H. Fox, *The evolution of the fishing village* (Oxford, 2001), 101).

41 T.N.A., *Resident aliens in the late middle ages*, www.englandsimmigrants.com/search using Minehead as the place of residence as a search term. Accessed March 2015.

42 P. Dryburgh and B. Smith (eds), *Handbook and select calendar of sources for Medieval Ireland* (London, 2005), 170. At least two other printed and reputable sources, one by Maxwell-Lyte, writing in the *Archaeological Journal* in 1880 state that this event took place in 1427, but Dryburgh quotes the original source as T.N.A., E 28/15/86 which relates to 1404.

43 N. O'brien, *Minehead fisherman at Carlingford in 1404* (2015) found at http://celtic2realms-medievalnews.blogspot.co.uk/2015/06/minehead-fishermen-at-carlingford-in.html accessed October 2015.

44 M. Kowaleski, "Alien' encounters in the maritime world of Medieval England' in *Medieval Encounters* 13 (2007), 116-9.

45 Hancock, *Minehead*, 237-8; T.N.A., REQ 2/4/399, Court of Requests pleading, late fifteenth century. A further incident regarding the capture of a Minehead fishmonger, Richard Chapman in 1482 and his imprisonment in Scotland is found in *M.H.S.* 2, 2.

46 S. Flavin and E. Jones (eds.), *Bristol's trade with Ireland and the continent 1503-1601*, B.R.S. 61 (2009), 4-100.

47 M. Kowaleski, 'Alien' encounters' 116-9; J. Black (ed.), *C.P.R. Henry VII* (1916), 2, 14; R. Dunning, *Bridgwater borough archives 1468-1485,* S.R.S. 70 (1971), 22.

48 T.N.A., E 179/169/92, m. 1, Somerset alien subsidy 1440, quoted in the T.N.A. website *Resident aliens in the late Middle Ages* at www.englandsimmigrants.com/person/58569 and person 58609 accessed March 2015.

49 T.N.A., CP 40/853 f507, Roper v Bayssher, 1475.

50 Dryburgh and Smith, *Handbook*, 285-7.

51 T.N.A., CP 40/888/f590, Roberdys v Hargate, 1484.

52 Dryburgh and Smith, *Handbook*, 281, 286, 290.

53 Kowaleski, 'The expansion', 437-8, 442. An Exchequer investigation into the lack of payment of salt customs in 1478 was found by Wendy Childs at T.N.A., E 122/253, divers ports' accounts, and brought to the notice of Kowaleski.

54 T.N.A., CP 40/629/d1721, Leonard v Nicholas, 1418, abbots were known by their first names. Leonard Lythenstoke was the Abbot of Cleeve in 1416 ('House of Cistercian monks: The abbey of Cleeve', in W. Page (ed.), *V.C.H. Somerset* 2 (London, 1911), 118). Given that Lythenstoke seems to have owned a ship in 1417 or 1418, it is not unlikely that he was the owner of the *Leonard* of Dunster in 1419, mentioned in this chapter, and possibly

the case in the court of Common Pleas caused the Abbot's vessel to be returned. Leonard 'Lytherenstoke', abbot of Cleeve also appeared to be in debt to two Devon men in 1418 (T.N.A., 40/629/d1543, Cole v Leonard and 40/629/d1612 Laurence v Leonard).

55 J. Chapman (ed.), *Calendar of Inquisitions Miscellaneous 1422-1485* (London, 2003), 101.

56 Chapman, *C.I.M. 1422-1485*, 162-3.

57 T.N.A., C 1/64/839, Chancery proceedings relating to the bailiff of Minehead, 1475-1485.

58 R. Fowler (ed.), *C.P.R. Edward IV, Edward V and Richard III* (London, 1901), 79.

59 *M.H.S.* 2, 2 and 9. John Thye's mercantile activity is indicated by dealings with Devon merchant William Clotworthy in 1477 (T.N.A., CP 40/861/ d945, Clotworthy v Tye and others, 1477).

60 J. Black, *C.P.R. Henry VI 1485-1494* (London, 1914), 172.

61 See *M.H.S. 2*, 2 for a fuller context of this event.

62 M. McIntosh, *Controlling misbehaviour in England 1300-1600* (Cambridge, 2002), 141.

63 M. Nathan, *The annals of West Coker* (Cambridge, 1957), 89-90.

64 M. Oppenheim, 'Maritime history', in W. Page (ed.), *V.C.H. Somerset* 2 (London, 1969), 248.

65 T.N.A, CP 40/466/f314, Carter v Riche, 1377; d746, Cartere v Hennsfeld, 1377; CP 40/483/f961 Cartere v Huwyssh and others, 1381; d924 Cartere v Legh, 1381.

66 M. Williams, 'A contribution to the commercial history of Glamorgan' in *The National Library of Wales Journal* 9 (1956), 192.

67 W. Bird (ed.), *C.C.R. Henry IV 1402-1405* (London, 1928), 453. Usser may have been Usher and Horton may have been Harton mentioned in the section relating to Owen Glendowr.

68 C. Woolgar, *The great household in late medieval England* (New York, 1999), 113.

69 Maxwell Lyte, *Dunster* 72, 79.

70 Maxwell Lyte, *Dunster* 72, 76.

71 Hancock, *Minehead,* 234-5; Maxwell Lyte, 'Dunster' part 2, 167; R. Fowler (ed.), *C.P.R. Henry V 1416-1422* (London, 1911), 358.

72 S.H.C., DD\L/P1/16/15, Luttrell papers, account of Philip Clopton, master of the *Leonard* of Dunster, 1417.

73 Maxwell Lyte, 'Dunster' part 2, 168.

74 S.H.C., DD\L P4/26/4 and P4/11/3, Luttrell papers, accounts. The references to slates and coal in 1426/1427 are courtesy of Mary Siraut via the Victoria County History project.

75 Maxwell-Lyte, 'Dunster' part 2, 175.

76 Stevens, *'Harbours'* 10-13.

77 T.N.A., CP 40/717/f618, Mersshfeld v Hygyns and CP 40/717/d1355, Trenode v Fyssher, both 1440.

78 T.N.A., E 122/19/10, Port of Bristol leger, 1473-1474.

79 Fowler, *C.P.R. Edward IV-Richard III*, 193.

80 E. Carus Wilson (ed.), *The overseas trade of Bristol in the later middle ages* (New York, 1967), 289.

81 Dryburgh and Smith, *Handbook*, 278-91. Hide decomposition is prevented through tanning. Untreated hides decompose through bacterial action but can be temporarily preserved through salting.

82 T. Reddaway and A. Ruddock (eds), 'The accounts of John Balsall, purser of the *Trinity* of Bristol' in *The Camden Miscellany* 23 (1969), 7, 15, 17, 24.

83 R.W. Dunning, *V.C.H. Somerset* 5 (1985), 143-171.

84 T.N.A., E 199/39/11, 47, Exchequer accounts relating to a Watchet fishery, 1385-1386.

85 H. Maxwell Lyte, 'Dunster and its Lord's' in *The Archaeological Journal*, 38 (1881), 72.

86 A. Hughes, *C.P.R. Henry VI 1429-1436* (London, 1907), 10, 15.

87 For details of the 1458 storm see S. Seyer, *Memoirs historical and topographical of Bristol and its neighbourhood* 2 (Bristol, 1823), 202.

88 J. Chapman (ed.), *Calendar of Inquisitions miscellaneous 1377-1388* (London, 1957), 78.

89 T.N.A., C 1/6/265. Chancery proceedings regarding the alleged destruction of Doniford Weir, 1406-1426.

90 J. Chapman (ed.), *Calendar of Inquisitions miscellaneous 1387-1393* (London, 1962), 198. It appears that John Melow of Dunster was a merchant. In 1389 he was indebted to people in Dunster and Barnstaple. (G. Morris, *C.P.R. Richard II* 3 (1900), 490).

91 Dunning, *V.C.H. Somerset* 6, 146-52 quoting Eton College, 61/RR/A/34.

92 www.medievalgenealogy.org.uk/fines/abstracts/CP_25_1_202_42.shtml acessed 19.5.14.

93 Dunning, *V.C.H. Somerset* 6, 146-52 quoting Eton College, 61/RR/A/34.

94 J. Harvey (ed.), *William Worcestre itineraries* (Oxford, 1969), 124. Webb has recently discussed this issue and has not found an alternative opinion from the Medieval period (A.J. Webb, *The Somerset coast c. 1350-1824*, S.R.S. 97 (2015), 31).

95 Dilks, *Bridgwater 1377-1399*, 242.

96 Institute of Historical Research, inquisitions, No. 121, www.history.ac.uk/cipm-18-part-ii accessed December 2014.

97 Chapman, *C.I.M. 1399-1422*, 259.

98 T. Hugo, *The history of Taunton Priory* (London, 1860), 48-50.

99 T.N.A., CP 40/483/f344, Michel v Ferror and others, 1381. The others included John Neth who might have been a relation of Nicholas Neth. Also in 1381, but at an unknown place, but likely to have been along the Parrett, Adam Kyneman accused Robert King of breaking a boat and submerging a cargo of coals (T.N.A., CP 40/483/f1003), and Thomas Carter accused Robert Legh of 'arresting a boat' (T.N.A., CP 40/483/d924).

100 www.historyofparliamentonline.org/volume/1386-1421/member/coullyng-robert and www.historyofparliamentonline.org/volume/1386-1421/member/cyscl-%28ayscll%29-robert both accessed February 2015.

101 J. Wright and R. Chelu, 'The Franciscan Friary and Civil War defences at Friarn Meadows, Bridgwater' in *P.S.A.N.H.S.* 151 (2008), 103.

102 Dunning, *Bridgwater*, 19.

103 Dunning, *V.C.H. Somerset* 6, quoting T.N.A., SC 6/968/17, 19-20, 22-4, 26, 28; SC 6/969/1, 5-7, 10, 12-13, 17-20, Bridgwater Castle reeve's accounts 1347-1414.

104 A. Hinds, *C.P.R. Edward III 1348-1350* (London, 1905), 180,

242.

105 Hinds, *C.P.R. 1348-1350*, 17, 113.

106 T.N.A., SC 8/156/7761. This document is undated, however, the National Archives give it a date *c.*1320. Whilst this may be correct, the date 1360 appears in the text as the document states that the matter occurred when Robert Plumpton was provost of Bridgwater. Table 3 shows that a Robert Plumpton exported grain from Bridgwater in the 1360s, hence the decision to use that date in the text.

107 Dilks, *Bridgwater 1377-1399*, xx-xxi.

108 A. Powell, *The ancient borough of Bridgwater* (Bridgwater, 1907), 190.

109 W. Bird (ed.), *C.C.R. Edward III 1369-1374* (London, 1911), 52.

110 T.N.A., SC 8/5/206, Ancient petition, 1321; C 241/103/117, Chancery certificate regarding a Bridgwater debt, 1332.

111 www.historyofparliamentonline.org/volume/1386-1421/member/cole-john-iii accessed Sept 2014. The reference to Cole's wheat and bean growing can be found in Gascon Rolls Online www.gasconrolls.org/en/. Research has shown that fourteenth-century wheat yields were about one quarter per acre; one quarter = 8 bushels. English agricultural output 1250-1850, can be found at www.basvanleeuwen.net/bestanden/agriclongrun1250to1850.pdf accessed Sept. 2014.

112 The Gascon Rolls project, www.gasconrolls.org/en/solrsearch/#q=blaunkpayn accessed Oct 2014.

113 Dilks, *Bridgwater 1200-1377*, xxxv. Another source, relating to the same event, states that in 1364 Godesland shipped 50 quarters of beans worth 4s (per quarter?) out of Bridgwater to Cork in his own ship on two occasions. The vessel which took 60 quarters of corn worth £20 from Bridgwater to Cork was a Waterford vessel. According to Godesland, Richard Dyere and a fellow bailiff did not arrest either of these vessels (H. Rodney (ed.), *Calendar of inquisitions miscellaneous* 3 (London, 1937), 206).

114 N. Rodger, *The safeguard of the sea* (London, 2004), 110.

115 W. Bird (ed.), *C.C.R. Henry IV 1399-1402* (London, 1927), 44, Bayonne vessel in Bridgwater loading beans and peas, 1400; www.gasconrolls.org/en/ 61/74, 61/88. The shipments in 1378 are referenced in J. Sherborne, *War politics and culture in fourteenth-century England* (London, 1994), 76. In 1381 there were discussions in Bridgwater regarding the ship of a Bayonne merchant, John Carsett (Dilks, *Bridgwater 1377-1399*, 130-1).

116 R. Isaacson (ed.), *Calendar Patent Rolls Edward III* 1364-1367 (London, 1912), 76-78.

117 S. Rose, *The wine trade in medieval Europe* (London, 2011), 68.

118 J. Black, *Calendar Patent Rolls Edward I 1301-1307* (London, 1898), 398.

119 W. Stevenson, *C.C.R. Edward II 1313-1318* (London, 1895), 565.

120 T.N.A., C 241/97/74; 99/25 and 100/50, Chancery certificates relating to Bridgwater mercantile debts, 1327-1329.

121 R. Isaacson (ed.), *Calendar Patent Rolls Edward III* 1350-1354 (London, 1907), 377.

122 Dilks, *Bridgwater 1200-1377*, 132. The vessel is referred to as of Donwych. Given that it belonged to Plumpton, this is a spelling error and the vessel actually was from Combwich. Adam Best had accounting dealings with a Salisbury man in 1381 (T.N.A., CP 40/483/f528, Butterlegh v Best, 1381).

123 R. Palmer, *English law in the age of the black death: 1348-1381* (North Carolina, 2001), 161.

124 www.gasconrolls.org/en/61/90.

125 Dilks, *Bridgwater 1377-1399*, 235.

126 Dilks, *Bridgwater 1377-1399*, 241-4; T. Dilks (ed.), *Bridgwater Borough archives 1400-1445*, S.R.S. 58 (1943), 5. Stone arrived at the quay in a boat in 1394 for town works (Dilks, *Bridgwater 1377-1399*, 234). It seems that in 1370, Coles sister, Juliana, was the wife of Blaunkpayn and that the couple lived in Ilchester opposite the church.(W. Baker, Ilchester almshouse deeds, 1200-1625 (Yeovil, 1866), 68.)

127 M. James and E. Veale, *Studies in the Medieval wine trade* (Oxford, 1971), 102-105.

128 Dilks, *Bridgwater 1200-1377*, 225.

129 D. Farmer, 'Millstones for medieval manors' in *Agricultural History Review* 40:2 (1992), 99, 106. On page 105 of this article there is a table of the prices of (Welsh) stones at Bridgwater from 1290-1410 along with prices of stones from other locations.

130 C. Gerrard, *Trade and settlement in medieval Somerset*, PhD thesis for the University of Bristol (1987), 185-6.

131 A. Erskine, *The accounts of the fabric of Exeter Cathedral Part 1*, Devon and Cornwall Record Society NS 24 (1981), 19-22.

132 Dilks, *Bridgwater 1377-1399*, 139.

133 Rodger, *Safeguard*, 110.

134 R. Marsden (ed.), *Select pleas in the Court of Admiralty*, First series (1892), 17, 166-72.

135 A. Hinds (ed.), *C.C.R. Edward III 1337-1339* (London, 1900), 323.

136 M. Hughes, 'The fourteenth century French raids in Hampshire and the Isle of Wight', in A. Curry, *et al* (eds), *Arms armies and fortifications in the hundred years war* (Woodbridge, 1991), 121, 131.

137 N. Gras, *The early English customs system* (London, 1918), 419-21, 429-30. Somerset exporters of about 20 cloths per year were Thomas de Babcary, Robert de Cheddar, John de Wrington and Walter de Taunton. It is clear that the customs officials were recording place of origin as a second name, probably for non-Bristol merchants, as the sphere of influence of the regional metropolis in Gloucestershire can also be traced through merchant second names too.

138 A. Hinds (ed.), *C.C.R. Edward III 1354-1360* (London, 1908), 431.

139 C. Dyer, *Everyday life in medieval England* (London, 2001), 172.

140 T.N.A., C 131/28/28; 241/150/146; 241/168/40; 241/168/55, Chancery Extents for debt and certificates, 1369-1381.

141 J. Munro, 'Medieval woollens: The struggle for markets' in D. Jenkins (ed.), *The Cambridge history of western textiles*, 1 (Cambridge, 2003), 273.

142 J. Chapman (ed.), *Calendar of inquisitions miscellaneous 1392-1399* (London, 1963), 71.

143 T.N.A., SC 8/216/10796, Ancient deed 1402; Chapman, *C.I.M. 1399-1422*, 95-6; Fowler, *C.P.R. Henry IV* 1, 520; F. Weaver (ed.), *Somerset medieval wills 1383-1500,* S.R.S. 16 (1901), 43-4; Dilks, *Bridgwater 1400-1445*, 26, 33-4.

[144] R. Fowler (ed.), *C.P.R. Henry IV 1408-1413* (London, 1909), 310. John Warde was a prominent Bridgwater in Bridgwater affairs around 1410 and was later termed a merchant (Dilks, *Bridgwater 1400-1445*, 171). Other possible Bridgwater people involved in the affair were Robert Skynner, Clement Busshon and Thomas Gwyn. Skynner and Gwyn are names that crop up in Bridgwater affairs in the early fifteenth century.

[145] W. Childs, *Anglo-Castilian trade in the later middle ages* (Manchester, 1978), 118.

[146] Weaver, *Wills 1383-1500*, 233.

[147] Dryburgh and Smith, *Handbook*, 291.

[148] Dilks, *Bridgwater 1400-1445*, 51.

[149] Dilks, *Bridgwater 1400-1445*, 104-5.

[150] Dilks, *Bridgwater 1445-1468*, 65.

[151] D. Farmer, 'Millstones for medieval manors' in *Agricultural History Review* 40:2 (1992), 99, 101.

[152] Dilks, *Bridgwater 1400-1445*, 50-2; Dilks, *Bridgwater 1445-1468*, 88.

[153] Dilks, *Bridgwater 1445-1468*, 4.

[154] Dryburgh and Smith, *Handbook*, 280, 284, 291.

[155] Dilks, *Bridgwater 1400-1445*, 16. In 1396 Somering owed a debt to Philip Bat(t), a person mentioned early in this chapter but not named in the published Bridgwater borough records, who had other debtors in the Crewkerne and Ilminster area. (T.N.A., CP 40/541/f293, Bat v Somering). No doubt Somering was purchasing goods to sell overseas.

[156] H. Ellis, *Original letters illustrative of English history* (London, 1827), 84.

[157] Dunning, *Bridgwater*, 24; Dilks, *Bridgwater 1377-1399*, xv-xvi; Dilks, *Bridgwater 1400-1445*, xi-xii. The most comprehensive analysis of John Kedwelly's career is to be found at K. Bevan, 'Clerks and scriveners: legal literacy and access to justice in late Medieval England', University of Exeter, 2013, D.Phil thesis, 226-9.

[158] Childs, *Anglo-Castilian trade*, 132.

[159] Carus Wilson, *Overseas trade*, 60-2.

[160] Fowler, *C.P.R. 1408-1413*, 201.

[161] Dilks, *Bridgwater 1445-1468*, xi-xii, 91. Further evidence of Founs's trade is the fact he was allegedly indebted to John Stone, a weaver/merchant from Taunton (T.N.A., CP 40/778/d1792, Stove v Founs or Founce).

[162] Dilks, *Bridgwater 1445-1468*, 128-9.

[163] B.L., Harl. MS. 433, tin traded in a Bridgwater vessel, 1480s. The Cupar or Cooper merchant family of Bridgwater seemed to have strong Cornish links in the late 1480s as the tin episode suggests. In 1480, Bridgwater merchant John Couper was owed money by two Cornish mariner/merchants including one from Fowey (T.N.A., CP 40/871/f831, Couper v Barbour and another, 1480).

[164] T.N.A., C 1/59/51 Chancery proceedings relating to John Pellycorn of Combwich and Samodio, 1475-1485. Samodio seem to have been an adversarial character, Between 1475 and 1485 he was persuing Bridgwater merchants William Poyle, Thomas Philips, Marurice Lee and Robert Cok for debts (T.N.A., C1/59/60).

[165] Fowler, *C.P.R. 1476-1485*, 365.

[166] Dunning, *Bridgwater*, 26.

[167] Weaver, *Wills 1383-1500*, 311.

[168] Dunning, *Bridgwater*, 26; S.H.C., D\B/bw/1431, 1432, Bridgwater borough water bailiffs' accounts, 1495 and 1505.

[169] T.N.A., www.englandsimmigrants.com/search searching Bridgwater as place of residence. Accessed March 2015.

[170] T.N.A., CP 40/861 indices.

[171] Ashford, 'Mercantile debt', 144-5.

[172] S.H.C., D\B\bw/197, Bridgwater borough legal papers, 1467; Dunning, *Bridgwater 1468-1485*, 30. John Kendale had trading links with Bordeaux merchants John de Bustomdan in 1474 and John de Cabay in 1477 from whom he may well have traded woad and wine for woollen goods (Dunning, *Bridgwater 1468-1485*, 17, 30).

[173] T.N.A., C 1/64/722, Chancery proceedings relating to the bailiffs of Bridgwater, 1475-1485.

[174] Weaver, *Wills 1383-1500*, 233, 247, 310.

[175] Dilks, *Bridgwater 1445-1468*, 2.

[176] Dilks, *Bridgwater 1445-1468*, 10, 53, 68, 82.

[177] S.H.C., D\B/bw/1985, Bridgwater borough water bailiffs' accounts, 1473.

[178] J. Black, *C.P.R. Henry VII 1485-1494* (London, 1914), 83.

[179] Dryburgh and Smith, *Handbook*, 279, 282-3.

[180] Dryburgh and Smith, *Handbook*, 284-5. An 'enduring' maritime link between Bridgwater and Wexford during the sixteenth century is noted by Taylor, *M.H.S.* 1, 4.

[181] Kowaleski, 'The expansion', 429-54; this reference is on page 438. The water bailiffs accounts quoted by Kowaleski are S.H.C. , D\B/bw/1985 and 1431, Bridgwater borough archives, water bailiff's accounts, 1473 and 1495.

[182] Childs, *Anglo-Castilian trade*, 99.

[183] Childs, *Anglo-Castilian trade*, 227.

[184] Dryburgh and Smith, *Handbook*, 279.

[185] D. Dawson, 'Bridgwater and pottery studies', 2013 found at www.bridgwaterarchaeology.org.uk/news/jubilee/dawson.pdf accessed May 2015.

[186] M. Aston and C. Gerrard, *Interpreting the English Village: Landscape and community at Shapwick* (Oxford, 2013), 62.

[187] J. Bell, curator of Glastonbury Abbey quoted in a BBC report 2011 found at www.bbc.co.uk/news/uk-england-somerset-13359242 accessed May 2015.

[188] J. Allen, M. Hughes and R. Tayler, 'Saxonorman pottery in Somerset: some recent research' in *P.S.A.N.H.S.* 154 (2011), 176.

[189] S. and J. Rendell, *Steep Holm pioneers* (Weston-super-Mare, 2003), 20-9. The Priory seems to have had most of its monks transferred off the island in 1260, though two were left and the Priory was rebuilt just before 1315, so the polychrome jug may well be fourteenth century. The sherds of the polychrome jug on display in Steep Holm museum, next to a photograph of Glastonbury's polychrome jug shows the two to be very similar.

[190] Aston and Gerrard, *Interpreting*, chapter 7; Bell, report 2011, found at www.bbc.co.uk/news/uk-england-somerset-13359242 accessed May 2015.

[191] J. Allen, 'Rediscovering Glastonbury Abbey excavations, 2011', found at www.glastonburyabbeysymposium.com/summary.php?&id=1016&rpn=summaries accessed May 2015.

[192] Dilks, *Bridgwater 1445-1468*, 74.

[193] Dryburgh and Smith, *Handbook*, 280, 285.

194 N. Gras, *The early English customs system* (London, 1918), 272, 419-21, 447.

195 Dilks, *Bridgwater 1400-1445*, xi-xii.

196 Dilks, *Bridgwater 1445-1468*, 37-8; Dunning, *Bridgwater borough archives 1468-1485*, 22.

197 Dryburgh and Smith, *Handbook*, 281, 284-5, 291.

198 O. Coleman (ed.), *The brokage book of Southampton 1443-44*, Southampton Record Series 4, 1 (1960); Clewer had affairs in Bridgwater in the 1440s (Dilks, *Bridgwater 1400-1445*, 119, 136).

199 T.N.A., E 122/19/1, Port of Bristol ledger, 1461-1462; Carus Wilson, *Overseas trade*, 213, 271; S.H.C., D\B\bw/191, Bridgwater borough archives, legal papers, 1482. It is not impossible that imported Welsh cloth was used for clothing for sailors or soldiers being recruited at the time for service against Lancastrians in Wales. Mariners were being recruited in Bridgwater in 1461 for action in Wales (D. Bret, *The Yorkist kings and the wars of the roses; part 1 Edward IV* (London, 2013), 107; H. Evans, *Wales and the Wars of the Roses* (Cambridge, 1915), 140-1).

200 Dunning, *Bridgwater*, 24.

201 A. Nocolini, *Commercio marittimo Genovese in Inghilterra nel medioioevo 1280-1495*(Genoa, 2007), 283. www.academia.edu/8769055/Commercio_marittimo_genovese_in_Inghilterra_nel_Medioevo_1280-1495, accessed December 2014.

202 Lawrence and Lawrence, *Bridgwater*, 59.

203 Peter Flemming has shown that Bristol's cloth exports shrank by over 80% after the loss of Gascony taking decades to develop other markets in Iberia (P. Fleming, *Time space and power in later Medieval Bristol*, 90, found at http://eprints.uwe.ac.uk/22171/2/TimeSpacePowerFinalVersion%20%283%29.pdf accessed January 2015).

204 R. Dunning, 'Bridgwater: Economic history' in *V.C.H. Somerset* 6 (1992), 213-23.

205 www.historyofparliamentonline.org/ accessed April 2015 under Robert Aysell, Robert Coullying and William Marchaunt of Taunton, John Blithe, Roger Chapman, Walter Doddesden, Walter Dyer, Richard Ferrour, Richard Groos, Thomas Hore, John Newmaster and Thomas Tanner of Wells.

206 T.N.A., C 1/204/55, 61. Chancery proceedings, 1493-1500 and 1500-1501.

207 W. Baildon (ed.), *Calendar of manuscripts for the Dean and Chapter of Wells 2* (London, 1914), 64-6.

208 J. Black (ed.), *C.P.R. Henry VI 1494-1509* (London, 1916), 502.

209 N. Gras, *The evolution of the English corn market from the twelfth to the eighteenth century* (Now York, 1915), 447; Black, *C.P.R. Henry VII 1485-1494*, 391.

210 Gras, *Evolution*, 283-86.

211 S.H.C., D\B/bw/1985, Bridgwater borough archives, water bailiff's accounts, 1473.

212 Dryburgh and Smith, *Handbook*, 279-85.

213 Dryburgh and Smith, *Handbook*, 279-85.

214 A. Cosgrove, *A new history of Ireland 2: Medieval Ireland 1169-1534* (Dublin, 2000), 503.

215 Allen, *et al*, 'Saxonorman', 167.

216 C. Mahoney, 'Pottery, ridge tile and ceramic water pipes' in T. James (ed.), *Excavations at Carmarthen Greyfriars 1983-1990* (1998), 17, 25, 28, 54.

217 Allen, *et al*, 'Saxonorman', 167, 173.

218 D. Dawson, 'Bridgwater and pottery studies' in *Bridgwater and district archaeological society, Jubilee* (Bridgwater, June 2013).

219 Wessex Archaeology, *Harold's house, Portskewett, Monmouthshire* (Salisbury, 2007) 20..

220 A. Forward, *The ceramic evidence for economic life and networks from twelfth to seventeenth century settlement sites in south Glamorganshire*, Phd thesis (Cardiff, 2013), 4, 8.

221 J. Allen, 'The medieval pottery found at Pigs paradise, Lundy in 2001', in *Annual reports of the Lundy Field Society*, 53 (2001), 136-40.

222 Anon, *Tresco Channel, Isles of Scilly, survey report* (2011), 27-39.

223 C. Mahoney, 'Pottery, ridge tile and ceramic water pipes' in T. James (ed.), *Excavations at Carmarthen Greyfriars 1983-1990* (1998), 21.

224 P. Stevens, *Four excavations in Kilkenny city, 1999-2001* (2000), 25.

225 Dilks, *Bridgwater 1400-1445*, 15.

226 S.H.C., D\B\bw/1009, Bridgwater borough apprenticeship indenture, 1424; Dilks, *Bridgwater 1400-1445*, 146. The full story of the conditions of the apprenticeship, whether it succeeded and the affairs of the Davey family has been recently researched by Niall O'Brein, an Irish historian of the medieval period. The findings are to be found at N. O'Brien, *Conditions of medieval apprenticeship in Bridgwater* (2014) (http://celtic2realms-medievalnews.blogspot.co.uk/2014/06/conditions-of-medieval-apprenticeship.html, accessed October 2014).

227 S.H.C., D\B\bw/1008, Bridgwater borough apprenticeship indenture, 1433.

228 Dryburgh and Smith , *Handbook,* 128. John Mey was a Bridgwater merchant in 1445 and constable in 1461 (Dilks, *Bridgwater 1445-1468*, I, 115).

229 T.N.A., www.englandsimmigrants.com using Somerset as place of residence and Irish as nationality.

230 S.H.C., D\B\bw/1985, Bridgwater borough water bailiffs' accounts, 1473.

231 W. Childs, 'Irish merchants and seamen in late medieval England' in *Irish Historical Studies* 32 (2000-1), 32.

232 *M.H.S.* 2, 2.

233 T.N.A., E 122/19/6; 19/7; 19/8; 176/27, Port of Bristol ledgers, 1469-1472.

234 Weaver, *Wills 1383-1500*, 313.

235 R. Fowler (ed.), *C.P.R. Henry IV 1405-1408* (London, 1907), 224. There does not appear to be any reference to Codeworth in the published records from the Bridgwater Borough archives but he is found six years later dealing with prisoners, Harfleur and trade on the south coast of England (Historical Manuscripts Commission, *The Manuscripts of the Corporations of Southampton and Kings Lynn: eleventh report, appendix; part III*(1887), 79).

236 Anon, *Rymer's Foedera* 9 (London, 1709), 164.

237 T.N.A., CP 40/629/d1341, Gardyner v Cley, 1418.

238 R. Fowler (ed.), *C.P.R. Henry V 1413-1416* (London, 1910), 370.

239 D. Gardiner, *A calendar of early chancery proceedings relating to west country shipping 1388-1493*, DCRS 21 (1976), 56-7. In

1442 Thomas Cradock of Bridgwater, merchant, along with Richard Cradock of Northam, (Barnstaple) merchant both were indebted to a Bristol merchant. (T.N.A., CP40/724/d1080, Court action in relation to debt, Burton v Cradock, 1442). No doubt the Cradocks were related. This helps explain why some of Thomas Cradock's alleged piratical activity took place in the Barnstaple area.

240 A. Bland (ed.), *C.P.R. Henry VI 1441-1446* (London, 1908), 247. The name of Colwell does not appear in the published Bridgwater Borough archives but in the 1440s Thomas Cradock lived in the town between the bridge and the church lending some credence to the claim of the Spaniard.

241 Dilks, *Bridgwater 1445-1468*, xii.

242 T.N.A. ,C 1/45/41, Chancery proceedings relating to the *Mighell* of Bridgwater, 1433-1443, or more likely 1467-1472.

243 *M.H.S.* 2, 2.

244 T.N.A. , C 1/135/131, Chancery proceedings relating to goods brought to Bridgwater, 1486-1515; T.N.A., E 326/5081, 5083, 5087, 3264, Exchequer ancient deeds, 1493-1499.

245 Dilks, *Bridgwater 1445-1468*, 44.

246 For illegal trade in 1347, see A. Hinds (ed.), *C.C.R. Edward III 1346-49* (London, 1905), 242; J. Edwards, 'The transport system of Medieval England and Wales' Ph.D. thesis (University of Salford, 1987), 323; S. Rippon, 'Waterways and water transport on reclaimed coastal marshland: The Somerset levels and beyond' in J. Blair, *Waterways and canal building in medieval England* (Oxford, 2007), 235. A modern map of the position of Rackley's wharfs is to be found at M. Richardson, *An archaeological assessment of Rackley* (Taunton, 2003), 14..

247 W. Greswell, *Chapters in the early history of Glastonbury Abbey* (Taunton, 1909), 9-10.

248 R. Palmer, *English law in the age of the Black Death 1348-1381* (North Carolina, 2001), 330.

249 The reference to Tanner using Rackley by 1388 is repeated tens of times on many types of sites on the internet, but I have been unable to track down the original documentary source. His biography is to be found at www.historyofparliamentonline.org/volume/1386-1421/member/tanner-thomas-1401 accessed April 2015.

250 T.N.A., CP 40/541/d36, Galeway v Haynes and another, 1396.

251 The data is extracted from the indices from the Court of Common Pleas found at http://aalt.law.uh.edu/Indices/CP40Indices/CP40_Indices.html , accessed June 2016, for 22 law terms spread between 1418 and 1498. The number of tanners, shoemakers and saddlers were recorded. Axbridge had 25, Taunton 14, Bridgwater 13, Milverton 10 and Wells only 6. Perhaps Axbridge was Somerset's most important leather processing town at the time.

252 S.H.C., DD\S\SBY/10, notification regarding Axbridge apprenticeship agreement, 1449.

253 T.N.A., E 122/19/10A; E 122/19/11, Port of Bristol legers, 1474-1476.

254 T.N.A., E 122/19/8, Port of Bristol leger, 1471-1472.

255 Dryburgh and Smith, *Handbook*, 282.

256 T.N.A., C 1/77/36, Chancery proceedings relating to Axbridge and Bristol merchants, 1485-1486.

257 Dryburgh and Smith, *Handbook*, 288-91.

258 Chapman, *C.I.M. 1399-1422*, 77.

259 G. Good *et al*, *Waterfront archaeology proceedings* (1991), 64; Powell, *Bridgwater*, 196-7.

260 Somerset Historic Environment Record number 32226 found at http://webapp1.somerset.gov.uk/her/query.asp searching under wharf and accessed January 2016; *M.H.S.* 2, 123.

261 T.N.A., C 241/117/436; 241/111/121; 241/169/34; 241/173/63, Chancery certificates relating to Bridgwater mercantile debts, 1339-1385. In 1338 Robert Cave owed £11 10s, in 1339 John de Cary owed £18, in 1380 Richard Warde owed a considerable £56 13s 4d and in 1385 John Kedwelly with Richard Ermyle owed £40 to Bristol merchants.

262 C. Gathercole, 'Somerset urban archaeological surveys (EUS)' at www.somersetheritage.org.uk/eus/bridgwater_eus.html, accessed June 2016.

263 T. Scrase, *Somerset towns: changing fortunes 800-1800* (Stroud, 2005), 64. These comments are based on the work of medieval historian M. Kowaleski. See also Kowaleski, *Local markets*, 268-9, 278.

264 W. Childs, 'The commercial shipping of south-western England in the later fifteenth century' in *The Mariner's Mirror* 83 (1997), 273, 289.

265 W. Childs, 'Irish merchants and seamen in Late Medieval England' in *Irish Historical Studies* 32 (2000-1), 22-43.

266 M. Kowaleski, 'Fishing and the fisheries in the middle ages: the western fisheries' in D.J. Starkey (ed.), *The commercial sea fisheries of England and Wales since 1300* (Barnsley, 2000), 28.

267 M. Duffy (ed.), *A new maritime history of Devon* 1 (London, 1992), 83.

268 Childs, 'Commercial shipping', 289.

269 The sphere of influence of Bristol, Bridgwater and Taunton merchants, amongst others, in fifteenth century Somerset is more fully explored and mapped in Ashford, 'Mercantile debt', 141, 144.

270 In 1390 when Somerset was the leading county in England for wool production, losing that position to Suffolk by 1470 when Somerset moved to second place. (J. Munro, 'Medieval woollens: the western European woollen industries and their struggle for international markets, *c.* 1000-1500' in D. Jenkins (ed.), *The Cambridge history of western textiles* 1 (Cambridge, 2003), 273).

271 Any unreferenced material relating to Richard Boyton in this biography is to be found at www.historyofparliamentonline.org/volume/1386-1421/member/boyton-richard-1422 accessed August 2014.

272 Dunning, *V.C.H. Somerset* 6, 92.

273 T.N.A., E 210/2614, Exchequer ancient deeds, 1419-1420.

274 M. Dawes (ed.), *C.F.R. Richard II 1391-1399* (London, 1929); P. Davies (ed.), *C.F.R. Henry IV 1399-1405* (London, 1931); P. Davies (ed.), *C.F.R. Henry IV 1405-1413* (London, 1933); P. Davies (ed.), *C.F.R. Henry IV 1413-1422* (London, 1934) using the indexes to identify Boyton's appointments.

275 Fowler, *C.P.R. Henry IV* 4 and Fowler, *Henry V* 2 using the indexes to find Boyton's appointments.

276 Fowler, *C.P.R. Henry IV* 4, 365.

277 Boyton's 'Nill account' for 1413-14 is to be found at T.N.A.,

E 122/25/3.

278 T.N.A., CP 40/677/f665, Boyton v Crook, 1430 and d/1328, Boyton v Cheddar, 1430.

279 Dilks, *Bridgwater 1400-1445*, 210, 213-4, 224-5, 236-7; Dilks, *Bridgwater 1445-1468*, 31, 35, 56.

280 www.historyofparliamentonline.org/volume/1386-1421/member/cave-thomas, accessed August 2014.

281 www.historyofparliamentonline.org/volume/1386-1421/constituencies/bridgwater , accessed August 2014.

282 T.N.A., WARD 2/57A/204/58, Bridgwater letter of attorney, 1420; WARD 2/57A/204/56, Bridgwater quitclaim, 1420.

283 T.N.A., CP 40/483/d387, Crich v Hardyng, 1381 and f499, Crich v Alfreton, 1381.

284 Dilks, *Bridgwater 1200-1377*, xxxiii, 95, 115-231; Dilks, *Bridgwater 1377-1399*, 2-232; G. Morris (ed.), *C.P.R. Richard II 1392-1396* (London, 1905), 340.

285 The surname is not present on the document.

286 Weaver, *Wills 1383-1500*, 194-5; T. Holmes, *The register of Bishop Stafford 1425-1443*, S.R.S. 32 (1916), 270; Dilks, *Bridgwater 1400-1445*, 125, 129, 137, 146, 150; Dilks, *Bridgwater 1445-1468*, 27-8, 41, 60-1, 91, 97, 105, 110; T.N.A., CP 40/758/f168, Davy v Brydde and others, 1450; T.N.A., CP 40/814/d1099, Davy v Lymbery and others, Davy v Smalle and others, CP 40/814/f168, Davy v Brydde and others, all 1465; S.H.C., A\CGS/38 bond for 100 marks, 1451; D\B/bw/838 Bridgwater borough archives, safe conduct papers, 1455; D\B\bw/1775 Bridgwater borough archives, constables, 1436; DD\bw/1/47 and 1/48 Pym manuscripts, leases, 1447 and 1452. See also N. O'Brien, *Conditions of medieval apprenticeship in Bridgwater* (http://celtic2realms-medievalnews.blogspot.co.uk/2014/06/conditions-of-medieval-apprenticeship.html, accessed October 2014).

287 T.N.A., E 122/26/14, Bridgwater customs account prepared by John Stone, 1486-1488.

288 T.N.A., CP 40/807/d1171, Braddon v Fitzjames, 1463 and CP 40/826/f76, ate Wyll v Fitzjames, 1468.

289 Dilks, *Bridgwater 1445-1468*, 107, 134.

290 T.N.A., CP 40/814/f726, Fitzjames v Dodyng, 1465 and f649, Fitzjames v Faux and Bevyll, 1465.

291 www.historyofparliamentonline.org/volume/1386-1421/member/fitzjames-james-1423, accessed August 2014. This article points out that James Fitzjames M.P. for Bridgwater in 1467 should not be confused with a namesake, dead by 1423, who was the town's M.P. in 1421. By the same token it should not be assumed that he was the same James Fitzjames who was controller of customs in Bridgwater in 1446, though it is not impossible. (A. Bland (ed.), *C.P.R. Henry VI 1446-1452* (London, 1909), 19).

292 Davies, *C.F.R. 1399-1405*, 132.

293 S.H.C., D\B\bw/114 Bridgwater borough archives, general pardon, 1402.

294 S.H.C., D\B\bw/1416, 679, 664 and 514, Bridgwater borough archives, deeds, 1405-1417.

295 T.N.A., CP 40/629/d1042, Gascoigne v Brouning and others, 1418 and f311, Gascoigne v Pareys and others.

296 http://www.historyofparliamentonline.org/volume/1386-1421/member/gascoigne-william-1423, accessed August 2014. All the substantial matters relating to Gascoigne derive from this source except those with separate references.

297 www.historyofparliamentonline.org/volume/1386-1421/member/gascoigne-william-1423, accessed August 2014.

298 S.H.C., D\B\bw/989, Bridgwater borough archives, deed, 1423.

299 P. Davies (ed.), *C.F.R. Henry VI 1430-1437* (London, 1936), 168, 169, 329; P. Davies (ed.), *C.F.R. 1437-1445* (London, 1937), 168; A. Hughes and A. Bland (eds), *C.P.R. Henry VI 1436-1441* (London, 1907), 313.

300 R. Fowler (ed.), *C.P.R. Edward IV 1461-1467* (London, 1897), 55.

301 T.N.A., E 122 25/40, Bridgwater customs accounts prepared by Gosse and Pytte, 1438-1439.

302 S.H.C., D\B\bw/902 and 1391, Bridgwater borough archives, deeds, both 1438.

303 Holmes, *The register of Bishop Stafford 1425-43*, S.R.S. 32, 270.

304 T.N.A., CP40/732/d435, Gosse v Lose, 1444; f917, Gosse v William and others, 1444.

305 P. Davies (ed.), *C.F.R. Henry VI 1452-1461* (London, 1939), 27.

306 T.N.A., CP40/768/d1114, Portman v Gosse, 1453.

307 Davies, *C.F.R. 1413-1422*, 291, 349 and accounts for his three years at T.N.A., E 122 25/14, 15 and 18, 1419-1422.

308 R. Fowler (ed.), *C.P.R. Henry IV 1399-1401*(London, 1903), 520.

309 S.H.C., D\B\bw/114 Bridgwater borough archives, general pardon, 1402.

310 http://www.historyofparliamentonline.org/volume/1386-1421/member/gosse-william , accessed August 2014. Gosse witnessed a quitclaim in Bridgwater in 1407 and some of his property was in Friarn Street (S.H.C., A\ATR\7, D\B\bw/664, 1026 and 985, Bridgwater borough archives, deeds, 1414 and 1424).

311 T.N.A., CP 40/758/d1067, Gunne v Portman, 1450.

312 Fowler, *C.P.R. Edward IV 1461-1467*, 55.

313 Davies, *C.F.R. 1413-1422*, 380-1 and Fowler, *C.P.R. 1416-1428*, 378. His accounts are at T.N.A., E 122 25/19 and 22, 1421-1423.

314 J. Roskell, T*he Commons in the parliament of 1422* (Manchester University press, 1954), 186.

315 T.N.A., WARD 2/57A/204/58, Bridgwater letter of attorney, 1420.

316 Bath and North-East Somerset Record Office, BC 151/2/95, release, 1424.

317 S.H.C., D\B\bw/755, 972, 901 and 1396, Bridgwater borough archives, deeds, 1423-1429.

318 T.N.A., WARD 2/57A/204/68, Bridgwater grant, 1419; WARD 2/57A/204/40, Bridgwater quitclaim, 1433.

319 T.N.A., CP 40/647/d830, Gunne v Plomer and others, 1422.

320 T.N.A., CP 40/717/f821, Gunne v Adam and others, 1440.

321 S.H.C., D\B\bw/389, 290, Bridgwater borough archives, deeds, 1464 and 1480.

322 Dunning, *Bridgwater 1465-1485*, 2, 7, 10, 11, 16, 23, 38, 40, 42, 44, 55, 68.

323 http://bridgwaterlife.co.uk/Mayors/Mayors%20of%201400.htm, accessed August 2014.

324 T.N.A., CP 40/853/d950, Hamelyn v Tysdale and others,

1475 and f570, Palmer v Cosyn (mayor of Bridgwater) and Hamelyn, 1475.

325 Dryburgh and Smith, *Handbook*, 279.

326 Hamelyn's will of 1493 is found at T.N.A., PROB 11/9/396 but is translated and printed in Powell, *Bridgwater*, 68-9. Hamelyn's alleged debt patterns are found in T.N.A., CP 40/888/d699, Hamelyn v Robyns and f323, Lancokes v Hamelyn, both 1484, and CP 40/895/d968, Mudeford v Hamelyn, 1486.

327 S.H.C., D\B\bw/1386, Bridgwater borough archives, deed, 1490; Feets of fines CP 25/1/202/42 no. 16 found at www.medievalgenealogy.org.uk/fines/abstracts/CP_25_1_202_42.shtml, accessed August 2014.

328 T.N.A., CP 40/951/d824, Bartlot v Hamelyn, 1500. There is one concern regarding this biography of Hamelyn. Different sources giving at least three names for Hamelyn's wife(s). Only further research can identify whether there were two Adam Hamelyns in Bridgwater during the same period and/or the sequence of any remarriages.

329 T.N.A., E 122/26/15 and 16, Bridgwater customs accounts prepared by Hamelyn and Hardying, 1489-1491.

330 J. Black (ed.), *C.P.R. Henry VI 1494-1509* (London, 1916) 54.

331 F. Weaver, 'Cleve Abbey' in *P.S.A.N.H.S.* 52 (1906), 35-8.

332 T.N.A., E 122/26/15, 16, Bridgwater customs accounts prepared by Hamelyn and Hardying, 1489-1491.

333 S.H.C., DD\AH/65/6/18, Huntspill deed, 1487.

334 Hughes and Bland *C.P.R. Henry VI 1436-1441*, 62.

335 Davies, *C.F.R. 1413-1422*, 13, 14, 192, 242, 251.

336 T.N.A., E 122/25/5, 8, 13, 14, Bridgwater customs accounts prepared by Mayne, 1416-1420.

337 S.H.C., DD\BW/1/20, grant of property, 1409.

338 Dilks, *Bridgwater 1400-1445*, 54.

339 T.N.A., CP 40/629/f667, Hastyng v Ponteys and Hastyng v Webbe, 1418; CP 40/647/f251, Hastyng v Colvyle, 1422; CP 40/717/d1361, Hastynges v Kyngston, 1440.

340 E. Green (ed.), *Pedes finium*, S.R.S. 22 (1906), 19, 64, 175.

341 Powell, *Bridgwater*, 67.

342 Dilks, *Bridgwater 1400-1445*, 89.

343 T.N.A., C 241/170/10, Chancery certificate relating to Bridgwater mercantile debt, 1383.

344 W. Bird (ed.), *C.C.R. Richard II 1381-1385* (London, 1919), 108, 396.

345 D. Quinn, 'Guide to English financial records for Irish history 1461-1558' in *Analecta Hibernica* 10 (1941), 61-2. (Extracted from T.N.A., E404/82); T.N.A., C 241/179/1, 36, Chancery certificates relating to Bridgwater mercantile debts, 1391.

346 T.N.A., CP 40/483/d904, Taillour v Henton, 1381.

347 T.N.A., CP 40/541/d308, Mortymer and Ford v Henton, 1396; CP 40/629/f311, Gascoigne v Henton, 1418.

348 Davies, *C.F.R. 1452-1461*, 148-9.

349 Dilks, *Bridgwater 1400-1445*, 76-7, 86, 119, 123; Dilks, *Bridgwater 1445-1468*, 5, 63.

350 Dilks, *Bridgwater 1445-1468*, 1, 8, 80-1.

351 Dilks, *Bridgwater 1445-1468*, 37, xi.

352 Dilks, *Bridgwater 1445-1468*, 76, 107, 114, xii.

353 It is assumed that these were not the outstanding debts of his father (T.N.A., CP 40/807/38, Laurence, Clowdesham, Troubrigge and Walshawe v Hill, 1463).

354 T.N.A., E 122/26/2, Bridgwater customs accounts prepared by Kendale and Hill, 1470-1471.

355 Dunning, *Bridgwater 1468-1485*, 11.

356 Dunning, *Bridgwater 1468-1485*, 20-1.

357 Dunning, *Bridgwater 1468-1485*, 40-1.

358 Dunning, *Bridgwater 1468-1485*, 28, 33-4.

359 Dunning, *Bridgwater 1468-1485*, 34 and "Bridgwater online" http://bridgwaterlife.co.uk/Mayors/Mayors%20of%201400.htm accessed 11.5.2014.

360 T.N.A., PROB 11/7/57 will of John Hill, 1481. An English translation is to be found in Powell, *Bridgwater*, 70.

361 Dunning, *Bridgwater 1468-1485*, 49-50.

362 Dunning, *Bridgwater 1468-1485*, 43.

363 Dryburgh and Smith, *Handbook*, 282-3.

364 T.N.A., CP 40/883/186f, ? v Hill, 1483.

365 T.N.A., PROB 11/7/267. Will of Thomasina Hill, 1485. A. Powell, *Bridgwater*, 70-1 has an English translation of the will.

366 T.N.A., CP 40/911/638d, Hill v Brown, 1490.

367 Davies, *C.F.R. 1452-1461*, 254-7.

368 T.N.A., CP 40/807/d878m Ryghtwyse v Hochyns, 1463 and CP 40/807/f755, Belham v Hochyns, 1463.

369 D.Quinn and A. Ruddock, *The port book of the reign of Edward IV* (1) Southampton Record Society 37 (1937), 63; T.N.A., CP 40/814/d1169 Hochyns v Savage and others, 1465 and CP 40/814/f904, Hochyns v Burnard and others, 1465.

370 Dilks, *Bridgwater 1445-1468*, 136.

371 G. Morris (ed.), *C.P.R. Richard II 1377-1381* (London, 1895), 431.

372 Dilks, *Bridgwater 1377-1399*, xxi.

373 Dilks, *Bridgwater 1200-1377*, xxxiii, 157-225; Dilks, *Bridgwater 1377-1399*, 14-195.

374 Davies, *C.F.R. Henry IV 1405-1413*, 31.

375 www.historyofparliamentonline.org/volume/1386-1421/member/joce-gilbert-1423, accessed August 2014.

376 http://en.wikipedia.org/wiki/Bridgwater_%28UK_Parliament_constituency%29#Bridgwater_borough.2C_1295-1870, accessed December 2014.

377 R. Fowler, *C.P.R. Edward IV and Henry VI* (London, 1900), 356.

378 Fowler, *C.P.R. Edward IV-Richard III*, 61; T.N.A., E 122/26/4, 12 and 16, Letters patent appointing Fitzjames as a Bridgwater customs official, 1464-1465, and Bridgwater customs accounts prepared by Kendale and Hamelyn, 1484-1485 and 1489-1491.

379 Ashford, 'Mercantile debt', 152-3.

380 T.N.A., CP 40/826/f67, Kendale v Croppe and Peyntour, 1468.

381 T.N.A., CP 40/895/d852, Ralegh v Kendale, 1486; CP 40/907/d1350, Bonde v Kendale, f760, Shore v Kendale, f109, Kendale v Kene and f760 Kendale v Bunce and others, all 1489.

382 Dilks, *Bridgwater 1200-1377*, xxxiii, 73-230.

383 www.historyofparliamentonline.org/volume/1386-1421/member/mayne-richard-ii, accessed August 2014. Appointments of collectors are printed in Davies, *C.F.R. 1413-1422*, 11, 13, 14, 192, 291, 294. Customs accounts prepared by Mayne between 1413 and 1421 remain at T.N.A., E 122/25/1, 5, 8, 13, 15.

384 T.N.A. CP 40/717/f311, Mayne v Horwode and Selwode, 1440.

385 Dilks, *Bridgwater 1200-1377*, 157, 172, 198.

386 Dilks, *Bridgwater 1200-1377*, 105-79, Father's inventory 89. William Bythesea's land was in Cannington where he purchased a messuage and 40 acres in 1310 (E. Green (ed.), *Feet of Fines 1307-1346*, S.R.S. 12 (1898), 19).

387 Dilks, *Bridgwater 1200-1377*, 173, 179, 189, 200.

388 Davies, *C.F.R. 1437-1445*, 58.

389 Dilks, *Bridgwater 1400-1445*, 129-152; Dilks, *Bridgwater 1445-1468*, 1-84, Moore's death is alluded to on 72, 84.

390 Chapman, *C.I.M. 1399-1422*, 141.

391 Carus-Wilson, *overseas trade*, 188.

392 Fowler, *C.P.R. 1408-1413*, 310.

393 T.N.A., WARD 2/57A/204/75, Bridgwater lease, 1409.

394 T.N.A., PROB 11/2A/332. Will of Nicholas Neth of Bridgwater, 1410. Also published in Weaver, *Wills 1383-1500*, 43-4.

395 S.H.C., DD\Bw/1/21, legal instrument delivering properties, 1411.

396 Dilks, *Bridgwater 1200-1377*, 35-102; T.N.A., WARD 2/57A/204/54, Bridgwater grant, 1345.

397 Isaacson, *C.P.R. 1350-1354*, 377.

398 T.N.A., E 122/26/5, Customs account prepared by Kendale, 1472-1473.

399 Dunning, *Bridgwater 1468-1485*, 49-51.

400 T.N.A., C 1/59/60, Chancery proceedings relating to Bridgwater merchants, 1475-1485; W. Childs, *Anglo-Castilian trade in the later middle ages* (Manchester, 1978), 191-3.

401 T.N.A., WARD 2/57 A/204/11, 34, 52, 76, 78, 82, Bridgwater grants and a lease, 1363-1373.

402 Dilks, *Bridgwater 1200-1377*, xxiii; Dilks, *Bridgwater 1377-1399*, 9.

403 Powell, *Bridgwater*, 124.

404 R. Isaacson (ed.), *C.P.R. Edward III 1370-1374* (London, 1914), 49.

405 T.N.A., C 241/158/38; 241/179/1 and 36, Chancery certificates relating to debts, 1376 and 1391.

406 www.historyofparliamentonline.org/volume/1386-1421/member/pitt-john accessed August 2014. Much of the information on John Pitt derives from this source but information on his customs appointments are found at Davies, *C.F.R. 1413-1422*, 380-83; P. Davies (ed.), *C.F.R. Henry VI 1422-1430* (London, 1935), 73; Davies, *C.F.R. 1430-1437*, 168-9, 171, 184, 329; Hughes and Bland, *C.P.R. 1436-1441*, 247, 313.

407 T.N.A., E 122/25/37, 38, 40, Bridgwater customs accounts prepared by Pitte, 1430-1439.

408 S.H.C., D\B\bw/672, 90 and 1397, Bridgwater borough archives, deeds, 1410-1428.

409 T.N.A., CP 40/629/f665, Pytte v Kyngesbury and Sall, 1418; CP 40/647/d679, May v Pyt, 1422.

410 West Glamorgan Archive Service, RISW GGF 1/118.

411 Dilks, *Bridgwater 1200-1377*, 95-210; Dilks, *Bridgwater 1377-1399*, 52.

412 T.N.A., E 122/28/9, Bridgwater customs accounts prepared by Sprott, 1466-1477.

413 Dunning, *Bridgwater 1468-1485*, 4.

414 T.N.A., CP 40/837/d501, Sprot v Crosse and others, 1470.

415 T.N.A., CP 40/841/f710, Gunthorp v Sprot, d1075, Baker v Sprot, both 1472.

416 T.N.A., CP 40/483/f517, Tomere v Betevylle, 1381.

417 www.historyofparliamentonline.org/volume/1386-1421/member/thomer-%28tomere%29-william and T.N.A., CP 40/541/f828, Wely v Thomer, 1396; Many references to Wely are found in Dilks, *Bridgwater 1377-1399*. Thomer was witness to many Bridgwater legal agreements between 1390 and 1404 (T.N.A., WARD 2/57A/204/2, 5, 8, 14, 71, 88, 90, 92, Bridgwater grants, quitclaims and an enfeoffment, 1385-1405. In 1407, a quitclaim (S.H.C., A\ATR/7).

418 Davies, *C.F.R. 1413-1422*, 78.

419 T.N.A., E 122/182/9 and 14, Customs accounts for Somerset coast prepared by Trenode, 1414-1418.

420 www.historyofparliamentonline.org/volume/1386-1421/member/trenode-richard-1442 accessed August 2014; Chapman, *C.I.M. 1399-1422*, 303-4.

421 T.N.A., CP 40/717/d1355, Trenode v Fyssher, 1440.

422 www.historyofparliamentonline.org/volume/1386-1421/member/ward-richard accessed February 2015.

423 Chapman, *C.I.M. 1399-1422*, 141.

Chapter Four

Chasing Wrecks Around the Beach: Detective Work on an Early Nineteenth-century Wreck Site at Minehead

Serena Cant

Introduction

FOR ALL OF ITS historic maritime importance, the English Bristol Channel coastline is sparsely populated with documented wreck events and known wreck sites, so that its wreck heritage is relatively poorly understood compared with the rest of England.[1] The violent winter storms of early 2014 provided an opportunity to redress the balance in scouring sand from the beach to expose three near-

Illustration 4.1: Distribution map of all recorded shipping losses around the coast of England, showing a clear under-representation in certain areas, such as the Bristol Channel. (© Crown Copyright and database right 2017. All rights reserved. Ordnance Survey Licence number 100024900)

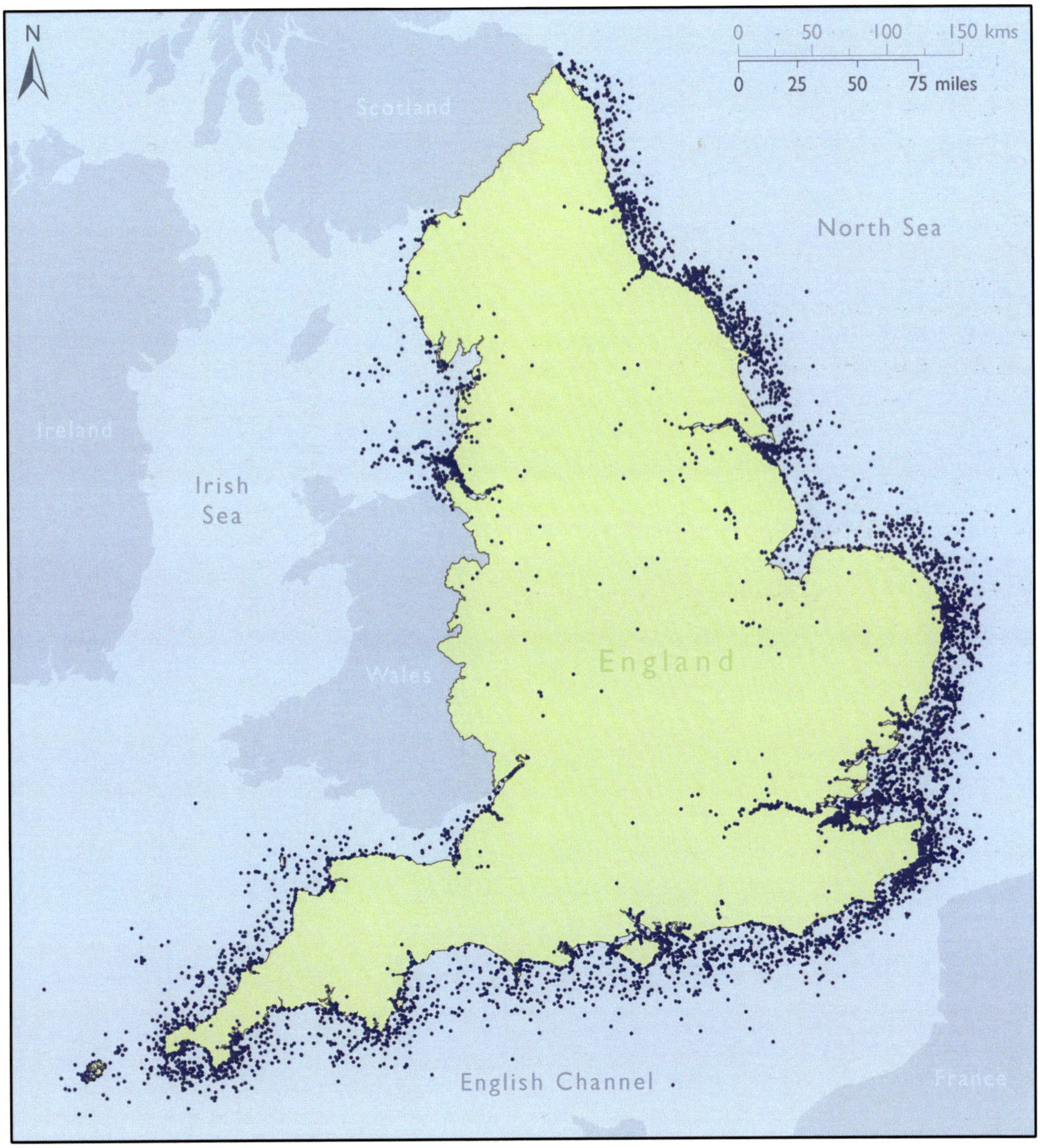

contemporary wrecks, one at Minehead and two at Northam Burrows in north Devon. All three wrecks have been seen from time to time before being re-covered, but sand erosion from all three in 2014 was sufficiently severe to ensure their continued exposure into 2016.[2]

A member of the public reported the Minehead find to English Heritage (now Historic England) with photographs showing the outline of a vessel with thick, sturdy timbers.[3] This appearance was entirely consistent with the sighting of a wreck in 1975 as a vessel outline with 'timbers, some 10in thick', before disappearing again.[4]

The 1975 site was, however, charted on the Strand at Minehead a quarter of a mile north-west of the 2014 site, and was attributed to the *Lamb*, driven ashore at Minehead Strand on 21 February 1735/6, while bound from Bristol with troops for Ireland.[5] Over 60 lives were lost. This attribution was, in part, based on the proximity of the charted location to the former Lamb Corner, said to have been named after the wreck, demolished in the early twentieth century redevelopment of Minehead.[6] Could the 2014 position, east of the 1975 sighting,

Illustration 4.2: The wreck at Minehead as seen in July 2015, looking to the seaward. The exposure of a single side suggests that the vessel is canted at an angle, probably as a result of the original wreck event: driven in on her beam ends or collapsing after going ashore. (© Copyright Historic England)

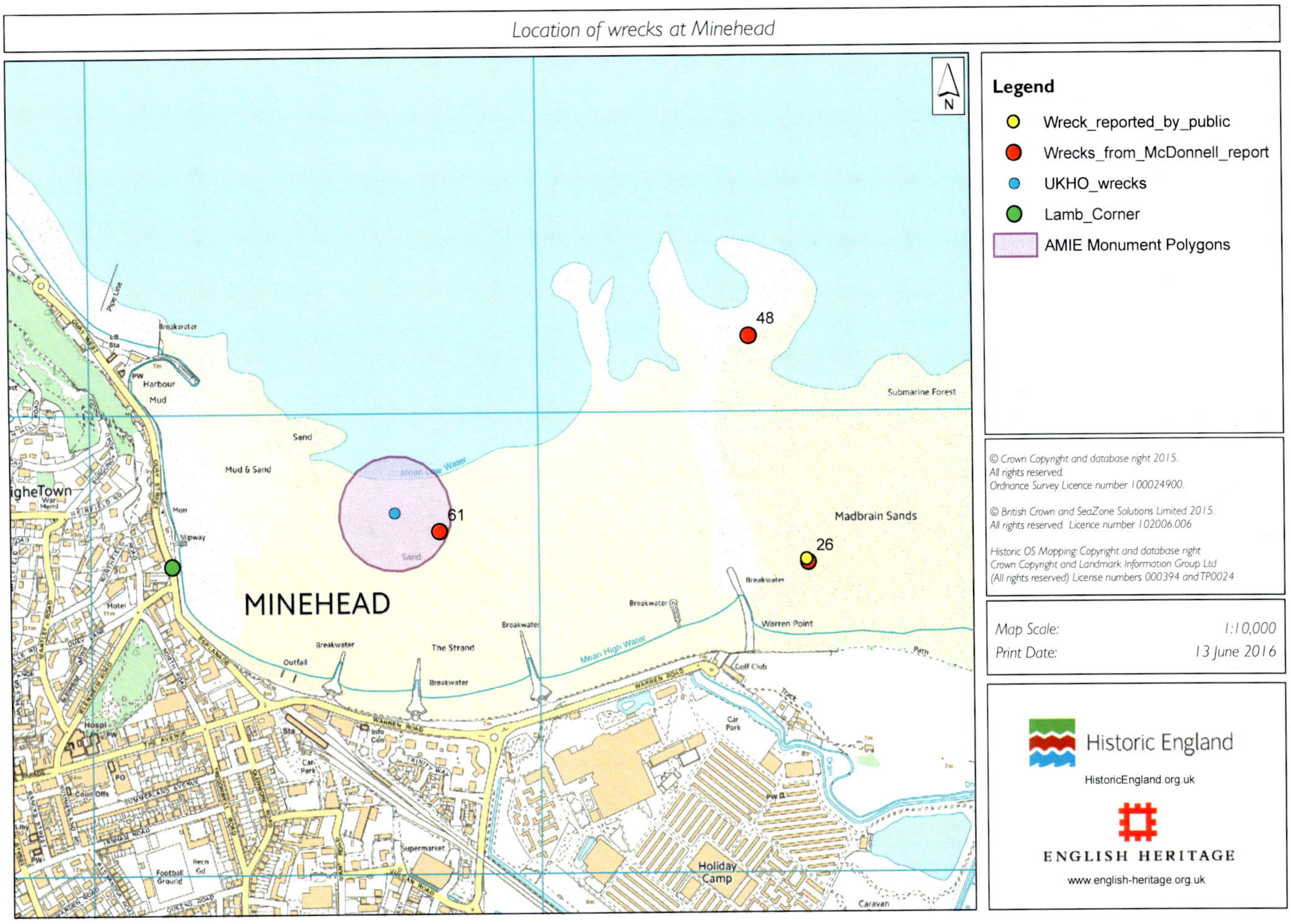

Illustration 4.3: Location map of the wreck at Minehead, showing the 1975 and 2014 positions and material seen in 2001 (© Copyright Historic England)

be confirmed as one and the same wreck site? If so, was it indeed the *Lamb*?

On both occasions, in 1975 and in 2014, the same conditions, namely winter storms, exposed a single wreck on Minehead beach. The 1975 sighting was charted in a position nearer to the mean low water mark and thus more exposed to the sea than the 2014 location higher up the beach. Given the level of sand erosion, it would have been reasonable to expect that exposure in this relatively sheltered location would also have been matched by any further exposures nearer to the water's edge, *i.e.* in the 1975 position.[7]

However, local enquiries in 2014 elicited that no vessel remains were seen in the 1975 position, confirmed on two subsequent visits by Historic England in 2015.[8] In turn this suggested some substance to the doubt expressed by the United Kingdom Hydrographic Office (U.K.H.O.) in charting the wreck as 'position approximate', fixed from seaward on board a vessel rather than on site at the beach.[9] In other words, the quoted co-ordinates did not necessarily chart the exact location of the wreck site. Indeed, foreshore wreck sites are characteristically charted as 'position approximate' around the entire English coastline.[10]

This suggested that the 1975 and 2014 appearances were variant reports of the same wreck, confirmed by intervening sightings. A 2001 study in advance of sea defence works at Minehead brought together the known archaeology on the beach.[11] The nearest structure to the approximate 1975 position in that study was a much smaller vessel, believed to be the remains of a dinghy or boat, but this lay 110m SE of the charted 1975 site and was therefore unlikely to relate to that site; see illustration 6.3.[12] On the other hand the 2014 site was illustrated with an accurate position given.[13]

Having confirmed its identity in that all sightings related to the same outline of a vessel with thick timbers, was it now possible to confirm the identity of the vessel in a more conventional sense, that is, its name and the circumstances of its loss? Such detective work for wreck sites is usually much harder to undertake than at first appears. Generally speaking, the further back in time one goes, the harder it is to find historical evidence for shipwrecks, whether tracing documentary details of historic shipwrecks, or matching a wreck site to a recorded event. Many shipwrecks were never documented at all, and of those that were, some records have since been lost: for example, religious houses often held the right to wreck on their coastal lands, but their records were sometimes lost or destroyed during the Dissolution of the Monasteries under King Henry the Eighth.

There are also biases in surviving evidence: medieval wrecks were usually only recorded if they were contentious, with some kings much more assiduous in investigating such cases than others, King Edward the Third (1327-1377) in particular.[14] Social factors also come into play: significant vessels, such as naval and East India Company ships, can be traced through a documentary trail of administrative and loss records. Whereas losses of small localised forms of fishing and trading vessels were less likely, until the nineteenth century, to leave behind much in the way of a documentary trail.

Public domain reporting of shipwrecks arrived with the earliest newspapers of the seventeenth century. Shipwreck news became a staple of the press, reaching an increasingly wide audience with the development of regional newspapers from the early eighteenth century onwards and the dedicated shipping journal *Lloyd's List* from the 1720s (although its earliest extant issue dates from 1740). Interestingly, the coal trade was so important to Tyneside that from its inception in 1711 the *Newcastle Courant* covered the wrecks of collier vessels, whether they occurred locally or further afield. By contrast, Bristol-based newspapers from the 1720s offered far less coverage of local shipping, so that in terms of eighteenth century wrecks the Bristol Channel is relatively under-represented, despite its numerous hazards and the region's undoubted maritime activity.

Attempts to identify any wreck site are thus fraught with these gaps and biases in the surviving documentary evidence, particularly so for Bristol and Somerset. The possibility that the sole match for a given wreck site might be a vessel for which the records have been lost (and therefore impossible to identify) is therefore not at all far-fetched.

The original suggestion of the *Lamb* for the 1975 site demonstrates further pitfalls of the identification process. Despite the sporadic nature of early eighteenth century wreck coverage, the *Lamb* is one of the better-documented wrecks for the period and region, making it an attractive identification. The scale and nature of the tragedy made it newsworthy enough to creep into the columns of some of England's earliest newspapers and even the foreign press.[15] Further details emerge from burial records at Minehead and Dunster and in a letter by the great sea captain Thomas Coram. At the time Coram was still campaigning for his Foundling Hospital in London and was concerned in the voyage. He had taken 'equal care to get a good master and a good ship' which was 'but 2 years old', and lost 'in the best wind that could blow at NE, tho' very fresh'.[16] As a result, the *Lamb* is unusually well-documented for an unremarkable vessel engaged on a quotidian voyage, but a well-documented wreck is not necessarily the correct identification, and the greater distance between the site's actual location and Lamb Corner also calls the attribution to the *Lamb* into question.

An alternative candidate for identifying the site has been suggested as the Norwegian barque *America*, which was explicitly recorded as striking Warren Sands in 1881, consistent with the actual location of the vessel remains.[17]

Examination of other candidates for the site during that period reveals, as predicted, a number of gaps in the records.[18] Following the *Lamb* in 1736 the next known reference to a wreck at or near Minehead is in 1770, with intervals of several years between each incident thereafter.[19] The sporadic nature of the wreck record may not be solely attributable to lack of surviving documentary evidence, but may also be due to local environmental conditions. Losses may have tended to occur particularly during the ENE gales that were noted in a 1701 map of the 'Town and Peer' as 'most destructive' to shipping and consistent with Coram's observations on the loss of the *Lamb* with the wind at NE.[20]

Site observations have shown that the wreck is some 30m long, with a minimum length of 16m revealed on previous exposures, fastened with both treenails (timber fastenings) and copper nails, and sheathed in timber.[21] Although used in ancient times, copper nails became more widespread in shipbuilding after the introduction of copper hull sheathing into the Royal Navy from the mid-

Illustration 4.4: (Opposite) Detail view of the timbers. At right, the loose copper nail is seen in context; travelling up the timber, the thin sheathing can be seen to be coming away, exposing a wooden peg (treenail). (© Historic England)

eighteenth century onwards, and the contemporary need to replace internal fixtures and fittings with iron or copper alternatives as traditional timber resources dwindled.[22] These innovations began to percolate down to lesser vessels from the late eighteenth to early nineteenth centuries, although their adoption was neither universal nor always necessary. The Minehead site is an excellent demonstration, however, of the principle that copper fastenings did not necessarily mean that a vessel was sheathed in timber, or vice versa.

The Minehead wreck benefited from the simultaneous investigation by Historic England in 2015 of the two Northam Burrows sites on Devon's Bristol Channel coastline (mentioned above). Stylistically very similar to the Minehead site, they had, however, only treenails for fastenings. The landward retreat of Northam's pebble ridge measured over time provided a dating framework to complement the internal evidence of their construction, and enabled the larger vessel to be identified as the probable wreck of the *Sally* in 1769, with the smaller one a possible Severn trow lost around 1800.[23]

The Minehead site's dimensions suggest it is a local coaster or short-range seafaring vessel, with its timber sheathing indicating it is a vernacular vessel. Its dual fastening technologies are from a transitional period in construction characteristic of the conservative tendencies of vernacular shipbuilding. Its copper nails suggest that the wreck is likely to post-date the introduction of copper sheathing, dating towards the end of the eighteenth or beginning of the nineteenth centuries at the earliest, and thus contemporary with, or slightly later than the Severn trow at Northam, built with treenails only. These observations appear to eliminate the *Lamb* as too early a candidate for the vessel remains at Minehead.

The next step was a physical investigation of the site for further clues to tally, where possible, with the available documentary evidence. A preliminary visit in July 2015 by Historic England yielded a loose

Illustration 4.5: Detail view of timbers looking westward towards the harbour at Minehead. The timbers in the middle and at extreme right show treenail holes, while the timber at extreme left illustrates a characteristic treenail hole erosion pattern. (© Historic England)

Illustration 4.6: (Above) The larger wreck at Northam Burrows, Devon, looking south-west towards the Westward Ho! end of the beach. Like the Minehead site in the smaller Minehead Bay, the Westward Ho! wreck was lost between two headlands. (© Historic England)

Illustration 4.7: (Below) The smaller wreck at Northam Burrows, another 'single-sided' wreck probably driven in under similar conditions to the vessel at Minehead, looking north-east. (© Historic England)

copper nail which was at risk of being lost to the sea and subjected to sacrificial analysis. Frustratingly, it proved inconclusive and was dated to 'between Roman times and the 20th century'.[24]

Dendrochronological analysis (tree-ring dating) undertaken in December 2015 was similarly fraught with difficulty. Species identification revealed that the vessel was constructed, unusually, of softwood pine and larch, yielding no matches within domestic reference data for its chronology. A worldwide search similarly elicited no match to date the timbers; it is easier to date timbers, such as English oak, for which reference chronologies are plentiful, because more examples exist.[25] Such softwood timbers are characteristic of shipbuilding in northerly climes, prompting a review of the Norwegian *America* as a possible match for the wreck site. She, too, was eliminated on further research, which revealed that she was immediately salvaged, broken up and sold in situ, with little, if anything, likely to remain.[26]

The known intervening wrecks between the *Lamb* and the *America* were then assessed for their potential as candidates for the site. One candidate, a little later than the Northam Severn trow, stood out in a bald statement in *Lloyd's List* in 1808: 'The *Bristol Packet*, Day, from Teingmouth [*sic*] to Bristol, is lost at Minehead'.[27] At first glance this appears uninformative, but 'at Minehead' is enough to indicate a stranding rather than a sinking offshore.[28] No other contemporary newspaper expands upon the story in more detail, but this in itself is not at all unusual at this period and is not necessarily to be regarded as suspicious at a time when wrecks were everyday occurrences nationwide.[29]

However, the *Bristol Packet* left a documentary trail elsewhere. Her entry in *Lloyd's Register* of 1808, identifiable by her master's name 'W Day,' shows her to be a vessel of 249 tons in the 7th year of her age, thus built around 1801.[30] Her disappearance from the 1809 edition confirms her loss (*i.e.* she was not refloated or repaired to sail another day).

More excitingly, her 1808 entry also reveals her to be New England-built, with pine topsides and wooden sheathing, consistent with site observations. It is also consistent with contemporary shipbuilding practice on the north-eastern seaboard of the United States and Canada, including the use of larch (known as *hackmatack* or *tamarack*), also present in the Minehead wreck.[31] Not, therefore, the *America*, but *an* American.

As the site demonstrates with only one side of the wreck visible, the vessel was most likely driven in on her beam end during a storm event, as was the smaller of the two wrecks at Northam. From the reporting date of 16 February 1808 for the *Bristol Packet*, it seems likely that such an event could well have been the 'excessively high gale of wind' reported at Bristol on the 11th to the 12th, which seems to have been felt countrywide and to have arisen principally from the NE, consistent with the most dangerous quarter for Minehead.[32] So far, therefore, in origin, date, and circumstances of loss, the *Bristol Packet* is the most plausible identification for the Minehead wreck.

As the vessel most closely matching the pine and larch-built wreck at Minehead, the *Bristol Packet* provides intriguing evidence of a strong transatlantic trade in ships themselves, which continued even after the breach following the American War of Independence (1775-1783).

Each of the three Bristol Channel wrecks investigated in 2015 thus illuminates a different aspect of the channel's characteristic trades 200 to 250 years ago. The larger wreck at Northam, the *Sally*, from Oporto, provides evidence for Bristol's importance as a centre of the wine trade; the smaller wreck of a Severn trow, by its very location on the Devon coast, is evidence of trow's development into a seagoing coaster.[33] All three are rare survivals: out of more than 11,000 documented wreck events in England for this period, only some 40 wreck sites so far have been identified. The majority are of significantly larger vessels such as warships, or East Indiamen. Wrecks of this era in the archaeological record are therefore rare; wrecks of lesser vessels rarer still, and the ability to attribute an identity very unusual.[34]

At the time of writing in December 2016, the Minehead wreck had just joined its counterparts in Devon as a scheduled site under the 1979 Ancient Monuments and Archaeological Areas Act. Scheduling is the preferred option for wrecks in the inter-tidal zone, accommodating both public access and enjoyment without restriction, but affording protection against deliberate damage and interference. Scheduling also recognises a heritage asset as being of national importance, in this case representative of a vessel type otherwise unknown in the archaeological record.

The wreck at Minehead has so far been reluctant to give up its secrets. A plausible candidate for its identification has been put forward, but cannot be confirmed without further formal survey of the surviving timbers. Its significance, however, in illuminating our understanding of trade in the Bristol Channel of the late eighteenth to early nineteenth centuries, is clear and all three wrecks borrow from one another in group value. They have enormous potential to be studied independently and together to illustrate the particular patterns of loss as well as use, characteristic of the Bristol Channel, as much part of their local environment as wrecks as they were when afloat and in service.

References

1 S. Cant, *England's shipwreck heritage: from logboats to U-boats* (Swindon, 2013), viii, 170, 242-3.

2 S. Cant, *Unknown wreck at Minehead, known as the* Lamb*: Preliminary Assessment of Site: 16.07.2015*. Unpublished report for Historic England.

3 Information supplied by Julia Race, 17 February 2014.

4 United Kingdom Hydrographic Office (U.K.H.O.), Wrecks Database record no. 12406.

5 National Record of the Historic Environment (N.R.H.E.), Historic England, maritime archaeology database record for the Lamb, ID 1383050. Before 1752 the English calendar ran 25 March to 24 March the following year, with the result that 24 March 1751 was the day before 25 March 1752, not a year previously. This quirk of the English calendar has an impact on wreck research, with a high incidence of wrecks during the winter months.

6 Located more or less at the junction of the present Quay Street and Esplanade, Minehead (J. Gilman, *Exmoor's maritime heritage* (Dulverton, 1999), 67-8). The source of the attribution is not known and may be local tradition, derived less from the presence of vessel remains than local knowledge of a historic event in this location attended with heavy loss of life. The name 'Lamb' is common enough that it may have nothing at all to do with the wreck.

7 Sand cover was eroded to such an extent that it was flung landward onto the footpath seaward of Warren Road, where it was still in situ in July 2015 (Cant, *Unknown wreck*).

8 Information supplied by Julia Race, 17 February 2014; Cant, *Unknown wreck*; S. Cant, *Unknown wreck at Minehead, known as the* Lamb: *second site visit: 14.12.2015*, unpublished report for Historic England.

9 U.K.H.O., Wrecks Database record no. 12406: 'position for filing only', after being taken by horizontal sextant angle, its position calibrated by sextant between two landmarks.

10 The discrepancy is characteristically around 0.25 or 0.5 mile out. For example, Formby on the north-west coast, Camber Sands on the English Channel coast, and Amble on the north-east coast, all recorded in the N.R.H.E. maritime archaeology database, Historic England.

11 R. McDonnell, *Minehead sea defence scheme: archaeological report: vol. i: assessment, survey and evaluation* (2001), 9-16

12 McDonnell, *Minehead*, 14, wreck no.61.

13 McDonnell, *Minehead*, 10-11, wreck no.26.

14 Cant, *England's shipwreck heritage*, 116-118.

15 *Derby Mercury*, 4 March 1735/6; *Caledonian Mercury*, 2 March 1735/6; *Oprechte Haerlemsche Courant*, 15 March 1735/6.

16 Somerset Heritage Centre (S.H.C.), D/P/du/2/1/3 burial register for St. George's Dunster, 1735-1736; D/P/m.st.m/2/1/3, 1735-6 burial register St. Michael's Minehead, 1735-1736; T.N.A., ADM 106/879/21 letter from Thomas Coram to the Principal Officers and Commissioners of His Majesty's Navy, 23 February 1735/6.

17 *Bristol Mercury and Daily Post*, 24 January 1881; U.K.H.O., Wrecks Database record no. 12406; N.R.H.E. record for the *America*, no. 1382577.

18 From the N.R.H.E. database, Historic England.

19 *Molly*, N.R.H.E. wreck no. 1383082. The following is indicative of the intervals between surviving documented records for vessels specifically stated as having stranded at or near Minehead (*Rose*, 1783, N.R.H.E. 1601376; *Anne*, 1791, N.R.H.E. 1336036; *Times*, 1802, N.R.H.E. 1338965; *Friends*, 1808, N.R.H.E. 1341064; *Industry*, 1817, N.R.H.E. 1003071; *Rose*, 1826, N.R.H.E. 1360314).

20 S.H.C., DD/L/1/58/15 Thomas Surbey, The Towns and Peer of Minehead, 1701, transcript in A.J. Webb (ed), *A maritime history of Somerset volume two* (Taunton, 2014), 166-7; T.N.A., ADM 106//879/21.

21 McDonnell, *Minehead*, 12; S. Cant, *Site visit to Westward Ho!,* unpublished report for Historic England.

22 M. MCarthy, *Ships' fastenings: from sewn boat to steamship* (Texas, 2005), 30, 101-114.

23 P. Keene, *Classic landforms of the north Devon coast* (Sheffield, 1986); B. Hughes, 'Attempting to name the large wreck on Westward Ho! beach' in *North Devon Heritage* 19 (2007), 8-12; Cant, *Unknown wreck*; S. Cant, *Unknown wreck … second site visit.*

24 D. Dungworth, *Minehead shipwreck: investigation of copper alloy nail*, unpublished report for Historic England (2015).

25 Information from Cathy Tyers, Dendrochronologist, Scientific Dating Team, Historic England, 26 February 2016.

26 *Bristol Mercury and Daily Post*, 24 January 1881.

27 *Lloyd's List*, 16 February 1808, no.4,229.

28 Examination of contemporary wreck records for England, N.R.H.E..

29 The same report is reproduced verbatim across all newspapers printing the notice, suggesting a single source. Alternative or subsequent accounts of a wreck usually derive from multiple sources and may amplify the bare details of an original report, but wrecks were so commonplace that the loss of a fairly ordinary vessel would not necessarily excite much attention, particularly if the vessel and its cargo were of low value and no lives were lost. In 1808 alone 222 wrecks have so far been discovered for the whole of England. Comparison of wreck reports in the N.R.H.E.

database.

30 *Lloyd's Register*, 1808, no. 412(B).

31 H. Thurston and W. Barrett, *The Atlantic coast: a natural history* (Vancouver, 2012), 82.

32 *Bristol Mirror*, 13 February 1808; *Morning Post*, 15 February 1808. As might have been expected for a gale from this quarter, the east coast was principally affected, so if it was this storm which resulted in the loss of the *Bristol Packet*, she seems to have been unlucky in catching the wind just at this quarter on the west coast, for no other wrecks are recorded locally for this storm, although plentiful elsewhere (N.R.H.E.).

33 *Wreck at Westward Ho!* National Heritage List for England, Historic England (N.H.L.E.), 1432418 https://historicengland.org.uk/listing/the-list/list-entry/1432418; wreck at Northam Burrows, N.H.L.E., Historic England, 1432949, https://historicengland.org.uk/listing/the-list/list-entry/1432949.

34 S. Cant, 'Devon's Shipwrecks' in *Heritage Calling*, accessed 15 August 2016 at https://heritagecalling.com/2016/08/15/devons-shipwrecks/.

Chapter Five

No Safe Haven: a Geologist's Perspective of a History of West Somerset's Ports

Eric Robinson, with an introduction by Philip Ashford[1]

The construction of Porlock, Minehead and Watchet quays: an historical and geologic perspective

THE OLDEST section of Porlock quay, perhaps dating from the sixteenth or seventeenth century, is the middle section where Hangman sandstone cobbles bonded with lime mortar are common; this section includes the sluice wall mentioned in 1650. To the north of this, at the end of the quay are the grey, more regular limestone blocks that arrived from Barry in 1767.[2] Finally, the section either side of the lock gates, using massive dressed sandstone and limestone blocks, may have been constructed in the 1850s.[3] Some of the superficial structures on the top of Porlock quay are constructed of softer, more recent local Triassic sandstone.

Illustration 5.2: Triassic sandstone superstructure at Porlock Quay (Garry Holden Photographics, 2016)

Illustration 5.1: Contrasting construction materials at Porlock Weir, Hangman sandstone and limestone from Barry used in the construction of the harbour wall. (Garry Holden Photographics, 2016)

Illustration 5.3: Contrasting construction materials, Hangman sandstone with dressed sandstone and limestone blocks, flanking Porlock Weir lock gate in 2016. (Garry Holden Photographics, 2016)

Minehead quay also has three visible subsections. Again, the oldest section, like at Porlock, is made of beach cobbles of Hangman sandstone. Some of these cobbles are enormous. Parts of this section probably date to the early seventeenth century when the quay was being developed, a phase of construction being completed in about 1622.[4] It was, perhaps, during this construction phase that rocks of up to one ton were floated by with casks and transported from the cliffs at Greenaleigh Point, about one mile to the west of the harbour. By 1633, Minehead's harbour wall was described as a 'fair stone key'[5] and there is a detailed description by a French visitor in 1644 of the extra-large stones placed on top of each other to form the harbour wall. Monsieur Le Gouz, stated that there was no mortar used in the piles of stone. If true, the mortaring of Minehead harbour might have been a later seventeenth-century improvement. Nevertheless, the undressed and irregular large Hangman grit visible today in a section of Minehead's harbour wall probably are ones that Le Gouz witnessed.[6]

In 1682, Colonel Francis Luttrell paid for strengthening the harbour. Rocks were brought by sea to the western side of the harbour and placed behind the quay to break the force of the waves. These rocks are still visible at low tide. The date of this maintenance, 1682, was marked with a plaque on the quay, but this memorial from 1682 is now gone.[7] The Greenaleigh Point Hangman sandstone cliffs, with almost vertical beds were observed and commented on by geologists during the early nineteenth century.[8] Towards the outer end of the quay is more regular work constructed of Hangman grit, which was the significant improvement of Minehead 'Peer' designed by Thomas Surbey in 1701 and constructed by engineer Daniel Dennell between 1704 and 1716. The material for the development of the quay, 'the ruff stone of all magnitude from 25 or 30 tuns downward … are to be got on the shore within two miles of the place' *i.e.* Culver Cliff.[9] Maintenance was needed again in 1799 when stone from Culver Cliff was brought by coastal vessel to the harbour.[10] A third obvious section is the outer end of the quay which is encased in concrete.

Watchet was described as having a 'fair stone key' in 1632.[12] This would probably have been made from the local lias. Then, during the 1640s, storms severely damaged the harbour facilities at Watchet

Illustration 5.4: Hangman grit at Culver Cliff, Minehead. This vibrant image summarises the folding of the strata and the pronounced joints perpendicular to the folded beds, providing strong rock masses that have proved ideal for the construction and maintenance of Minehead Harbour. (Kester Webb[11])

according to a memorial from the 1660s.[13] The poverty and disorder of the time, caused by the Civil Wars, meant that the damage was not immediately attended to. Not until the late 1650s and early 1660s was money being raised locally and through 'briefs' read across the country as far afield as Yorkshire and London. One brief from Dorset stated that money raised was for the 'reparation of their key or piere' whilst another from Gloucestershire related that 'the harbour being

Illustration 5.5: Rarely seen, massive Hangman grit rocks from Culver Cliff 'behind' Minehead harbour, reminiscent of the heap of rocks that Le Gouz witnessed and, as the text indicates, some of which may have been gathered and placed in position in the seventeenth century. (Philip Ashford, 2017)

decayed by the violence of the sea and the whole town being in danger of being undermined'.[14] It was reported in 1677 that the 'key is ruined', presumably it was never properly re-instated after the storms of the 1640s.[15] Again, in 1701, it was being reported that Watchet harbour had 'of late' been washed away by the 'fury of the sea'.[16] Whether this report was a re-publishing of old news or whether more damage occurred in the 1690s is not known. What is sure is a bill concerned with the repairing of Watchet harbour and 'key' was presented to the Commons in 1705;[17] the Earl of Egremont obtained the appropriate Act of Parliament in 1708.[18] An image of the state of the development of the stone quay from the 1820s and particulars of the development of West Quay, which occurred in the early 1860s at the same time of the development of the West Somerset Mineral Railway, is detailed elsewhere.[19] The geologic materials now found in Watchet quay are detailed below.

No Safe Haven

Few coasts can be as challenging for vessels as that which forms the southern shoreline of the Bristol Channel between Hartland Point and Portishead. The beetling cliffs, the tallest on the English coast, have no natural harbours to run to in the face of the onshore storms which sweep the south west of England from the Atlantic.[20] Throw in the exceptional tidal range and the swirling longshore currents and the hazards are and were formidable.

The cliff coast in question has a relatively simple geology. From Ilfracombe through Lynton and Porlock to Minehead, they are of the geological unit of time known as the Hangman grits; a series of bands of hard and resistant muddy sandstones separated by thinner mudstone units, creating the stepped profiles which encouraged the climbing traverses pioneered by the botanist, Newell Arber.[21] His climbs and descriptions of the north Devon and west Somerset cliffs have been extended and illustrated by Kester Webb and his friends. In several respects, the text here and understanding of the Hangman grits has been extended by the account of the coast by Kester Webb who has described its stratigraphy and weathering in the cliff. His accounts are dramatically illustrated by photographs and artistry featuring cliffs he daringly explored as a climber.[22] The well jointed strata allowed blocks and slabs to be removed for the building of reliable sea walls and harbours over several centuries at Porlock and Minehead.

The near-continuous cliff wall is only briefly broken by narrow inlets where the strong bedding and jointing at right angles have been exploited at Combe Martin and to a lesser extent at Lynmouth, never quite affording safe haven for sailing boats, including the working ketches and brigs plying their trade to the Welsh coast and beyond. It was this situation that encouraged the building of the limited number of ports, such as Porlock and Minehead. Their piers and breakwaters were devised to utilise the limited local natural features, as well as good access to land routes connecting them to the farming communities of

Illustration 5.6: Hangman grits at Selworthy Sands at low tide as painted by local artist Kester Webb. This artistic impression is a rarely seen view due to inaccessibility and dangerous tides. (Kester Webb, 1990s)

Illustration 5.7: Intensely folded Hangman grits at Hurlstone Point on a high tide. The arch formed in a fold is locally known as 'Gull Hole' (Kester Webb, 1990s)

Exmoor and west Somerset. These enterprises called for suitably tough and resistant stone for the structure; stone which, given the transport limitations of earlier centuries, was available from coastal sites.

Illustration 5.8: Bristol Channel coastal geology from Combe Martin to Watchet (Philip Ashford, 2017)

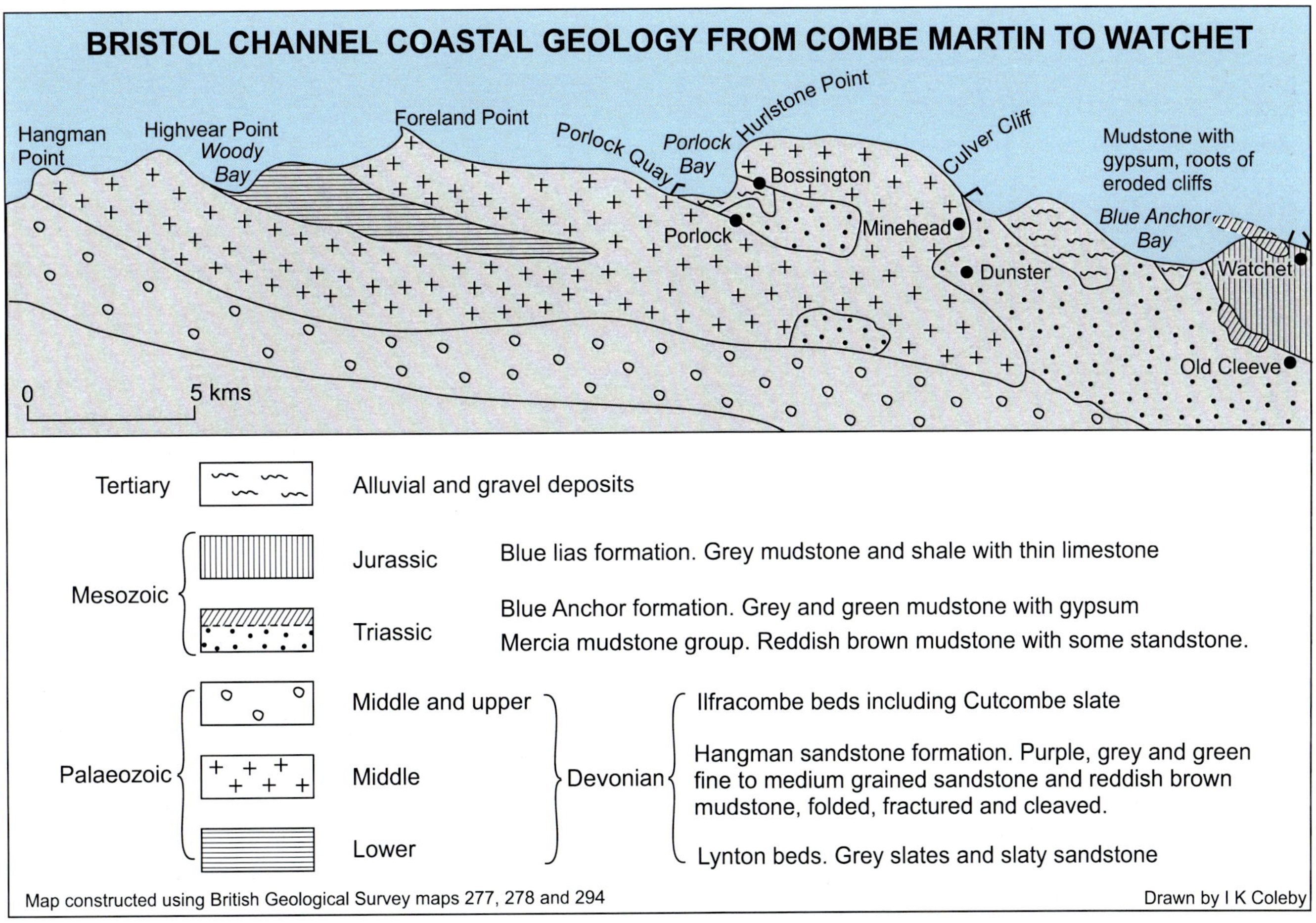

The geological materials of the ports and piers[23]

Hangman grits. Distinguishing 'suitable' from the 'less suitable' eliminates several local stones which, while widely used in vernacular buildings in the Exmoor area, would prove vulnerable to weathering and especially the attack of the sea. In the circumstances the very stone of the cliffs invited use. The Hangman grit freely breaks into slabs in lengths up to 1 ½ metres and up to ½ a metre thickness, easy to detach and manhandle. Fallen from the cliff, the slabs can be rounded and lose their edges as the stone is worked by the backward and forward movement of the tides. This working if anything improved the cliff stone. On other counts, the Hangman grit must qualify as the hardest of local stones; the sand grains were bonded in a muddy matrix impossible to penetrate and exploit, as would be the case with most sandstones where there is pore space between the grains. It had to be an advantage that the Hangman slabs were where they were wanted, requiring minimum effort in their transportation, as we see at Porlock Weir and Minehead.

Local Old Red Sandstone. For the seawall copings and the top surfaces of several piers, a coarse grained sandstone, red in colour, could be compared with the Lower Devonian sandstones from South Wales and the Clevedon coast, fluviate offshore deposits which grade southwards into the marine limestones of

Illustration 5.9: Hangman sandstone used in the wall at Porlock (Garry Holden Photographics, 2016)

Illustration 5.10: Hangman sandstone used in the construction of the quay at Minehead (Garry Holden Photographics, 2016)

Devon. Options for sources include one-time quarries around Clevedon and Portishead which were conveniently close to the coast for transport. Other possibilities must include the Brownstone outcrops behind Newport, and further upriver to the Forest of Dean outlet through the well-engineered port at Lydney. For both options, we have the established traffic from Watchet supplying iron ore from the Brendon Hills to the blast furnaces of Ebbw Vale, for which the return cargoes were Forest coal and timber. Dressed stone of the sizes we recognise in our ports could have been a weighty cargo which could have compensated for the awkward loads of coal, stabilising the brigs and ketches in the period post-1850.

Visibly, gritstones, the cement of the Old Red sandstones, is siliceous and tough enough to make the stone strong against weathering and the impact of tides. In contrast, most of the local New Red sandstones, quite suitable for domestic buildings, have a lime cement to the sand grains, a bonding which is more easily leached, giving them a friable character and weakness against seawaters. White quartz pebbles in some of the stone copings could identify the well-known quartz conglomerate of the Forest of Dean and Chepstow.

Local Jurassic rocks. Within the lower Jurassic of the coast, the crystalline and hard limestones we call Blue lias, can be (and was) involved in coastal engineering. The stone which is used in street paving and kerbstones when well cemented, with sand and lime mortar, can be found in some piers and seawalls.

At Minehead, in the post-1900 sea wall at the top of Quay Street, a softer mudstone variety of lias, probably from the cliffs of South Glamorgan between Nash Point and St Donats was dressed into slabs about 60 cms by 25 cms, and laid like bricks in the seawall by the slipway. Softer by nature, the stones have lost their sharp margins. As walling, the sound mortaring makes them suitable for the stretches of the harbour between the Hangman grit 'bolsters'. The availability of lias from the reefs and ledges of the coast of Blue Anchor and Watchet made the lias a natural choice, if not the best stone for the purpose of incorporating into pier and harbour walls at Watchet.

Illustration 5.11: Old Red sandstone, quarry-dressed, into slabs of about 90 cms in length, used as copings to sea walls and piers. Watchet west pier provides a good example. Innumerable Bristol Channel coastal vessels traded between Watchet and Lydney between 1865 and 1914. For example, the *Thomas and Sarah*, repaired at Watchet prior to 1 July 1868 later sailed from Lydney to Watchet with coal and may well have brought some sandstone.[24] (Garry Holden Photographics, 2016)

Illustration 5.12: Imported Old Red Sandstone copings and local Blue lias in the West Pier wall at Watchet. The date stone marks the construction of this section of the wall. (Garry Holden Photographics, 2016)

Illustration 5.13: Blue lias, probably from the cliffs of South Glamorgan by Minehead Harbour slipway provide a contrast to the Hangman grits of the older quay wall to the right of the photo. (Garry Holden Photographics, 2016)

More recent coastal engineering

With time, the practices from other coasts have come to our area. Mainly this involves structures in concretes, reinforced with dressed stones from the Carboniferous limestones of Mendip and South Wales quarries, examples of which can be seen at Watchet, Blue Anchor and Minehead.

Other protections against the attack of the sea come with the introduction of armour stone, rough-

Illustration 5.14: Mendip Carboniferous limestone from the quarries of Frome (Tor Quarry). Blocks of this dark stone, are rich in fossils and was used in the sea wall protecting the cliff below West Street, Watchet (Garry Holden Photographics, 2016)

hewn blocks of igneous rocks from Scottish 'superquarries' situated on deepwater anchorages on Lewis or at Loch Linnhe. Along with these gabbros and schists, Mendip quarries have supplied limestone, delivered by Foster Yeoman in their own freight trains using the West Somerset Railway. Once again, transport by sea or rail has counted in the dispersal of these bulky additions to our coasts.

So much for the materials; what remains is to discuss the process of marine sedimentation which have an importance in the history of our ports.

Geomorphology and future prospects

At all times it is wise to work with nature as far as possible. This is abundantly illustrated in the history of our Bristol Channel ports. Initially, defence was needed against the longshore drift of currents as well as periodic storms. Once protective piers had been constructed using suitable stone, those same currents became the means of contributing to their defence by trapping a constant flow of beach gravels and sands behind the piers, such as at Porlock and Minehead.

Geomorphology is a very important branch of geology as we seek to understand the process of sedimentation and the production of our standard rock types. While we regard Empedocles as our first expert for his comment that 'One can't step in the same stream twice' the dynamics of the process was best outlined by Charles Lyell in his 'Principles' when he said that the 'present is the key to the past'.[25] This is the reasoning which allows us to speculate that the Old Red Sandstone gritstones developed in ways that can be seen in modern deltas. Dynamic processes operate when sands and gravels have to be removed at Minehead and Porlock harbours as they are soon replaced by similar materials from our beaches and shoreline. We need to recognise that the flow of

Illustration 5.15: Rock armour, sourced from Scotland protect the cliffs of West Beach, Watchet at high tide (Garry Holden Photographics, 2016)

Illustration 5.16: Shoal of Hangman sandstone pebbles trapped to the east of Minehead pier blocking the entrance to the harbour, 2015. (Eric Robinson)

beach materials which can re-inforce our harbours, can produce the demise of Porlock Weir as a working port.[26] Similarly, the gravel shoal that periodically blocks the entrance to Minehead harbour to ships of modest draught will continue to appear.[27] Local solutions might be introduced such as groynes or spurs to trap the flow for example. The reason why beach materials are not piled high against the west pier at Watchet is because of the flushing-scouring action of the Watchet stream which enters the Bristol Channel immediately alongside the western exterior of the pier. Aerial photography reveals a plume of beach material washed hundreds of metres out to sea by the action of this stream when in spate. Overall, however, the best solution would be to have a national agency taking account of coastal erosion. A

Illustration 5.17: The Washford stream entering the Bristol Channel to the west of Watchet's West Pier (Eric Robinson, 2015)

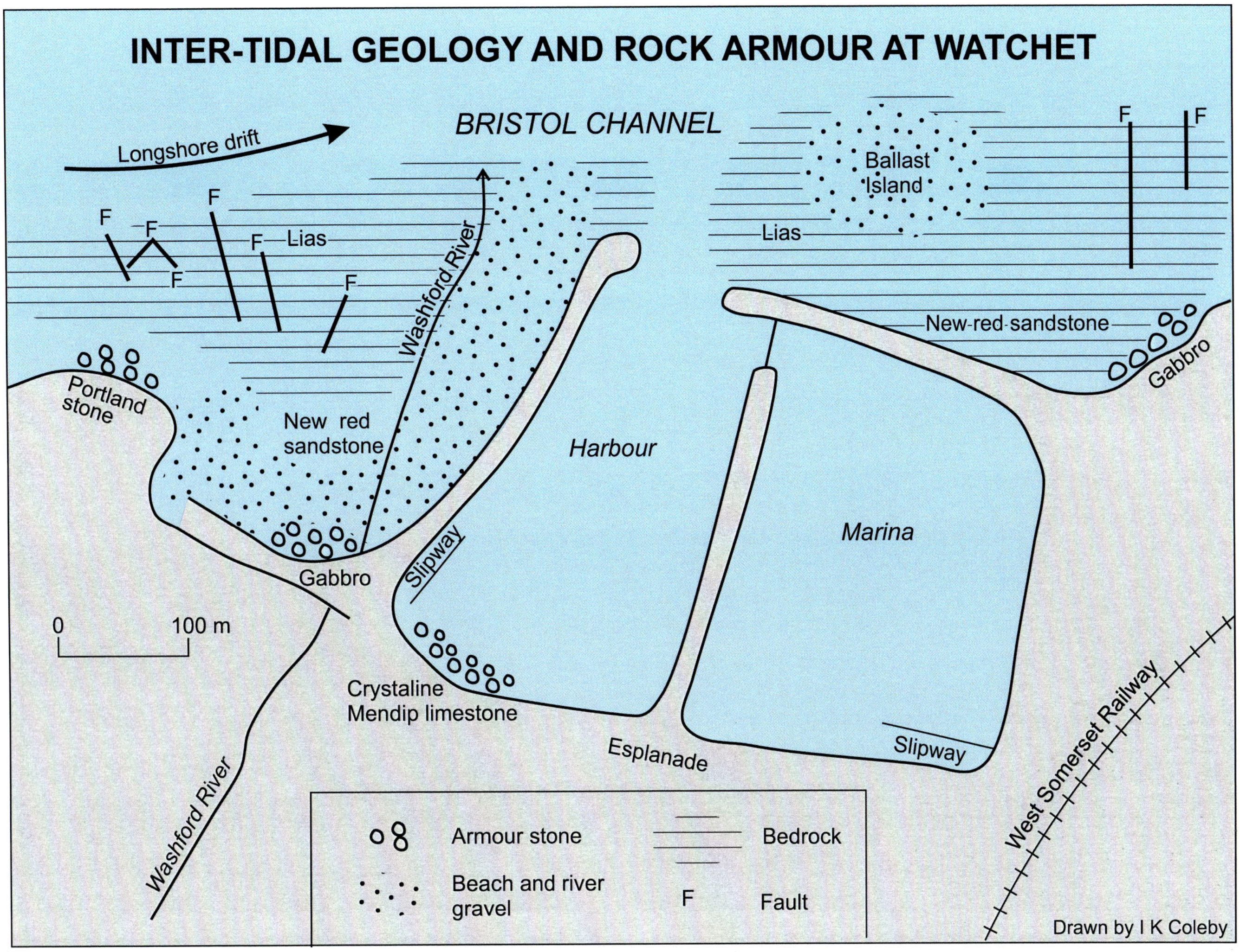

Illustration 5.18: A plan of the inter-tidal geology and rock armour at Watchet (Eric Robinson, 2017)

balance needs to be struck between coastal loss impossible to counter except at unacceptable expense and the complimentary silting up of other areas. Coastal engineering research is badly needed.

References

1 This paper is in two parts. The first part was written by Philip Ashford, showing the historical documentation of Porlock, Minehead and Watchet's man-made harbours. The main part of this chapter, under the heading 'No safe haven' was written by Professor Eric Robinson.

2 *M.H.S.* 1, 48-9.

3 S.H.C., DD/BR/bn/19 Porlock harbour accounts, 1854-5.

4 M. Siraut, 'Minehead Harbour', (undated) www.victoriacountyhistory.ac.uk/explore/.../minehead_harbour.doc, accessed 18 Apr. 2014.

5 T.N.A., E 134/8Chas1/mich48 litigation relating to Aberthaw, Glamorganshire, 1632-3.

6 *M.H.S.* 2, 52.

7 J. Gilman and S. Lloyd, *From curragh to ketch: The story of Minehead's quay town* (Minehead, 2012), 15, 31.

8 L. Horner, 'Sketch of the geology of the south-west part of Somersetshire' in *Transactions of the Geological Society* 3, (1816), 345.

9 *M.H.S.* 2, 160, 171.

10 Gilman and Lloyd, *From curragh to ketch*, 38, 45-6.

11 Sadly, Kester Webb died in late 2016 so the authors can but posthumously thank him for his contribution of images for this chapter.

12 T.N.A., E 134/8Chas1/Mich48 litigation relating to Aberthaw, Glamorganshire, 1632-3.

13 R.W. Dunning *et al* (eds.), *A history of the county of Somerset* 5 (1985), 143-71.

14 Briefs regarding Watchet restoration from Yorkshire and London are in G. Farr, *Ships and harbours of Exmoor* (Dulverton, 1970), 45; from Dorset, in *S.D.N.Q.* vol. 20, 203 and from Gloucestershire in B. Blacker (ed.), *Gloucestershire Notes and Queries* 2(1882), 136. On page 83 of A. Wedlake's, *A history of Watchet* (Dulverton, 1973) and other locally published books in the latter quarter of the twentieth century, the statement appears that Watchet's harbour was damaged in winter gales in 1658. Other local authors have repeated this published assertion and the same statement is to be found on page 116 of *M.H.S.* 1. However, documentary evidence suggests that the sequence of events repeated in this chapter is the correct one. It is likely that the error arose when evidence of the briefs was found from

the late 1650s, therefore authors associated the timing of the briefs with the timing of the damage to the quay.

15 L. Roberts, *The merchants map of commerce* (London, 1677), 290.

16 R. Morden, *The new description and state of England* (London, 1701), 142.

17 *Journal of the House of Commons* 15 (1705), 487, 525.

18 *M.H.S.* 1, 116.

19 *M.H.S.* 1, chapter 7.

20 D. Webb and E. Webb, *The hidden edge of Exmoor* (Kingston Bagpuize, 2011), 92 where it is stated that the highest English cliff is 700 feet, at Great Hangman Hill in North Devon.

21 E. Arber, *The coast scenery of north Devon* (London, 1911). Arber was a botanist, but also a geologist. His was a life-time study of the massive cliffs of Devon and Somerset as an aspect of coastal geomorphology. His studies involved him in hair-raising cliff climbs and horizontal traverses of the banded grits of the Hangman sandstone.

22 Webb and Webb, *Edge of Exmoor*, is full of images and accounts throughout.

23 Though clearly important, the geology of piers and harbours in Somerset seems to be an overlooked topic, as is the foreshore as a source of construction materials. In a recent publication by English Heritage, A. King, *A building stone atlas of Somerset and Exmoor* (Swindon, 2011), no coastal source of stone is acknowledged and no maritime structure is illustrated or discussed.

24 S.H.C., DD\RSS/1/8/16 crew list for the *Thomas and Sarah*, 1868.

25 'The present is a key to the past', a much used geologists phrase, is a synopsis of a typically more verbose early nineteenth century quotation from Charles Lyell. 'The geologist who yields implicit assent to the truth of these principles, will deem it incumbent on him to examine with minute attention all the changes now in progress on the earth, and will regard every fact collected respecting the causes in diurnal action, as affording him a key to the interpretation of some mystery in the archives of remote ages'. (C. Lyall, *Principles of geology* (London, 1830), 165).

26 The centuries long struggle to keep Porlock Harbour clear of pebbles moved by longshore drift is detailed in *M.H.S.* 1, 49-50.

27 Such beach material was a problem in the entrance to Minehead harbour in 1701, stimulating major civil engineering works (*M.H.S.* 2 chapter 4, especially page 177), and most recently formed in 2015, being removed in early 2016. A slightly smaller shoal re-formed over the winter of 2016-2017.

Chapter Six

Seamen's Religious and Social Welfare, 1817-1983

Alston Kennerley

Introduction

SEAFARERS INTERACTED with particular sections of coastline directly because they belonged to one of its ports, or because the ships in which they were currently serving happened to call at one of the ports, and indirectly if in ships passing along those coastal waters. In both cases, since time immemorial various forms of local response may be identified. From Elizabethan times the parish-based poor law was supposed to cater for those in need of physical relief, and this included seafarers belonging to Somerset ports such as Watchet and Minehead where the overseers, as the parochial authorities were termed, were responsible for the destitute. Seafarers in need who were outsiders depended on local good will or more specific charitable provision. At what may now seem quite small ports it may be possible to discover ancient mariners' almshouses or mutual aid funds (which may include widows and orphans), and seamen's or fishermen's chapels. Religious practices, including blessing newly built vessels, blessing a fishing fleet about to sail, and preaching sermons addressed at seafarers, have roots back to the dawn of recorded history. Welfare provision along the coast also includes the establishment of coastal marks (including lights), pilotage, rescue services and the physical support of shipwrecked seafarers. Social care for seafarers is writ large in major ports such as Bristol, where the Society of Merchant Venturers provided almshouses and made payments to seamen and their families who had fallen on hard times. This could include ransom money to free those in slavery abroad. Social and religious support of seafarers at Bristol lies outside the scope of this volume, but there are nineteenth-century aspects of more than local significance which relate to Somerset, namely the 1823 Bethel Flag controversy and the Reverend John Ashley's religious mission amongst shipping in the Bristol Channel in the 1830s and 1840s.[1] Off Portishead (from 1869) was moored the industrial training ship *Formidable*, while the mid channel island of Flat Holm was the site of an isolation hospital between 1883 and 1937.

Illustration 6.1: The Revd John Ashley (Reproduced courtesy of the Mission to Seafarers)

It was in the late eighteenth century that the religious revivalism of the period began to make its mark amongst seamen. By the end of the wars with France a spontaneous revivalism movement amongst merchant seafarers on the River Thames was carried to most British ports and to many overseas ports by ships' captains.[2] This provided the basis for the founding of numerous seamen's mission societies, such as the Bristol Seamen's Friend Society (founded in 1820). A least sixty were formed in Britain which served to unite local outreach, but, in addition, the practice of some ships' masters when in port of holding *ad hoc* services for any seamen aboard their ships, maintained the spontaneous spirit of religious revivalism in the decades which followed. Key elements uniting the movement were the early establishment of a logo and flag (in 1817) and the efforts of a Baptist minister, Reverend George Charles Smith, who was frequently present at the founding meetings of societies. He provided the movement with its shared literature, including printed tracts and, particularly, its monthly organ, the *Sailor's Magazine* (from 1820) which, with much other material, reported the activities and meetings of this mass of independent but related societies and of individuals.

Illustration 6.2: The Bethel flag, introduced in 1817, was in regular use aboard ship and on Seamen's Bethel buildings into the twentieth century. It still appears today, and the star and dove elements from it today form the logo of the Sailors' Society. Here it is on a plate from the Plymouth Seamen's Bethel (Alston Kennerley Collection)

Smith certainly carried the religious message into Somerset. In 1817, on horseback, he conducted an open air preaching mission, after the manner of John Wesley, the founder of Methodism, along the north Devon coast, and as far as Minehead and Watchet.[3] In London he founded the British & Foreign Seamen's Friend Society and Bethel Union in 1819, effectively the parent society of the early seamen's mission movement, which the present day Sailors' Society includes in its ancestry.[4] But the Bethel Flag was already in use before he became active at the national level. Nevertheless he recognized its importance and the Flag's use was systematically recorded in the *Sailor's Magazine*. For example, amidst reports of the formation of a society at Bideford and Appledore, the Bethel Flag at New York, and a seamen's library at Poplar, London, is a report of the hoisting aboard ship of the Bethel Flag at Bridgwater in March 1822. This event at Bridgwater included a service, preaching and the distribution of tracts, which, with the Flag, had been purchased from money raised by local subscriptions.[5] That flag was borrowed for the first such service at Watchet aboard the Watchet schooner, *Britannia*, owned by Messrs Royal and Hole. The Reverend Mr Gabriel of Stogumber, a former naval seaman, merchant ship master and Baptist minister, preached, and announced the intention of forming the Watchet Bethel Union Society, a room having been obtained for meetings.[6] Within months the use of houses on or near the quays at Porlock, Porlock Weir and Minehead had been obtained, and Bethel flags were flown and services were attended by seamen in port and by local residents.[7]

It was in 1823 at Watchet and Minehead that flying the Bethel Flag fell foul of local Customs and Excise officers. They asserted that the flying of flags without proper authority contravened the law and could lead, on prosecution and conviction, to a fine of £500. The matter was referred to Smith who consulted the London Bethel Society's president, Admiral Lord Gambier. In an exchange of letters the local officers stood their ground despite letters from Smith and Gambier, in which the numerous occasions the flag had been flown elsewhere aboard ships, including naval vessels, were pointed out, and that the Act upon which their case was based only applied to naval flags.[8] It took a letter from the Commissioners of Customs in London to this effect before the local officers backed down. It was characteristic of Smith, that having won the point, he should rub it in by publishing all the exchanges in a pamphlet together with a short history of the Bethel movement amongst seamen. This no doubt reached most ports in the United Kingdom and strengthened the right of ships' masters, as well as supporters ashore, to fly the Bethel flag.

The Reverend John Ashley (an Anglican clergyman with a private income), came on the scene after the Bethel movement had become well established. He was seeking a parish in 1835 when he visited Clevedon, when his attention was caught by Steep Holm and Flat Holm, their residents and later, the shipping anchored in the vicinity.[9] He hired local vessels to minister to the islanders and then, declining the offer of a parish, extended his activities to the ever present shipping, and to ports on both sides of the Bristol Channel. The anchorages off Portishead and at King Road at the mouth of the River Avon became regular locations for his visiting ships and for religious services. Soon his activity embraced ports in north Devon, Somerset, south Wales and up the River Severn, taking in the islands and favoured shipping anchorages such as those off Penarth and ones used by Severn trows.

Very gradually his self-imposed task gathered financial backers, and in 1837 the Bristol Channel Mission Society was formed. Its report for 1839 to 1841 contains thirty pages listing donors and annual subscribers. Indicative of the scale and geographical spread of donations are John Ames (Lyme Regis) £20, Evan Bailie & Sons £10, Robert Bright £10, Mrs Burges (Brislington) £5, C.E. & W.E. Bernard £5. Annual subscribers of a pound or a guinea included Revd Dr Ashley (Shirehampton), Capt. P. Brett R.N., Miss Burroughs (Ashton). There was an obvious need for a dedicated vessel (the *Eirene*) and its keel was laid at Pill, a base for local pilots and possibly another Somerset location for the Bethel movement. Preaching sermons raised at, for example, Weston-super-Mare £68, Taunton £49 and Bedminster £21. When the *Eirene* was finished in 1840 (at a cost of £1,342), her hold had been fitted up as a chapel, able to accommodate 60 or 70 seamen. Manned with a professional master and crew, she rapidly became a familiar and popular sight in all weathers up and down the Channel. Crew wages for 1841 and 1842 came to £427, and Ashley was able to accept remuneration of £300 for 1839 to 1841. He devised his own set of signal flags to indicate when services were to be held and circulated cards for display aboard ship, an effective means of publicising his activities.

Ashley's reports emphasise the religious dimension: evangelisation, services, prayer, *Bible* reading, literature sales and religious counselling. But the existence of this informal sea-going 'coastguard' must have been an effective channel of up-to-date

Illustration 6.3: The Mission Cutter *Eirene* (Reproduced courtesy of the Mission to Seafarers)

Illustration 6.4: The Missions to Seamen Bristol Channel Branch steam launch *Eirene*, with anchored shipping in the Bristol Channel in the late nineteenth century (*Fifty years with our sailors*, 48)

local shipping information reaching maritime and welfare authorities ashore. It provided a model for similar seamen's mission activities afloat in other parts of the country and especially for the soon-to-develop national Church of England Society, The Missions to Seamen in 1856, today's Missions to Seafarers. Fifteen years of intensive labour took a physical toll, and Ashley was forced to give up in 1850. Although he had canvassed support through preaching at Sunday services in Anglican churches, extensively in Somerset, Gloucestershire and south Wales, running a vessel which did not earn its keep was expensive, and the Society was by no means over endowed. Despite being reorganized as the Bristol Channel Seamen's Mission in 1845, it struggled on and was further reorganized at the Bristol Missions to Seamen in 1855. Meanwhile, the need for a national Anglican society was recognized, leading to the formation of the Missions to Seamen. Although a few local Anglican societies had been formed in the 1820s, Anglicans had often lent their support for seafarers' welfare to the Bethel movement. The new society sought to unify Anglican provision nationally and internationally. Thus in 1858 the Bristol Society merged with the Missions to Seamen. Operating from Bristol as the Bristol Channel Branch, the work afloat pioneered by Ashley was continued, though with an emphasis on the Somerset side of the Bristol Channel. Although the Mission to Seafarers venerates Ashley's efforts as its roots, recent research argues that the national mission was a separate establishment with which the remnant of Ashley's mission later merged.[10]

While the initiation of seamen's Bethel activity in Somerset in the 1820s is well established, evidence is uncertain for its continuation later in the

Illustration 6.5: The inside of the mission chapel of St Peter on the quay at Minehead, *c.*1950 (Adrian Webb Collection)

nineteenth century. However, at Minehead the mission chapel of St Peter on the quay was created from a merchant's cellar in 1910. The cellar had been donated to Minehad at the same time as an almshouse complex by Robert Quirke, a local merchant and mariner. This would have been a typical initiative on behalf of seamen and fishermen. It is still in use as a place of worship. Similarly, the building now occupied by Watchet Museum is reported as being in use as late as 1907 as a seamen's chapel. In contrast to this the Bristol Seamen's Friend Society, with its floating chapel at the Grove, Bristol became an established feature. But the rise of the Mission to Seamen with a strong branch based in Bristol ensured the continued outreach and not only the work afloat in the Bristol Channel. Later in the century it established a seamen's institute at Portishead, and for Bridgwater and Burnham it maintained a Scripture Reader, the Missions to Seamen title for its lay seamen's missionaries.[11] This provision lasted well into the twentieth century, as did the work at Avonmouth and Bristol docks. Today the focus has moved to the Royal Portbury Dock, where, through the Port of Bristol Seafarers Centre, there is an ecumenical welfare presence in which the Mission to Seafarers, the Sailors' Society and the Apostleship of the Sea (a Roman Catholic organisation formed in 1920) share the physical resources in providing spiritual and social welfare for today's seafarers.

The Bristol branch of the Missions to Seamen acquired another sphere of religious outreach, in connection with future boy seamen training in T.S. *Formidable*, moored off Portishead. Often referred to as the Bristol training ship, this was Somerset's contribution to the civilian stationary training ship movement. At its height in the 1880s there were over twenty such vessels scattered around the United Kingdom coastline.[12] Two were fee-paying officer cadet boarding establishments, five were orphanages, eleven, including T.S. *Formidable*, were operated under the Industrial Schools Acts, and three under the Reformatory Schools Acts. Only boys sent to the last category had been convicted of an offence, but those sent to the industrial schools were sent under court orders, as they were deemed as being in need of care and protection. T.S. *Formidable* was licensed and inspected by the Home Office, and could receive boys from any part of the country, but most came from Bristol and Somerset. The ship was both an

Illustration 6.6: The National Nautical School, 2015. Following its closure in 1983 the building is now part of a private gated community known as Fedden Village. (By Lewis Clarke, CC BY-SA 2.0, https://commons.wikimedia.org/w/index.php?curid=51282402)

Illustration 6.7: T.S. *Formidable* and the tender *Polly*, pre 1907. To the left is pictured Mr Henry Fedden and to the right Mr Augustine Woodward two of the principal founders (National Nautical School, *National Nautical School Jubilee Year 1954* (1954))

elementary school and a vocational training establishment in which the primary training was seamanship. Boys were literate and numerate on leaving, and between 1869 and 1909 of the 3,700 boys discharged 2,312 were found jobs as boys in merchant ships.[13] T.S. *Formidable* was licensed for 300 boys and in 1878 was reported as being full. The staff numbered twenty, which included three schoolmasters, and five seamen instructors. Boys also received instruction from tradesmen: carpenter, tailor, shoemaker, cook and blacksmith, and the bandsman and gunner. There was a sea-going tender, *Polly*, for summer cruises, an infirmary ashore, and a shipping agent was employed to find berths at sea for boys who left. The Mission to Seamen chaplains in a sense for many years were visiting staff, taking not only regular services but also confirmation classes and burial services, the ship not being immune from accidents and illnesses. In 1906 the establishment moved ashore into new buildings on a site adjacent to where the ship had been moored. It was renamed the National Nautical School, and in 1912 acquired a chaplain and its own chapel dedicated to St Nicholas. In 1933 it became an approved school. In its later years the school became a leading provider of trained sea catering staff. It closed in 1983 and the buildings were converted into private residences.

Undoubtedly Dr. Ashley would have visited the Bristol Channel islands of Steep Holm and Flat Holm, but the use of the latter as a location for an isolation hospital came long after his time. Established by Cardiff Borough Council in 1883 it was one of a national network of similar hospitals founded in the late nineteenth century in the battle against imported diseases and their containment.[14] The risk was mainly from persons entering the United Kingdom from parts of the world where there were outbreaks of contagious diseases, such as cholera. High on the list were seafarers in merchant ships. Indeed, the first patients on Flat Holm were cholera cases from the steamer *Rishanglys* which had arrived at Cardiff from Marseilles with cholera aboard. Flat Holm was farmed and its produce was sent to Cardiff for sale. In addition Flat Holm had temporary residents, including a military detachment and lighthouse keepers, which made the establishment of the hospital a contentious issue. Nevertheless, seamen were accommodated in a tented hospital. In 1886 Flat Holm was leased from the Marquess of Bute, its owner, and a more permanent hospital structure was erected. Seafarers from several other ships and other ports apart from Cardiff were received over the following years. Even Barnstaple, Bridgewater and Watchet had nominal arrangements to send cases there should they occur. By the 1930s alternative arrangements had been made and the hospital at Flat Holm was redundant.

Conclusion

The boundaries adopted for the Maritime History of Somerset series recognise a coastline on the Bristol Channel extending south westerly from the mouth of the River Avon to the boundary with Devon. This area excludes the major port of Bristol where seafaring well-being agencies in the region were generally based. But such services move with the times and provision migrated to Avonmouth, and more recently to Portbury (south of the River Avon) where The Mission to Seafarers has a seafarers' centre continuing the ministry initiated by John Ashley nearly 200 years ago. The examples discussed above show Somerset was as much involved in the various facets of seafaring welfare provision as other parts of the British Isles. They also demonstrate how minor ports and locations abutting Somerset's coastline were not ignored. Today much of charitable social welfare provision for seafarers has been assumed by the welfare state, but visiting seafarers, as itinerants, continue to value the support seafaring missions are able to provide.

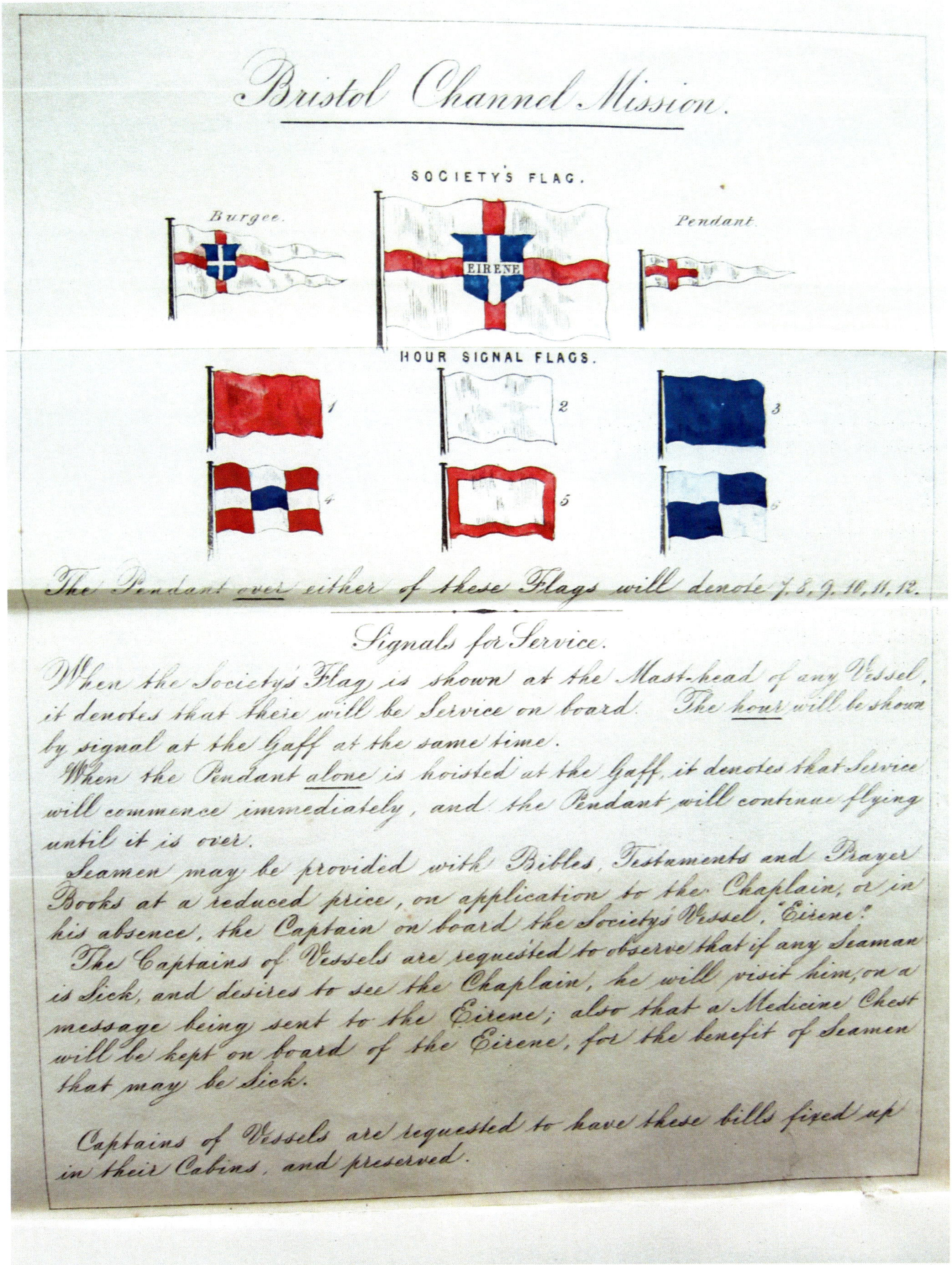

Bristol Channel Mission.

SOCIETY'S FLAG.

Burgee.

EIRENE

Pendant.

HOUR SIGNAL FLAGS.

1 2 3 4 5 6

The Pendant over either of these Flags will denote 7, 8, 9, 10, 11, 12.

Signals for Service.

When the Society's Flag is shown at the Mast-head of any Vessel, it denotes that there will be Service on board. The hour will be shown by signal at the Gaff at the same time.

When the Pendant alone is hoisted at the Gaff, it denotes that Service will commence immediately, and the Pendant will continue flying until it is over.

Seamen may be provided with Bibles, Testaments and Prayer Books at a reduced price, on application to the Chaplain, or in his absence, the Captain on board the Society's Vessel, "Eirene."

The Captains of Vessels are requested to observe that if any Seaman is Sick, and desires to see the Chaplain, he will visit him, on a message being sent to the Eirene; also that a Medicine Chest will be kept on board of the Eirene, for the benefit of Seamen that may be Sick.

Captains of Vessels are requested to have these bills fixed up in their Cabins, and preserved.

Illustration 6.8: The Reverend John Ashley used this simple signal code to advertise to nearby vessels when a service was about to take place aboard the ship flying the flags. The cards depicting the code were often framed and displayed aboard ships (*Report of the Bristol Channel Mission Society* . . ., 1839-1843 courtesy of Bristol Reference Library)

References

1 For a recent study of Ashley's life, including his mission to seafarers see R.W.H. Miller, *Dr. Ashley's Pleasure Yacht: John Ashley, the Bristol Channel Mission and all that Followed* (Cambridge, 2017).

2 R. Kverndal, *Seamen's missions: their origin and early growth: a contribution to the history of the Church maritime* (Pasadena, 1986) is the definitive work on the rise of seamen's missions. See also A. Kennerley, 'British seamen's missions and sailors' homes, 1815-1970: voluntary welfare provision for serving seafarers' (unpublished PhD thesis, CNAA/Polytechnic South West [Plymouth], 1989), and A. Kennerley, 'The British contribution to seafarers' welfare in Mediterranean and Black Sea ports since the 1820s', *Mariners' Mirror*, 93:1 (February 2007), 65-82. Mission histories include: The Missions to Seamen, *Fifty years with our Sailors* (London, 1906); G.A. Gollack, *At the Sign of the Flying Angel* (London, 1930); L.A.G. Strong, *Flying Angel: the story of the Missions to Seamen* (London, 1956); Bill Down, *On course together, the Churches' ministry in the maritime world today* (Norwich, 1989); R.W.H. Miller, *One Firm Anchor: The Church and the Merchant Seafarer* (Cambridge, 2012).

3 Kverndal, *Seamen's missions*, 170.

4 The Sailors' Society actually sees the formation of the Port of London Society for Promoting Religion among Merchant Seamen in 1818 as its beginning, then the 1919 Society, followed by the British & Foreign Sailors' Society formed in 1833, which was renamed British Sailors' Society in 1925, and then British & International Sailors' Society in 1995 (see the sources in note 2 above).

5 *Sailors' Magazine*, vol. III (1822), 170-1; see also 291-2.

6 *Sailors' Magazine*, vol. III (1822), 370-1.

7 *Sailors' Magazine*, vol. IV (1823), 196.

8 *Sailors' Magazine*, vol. IV (1823), 101; G.C. Smith (ed.), *Minehead & Watchet officers and the Bethel Flag* ... (Bristol, 1823).

9 Kverndal, 382-6.

10 Miller, *Dr. Ashley's Pleasure Yacht*, 103-108.

11 Missions to Seamen, *Annual reports* (1882), 35; (1915), 115.

12 A. Kennerley, 'Ratings for the mercantile marine: the roles of charity, the State, and industry in the pre-service education and training of ratings for the British Merchant Navy, 1879-1939' in *History of Education*, vol. XXVIII, no. 1 (March 1999), 31-51.

13 A. Kennerley, 'The education of the Merchant seaman in the nineteenth century', unpublished MA thesis, University of Exeter, 1978, appendices 10e and 10f, T.S. *Formidable*: extracts from statements of admissions and discharges.

14 J.R. [Morgan-]Guy, 'Hulk and Holm: England's offshore battle against cholera', *Proceedings: XXX International Congress of the History of Medicine* (Düsseldorf, 31 August – 5 September 1986), 833-7; 'The Cholera Hospital: Flat Holm isolation hospital, 1884-1937' in B. Jory, *et.al* (eds), *Flat Holm: Bristol Channel Island* (Wincanton, 1995), 84-97;

Chapter Seven

West Somerset's Maritime Stone Trade, 1400-1900

Philip Ashford

Introduction

ROCK AND STONE was a cargo that does not figure in the surviving customs accounts for the Somerset ports prior to 1900. Fortunately, evidence for the importation and exportation of stone and its usage can be found in other records from which some aspects of Somerset's stone trade can be reconstructed. Furthermore, given that stone is often a lasting material, physical remains of the trade in stone brought to west Somerset harbours and strands still exists. Similarly, where Somerset stone is found further afield the material provides evidence of stone exports.[1] This chapter is divided into two parts. The first examines how natural materials from the coast were used in construction and as exports. Secondly, how imported materials have been used in west Somerset and where they came from.

Local construction and exports

Perhaps the earliest use of cobbles of the Hangman sandstones was on the beaches of Porlock and Minehead themselves. The cobbles were moved into roughly coursed 'V' formations to form medieval tidal fish weirs.[2] Weirs, still visible today especially at low Spring tides, have arms up to 70 metres long, four metres wide and up to a metre high.[3] Such fish weirs are numerous along the west Somerset coast as far as Lilstock. Documentary evidence for Dunster's weirs dates back to the eleventh century, with fifteenth and sixteenth century references to others in neighbouring parishes.[4] Those in the far west of the county are composed of Devonian aged beach material, mainly Hangman sandstone, whilst others east of Dunster are composed of Triassic or Jurrasic beach material. The 'Lord's weir at Watchet, probably made of local lias stone, was still standing in 1475, but stone was carried away, probably sold, to Wales in 1480.[5] In 1614, further east at Stoford, in the manor of Week Fitzpaine, the tenants from

> time beyond the memory of man at their pleasure … have digged and carried away stone between the Chesil and low water mark from Chinkmere to Wyppell for the building and repair of their houses within the said manor and other necessary uses.[6]

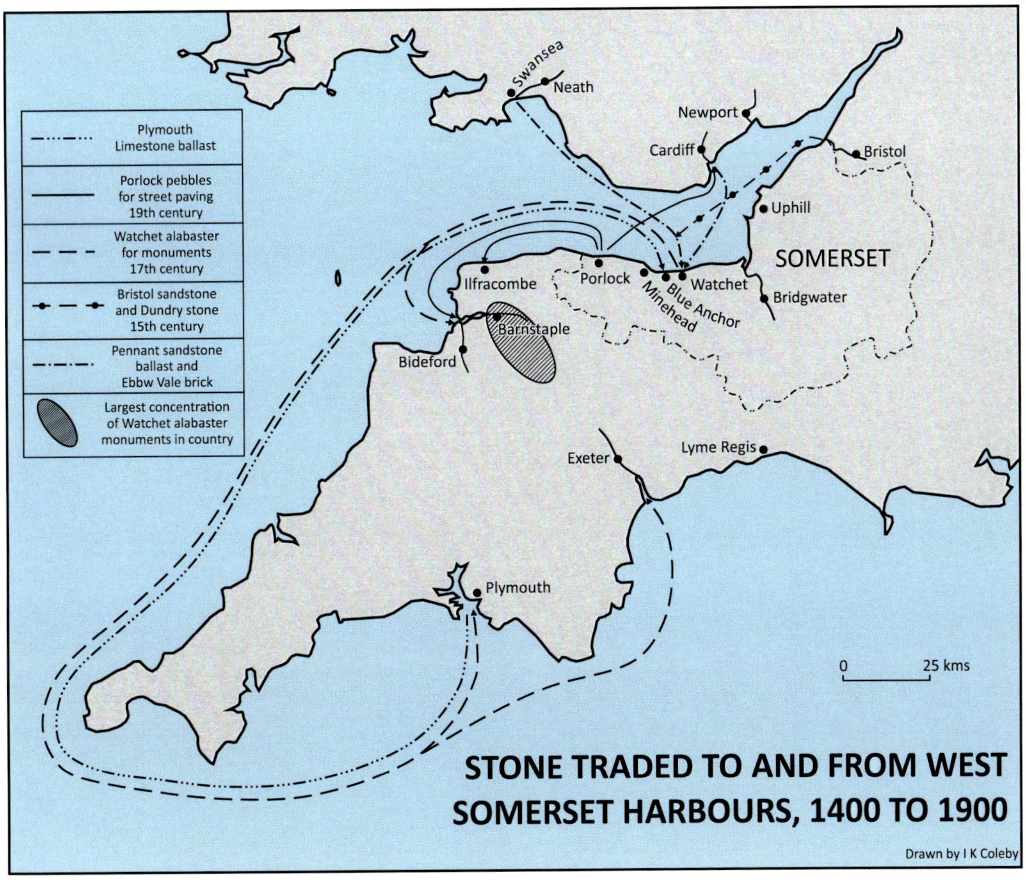

Illustration 7.1: Map illustrating aspects of stone traded to and from ports and harbours in west Somerset, from 1400 to 1900 (Reg Highnam, 2017)

Illustration 7.2: Gore Point, Worthy and Porlock Weir at low tide. Two small pools can be seen at Gore Point. These are the pools behind fish weirs made of Hangman sandstone pebbles and boulders. (Elliot Lowe, 2014)

The material in question would have been Jurassic lias.

Much later, the expansion of Cardiff in the 1850s created a demand for street paving in order to improve drainage and the durability of its carriage-ways. Previously, the streets had been cobbled by stones from the River Taff, but fresh supplies, of what proved to be superior paving cobbles, for 'pitching the streets' were obtained from Porlock and Minehead. Between 1856 and 1858 at least eight named streets were cobbled to the 'great satisfaction' of the Cardiff authorities, using the Hangman sandstone pebbles from west Somerset.[7] No doubt the trade continued, for the same reason, since it is clear that the *Fanny*, one of Porlock's most long-lasting trading vessels, exported pebbles to Cardiff twice in 1864 and continued to take pebbles to south Wales up until at least 1867. At this time the vessel was owned by William Pulsford and Robert Marley was the master.[8] Porlock pebbles were also taken to Newport; for example, the *Unity*, with Stevens as master, arrived at Newport in June 1856 from Porlock with 'stones'.[9]

Porlock pebbles were also used to help pave the streets of two Devon towns. Pebbles ordered by Barnstaple Council in 1877 had not arrived from Porlock by early October. A member of Barnstable Council travelled to Porlock to order a further cargo in October 1882. Pebbles were ordered from Mr Marley of Porlock in June 1886, at least two more cargos in 1887, one of which was delivered by the *Elianor and Mary* in May 1887. Later, in July 1887 a further two cargoes of Porlock pebbles were ordered by Barnstaple Urban Sanitary Authority. The *Samuel* delivered a cargo of pebbles to Barnstaple from Porlock in July 1889 and finally, in April 1893, the *Mary-Grace* arrived in Barnstaple with a cargo of Porlock pebbles for the town council.[10] As far as Ilfracombe was concerned 70 tons of Porlock pebbles were ordered in June 1860 because extensive repairs were needed for parish roads. However, in 1879 an offer by Mr Marley of Porlock to deliver pebbles at 3s 2d a ton was rejected. Despite this a cargo of Porlock pebbles arrived in Ilfracombe in March 1889 to mix with local stone for paving some of its streets.[11] In 1877 three cargoes of Porlock stones were ordered for the streets of Plymouth.[12]

Porlock was not the only west Somerset location to provide Hangman sandstone pebbles for Wales. In 1866, the *Stag* of Minehead, Henry Pulsford being the managing owner, sailed from Minehead to Cardiff six times with pebbles and a Watchet vessel, the *Tredegar*, collected pebbles from Minehead in 1872.[13] Observant geologists may well find these Hangman sandstone pebbles used as paving material at Neath and Swansea; both were common destinations of those vessels.

Porlock pebbles or cobbles were also used for garden pathways, courtyards and pavements in Porlock, Bossington and as far inland as Holt Ball Farm, Luccombe for example. Larger Hangman sandstone cobbles were used in the construction of whole houses on Porlock beach, in garden walls, such as at Bossington, as well as agricultural buildings. The regularity of some of the cobbles is due to the fairly even width of the natural beds of the Hangman sandstone as it outcrops on the Exmoor coast, often with a near vertical angle of dip. This regularity makes the cobbles particularly suitable for 'cock and

Illustration 7.3: Paving with pebbles (or cobbles) outside of St Michael's church, Minehead, *c.*1930. The scene must have been very similar to street developments in Cardiff, Newport, Barnstaple, Ilfracombe and Plymouth in the second half of the nineteenth century, all locations that received pebbles from west Somerset by ship. (Philip Ashford Collection)

Illustration 7.4: Whole Hangman sandstone pebbles used in garden walls at Bossington (Garry Holden Photographics, 2016)

Illustration 7.5: Dressed Hangman sandstone pebbles used for a chimney at Bossington (Garry Holden Photographics, 2016)

Illustration 7.6: Fishermen's cottages on the beach at Porlock Weir constructed of Hangman sandstone pebbles (Garry Holden Photographics, 2016)

Illustration 7.7: A camouflaged World War Two pillbox at Porlock Weir. Hangman sandstone pebbles overlay the concrete (Garry Holden Photographics, 2016)

Illustration 7.8: The forecourt of the Castle Hotel in Porlock constructed of local Hangman sandstone pebbles (Garry Holden Photographics, 2016)

Illustration 7.9: A twenty-first century pavement in Dunster's High Street, flanked by Hangman sandstone pebbles used for pavement and gutter construction (Philip Ashford, 2016)

Illustration 7.10: A sloping Hangman sandstone pebble apron around a cottage at Bratton, Minehead designed to clear water drips from the thatch and move the water away from the footings. (Garry Holden Photographics, 2016)

Illustration 7.11: A domestic dwelling west of St Michael's church, Minehead. This building was created from a converted barn made of Hangman sandstone pebbles (Philip Ashford, 2016)

hen' coping stones on wall-tops.

Though hard to work and dress, Minehead Hangman sandstone cobbles were successfully split width-wise in the nineteenth century to provide a flattish face. This free building material was used by the Luttrell estate to build whole streets of terraced houses, such as Selbourne Place, Minehead. The new houses were rented out to local residents when the town was expanding due to the coming of the railway to Minehead in 1874.

Illustration 7.12: Selbourne Place, Minehead built principally of split Hangman sandstone pebbles from Minehead beach in the second half of the nineteenth century. (Garry Holden Photographics, 2016)

In contrast to the hard Hangman sandstone, the pinkish alabaster (anhydrous calcium sulphate) ground down to make gypsum, from Watchet's alabaster cliff on West Beach is too soft for exterior work. Nevertheless, it does form the key stones above the nineteenth-century windows of a house in Swain Street, Watchet. Watchet alabaster was used in medieval times for carving figures for the early fifteenth-century tombs of Sir Hugh Luttrell and his wife,[14] the pictorial alabaster memorial stone to Elizabeth Luttrell d. 1493[15] and the effigy of Thomas Luttrell carved about 1570,[16] all of which are still visible in Dunster church. Whether the plaster bought by the manor of Porlock from Watchet, and probably delivered by boat, in 1420 was from gypsum, or lime from the blue-grey Jurassic Limestone for making mortar is not known.[17] The alabaster effigies of Sir John and Lady Harrington in Porlock church are early fifteenth century and it was supposed that two alabaster chimney pieces visible in Worthy Manor House, Porlock, in the nineteenth century, were of a similar age.[18] The alabaster used at these locations is likely to have come from Watchet, as is the alabaster in the Tudor arches in the great hall at Binham Grange, Old Cleeve.[19] Since alabaster is not found in Bristol, it is just possible that alabaster tables and alter screens exported in Bristol ships to Gascony, Spain and Portugal in the 1470s and 1480s were carved from the raw material derived from the cliffs at Watchet.[20]

Illustration 7.13: Detail of a dressed Hangman sandstone pebble wall in Selbourne Place, Minehead. (Garry Holden Photographics, 2016)

A description, by Thomas Gerrard, of Watchet's alabaster industry from the first decades of the seventeenth century stated that it was used for making tombs and chimney pieces.[21] This is borne out by the fact that thirteen alabaster effigies of local dignitaries were made between 1603 and 1632 and installed in Somerset churches (listed at Appendix 1); there may have been more which have not survived the ravages of Victorian restoration. Of the thirteen effigies, ten are in west Somerset leading to the suggestion that the raw material supply was indeed from Watchet cliffs. Furthermore, a few Somerset church fonts such as the one in Williton church,

Illustration 7.14: The fifteenth-century alabaster effigies of Sir John Harrington (d.1418) and Lady Elizabeth Harington (d. 1471) in Porlock church. It is likely that the alabaster was from Watchet and would have been brought to Porlock by boat. (Philip Ashford, 2016)

Illustration 7.15: The fifteenth-century pink alabaster effigy of William Canynges (1399-1474). Canynges was Bristol's richest merchant in the mid fifteenth century, with a fleet of nine ships and 800 sailors. In his later life he became a churchman and is dressed as such in this effigy at St Mary Redcliffe, Bristol. It is not unlikely that the pink alabaster came from Watchet. If so, it is likely to have been transported there by a local trading vessel rather than one of Canynges's large ships. Alabaster alter screens are more likely to have been traded in Canynges's ships. (Philip Ashford, 2016)

dated 1666,[22] and at Elworthy were made of Watchet alabaster.[23] This alabaster would have left the cliff by cart for these two local destinations. In addition, there is evidence that there was an active export trade of alabaster from Watchet during the early seventeenth century. Documentary evidence in the record of Watchet quay duties from 1621 (payable to the lord of the manor) reveals a duty of 4d per ton was placed on alabaster, the same as tonnage duty for freestone and one penny more than grindstones.[24] Physical evidence of the locations of alabaster effigies in churches from this period in Bristol and Bath, Gloucestershire and Devon can be found next to, or near, navigable parts of the rivers Avon, Severn, Taw, Torridge, Tamar, Teign and Exe. Also, Watchet alabaster is known to have been used for early seventeenth-century church wall memorials at Michaelston-y-Fedw (half way between Cardiff and Newport) and possibly at Margam (near Port Talbot). See Appendix 2.

Research by R. Firman of Nottingham

Illustration 7.16: Effigies of Henry and George Wyndham dated 1624 in St Decuman's church. The pink alabaster must surely have come from the Watchet cliffs. (Philip Ashford, 2016)

University has shown that if the whole of the seventeenth century is considered, there are at least 39 monuments in churches within 10 miles of Barnstaple made wholly or largely of Somerset alabaster from the Watchet area. There are lesser concentrations near Plymouth and Exeter. Firman states that he was not qualified to forward geological or social reasons for those concentrations, but it is clear from the maritime history perspective that there were strong trading links between Watchet and the Barnstaple area, especially during the seventeenth century.[25]

The alabaster trade continued during the eighteenth and nineteenth centuries. Eyewitness to this was Daniel Defoe, who may have walked on Watchet beach in the 1740s, who commented that the alabaster which fell from the cliffs was transported to Bristol by coaster.[26] The export of alabaster from Watchet was later noted in the 1780s[27] and in 1798 it was observed that the export of gypsum from the cliffs was part of Watchet's maritime trade.[28] In the 1830s the main destinations for Watchet gypsum were Bristol and Swansea.[29] Significant expenditure by the Earl of Egremont enabled craftsmen in the late 1830s to use a considerable amount of Watchet alabaster in the interior restoration of Sampford Brett church, the style of which upset contemporary commentators.[30] Also in the 1830s, a prominent geologist, Henry de la Beche, noted that the still considerable deposits of alabaster were in the cliffs to the west of Watchet.[31] Many 'vast blocks' of gypsum (alabaster) from layers of up to 'three feet deep' piled on each other were noted at the base of the cliffs to the west of Watchet.[32] South of Taunton, the font of Buckland St Mary's church, restored in the late 1850s, has panels made of Watchet alabaster.[33]

Fig. 24.

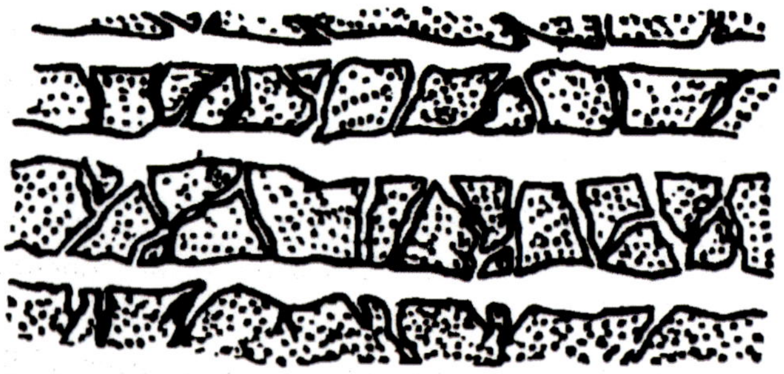

Illustration 7.17: Alabaster formations found in the cliffs near Watchet. (Henry de la Beche, *Report on the geology of Cornwall, Devon and west Somerset* (London, 1839), 196). Note the white alabaster layers which may be 60 cms or more thick with smaller inter-connecting veins.

Illustration 7.18: The sea-cobbled floor of the porch of Old Cleeve church showing the intriguing design of yellowing alabaster pebbles in the shape of a heart. Part of the diamond shape is also illustrated along with the presumed date of design, 1614. The alabaster pebbles derived from the cliffs near Blue Anchor. The fact that there are two playing card motifs on the floor of a church porch, dating from the early seventeenth century, is an intriguing one (Philip Ashford, 2016)

In 1857 a Bridgwater merchant, Alfred Barham, paid £100 to lease the right to search for and quarry alabaster on the cliffs and beaches of Old Cleeve manor, west of Watchet. The enterprise must have been profitable since he renewed the lease in 1860, paying £150. [34] Quarrying alabaster continued along the coast belonging to the lord of the manor of Old Cleeve during the 1870s, since Barham Brothers of Bridgwater were quarrying for gypsum at Blue Anchor in 1872. Transporting gypsum from the coast at Blue Anchor was more difficult than from Watchet. Though no harbour lay beneath the quarry, a sandy patch below the cliffs known as 'The Berths' was cleared of rocks and marked with tall posts to facilitate mooring, berthing and loading. The quarry is said to have contained a small railway for transporting the stone to the loading pier, now entirely vanished, and from thence it was lowered to the ships, probably with the help of a shoot. The ships, which are likely to have been ketches, had to carefully pick the right weather, for despite the prevailing westerly winds, it was all too easy to be caught on a lee shore. Once away vessels returned to Watchet where the gypsum was used in paper-making, or shipped to Bristol where the poorer quality broken alabaster or gypsum could be easily crushed for plaster-of-Paris, and the finer larger pieces reserved for carving.[35]

Shipments of alabaster, 30 tons a time, were taken to Minehead from Watchet in the 1870s and 1880s.[36] One vessel carrying gypsum from Watchet in 1871 was the *Tartar*, the managing owner was Thomas Widlake who would have profited from this sale of gypsum to merchants in Waterford, Ireland.[37] In 1873 a Bridgwater schooner of 80 tons taking gypsum, probably from Watchet, to Waterford struck rocks just east of Ilfracombe.[38] During the 1890s several shiploads of gypsum, or gypsum stone were taken every year from Watchet to south Wales in vessels of between 20 and 70 tons. The predominant destination was Swansea where the purchaser was Vivian and Sons, but a few shiploads were taken to

Newport. This seems to have been a winter trade since most sailings were between November and April.[39] Alabaster stone was also taken to Swansea in September 1891.[40]

Also outcropping on the Watchet beach, east of the harbour is a blue-grey muddy Jurassic limestone. This limestone has been burned in kilns for centuries and makes natural cement. It has long been used for harbour walls and docks which needed quick-setting hydraulic cement. In the nineteenth century slabs of this limestone were collected from the beach near Splash Point at low tide, brought up the slipway by cart and burned in a kiln in Goviers Lane. Watchet lime was traded throughout the Bristol Channel region and further afield.[41] Hydraulic lime, which had the property of setting underwater, was, in 1756, transported in 80 cider barrels from Watchet to Plymouth for use on John Smeaton's Eddystone lighthouse.[42] The excess from this most famous of engineering projects, seven years later, was used by Smeaton for underwater engineering when the Calder, Yorkshire, navigation was being improved.[43]

In 1798 an observer stated that the pebbles of lias, left on the beach by the tide at Watchet, were the stone 'from which the greatest advantage is derived'.[44] He went on to comment on the use of manufactured lime mortar for making bridge piers. The presence of this 'blue lias limestone of Watchet, so admirably adapted for aquatic building' was, in 1845, one of the trades that the proposed new railways into this part of west Somerset hoped to capture from coastal vessels.[45] However, despite the coming of the railway to Watchet, stone, probably limestone continued to be transported by ship; for example Cardiff in 1872 and Swansea in 1897 and 1899 received shiploads of Watchet limestone.[46] Presumably the existence of this trade indicates that railway freight costs had not yet completely undercut shipping prices between Watchet and parts of south Wales as had been hoped by the railway developers.

The geologist's eye and evidence of stone imports through West Somerset ports

One commonly imported stone, limestone, used in many Somerset coastal lime kilns from at least the sixteenth century and used for making mortar, or for spreading on farmland, leaves little or no evidence as it was burned. In the 1830s Porlock vessels visited Porthcawl in ballast and brought limestone back to Porlock kilns, such as in July 1830 by the *Betsy* (mastered by Perkins) and in the *Harriet* (mastered by Poole). Perkins and the *Betsy* were in action in the same trade in March 1843.[47] During the 1860s and 1870s local vessels frequently brought back stone to Watchet, commonly Carboniferous limestone from Uphill, from Barry to Minehead and Newton to Porlock.[48] Thus, in the case of Porlock, the ancient connection with Newton seems to have continued until almost the end of the era of the coastal trading under sail in the Bristol Channel.[49]

Documentary evidence for Cornish slate and Bristol stone, arriving at Dunster by ship during the early fifteenth century, is mentioned elsewhere in this volume. The Bristol stone was red sandstone and was used to make a 'new', early fifteenth-century, gatehouse, still visible today, which was subsequently roofed with Cornish slate.[50] Blue lias was one of the rocks used to construct the nave and tower of St Michael's church at Minehead in the fifteenth century.[51] It is likely to have come from Blue Anchor, or the cliffs and foreshore around Watchet and brought to Minehead by boat.[52] Within the church there is evidence for other Bristol stone arriving in west Somerset, probably by ship; Dundry stone was used for an effigy of a fifteenth-century cleric, likely to have been Richard of Bruton, Minehead's vicar from 1401 to 1406. The Dundry stone canopy to the effigy is thought to have been carved much later, about 1460.[53]

Within feet of Watchet harbour itself is a garden wall which is partially constructed of Carboniferous Pennant sandstone, probably from south Wales though some is found in the Bristol area. The most likely explanation being that it was constructed from ballast removed from vessels arriving at Watchet to load Iron Ore for the Dowlais Iron Company in the nineteenth century. More significant is the rank of fine terraced houses on the north side of West Street, and a substantial three-story house in Swain Street made of Plymouth limestone. Again, the most likely scenario is that vessels from south Devon arrived at Watchet in ballast having taken coal to Plymouth from south Wales. They would then load Iron Ore to take back to Wales on the homeward leg. Between 1864 and 1914 there were innumerable voyages made by coastal vessels plying between Plymouth, Watchet and south Wales, many recorded as carrying stone or ballast. An example was the *Friends* which carried

Illustration 7.19: A house made of Plymouth limestone near Watchet harbour (Garry Holden Photographics, 2016)

stone and ballast in 1870 and visited Plymouth and Watchet.[54] The terraced houses of West Street, Watchet, have windows and doors surrounded by yellow Ebbw Vale brick, which was brought to this part of west Somerset in part exchange for iron ore between 1855 and 1914; the Ebbw Vale Company rented property on Watchet Esplanade in 1866.[55] The name 'Ebbw Vale' is even found printed on fine yellow brick moulded gate post coping stones at the bottom of Goviers Lane, Watchet.[56]

Conclusion

There are a variety of geological types, useful for vernacular and other construction purposes, such as quays, or for artistic and industrial usage, outcropping along the west Somerset coast from Porlock to Watchet. The cliffs and beaches have long been exploited by local people and businesses partly because they were easily accessible by sea. Some of the rocks or pebbles have been carried inland, whilst others were sent as cargoes to destinations around the Bristol Channel and occasionally beyond. Beach material has also been used as ballast when vessels sailed from the Somerset coast to Wales to bring back coal or limestone. Other geological material arrived in the west Somerset ports, either directly for construction, or as ballast which had at times been turned to commercial use.

The combination of the lasting nature of stone, the survival of some documentation relating to its trade and the expert knowledge of geologists, has meant that new light can be shed on this aspect of maritime history. In many cases the results of the endeavours of stone merchants and masons are as visible today as when the stone was first traded and worked, a link back to Somerset's vibrant maritime past. The trade in Watchet's liassic limestone, alabaster and gypsum from the seventeenth to the nineteenth century has meant that the coastline was quarried for mercantile gain. This must have increased the rates of erosion along parts of the west Somerset coast, especially in the Watchet area where the rocks are much softer than those to the west of Minehead. Combined with funeral monuments, church fonts, cobbled streets, domestic buildings and other uses, the stone trade has left its mark not only on Somerset but across the region.

Illustration 7.20: Pennant sandstone from south Wales, the brown stones in a garden wall by Watchet harbour (Garry Holden Photographics, 2016)

Appendix 1. Early seventeenth century west of England alabaster effigies in Somerset churches, 1603-1633

Batholamew Barnes and family, Bath Abbey, 1605.
Lady Waller, Bath Abbey, 1633.
Rachel Portman, Bickenhall, 1632.
George Farwell, Bishop's Hull, 1609.
Francis Kingsmill, Bridgwater, 1620.
William Brewer, Chard, 1618.
Sir William Bassett, Claverton, 1613.
Sir John Stowell and his second wife, Cothelstone, 1603.
John Colles, Pitminster, 1607.
John Colles, Pitminster, 1627.

Henry and George Windham, Watchet, 1624.
Chief Justice Popham, Wellington, 1607.
Humphrey Windham, Wiveliscombe, 1622.

Source: A. Wickham, *Churches of Somerset* (London, 1965), 73-4. Given that, according to Wickham, alternative sources of alabaster that might be used for effigies in Somerset during the early seventeenth century would be from Derbyshire or Italy, and given that there were no maritime links with Derbyshire and that Somerset did not have significant maritime links with Italy at the time, the most likely explanation for this group of west Somerset alabaster effigies is that the source material came from an area of coast stretching from Blue Anchor to Watchet. Information has also been consulted on the Church Monument Society's website churchmonumentssociety.org accessed April 2016.

Appendix 2. Alabaster effigies in other west of England and Welsh churches and Cathedrals, 1600-1644

Bristol
Sir Richard Berkeley, Lord Mayor's chapel, 1602.
Sir George Snygge, Holy Trinity St Philips,1617.

Gloucestershire
Henry, 17th Lord Berkeley, Berkeley, 1615.
Alderman Abraham Blackleech, Gloucester Cathedral, 1639.
William Culpepper, Miserden, 1640, 1644.

Devon
Elizaeus Hele, Bovey Tracey, 1626.
Bishop William Cotton, Exeter Cathedral, 1621.
Bishop Valentine Carey, Exeter Cathedral, 1626.
Rector John Downe, Instow, 1633.
Sir Arthur and Lady Harris, Lifton St Mary, 1618, 1630.
Elizabeth Elford, Sheepstor, 1641.
John Grenville M.P., Tavistock St Eustacius, 1600.
William Bourchier and wife, Tawstock St Peter, 1623.

Glamorganshire
Unknown, Michaelston-y-Fedw, early 17th century.
Unknown, Margam, early 17th century.

Source: Church Monument Society pages relating to Bristol, Gloucestershire and Devon found online attheir website churchmonumentssociety.org accessed April 2016. Excellent images of all these monuments are to be found at these interesting websites. The information relating to Watchet limestone monuments in South Wales derives from M. Statham, 'A history of the use of alabaster deposits of South Wales and South-West England' in *Welsh Stone Forum* 13 (2016), 10-11.

References

1 This chapter compliments sections in chapters 1 and 3 where exports of Somerset stone via the Avon and the Parrett are explored.

2 D. Webb and E. Webb, *The hidden edge of Exmoor* (Kingston Bagpuize, 2011), 28, has an excellent photo of one at Culver Cliff, Minehead. Stunning aerial photos of those at Porlock and Minehead are to be found in H. Riley and R. Wilson-North, *The field archaeology of Exmoor* (Swindon, 2001), 158-9. A reference in Riley and Wilson-North points out that wooden structures associated with other fish weirs found along the Severn Estuary date back to the eighth or ninth centuries, so the use of the Hangman sandstone to construct fish weirs could date to the Anglo-Saxon period.

3 Somerset Historic Environment Record number 35926 found at http://webapp1.somerset.gov.uk/her/details.asp?prn=35926 accessed February 2016.

4 Somerset Historic Environment Record number 33776 found at http://webapp1.somerset.gov.uk/her/details.asp?prn=33776 accessed February 2016.

5 W. Page, *Victoria County History of Somerset* volume 2 (London, 1906), 160.

6 S.H.C., DD/X/WI/34 survey of the manor of Week Fitzpaine, 1614.

7 *The Cardiff and Merthyr Guardian, Glamorgan, Monmouth and Brecon Gazette*, 30 April 1859, under the headline 'Cardiff sanitary and other works 1856-1858'.

8 S.H.C., DD\RSS/1/4/10, 1/5/53, 1/6/57 and 1/7/124 Port of Bridgwater crew lists which give details of vessel ownership, crew, destinations and cargoes of Bridgwater vessels in particular years, 1864-1867.

9 *Monmouthshire Merlin,* 21 June 1856.

10 *The North Devon Journal,* 4 October 1877, 19 October 1882, 24 June 1886, 26 May 1887, 14 July 1887, 18 July 1889 and 20 April 1893.

11 *The North Devon Journal,* 7 June 1860, 14 August 1879 and 28 March 1889.

12 *The Exeter and Plymouth Gazette,* 16 September 1877.

13 S.H.C., DD\RSS/1/6/51, 1/8/104 and 1/17/97 for example. Port of Bridgwater crew lists which give details of vessel ownership, crew, destinations and cargoes of Bridgwater vessels in particular years.

14 E. Robinson, *A geology of Watchet walls* (Watchet, no date). This undated pamphlet is available at Watchet Museum, Watchet Conservation Society website http://www.watchetconservationsociety.co.uk/features_alabaster.html accessed February 2016.

15 Elizabeth Luttrell's memorial, http://www.victoriacountyhistory.ac.uk/explore/items/dunster-castle accessed March 2016.

16 A. Wickham, *Churches of Somerset* (London, 1965), 73.

17 C. Chadwyck-Healey, *The history of part of west Somerset* (London, 1901), 423.

18 W. Hook, *A history of the ancient church of Porlock* (London, 1893), 76.

19 http://www.binhamgrange.co.uk/ and Period property of the month, http://www.periodproperty.co.uk/ppuk_discovering_ppom_200901.shtml accessed March 2016.

20 F. Cheetham, *English medieval alabasters* (London, 1984), 47, refers to exports in 1478, as do Bristol customs accounts for 1485, transcribed for the Cabot project and kindly

supplied by Dr Evan Jones of the University of Bristol.

21 E. Bates (ed.), *The particular description of the county of Somerset*, S.R.S. 15 (1900), 12. In this source, Thomas Gerrard of Trent, Dorset, makes the geologically unsound statement that the alabaster was mined at Minehead. This cannot have been the case as the cliffs at Minehead are the older Hangman sandstone. It is not until the cliffs to the east of Blue Anchor are reached that the appropriate geological formations occur, continuing past Watchet. Interestingly, William Gerrard (d.1604) of Trent, who must have been a relation of Thomas, has a monument in Trent parish church partially made of pink alabaster. Thomas probably made his comment regarding the Watchet Alabaster industry knowing the origin of this particular piece of alabaster. (Dorset, Church Monument Society, found at www.churchmonumentssociety.org/Dorset.html, accessed April 2016).

22 Robinson, *Watchet walls.*

23 Details of the architecture, including the alabaster font are to be found at 'Church of St Martin, Elworthy', www.visitchurches.org.uk/Ourchurches/Completelistofchurches/Church-of-St-Martin-of-Tours-Elworthy-Somerset/ accessed February 2016.

24 S.H.C., DD/WY M/4038 box 2 survey of the manor of Williton Fulford, 1621. I am grateful to Dr Adrian Webb for this reference.

25 R. Firman, 'Somerset alabaster, the Devon connection' in *Church Monument Society Newsletter* 9 (1994), 34-6. A copy of this article with other notes and distribution maps of the subject are found elsewhere (S.H.C., A\CUR/3 documents relating to Somerset alabaster *c*1990s).

26 D. Defoe, *A tour through the whole island of Great Britain* (London, 1748), 21.

27 J. Collinson, *The history and antiquities of the county of Somerset* 3 (Bath, 1791), 486.

28 W. Gilpin, *Observations on the western parts of England* (London, 1798), 168-9.

29 De la Beche was director of the Ordnance geologic survey. It is clear from sketches of the alabaster veins that De la Beche walked along the foreshore at Watchet. He was no stranger to the Bristol Channel, having sailed from King Road to the Carribean for geologic research in 1823 (H. de la Beche, *Report on the geology of Cornwall, Devon and west Somerset* (London, 1839), 504).

30 Anon, *The Ecclesiologist* (Cambridge, 1842), 110.

31 De la Beche, *Geology*, 196-7.

32 L. Horner, 'Sketch of the geology of the south-west part of Somersetshire' in *Transactions of the Geological Society* 3 (London, 1816), 345.

33 Anon, *The Building News,* 10 (London, 1863), 704.

34 M. Siraut, *Watchet alabaster*, found at www.victoriacountyhistory.ac.uk/explore/sites/.../watchet_alabaster.doc accessed February 2016.

35 This material regarding shipments of alabaster from Blue Anchor in the 1870s derives from the notes of the late Hilary Binding, who was working on a chapter for this volume before she so sadly died in 2015. Hilary's contribution to researching and writing about west Somerset history was immense.

36 Siraut, *Watchet alabaster.*

37 S.H.C., DD\RSS/1/15/36 Port of Bridgwater crew list, 1871.

38 'Wrecks off c. Wexford' found at www.irishwrecksonline.net/Lists/WexfordListC.htm accessed February 2016.

39 *South Wales Daily News*, examples of shipping movements reported in 28 August 1888, 4 May 1889, 6 May 1890, 11 February 1891, 7 May 1891, 7 October 1891, 31 May 1892, 16 May 1893, 3 January 1894, 22 February 1894, 7 April 1894, 3 April 1895, 25 April 1896, 21 December 1896, 13 February 1897, 16 September 1898, 11 November 1898, 13 March 1899 and 18 November 1899; *South Wales Daily Post* 13 May 1895. Vivian and Sons were a metallurgical and chemical business in the lower Swansea valley. They made artificial manures, fertilizer from imported commodities. The gypsum was probably used for this.

40 *South Wales Daily News,* 10 September 1891.

41 Robinson, *Watchet walls.*

42 P. Stainer, *Somerset in the age of steam* (Taunton, 2003), 30.

43 C. Pasley, *Observations on lime, calcareous mortars, stuccos and concrete* (London, 1838), 181.

44 Gilpin, *Observations*, 169.

45 Anon, *The Economist* 3 (1845), 881.

46 *The South Wales Daily News*, 25 April 1872 and 1 November 1897; *The Weekly Mail*, 28 October 1899.

47 *The Cambrian*, 3 July 1830 and 11 March 1843.

48 S.H.C., DD\RSS/1.1.135, 1/19/111, 1/4/50, 1/21/92 and 1/18/52 Port of Bridgwater crew lists, 1860s and 1870s.

49 Porlock vessels traded with Newton during the early seventeenth century (*M.H.S.* 1, 53-4).

50 O. Garnett, *Dunster Castle, Somerset* (London, 2003), 30.

51 Anon, Parish church of Saint Michael, Historic England, found at https://historicengland.org.uk/listing/the-list/list-entry/1207000 accessed February 2016.

52 R. Edwards, *Exmoor geology* (Tiverton, 2000), 38-9 has a fine colour image of the tower but comments that Blue lias is also found in Selworthy parish which may mean there was an alternative source for the stone in the tower and nave.

53 Anon, *Guide to St Michael's church, Minehead* (Minehead, 2012), 6.

54 S.H.C., DD\RSS/1/14/47 Port of Bridgwater crew lists, 1870. This is but one of the many crew lists which detail coastal vessels trading between Plymouth and the Somerset ports in the Bristol Channel in the 1860s and 1870s. However, during the 1740s and in 1771, hoys arrived in Watchet during the summer months to collect wood for the Royal Navy; thus, it is possible that Plymouth limestone rock came to Watchet as ballast in those vessels. (T.N.A., ADM 106 series 1003/240; 1023/69, 106, 123, 143, 167; 1056/103; ADM 354 series 125/129; 128/199; 132/72).

55 Robinson, *Watchet walls*; SHC, DD\CCH/3/5, Solicitor's papers relating to leases, 1865-1873.

56 Robinson, *Watchet walls.* A fine image of these coping stones and the Ebbw Vale name imprint is to be found on the Watchet Conservation Society website found at www.watchetconservationsociety.co.uk/features_welshbrick.html accessed February 2016.

Chapter Eight

Copper Ore to Swansea: a Little Known Trade from the Historic Port of Combwich, 1791-1820

Peter Skidmore

Introduction

COMBWICH, A SMALL port near the mouth of the River Parrett, is mentioned in records dating back to the fourteenth century when corn shipped to Ireland was the main component of the trade.[1] The trade in agricultural products continued through to the eighteenth and nineteenth centuries when members of the farming community were investing in vessels for the trade. Grahame Farr in writing on the creek of Combwich in Victorian times, reported that the Combwich Farmers' Association built up a small but efficient fleet of vessels with the millers, maltsters and yeomen of Spaxton, Nether Stowey, Otterhampton and other nearby centres using Combwich because it was nearer than Bridgwater.[2] Eighteenth century port books for Bridgwater, of which Combwich was a subsidiary port for customs purposes, show the diversity of the outgoing trade that existed at that time with cargoes of fruit, cider, elm timber, flax and linen yarn being recorded in the outgoing trade in 1775.[3] There was also a trade in bricks and tiles manufactured from local clay to which Combwich would have contributed. A brick works was built there in 1832 by Henry Leigh, the son of another Henry Leigh a Cannington merchant and shipowner who was one of the leading owners of vessels listed in the Bridgwater registers. Shipments of bricks were made to ports throughout the south west and the requirement for fuel to fire the kilns further enhanced the coal trade from South Wales.

The copper ore shipped from Combwich was mined on the northern fringe of the Quantock Hills in and around the parish of Dodington where the Marquis of Buckingham (1753-1813) inherited land from the previous owner, Lord Melcombe, in 1762. The Marquis, educated at Eton and Christ Church

Illustration 8.1: The 1878 Salcombe built ketch *Sarah Jane* alongside Combwich Quay. (Rod Fitzhugh Collection)

Oxford, was a prominent British statesman, the second son of George Grenville, Prime Minister of Great Britain. He was returned to Parliament as one of the Members for Buckinghamshire from 1774 to 1779 when he succeeded his uncle as the second Earl Temple and moved to the House of Lords. In 1782 Buckingham became a member of the Privy Council and was appointed Lord Lieutenant of Ireland in the Rockingham ministry.[4]

We do not have substantive records of mining activities until the Marquis's period of tenure. Records, known as the Stowe manuscripts, are held in the Henry Huntington Library, San Marino, California and an extensive collection of microfilm copies of the documents are available in the Somerset Heritage Centre in Taunton. The records include maps, plans of the mines and letters dated from 1786. The letters include letters to the Marquis from his estate agent, initially Richard Camplin and later Scrope Bernard, letters between the estate agent and the Marquis's mining agent William Jenkin (1738-1820), and between Jenkin and the various mining captains he appointed. The records also report on mining activities on land owned by the Marquis in the Mendips around Bleadon, Banwell and Loxton where lead, fluorospar, and calamine were mined.

Jenkin, a Cornishman from Redruth, was an important figure in the Cornish copper industry. He was a qualified sampler and assayer of copper ore and was appointed as the Inspector Sampler for the Cornish Metal Company in 1785. This gave him responsibility for purchasing practically all the copper ore produced in Cornwall which at that time amounted to some forty to fifty thousand tons per annum. He also had interests in a company for the transportation of ore overland, while outside of the industry he was the agent for the owner of the Lanhydrock, estate, one of the largest estates in Cornwall. Unsurprisingly Jenkin often found it difficult to fulfil all of his responsibilities and there were occasions when the Marquis was asked to write to his employers, in Cornwall, to obtain permission for him to be temporarily released from his commitments there to make visits to Somerset.[5] Jenkin's 'out' letters, which covered all his business interests, have survived and are held in a series of bound volumes in the Courtney Library at the Royal Institution of Cornwall in Truro. The library also holds a set of transcripts of the Jenkin letters relating to Buckingham's mines prepared by Ruth Phillips.[6] The letters provide another valuable source for research, although they start in 1790 four years later than the Buckingham records. Account ledgers have also survived and are held in a separate collection in the Cornwall Record Office.[7]

The letters are almost exclusively about activities in Cornwall amongst which there are many relating to the Marquis's mining interests in the parish of Gwennap, which no doubt accounted for the relationship with Jenkin being established. Although there is a vast collection of letters, those relating to the Somerset activities are relatively easy to find. In addition to the transcriptions held by the Courtney Library, A.K. Hamilton-Jenkin, a descendant of William Jenkin, produced lists of references to assist J.R. Hamilton and J.F. Lawrence who researched the mining activities around Dodington and reported on their work in a book published in 1970 with a second edition added in 2008.[8] Hamilton-Jenkin also produced two files of research notes one consisting of correspondence and the second of newspaper cuttings and other ephemera.[9] Penny Watts-Russell also kindly carried out a search of her transcriptions to provide a further list of references for this project.

Although not within the scope of this study, the Jenkin letters relating to mining activities in the Mendips include a reference to a proposal to use a wharf near Batch on the River Axe for shipping fluorspar mined at Banwell Hill.[10] Unfortunately there are no subsequent references to actual shipments to provide a basis for a future study.

Mining in Dodington

References from Hamilton and Lawrence's work were used alongside information from primary sources to prepare the following summary and provide a background to the accounts of the shipping activities.

There were two discrete phases of mining activity at Dodington covered by the Buckingham and Jenkin records, from 1786 to 1801 and from 1817 to 1821. The two phases were conducted by different groups of investors. Records of the first phase start with the English Copper Company already working in Dodington in 1786. They were followed by the Mines Royal Mineral and Battery Work Society, who were awarded a lease in 1787, together with some other smaller concerns.[11] There are no references to Jenkin being involved with any of these concerns and it would appear that he had no responsibility for their work.

Jenkin was involved when the Fox family were awarded a lease, having been influential in their decision to invest. The lease was awarded in 1792, the mine during the previous year having produced ore worth about £1,400.[12] The Foxs were a Quaker family principally based in Falmouth but with branches elsewhere in the South West. A syndicate of family members was awarded a lease in 1792. The family held 44 of the 64 shares, with the Marquis holding 16 and Jenkin and representatives of Stephen Maltravers 2 shares each. The holders within the Fox family included George C. Fox & Sons, merchants of Falmouth, with the largest holding of 19 shares; the company incorporating George Croker Fox, Robert Were Fox and their mother Mary Fox. The Perran Wharf Company in which George Fox, son of Edward Fox a Wadebridge merchant was in partnership with William Phillips of Penryn, held 17 shares leaving Edward Fox himself and his brother, Thomas Fox of Wellington, holding 2 each. [13] It was also standard practice for the landowner to include a requirement to pay dues in the conditions of the lease on the sales of the material raised. In this instance a copy of the lease could not be found although there is a reference to dues in one of Jenkin's letters to Camplin advising him that the Fox family were asking if the Marquis could abate his dues, which confirms that they were included although we do not know the level.[14] The investment by the Foxes followed a visit to the mines in 1786 by Thomas Fox with associates from Wellington, after which a relatively long period elapsed before they were prepared to invest, although at the time of the visit the visitors were reported as commenting 'that there is doubtless a great deal of copper in this parish and neighbourhood'.[15]

Throughout the first phase Jenkin reported to the Marquis through his estate agent. He also liaised with the Fox family and arranged the sales of the ore to the smelters. Jenkin had a close relationship with the Fox family as a fellow Quaker, having successfully applied for membership of the Society of Friends following his second marriage to Honor Roberts of Marazion, a devout Quaker, in 1790.[16] The responsibility for recruitment of the mine captains also lay with Jenkin and he occasionally recruited miners, all from Cornwall. Mathew Grose was the first captain at the Garden Mine while his brother Samuel Grose and John Penrose had responsibilities elsewhere. Mathew Grose was moved by Jenkin to Loxton in the Mendips in 1788. There may have been an underlying purpose for the move because Mathew had a habit of making overly optimistic reports of prospects to Camplin, either through inexperience or enthusiasm to please, which on occasions led to friction between Jenkin and Camplin when Jenkin had a more conservative view. John Penrose replaced

Illustration 8.2: A map showing locations relevant to the text (Adrian Webb)

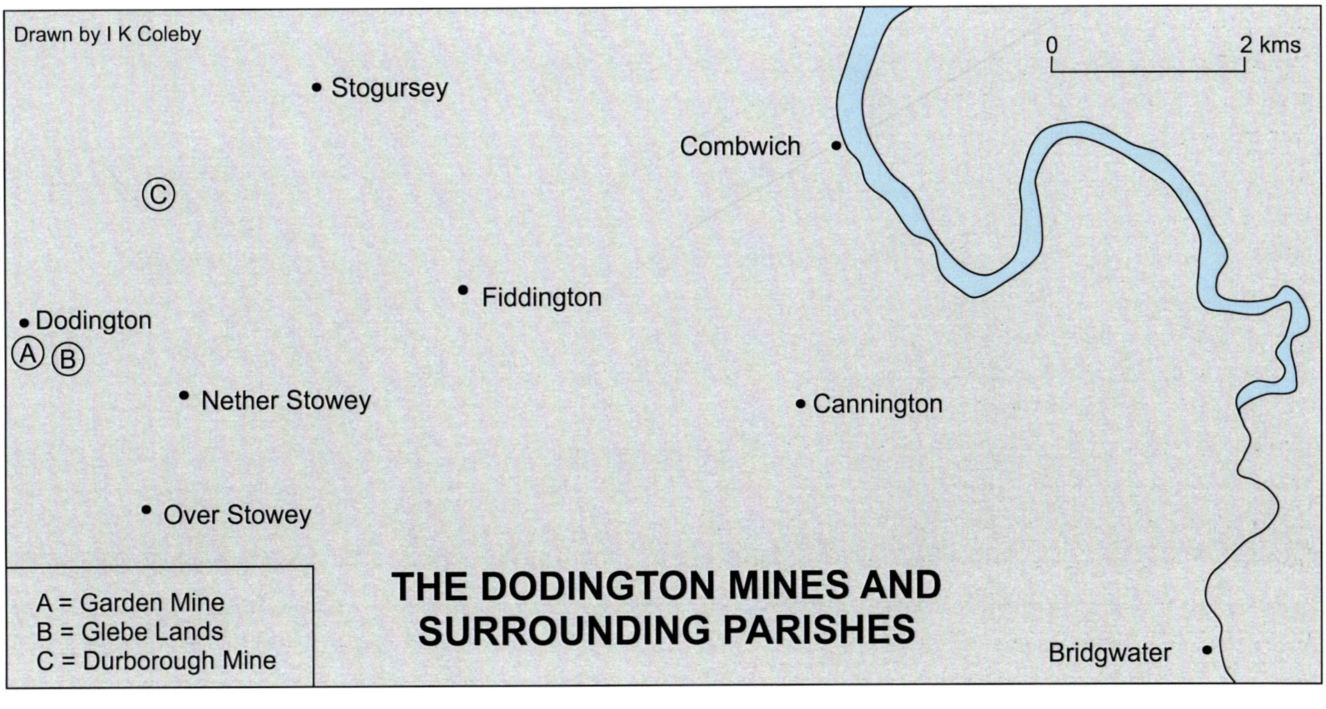

Mathew Grose and was joined by Samuel Grose who was appointed senior mine captain at Dodington in April 1791.[17]

Mining was initially confined to a rectangular piece of land in Dodington. Later the adits were extended into the adjacent Glebe Land and into Durborough Hill with leases obtained from the landowners for the ore to be extracted.[18] The mining area is shown on the map included as Illustration 8.2. Illustration 8.3 is a plan of a section of the mine and Illustration 8.4 is a photograph taken on an exploration in the 1960s showing the conditions in which the men worked.

Unfortunately the mining in which the Fox family was involved did not prosper. Over nearly ten years of operation costs invariably exceeded the income from sales and the principal investors eventually felt that it was not worth continuing. On 12 March 1801 George Croker Fox, representing the largest individual shareholder, wrote 'it is our present intention to give up all those mines where we have been so long sinking money and no prospect of being paid or rather repaid'.[19] Jenkin, however, remained convinced that a successful outcome could still be achieved by sinking a shaft to 30 fathoms and mining at a deeper level. This would have required the installation of a steam engine and pump to clear the workings of water at a cost of around £10,000 which the first group of investors were not prepared to consider. Indeed it was sixteen years before the second group of investors took a lease and implemented this strategy, sufficiently confident that the investment would be worthwhile.

The second period of operation from 1817 to 1821 was led by a group of local investors assembled by Thomas Poole (1765-1837) of Nether Stowey, a philanthropist and pillar of the community. The group included two local investors, Edward Sealy (1778-1864), and Sons bankers and Richard Symons, an attorney at law, both of Bridgwater, and some of Poole's London business associates. Their decision to invest followed a period of lengthy consultation on the prospects for the venture and a search for sponsors. The opinion of the renowned Humphry Davy was sought in 1806, who warned of the difficulties in predicting the likely outcome stating 'the indications would be favourable if the mine was

Illustration 8.3: An extract from a plan of the Buckingham mines in the manor of Dodington. (S.H.C., DD\HSE/1)

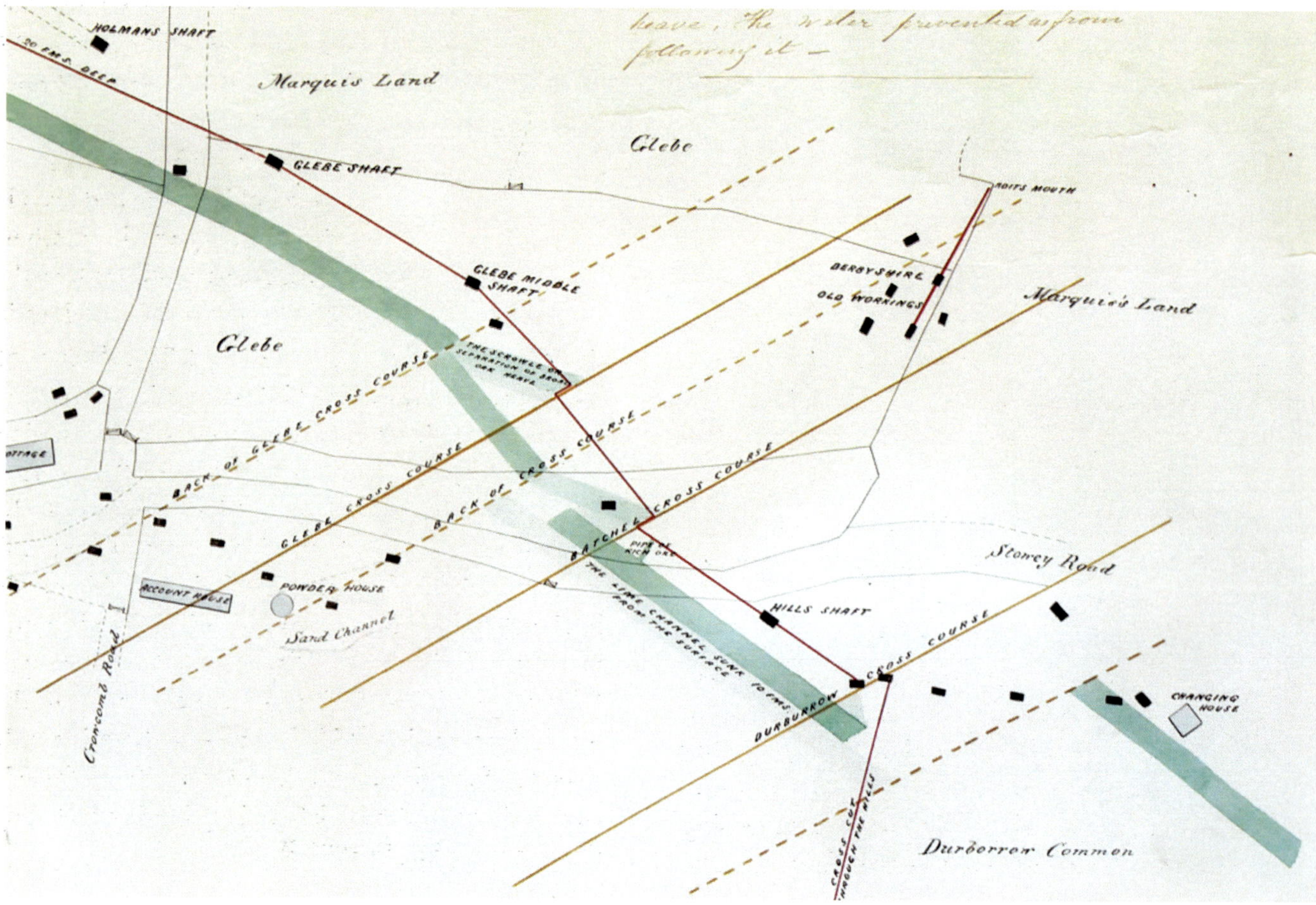

Illustration 8.4: An exploration of the Buckingham adit in the 1970s. (Nick Chipchase Collection)

in Cornwall but in a shell limestone of late formation, which existed at Dodington, there had not yet been any instances of great copper mines' and with only limited funds available he decided not to invest.[20] Poole nevertheless proceeded and submitted a proposal for re-opening the mine to the Marquis in 1806.[21] Jenkin was invited to Dodington in 1807 to meet with Poole and his fellow adventurers, together with Samuel Grose and an associate, John Chester, to discuss the prospects.[22] Jenkin formed a friendship with Thomas Poole during this visit declaring that he had been 'received with great civility and hospitality in his house'. In the following year Poole travelled to Cornwall to see the mines and the 'gigantic machinery employed about them' and stayed with Jenkin for a fortnight.[23]

Despite this personal relationship, however, Jenkin did not invest in the venture; although he was enthusiastic about the prospects of mining at a lower level he is reported as having lacked confidence in the mining abilities of the new adventurers.[24]

A lease was not applied for until some years later in 1817 and was granted for a term of 21 years with the condition that the adventurers would make an investment of £8,000 in the first six years, including the purchase of a steam engine of 50 nominal horse power. Illustration 8.5 shows the engine house erected on the Glebe land.

Buckingham was a shareholder, as he had been in the first period. Mathew Grose was employed as the mine captain, his activities in the Mendips having come to an end. The absence of mining references in Jenkin's letters in this period suggests that he was not called upon for advice. Jenkin's role, and later that of his son Alfred (1792-1872), following his death in 1820, appeared to be solely to act as agents for selling the ore. Alfred took on many of his father's roles following his death, having been sent away to school in Epping and eventually being apprenticed as a land surveyor following an initial desire to pursue a career in the medical profession.[25] Unfortunately the mine only operated for a short period, and was offered for sale with its associated materials and equipment, including the steam engine, in 1822.[26]

Illustration 8.5: The remains of the Buckingham Mine Glebe Engine House, with Hinkley Point Nuclear Powerstations "A" and "B" in the background, 2017. (Adrian Webb)

The South Wales Smelters

It seems appropriate to include a brief section on the customers, the South Wales smelters, since they feature extensively in the shipping accounts. The industry has been extensively researched and there are excellent reference works from which information can be gleaned on the smelters named in the Combwich accounts.[27]

The ownership of the smelting concerns was split between manufacturers and miners. The manufacturers principally from London, Birmingham and Bristol invested to protect their supplies from exploitation by the smelters and, at the opposite end of the chain, miners invested to protect their ore prices and supply outlets. The purchasers of Dodington ore came from both categories. The Birmingham Mining and Copper Company were manufacturers who were in a co-operative venture based on Redruth mining, Swansea smelting and Birmingham manufacture. The Bristol Brass and Wire Company had smelting interests and included manufacturing in the form of wire drawing mills on their site in Swansea, while another Bristol based company, the John Freeman & Co. Copper Company, smelted at the White Rock Copper works in Swansea.[28] The Crown Copper Company, based in the Neath valley at Neath Abbey was another company established to supply Birmingham's metal requirements just before the end of the eighteenth century.[29] Non-ferrous metal smelting was first established in the Neath Valley late in the sixteenth century before moving to Swansea.[30]

John Vivian from Cornwall and Thomas Williams from Anglesey were the two major mining investors. Vivian acquired a stake in the Cheadle Smelting Company at Penclawdd in 1800 and in 1809 built a new works at Hafod on the west bank of the River Tawe, just above Swansea. Vivian's son and grandson went on to manage the works at Hafod which established him as one of the acknowledged leaders in the British copper trade.[31]

Thomas Williams of Anglesey was known as the

'King of Copper' through his many smelting investments based on ore from his Parys Mine on Anglesey. He acquired the Upper Bank Works in Swansea in 1782 and one of his associates, the Stanley Company, took over the Middle Bank works in 1787. Williams in his heyday had a powerful hold on the smelting industry with other smelting interests in Amlwch on Anglesey and St Helens near Liverpool. Following his death in 1802 his son managed the Middle Bank works together with the Grenfells, a London based Cornish family with interests in mining and banking.[32]

Shipments from Combwich

The records found for the shipments are shown in Table 8.1 and are all taken from the Jenkin letters. Only one reference was found in the Buckingham letters which was to an estimated 100 tons of ore being ready for shipment in 1791, but no shipping details were provided.[33] Apart from the final two records all are for the first period of operation. The shipments were all from Combwich, but unfortunately it is impossible to trace the clearances of the vessels in shipping records. The port books for Bridgwater are not extant for the end of the eighteenth century and there are no local newspapers with shipping lists published at that time. There are, however, shipping lists for the destination ports in South Wales. The *Cambrian* newspaper included lists for the South Wales ports from the start of publication in 1804, although unfortunately, when searched, no records of copper ore shipments arriving from the River Parrett could be found.[34]

It is unfortunate that Jenkin was not more closely involved with the shipping as he was for the Cornish ore shipped from Portreath. For Portreath he often listed in his letters vessels waiting to load and vessels dispatched for the smelters. He also had frequent contact with Henry Bath, the leading shipping agent in Swansea, often expediting the provision of vessels to transport shipments of ore. Of course this was a much larger scale operation with the control of shipping essential to maintain a consistent supply of ore to keep the smelters operating.

The responsibility for arranging shipping at Combwich was delegated to the mine captain who was asked to procure vessels as and when a parcel of ore had been assembled ready for sampling and weighing. It was traditional to load the ore onto the vessel immediately after weighing in the presence of the smelter's representative. In the one instance where a vessel was identified it was found to have been registered in the Bridgwater shipping registers to local owners. It was probably representative of the vessels used since many of the requests came at short notice. All the shipments went to Swansea with the exception of one which went to Neath. The shipments are listed chronologically in table 8.1 and the following narrative provides a background to each shipment and sale transaction.

Table 8.1: Copper Ore Shipments from Combwich, 1791-1820

Shipment No.	Date	Source	Buyer	Where to	Source	Quantity		
						ton	cwt	qtr
1	29 Sep 1791	HJ/1/1	Birmingham Mining and Copper Company	Swansea	Buckingham	40	0	0
					Durborrow	5	0	0
2	19 Mar 1794	HJ/1/2	John Freeman & Co. Copper Company	Swansea	Buckingham	89	15	0
					Glebe	2	12	1
3	15 Jan 1796	HJ/1/3	Thomas Williams, Middle Bank	Swansea		74	2	0
4	15 Apr 1798	HJ/1/5	Bristol Brass and Wire Company	Swansea		56	19	2
5	31 Jan 1800	HJ/1/5	Bristol Brass and Wire Company	Swansea		57	13	1
6	4 Dec 1801	HJ/1/5	Parys Mine Company	Swansea		42	19	0
7	20 Oct 1820 (est.)	HJ/2/4	Middle Bank	Swansea		70		
8	16 Nov 1820 (est.)	HJ/2/4	Crown Copper Company	Neath		27	7	2

Source: Courtney Library, HJ/1/1-60, letters 1790-1906, HJ/2/1-10, letters as agent for William Grenfell & Co and the Crown Copper Company, 1814-1853.

Shipment No. 1

In a letter dated 1 June 1791 Jenkin advised Camplin there was a parcel of Buckingham ore that must be sold soon. Jenkin found it difficult to release himself from his duties in Cornwall for an extended period, but believed he could be spared for three or four days which would allow him time to carry out the sampling. He proposed that Samuel Grose and John Penrose, the two mine captains, get the ore ready for him to sample and weigh together with agents of the Birmingham Mining and Copper Company who were interested in buying the ore.

In the letter he also alluded to an issue existing between the Marquis and the Fox family relating to their investment in the Loxton mine by saying that that R.W. Fox might accompany him if it was possible to allot a day to settle the business between them. Jenkin continued by saying that the matter had given him great uneasiness of late and he heartily wished he had never proposed their (the Fox family) taking up any concern in the Somerset mines.[35] In an earlier letter to Camplin, on 5 May Jenkin had advised him that the Foxs were ready to give up the mine.[36]

A letter to John Penrose and Samuel Grose on 29 September 1791, advised them that the ore had been sold to the Birmingham Company with 40 tons of Buckingham ore fetching £13 18s per ton and 5 tons of Durborrow ore £8 2s per ton.[37] On 15 November a letter to Camplin advised him of the sale and stated that the Birmingham Company offered to contract to take future shipments at a fixed standard but he did not feel warranted to make a bargain with them.[38]

Shipment No. 2

It is three years before we find another shipment which was bought by the John Freeman & Co Copper Company of Bristol; the shipment was made on 19 March 1794. Jenkin wrote to Thomas Fox at Wellington in late December 1793 advising him that the contract had been made at a standard of £82 per ton of fine copper and that he intended to travel to Combwich in late January along with the buyer's agent, Paul Penrose, to sample and weigh the ore. He also mentioned that they needed to discuss the best method of proceeding with the lease.[39] This subject is taken further with the Marquis's agent, now Scrope Bernard, in a letter to him on 19 February when he raised the subject of the unease that existed within the Fox family. The information he imparted had been gleaned from a meeting the day before with Robert Were Fox and his brother who indicated that fellow investors Fox, Phillips and Fox & Co wanted to reduce their shareholding and would offer the Marquis half their share at two thirds of the cost. The Fox family also wanted the Marquis to consider abating his dues, or indeed temporarily suspending them, until 'the mine could better bear it'. Jenkin expressed the view that he considered that the prospects might be improved at a lower level of mining, but felt he could not press the adventurers to risk their money in the necessary investment given their present dissatisfaction.[40] A letter from Jenkin to Scrope Bernard on 19 March advised him that the ore had been weighed, and sampled and the weights and prices were 89 ton 15 cwt of Buckingham ore at £12 4s per ton and 12 ton 2 cwt 1 qtr of Glebe ore at £7 2s per ton.[41]

Shipment No. 3

For the next shipment, two years later, G.C. Fox & Sons decided to take responsibility for the sale of the ore using their relationship with Thomas Williams. In late 1795 Fox and Sons were advised that a parcel of ore was going to be carried to the shipping point, Combwich, in about four weeks time and Samuel Grose would arrange to get a vessel to take it to Swansea.[42] On 14 January 1796 they were further advised that half the ore was at Combwich, but Samuel Grose had not received any directions from them to get a vessel and therefore he, Jenkin, had instructed him to get a good vessel as soon as possible and get it insured.[43] A dispute then occurred with G. C. Fox & Sons wanting payment to be made according to the weight and sample as delivered to Swansea instead of at the point of shipping which was the traditional way. Jenkin disagreed with this but stated that the difference is probably 'more in words than substance' and instructed Samuel Grose to let it be delivered to Middle Bank, Swansea and apply to Thomas Williams there for him to sample and weigh the ore.[44]

Shipment No.4

In April 1798 Jenkin wrote to Samuel Grose to advise him of his imminent visit to Somerset with Captain Morcom the representative of the Bristol Brass and Wire Company to weigh and sample ore at

Combwich. He asked him to use his utmost endeavour to engage a vessel to take the ore onboard directly after weighing in the presence of Captain Morcom.[45] While still in Stowey, Jenkin wrote to Scrope Bernard to advise him that the weighing and sampling had taken place and stated that the weight was 56 ton 19 cwt 2 qtr with an estimated sale price of 12 or £13 per ton; the samples were to be assayed on his return to Cornwall to set the final price in the normal way.[46]

Shipment No. 5

Another parcel of ore was ready for sale in June 1799. Again G.C. Fox & Sons insisted on deciding where the ore was sold and they undertook to write to one of the copper companies to contract for its sale. Jenkin in correspondence with Samuel Grose tells him of the current buoyancy of the market with ore selling at the standard of £120 per ton of fine copper, while at the same time expressing fears that this may not last as the government is acting to reduce exports to India for the benefit of the Birmingham manufacturers.[47] Despite the action proposed by G.C. Fox & Sons, Jenkin remained active in looking for a buyer for the ore and advised Scrope Bernard that he was endeavouring to make a contract for the sale of about 45 tons of ore at the mines which he believes will sell for £600. A sum which he stated would again be considerably 'short of the cost of getting it'.[48] It was September before it was reported that a bid of £115 per ton standard was received from the Bristol Wire and Copper Company. G.C. Fox & Sons were asked if this is acceptable, or would they prefer to wait until the following Spring with the possibility that prices might be better. They were advised that Samuel Grose will get the ore carried to Combwich for sampling and weighing, but this would require a month because he has a limited number of sacks and only one farmer to carry it.[49] A deal is struck within a week with Morcom, the agent of the Bristol Wire and Copper Company, at a standard of £116 per ton.[50] The shipment, however, is delayed by a message from Samuel Grose stating that there was no proper place for receiving the ore at Combwich at that time but he was told to get as much ore as possible from underground and to get a regular sample before removing it from the 'strakes'.[51] Clearly the situation had been resolved by November when Jenkin advised Samuel Grose that he planned to be in Combwich on 22 December with Morcom to sample and weigh the ores. G.C. Fox & Sons were advised on the same date that the ores were nearly ready for sampling and they should be worth about £1,000, the quantity to be weighed having increased by that time.[52] On 9 December Samuel Grose was told to have the men at Combwich by the 20th and if possible to engage a good vessel to take the ores as in the previous year.[53] Scrope Bernard was informed soon after that a contract for the sale of the ore, which was expected to weigh around 56 tons, had been agreed with the Bristol Wire Company.[54] There is no reference to the actual loading and shipping of the ore, but in a letter in January to G.C. Fox & Sons they were informed of the terms of the settlement reached with the Bristol Company with 57 ton 13 cwt 1 qtr being sold for £20 2s 6d per ton realising £1159 16s 5d.[55]

Shipment No. 6

The final shipment in the first phase came soon after in 1801 which coincided with the closure of the mine. In September of that year Jenkin wrote to Thomas Fox at Wellington to advise him that they were now in treaty with Vivian of Truro for the sale of the ore with Vivian said to be buying on behalf of Thomas Williams or Pascoe Grenfell.[56] Later that month a letter to Samuel Grose urged him to 'hasten' all the ore to Combwich for sampling and weighing, advising him that he, Jenkin, would come up to do the work. He further stated that if possible he would like to ship the ore while he was still there and asked if a vessel could be acquired to take the ore in as it was weighed with the usual freight cost from there to Swansea.[57] A letter to G.C. Fox & Sons on 21 September 1801 advised them that Vivian will not give more than £114 per ton standard which at first the adventurers were reluctant to accept but finally agreed to.[58] Scrope Bernard was advised of the outcome and told that it was expected that the ore, estimated as being about 40 tons, would be weighed and sampled in mid November and that the adventurers then wished to give up the mine.[59] A letter to Scrope Bernard on 12 December informed him that the ore, which weighed 42 ton 19 cwt had been delivered to the Parys Mine Company of which nearly 8 tons was raised in the Glebe lands. The letter also refers to dues with Jenkin stating that the Marquis abated them to $^{1}/_{20}$th for the last parcel of ore sold and asking 'what part is to be paid of the present parcel'.[60]

Shipment Nos. 7 and 8

In the second phase of operation the only shipment found was one in 1820 which was eventually split into two. William Jenkin's son, Alfred, who had been retained by the new lease holders to sell the ore following the death of his father, responded to a letter from Mathew Grose, the mine captain, in August 1820 to say that he was ready to sell a parcel of 100 tons provided they could agree on the terms of the sale which would depend on the produce, *i.e.* the assay of the samples when taken.[61] Jenkin decided that the ore should be shared between the Middle Bank works in Swansea and the Crown Company in Neath, with the Middle Bank to receive the major share. This was subsequently found not to be possible because the ore could not be weighed where it was in Combwich and would have to be weighed on arrival at the works. Alfred Jenkin wrote to Michael Allen at Neath to advise him that Williams and Grenfell, the owners of the Middle Bank works, would receive the whole of that consignment with the Crown Company's share coming out of the next 'lot'.[62]

Shipments 7 and 8 are the only ones where the names of the vessels are given. On 16 October Alfred Jenkin informed J.B. Jenkins, the smelters representative, that a parcel of about 100 tons would probably be shipped in two to three days time on board two vessels, the *Friends* and the *Friends Increase* for the Middle Bank works in Swansea. He reiterated that the ore would have to be weighed on arrival with someone from the miners being present to see it done. Jenkin further advised that the captains of the vessels were to be paid the freight charge in accordance with the bills of lading, whatever the consignment weighed.[63] On 16 November Jenkin wrote to Jenkins again telling him that the remainder of the Buckingham ores had been sent to him contrary to his wishes and for the consignment to be delivered to the Crown Works at Neath.[64] The *Friends Increase* subsequently sailed from Swansea to Neath which incurred a further £4 per ton in freight charges.[65]

The vessels

The registration record for the *Friends Increase* was found in the Bridgwater shipping register for 1813. The vessel could be positively identified because the name of the master, James Hensley, was also given. The vessel was a square-sterned schooner of 46 $^{40}/_{94}$ tons burthen registered on 26 July 1813 with John

Illustration 8.6: Unknown vessel in Combwich Pill around the end of the nineteenth century (Rod Fitzhugh Collection)

Callen, a merchant of Otterhampton and Francis Hole and Joseph Wood, mariners of the same place, listed as subscribing owners together with Henry Leigh a Cannington merchant listed as a non-subscribing owner. James Hensley was the fourth master of the vessel having been appointed on 2 March 1820.[66]

There is a registration record on 6 February 1806 for a vessel named *Friends*, which was a square-sterned brigantine of $73^{43}/_{94}$ tons burthen but the vessel cannot be positively confirmed as being the vessel used because the master is not named; vessels of the same name often appeared in the same register. In this case, however, there is a high degree of certainty that this was the case since there was only one *Friends* in the register. Again the vessel was in local ownership with John Callen and Henry Leigh both subscribing owners.

Conclusion

The Buckingham and Jenkin archives between them provide a rich source of information on mining activities on the Marquis of Buckingham's land at Dodington in Somerset. Hamilton and Lawrence have made full use of the sources in their research of the mining activities and have produced two editions of an excellent publication on the subject. This work has investigated the downstream activities, the marketing and shipping of the ore, which the Jenkin letters cover in great detail.

Unfortunately a complete set of accounts could not be found to compare the quantities raised with the quantities shipped. At the end of the first phase of operation, however, Jenkin reported that the value of ore returned over the period of operation had been around £8,000.[67] Taking an assumed average price of £15 per ton this would equate to a total of about 550 tons being raised, which is close to the total tonnage of the shipments in Table 8.1 which amounted to just over 466 tons. Unfortunately no similar statement of production could be found for the second period making a similar comparison impossible, although it is almost certain that there was more than the one shipment, divided into two, that was found.

The quantities shipped were insignificant when compared with the Cornish output but nevertheless the mining was an important activity in the Quantocks at the time and added another element to the trade portfolio of the port of Combwich.

On the assertion made at one stage that no suitable place was available at Combwich to store the ore, one possible reason was a report that a sample previously sent for assay contained brick dust; no doubt an unfortunate consequence of the ore sharing storage with products of the principal industry in the port.

References

1 R.W. Dunning (ed.), *A history of the county of Somerset*, 6 (1992), 85.

2 G.C. Farr, *Somerset harbours including the port of Bristol,* (London, 1954), 117-8.

3 The National Archive (hereafter T.N.A.), E 190/1127/5 Bridgwater customs port book, Jan.-July 1775.

4 *Encyclopaedia Brittanica* (19 Jan 2010).

5 S.H.C., T\PH\hamn/1 letter from Richard Camplin to the Marquis at the request of William Jenkin, 17 Sep. 1786.

6 The letter books are held by the Courtney Library (hereafter C.L.) the letters include HJ/1/1-60, letters 1790-1906, HJ/2/1-10, letters as agent for William Grenfell & Co and the Crown Copper Company, 1814-1853 and HJ/3/1-14 ledgers and cash books, 1765-1870.

7 Cornwall Record Office (hereafter C.R.O.), AD 1219/5/5, financial papers of the Jenkins, Phillips and Abbot families, 1794-1870.

8 J.R. Hamilton and J.F. Lawrence, *Men and mining on the Quantocks* (Bracknell, 1970), is cited below as M&M ed. 1). The second edition of the work, which significantly adds to the detail some of which was acquired by site survey, was published in 2008 by the Exmoor Mines Research Group supported by Somerset Industrial Archaeology Unit, is hereafter cited as M&M, ed., 2.

9 S.H.C., DD\X\HAM/1 and 2.

10 C.L., HJ/2/1. Letter from Jenkin to Williams and Grenfell, Copper Office, London, 8 Apr 1814. Batch is shown on the 1901 Ordnance Survey Map for Somerset, sheet 16SE. Fluorospar was used as a flux in copper smelting.

11 M&M, ed., 1, 38-9.

12 S.H.C., DD\X\HAM/1, Letter to Richard Phillips, 1 March 1792 Jenkin reported that he and George and Robert Fox had met with the Marquis recently and had taken the mine 'off his hands'.

13 S.H.C., DD\X\HAM, A.K. Hamilton-Jenkin research notes. Shareholding as at 12 March 1801. Perran Wharf was a trading company with extensive interests in the exportation of tin and importing deals and spars, principally from the Baltic. It was owned by a partnership known as Fox, Phillips and Fox for which a 1786 partnership agreement exists and is held in the Cornwall Record Office as TLP/726. The information on the constitution of George C. Fox and Sons is taken from S.H.C., DD\X\HAM/1, Printer's text.

14 C.L., HJ/1/2, Jenkin to Scrope Bernard, 19 Feb. 1794.

15 S.H.C., T\PH\hamn, Jenkin to Richard Camplin, 10 Sep.

1786.

16 A.K. Hamilton Jenkin, *News from Cornwall: with a memoir of William Jenkin* (London, 1951), 4-5.

17 M&M ed. 1, 99.

18 M&M ed. 1, 32-3.

19 C.L., HJ/1/5, Jenkin to Scrope Bernard, 12 Mar 1801.

20 M&M ed. 1, 59.

21 S.H.C., DD\AH/14/7/25, Proposal dated 26 April 1806.

22 Cornwall Record Office (hereafter CRO), AD1219/5/5 ledger 96-10.

23 *News from Cornwall,* 134-5.

24 M&M ed. 1, 60-1.

25 *News from Cornwall,* 135, 140 and 145.

26 A notice of sale appeared in the *Royal Cornwall Gazette* on 20 July 1822. The mine was to be sold by auction at the premises by R. Down, an auctioneer of Bridgwater on Tuesday 22 August 1822, the sale to include all implements and materials including a steam engine and pumps.

27 The reference sources used were,: S. Hughes, *Copperopolis, landscapes of the early industrial period in Swansea* (Aberystwyth, 2000); D.B. Barton, *A history of copper mining in Cornwall and Devon* (Truro, 1968); J.R. Harris, *The Copper King,: a biography of Thomas Williams of Llanidan* (Liverpool, 1964).

28 Barton, *A history*, 38; Hughes, *Copperopolis*, 29, 41, 46, 192.

29 Barton, *A history*, 39.

30 Hughes, *Copperopolis*, 16.

31 Harris, *The Copper King*, 20-1.

32 Hughes, *Copperopolis*, 47.

33 S.H.C., T\PH\hamn, 10 Sep. 1786.

34 The *Cambrian* newspaper is available on line through the National Library of Wales website.

35 C.L., HJ/1/1 Jenkin to Richard Camplin, 1 June 1791.

36 C.L., Ruth Phillips transcripts, L.B. 90-92, Jenkin to Richard Camplin, 5 May 1791.

37 C.L., HJ/1/1 Jenkin to John Penrose and Samuel Grose, 29 Sept. 1791. The price paid per ton was based on a standard price per ton of fine copper with an assay of samples determining the purity and the price paid. The standard changed with market conditions.

38 C.L., HJ/1/1 Jenkin to Richard Camplin, 15 Nov. 1791.

39 C.L., HJ/1/2 Jenkin to Thomas Fox, 21 Dec. 1793.

40 C.L., HJ/1/2 Jenkin to Scrope Bernard, 19 Feb. 1794.

41 C.L., HJ/1/2 Jenkin to Scrope Bernard, 19 Mar. 1794.

42 C.L., HJ/1/3 Jenkin to G. C. Fox & Sons, 25 Dec. 1795.

43 C.L., HJ/1/3 Jenkin to G. C. Fox & Sons, 14 Jan. 1796.

44 C.L., HJ/1/3 Jenkin to Samuel Grose, 15 Jan. 1796.

45 C.L., HJ/1/5 Jenkin to Samuel Grose, 4 Apr. 1798.

46 C.L., HJ/1/5 Jenkin to Scrope Bernard, 15 Apr. 1798.

47 C.L., HJ/1/5 Jenkin to Samuel Grose, 15 June 1799.

48 C.L., HJ/1/5 Jenkin to Scrope Bernard, 26 June 1799.

49 C.L., HJ/1/5 Jenkin to G.C. Fox & Sons 21 Sep. 1799.

50 C.L., HJ/1/5 Jenkin to Samuel Grose, 28 Sep. 1799.

51 C.L., HJ/1/5 Jenkin to Samuel Grose, 5 Oct. 1799.

52 C.L., HJ/1/5 Letters to Samuel Grose and G.C. Fox, 29 Nov. 1799.

53 C.L., HJ/1/5 Jenkin to Samuel Grose, 7 Dec. 1799.

54 C.L., HJ/1/5 Jenkin to Scrope Bernard, 13 Dec. 1799.

55 C.L., HJ/1/5 G.C. Fox & Sons, 31 Jan. 1800.

56 C.L., HJ/1/5 Jenkin to Thomas Fox, 11 Sep. 1801.

57 C.L., HJ/1/5 Jenkin to Samuel Grose, 17 Sep. 1801.

58 C.L., HJ/1/5 G.C. Fox & Sons, 21 and 28 Sep. 1801.

59 C.L., HJ/1/5 Jenkin to Scrope Bernard, 10 Oct. 1801

60 C.L., HJ/1/5 Jenkin to Scrope Bernard, 4 Dec. 1801.

61 C.L., HJ/2/4 Alfred Jenkin to Mathew Grose, 15 Aug. 1820.

62 C.L., HJ/2/4 Alfred Jenkin to Michael Allen, 19 Oct. 1820.

63 C.L., HJ/2/4 Alfred Jenkin to J.B. Jenkins, 16 Oct. 1820.

64 C.L., HJ/2/4 William Jenkin to J.B. Jenkins, 16 Nov. 1820.

65 C.L., HJ/2/4 Alfred Jenkin to Edward Sealy & Sons, 28 Nov. 1820.

66 S.H.C., DD\RSH/1, Bridgwater shipping registers, 5/1813, *Friends Increase.*

67 C.L., HJ/1/5 Jenkin to Scrope Bernard, 4 Dec. 1801.

Chapter Nine

A Brief History of Somerset Coast Sea Level Changes and Extremes, with Special Emphasis on the 1607[1] Flooding Event

David Pugh, Philip Ashford and Kevin Horsburgh

ALL COASTLINES are in a continual state of flux. Some 125,000 years ago when polar glaciers were at a minimum, global sea levels were many metres higher than today. At the other extreme, as recently as 20,000 years ago during the most recent glacial maximum, sea levels were generally as much as 200 metres lower than today. Today's sea bed of the Bristol Channel was mostly habitable land. As the glaciers receded sea levels rose until they stabilised near the present levels about 7,000 years ago. Around that time, the coast of Somerset took the shape that we map today.[2]

By virtue of its geometry, orientation with respect to prevailing storm winds, and a mean spring tidal range of 12.2 metres, the Bristol Channel and its surrounding regions are particularly susceptible to flooding. About 120 km^2 of the Somerset Levels are at or below sea level and these traditional flood plains routinely suffer inundation.

It is easy to forget how on a daily basis Somerset is a county predominately under the influence of the sea: economically, geographically, socially, and above all as a result of its continual geological reshaping, by rivers, by tides and by currents. With so much of the county lying close to and just a few metres above mean sea levels, there is an ongoing battle between land and sea. As a result, vast areas of Somerset are vulnerable to flooding, both by freshwater from the rivers, and by salt water when the sea breaks through coastal defences. And after flooding, the water can be slow to drain away.

Flooding is most probable in winter. It is likely that the earliest inhabitants of the low-lying Somerset Levels were summer migrants from the surrounding hills. Freshwater flooding, following heavy and prolonged rain, occurs mostly in winter, as most spectacularly shown recently in the winter of 2013-14. The highest tidal sea levels are usually in March and September, but winter storms can raise the predicted tidal sea levels by several metres.

The most famous recorded local inundation from the sea was the notorious flooding of January 1607. In our account we describe the 1607 event in some detail, based on recorded observations and personal accounts. We also look at the scientific analyses of the event, related to contemporary tidal and weather conditions. The 1607 event was an extreme event in a continuous spectrum of lesser flooding events. Here we also review the records of other marine inundations.

We take the boundaries of the Somerset coast as extending from Hurlstone Point in the west, to Avonmouth in the east, a direct distance of 67 kms. Because the sea does not recognise our terrestrial boundaries, it is necessary to avoid severe geographic restrictions in our descriptions: for the full picture, we include some data from further west down the Bristol Channel. Before looking at historical flooding events we describe the present-day sea level regime to give a context for appreciating the extreme historical events we discuss later.

Part 1: Present sea level variations

Sea levels change rapidly over hours (described as tides) and days (influenced by storms), and over much longer time scales due to climate change and vertical land movements. At one extreme we have wind waves, followed by the twice-daily tides, effects of storms, right through to the long-term mean sea level changes, over decades and centuries, associated with climate change and global trends.[3] At any time, the observed sea level comprises the 'tidal' elevation due to astronomical forces plus the weather-generated 'surge'. If a large surge coincides with high water during a spring tide then the consequences can be devastating.

Globally, coastal flooding caused by cyclone-generated surges has been responsible for huge losses of life, most notably in the Bay of Bengal where 250,000 people were killed in November 1970. There were an estimated 140,000 fatalities when a storm surge struck Bangladesh in April 1991. The worst fully recorded storm surge in Britain occurred in the North Sea on 31 January 1953 claiming over 300 lives in England and a further 1,800 in Holland.[4]

Measurements

Measurements of sea levels in the Bristol Channel region are limited. Two long-term tide gauges operate as part of the Environment Agency National Network, one at Avonmouth, and one at the Hinkley Point nuclear power station. The Avonmouth gauge data is available since 1924 and data from Hinkley Point starts from 1990.[5] *Admiralty Tide Tables* contain tidal data, based on short periods of observation, for several coastal sites as discussed in the next section.

Tides

The most evident changes of sea level in the Bristol Channel are of course those due to the twice-daily tides, driven by the gravitational forces of the moon, and to a lesser extent the sun. These tides are generated in the main ocean basins, from where they spread as waves onto the surrounding shallower continental shelf seas. Figure 9.1, which shows the tidal changes at Hinkley Point over the month of March 2015, illustrates the twice-monthly spring-neap cycle in the tidal range. The zero level is Admiralty Chart Datum, defined as being approximately the level of Lowest Astronomical Tide (L.A.T.).[6]

From the Atlantic Ocean, the tides travel as waves travel up the Bristol Channel to the east; it is then reflected back down-Channel. This is, though of course on a much bigger scale, very like water sloshing back and fore in a domestic bath. The length and depth of the Channel mean that the tide ranges increase very much from west to east. Technically, oceanographers describe this a 'standing wave'.[7]

As well as increasing in range, the Bristol Channel tides also have the property that although the times of high water increase from west to east to the head, all the high-water times across the region are quite close, to within an hour or so. In Figure 9.2a the ranges of the average tides, *i.e.* the difference between the high and low water levels, are plotted against distance in kilometres, down-Channel and up-Channel from Hurlstone Point zero on the horizontal axis. For a fuller picture, we have included Appledore and Ilfracombe, in Devon. This shows how the average tidal range nearly doubles from Appledore to Avonmouth. Figure 9.2b compares the times of high tide: high tide at Avonmouth is only an hour later than high tide at Hurlstone Point.

The range of the tides increases and decreases regularly over a period of two weeks depending on the adding and subtracting of the sun's tidal effects to the moon's tidal forcing; this cycle is related to the lunar illumination cycle. This modulation of the tidal ranges is shown in Figure 9.1. Ranges reach a

Figure 9.1: Changes in the tidal heights and ranges for March 2015, at Hinkley Point

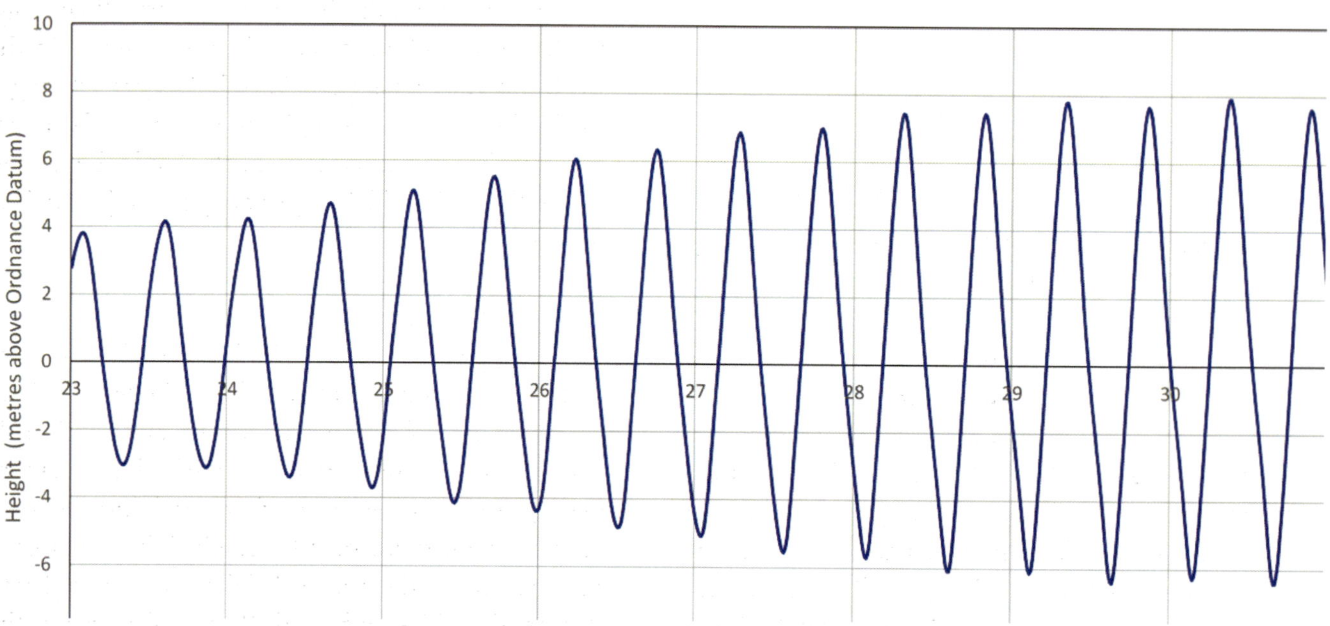

Note: H.A.T. and L.A.T. are Highest and Lowest Astronomical Tide respectively. M.H.W.S. and M.H.W.N. are the average levels of High Water on spring and neap tides respectively. M.L.W.S. and M.L.W.N. are the corresponding low water levels. Source: David Pugh.

Figure 9.2a: Ranges of the average tides at Ilfracombe, Appledore, Watchet and Avonmouth, 2017.

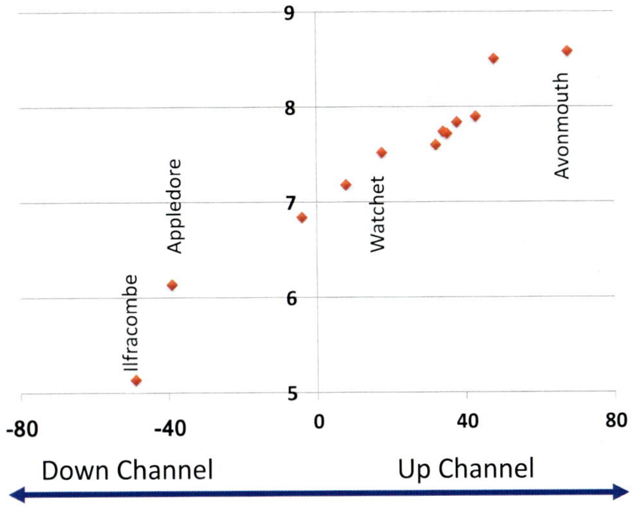

Note: The differences between the high and low water levels, are plotted against distances in kilometres, down-Channel and up-Channel from Hurlstone Point. Source: David Pugh.

Figure 9.2b: Comparison of high tide times at Ilfracombe, Appledore, Watchet and Avonmouth, 2017.

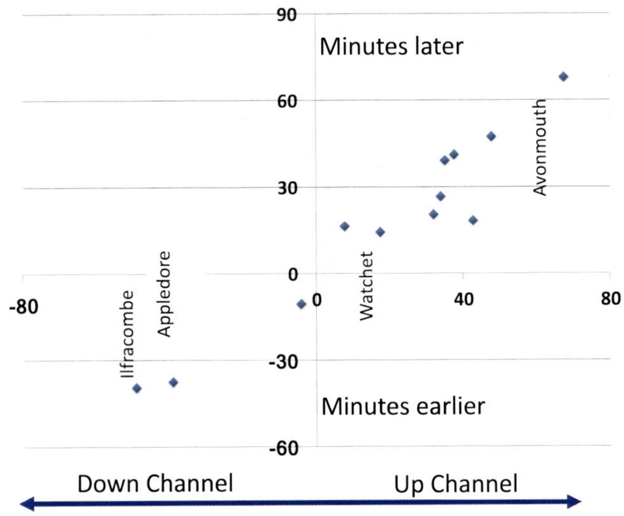

Note: High tide at Avonmouth is only an hour later than high tide at Hurlstone Point. Source: David Pugh.

maximum (fifty per-cent more than the average), a couple of days after full and new moon. These are the Mean High Water and Mean Low Water Spring Tides (M.H.W.S. and M.L.W.S.). For tides, 'spring' means 'lively', not 'occurring only at a particular season of the year'! In between we get the much smaller ranges of the neap tides, usually fifty per-cent less than the average termed Mean High Water Neaps (M.H.W.N.) and Mean Low Water Neaps (M.L.W.N.). The highest and lowest possible predicted tides due to the effects of the Moon and the Sun acting together are called the Highest Astronomical Tide (H.A.T.), and Lowest Astronomical Tide (L.A.T.). These extremes were nearly reached at the end of March 2015 as shown in Figure 9.1.

Table 9.1 summarises the various tidal levels for Hinkley Point and Avonmouth, and shows the greatest tidal range (H.A.T. less L.A.T.) at Avonmouth is 14.8 metres. At Hinkley Point the greatest tidal range is slightly less than at Avonmouth, at 13.0 metres. Levels are given to Admiralty Chart Datum, a level always close to L.A.T., and also to Ordnance Datum Newlyn, the British land levelling datum, which approximates to Mean Sea Level at Newlyn in Cornwall from 1915 to 1921.

Table 9.1: The various tidal levels for Hinkley Point and Avonmouth.

	Hinkley Point		Avonmouth	
	A.C.D.	O.D.N.	A.C.D.	O.D.N.
H.A.T.	12.8	6.9	14.7	8.2
M.H.W.S.	11.5	5.6	13.2	6.7
M.H.W.N.	8.4	2.5	9.8	3.3
M.L.W.N.	3.6	-2.3	3.8	-2.7
M.L.W.S.	0.8	-5.1	1.0	-5.5
L.A.T.	-0.2	-6.1	-0.1	-6.6

Note: Values are given in metres. A.C.D. is Admiralty Chart Datum and O.D.N. is Ordnance Datum Newlyn.
Source: Estimated from *Admiralty Tide Tables* and B.O.D.C. sources (David Pugh and B.O.D.C.).

For Avonmouth, the extremely large tidal range is often said to be the second greatest range in the world. Although comparable with the greatest ranges worldwide, there are two places in Canada, Burncoat Head in Nova Scotia, and Leaf Bay in Labrador, where the spring tidal ranges are greater (up to 16.0 metres)![8]

Weather effects

The tides predicted in Tide Tables from the positions of the Moon and Sun are regular and reliable. There is no evidence of significant changes in tides globally over recent centuries. Locally where harbour changes occur, for example following dredging or jetty construction, there may be small differences over time. However, the sea levels 'observed' from day to day as the tides ebb and flow, differ from the predicted levels because of the influences of the weather, an effect known as 'surging'. High air pressures depress sea levels, pushing them down; and low air pressures raise them. The main weather influence on sea level is due to the winds; the effect depends on both the wind speeds and direction. A detailed model study has shown that winds from the south, southwest and west are the most effective for lifting sea levels in the Bristol Channel.[9] At Avonmouth the southwest and westerly winds are most effective for raising levels, whereas further down-Channel southerly winds have most effect.

Figure 9.3: The probability of weather adding to or subtraction from predicted tidal levels.

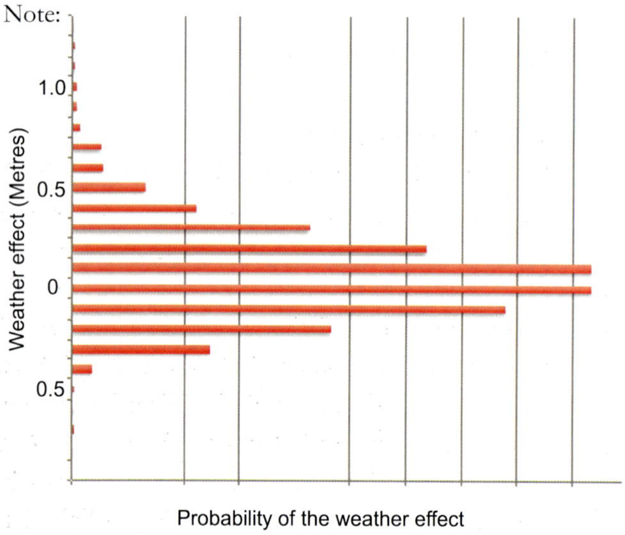

Positive values are adding to predicted tides. Weather effects above one metre are very rare, but do occur on extreme storms. Source: David Pugh.

Figure 9.3 shows the probability of weather adding to or subtracting from predicted tidal levels. Positive values are adding to predicted tides. The most 'probable' effect is zero or an increase of 0.1 metres above predicted tide levels. There is a long 'tail' at the top of the diagram of weather adding to predicted tidal sea levels. In 2015, the maximum additional weather effect resulted in an addition of 1.25 metres to the predicted height; the biggest reduction of predicted sea levels was 0.8 metres.

Extreme levels

The highest water levels recorded in the Bristol Channel during the last century were in the storm surge of 13 December 1981.[10] The peak surge of around 1.5-2 metres arrived very close to the time of high water, and although neither the tide nor the surge were exceptional the combination was disastrous. Flooding was severe and considerable damage was done to property and agricultural land.

Consider a recent extreme example. On 3 January 2014, a storm originating south of Nova Scotia hit the British Isles and caused sea level along the entire west coast of Britain to rise from 0.5 to 1.0 metres higher than predicted. At Hinkley Point the levels were 0.64 metres higher than expected, and the total observed level reached 13.35 metres above Chart Datum.[11] This is 0.55 metres higher than the highest predicted tides (H.A.T.) in Table 9.1. In this event, the extreme surge coincided with a predicted high tide of 12.7 metres.

On average the level reached in January 2014 will be reached about once every 15 years. Neither predicted very high tides, nor severe storms are sufficient to give *total* extreme observed levels and potential flooding. The very highest levels occur when a large surge and a large spring tide coincide.

Table 9.2 shows the most extreme observed levels at Avonmouth and Hinkley Point over the period of modern sustained measurements. At Hinkley Point the January 2014 level was 0.1 metres higher than anything observed in the period from 1990 to 2012. Note that the very high level levels of February 1997 and March 2006 appear near the top of both lists, showing the regional nature of potential flooding.

Table 9.2: The most extreme observed levels at Avonmouth (1961-2012) and Hinkley Point (1990-2012) over the period of modern sustained measurements.

Avonmouth			Hinkley Point		
A.C.D.	Time	Date	A.C.D.	Time	Date
15.00	08:00	26-Feb-90	13.26	08:45	10-Feb-97
14.97	08:00	04-Dec-94	13.16	07:15	30-Mar-06
14.93	09:15	10-Feb-97	13.12	08:15	30-Mar-98
14.85	07:45	30-Mar-06	13.12	19:30	08-Oct-06
14.84	20:15	28-Oct-96	13.07	07:30	04-Dec-94
14.80	20:00	08-Oct-06	13.05	07:45	02-Mar-10
14.79	20:45	24-Feb-97	13.04	08:00	30-Aug-92
14.78	08:45	30-Mar-98	13.03	20:00	29-Mar-98
14.73	09:00	30-Jan-75	13.01	19:30	09-Sep-10
14.72	09:00	09-Feb-74	13.01	07:15	10-Mar-01
A.C.D. is 6.5 m below O.D.N.			A.C.D. is 5.9 m below O.D.N.		

Note: Values are given in metres. A.C.D. is Admiralty Chart Datum and O.D.N. is Ordnance Datum Newlyn.
Source: Estimated from Admiralty Tide Tables and B.O.D.C. sources (David Pugh and B.O.D.C.).

Long-term changes

There is no evidence globally, or around the United Kingdom, that tidal ranges have changed much in the past few centuries, nor are there known trends in the storm effects on sea level. However, there are known increases in global average sea levels, and hence local mean sea levels over decades and centuries. In the twentieth century, mean sea levels rose by about 0.20 metres globally, a rate of rise also recorded at Pembroke Dock across the Bristol Channel in Wales, from 1832 to 2016. It is reasonable to suppose that sea levels along the Somerset coast have also risen at a similar rate over this time. For comparison with modern statistics, extreme historic flooding levels need to be adjusted for the effect of vertical land movement due to recovery from the weight of the last glaciation and other ongoing geological adjustments. In this region, a value of land rise of about 0.4 millimetres per year has been estimated.[12]

Part 2: Coastal flooding . . . an ongoing saga

The 1607 inundation has been moderately well documented given the limited capabilities of the time. Going further back in history, reports are less reliable and the details are scarce, often based on oral tradition. Table 9.3 gives some relatively recent documented events. Notably in 1484, some 200 people were drowned after flooding due to high tides and gales. Apart from 1607, other documented events were less devastating.

The outstanding event of 1607, in which so many people drowned, is the subject of this chapter. On 30 January 1607, a huge tidal surge caused large areas of Somerset, as well as parts of South Wales and estuarine parts of Gloucestershire and Devon to be inundated with water. The disaster had a significant impact on the local economy, and the event was seized upon by Puritan pamphleteers who used it as evidence of God's anger with the established church.

Part 3: Somerset's flood of 1607

Documentary evidence

The flooding of Somerset and Monmouthshire in January 1607 is well documented, with most later commentators drawing on four primary sources for regional information. The first three are chapbooks or pamphlets from 1607 titled *A true report of certain wonderful overflowings of waters in Somerset, Norfolk and other parts of England A.D. 1607,*[24] *God's Warning to his people of England* [25] and *Lamentable newes out of Monmouthshire in Wales.*[26] A fourth account can be found in William Camden's *Britannia* published in 1789.[27]

Table 9.3 Documentary evidence of Somerset sea floods, 1316-1798

Date	Recorded damage	Notes
Before 1316	Agricultural land flooded at Stockland Bristol by seawater reducing profitability.[13]	
15 Oct. 1484	Wall broken at Bleadon by ferocity of the sea and land flooded.[14] Along the Avon and at Bristol land was flooded and many properties affected. Salt and wool in merchant cellars destroyed. 200 people drowned. Ships lost in King Road.[15]	There was a huge gale so there was clearly a deep depression with a steep pressure gradient.
20 Jan. 1606/7	Flooding from Blue Anchor to Bristol and as far in-land as Glastonbury; as per this chapter.	The most widespread and significant historic sea-flood.
27 Nov. 1636	Sea walls at Kingston Seymour and Clevedon overtopped. Cellars in Bristol flooded.	One foot lower than 1607 flood.[16]
Mid October 1666	Tide rose over quays at Bridgwater and flooded cellars and houses.[17]	
1703	Great damage to shipping at Minehead, Huntspill sea wall destroyed and land flooded to depth of four feet.[18] Sea wall was broken at Kingston Seymour with sea water flowing up to six miles inland. Cattle and sheep drowned and many 'mows' of hay and corn destroyed.[19] Shipping destroyed in King Road and Hung Road and Bristol properties flooded.[20]	The 'great storm'.
9 Jan. 1737	Water rose over quays and flooded property at Bridgwater. Sea wall near Highbridge damaged, land flooded, sheep drowned, bridge damaged.[21]	A' great gale' so there must have been a low pressure area with a steep pressure gradient.
11 Sep. and Nov. 1798	Sea wall damaged at Huntspill by storms and on 11 September a boat was driven several hundred yards inland.[22]	Perhaps coast exposed by erosion at Steart in 1793.[23]

Note: Sources are shown in the references at the end of this chapter.

Further accounts can be found in works by John Stow published in 1631[28] and the diary of Walter Yonge published in 1848.[29] From those contemporary, or near contemporary writings, it can be inferred that the flooding extended some 40 kms along both banks of the Bristol Channel to a depth of 2-3 metres. Illustration 9.1 shows the affected regions in Somerset, and identifies those villages mentioned in the source materials. Estimates of the number of lives lost vary considerably. Yonge's diary records 500 fatalities, and Keys estimated as many as 2,000 may have died.[30]

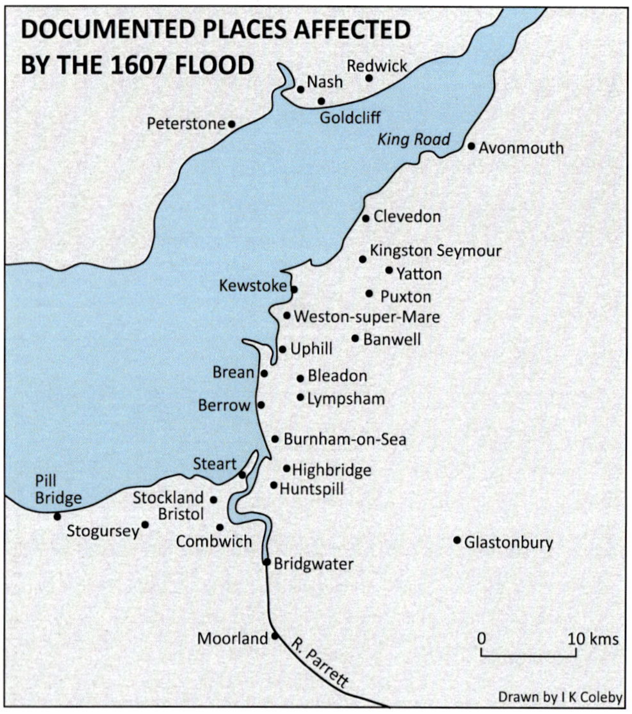

Illustration 9.1: Places documented as being affected by the 1607 flood in the Bristol Channel area. Note that many markers in the River Brue catchment area that would have shown the documented extent of the flood in this vicinity were removed over 200 years ago, including the one in St Benedict's church at Glastonbury. (Philip Ashford and Kevin Horsburgh).

The high water that drove up the Bristol Channel on the morning of 30 January 1607 started its trail of damage at Appledore and Barnstaple on the north Devon coast where a 60 ton laden ship was grounded and buildings were flooded.[31] It soon arrived at Lynmouth in north Devon, some 30 miles further east, where the paraphernalia of the herring industry, likely to have been stake nets and smoking houses, were destroyed.[32] However, to date, no incontrovertible evidence of any damage caused by the flood at Porlock and Minehead has been found. There is no record of damaged coastal property, and the burial registers for both Minehead and Porlock parishes do not have any indication of increased numbers of burials, or any marginal comments in the registers alluding to the event. Minehead's burial register from the period is replete with interesting detail and comments, including unusual deaths,[33] so it is very likely that the extraordinary event of the 1607 flood would have raised some mention if any local people had drowned. It is quite likely that the Porlock and Minehead marshes did flood, but since they were then largely uninhabited, apart from at Bossington near Porlock, there may have been little structural damage or drowning of people. However, in 1608 or 1609 George Miller of Minehead, who sustained 'loss by sea', was awarded £6 by the Quarter Sessions.[34] The award may result from losses sustained during the 1607 flood, but could alternatively derive from some other loss at a different time.

Illustration 9.2: An exceptional high sea level floods Porlock Marsh in April 1997 (Peter Ashford).

The most westerly construction in Somerset known to have been damaged by the 1607 salt water inundation was Mould or Mowthe Bridge. The residents of Carhampton and Williton were charged by the Court of Quarter Sessions to raise funds for its rebuilding and replacement, giving some credence to the suggested whereabouts of the structure. The bridge which contemporaries stated 'lyeth near the full sea mark' was 'borne away by the great flood' and the expense of its replacement caused local residents and gentry great perplexity for the next two years. More time was required to complete the task.[35] It is likely that the bridge in question crossed a stream entering the Bristol Channel near Home Farm, and is now known as Pill Bridge, on the coast road at Blue

Anchor on the boundary of Carhampton and Old Cleeve parishes.

Illustration 9.3: The modern water outlet at Pill Bridge, Blue Anchor. The stream passes under the causeway road and sea wall. This could have been the location of Mowthe Bridge which was damaged by the 1607 flood. (Elliot Lowe, 2014)

Further east at Stockland Bristol, it was recorded that the flood went over Stocklinch Marsh and so over Steart Point. Then at Combwich the passage was 'devoured by the flood',[36] such that the only way over the river was by boat. Since the passage would have involved a boat anyway, this is taken to mean that the slips and/or wooden quays, as well as secured boats, were inundated and probably washed away.

As to the human cost of the flood to the west of Bridgwater, at Stogursey, Joanne Pound, Joan Campline and her child were all buried two days after the flood, with their deaths attributed to drowning by the 'sea overflowing'. Perhaps these victims of the flood lived in the Stolford area, but it is surprising that the parish burial records, which are continuous for this period, show no further indications of the effect of the inundation. Furthermore, the fact they were buried within two days[37] means that the bodies were probably found the day before. Also at Stockland Bristol, John Williams who had married Joan Baylie, also of Stockland, before January 1607, suffered a loss worth £40 'in the great flood' which included his house. John then became itinerant and was picked up and tried as a wandering man by local justices in north-east Somerset in 1608. He had spent the night before the hearing in the church porch of Freshford.[38] In the same area of west Somerset, an estate survey of 1612 recites tenancy agreements made in late Tudor times to particular individuals who often renewed their leases after the 1607 flood indicating the survival of many of the inhabitants.[39]

Illustration 9.4: An extract from a map of the Stolford and Stockland Bristol area in 1612, just five years after the flood of January 1607. Stolford is just to the south of 'Wall Common' marked on the map, and Stockland Bristol's position is off the south-east corner of the map. Note the depiction of two windmills at the edge of Wall Common. This low lying flat land was inundated during the flood. (S.H.C., DD/X/WI 34)

A contemporary diarist, Walter Yonge from east Devon, commented on the state of affairs in January 1607, which he may have heard reported from the Bridgwater area. He noted how two villages and one market town were overflown and reports of 500 people drowned, as well as many sheep and cattle;[40] probably referring to Huntspill, Berrow and Brean. It is very likely that the Parrett sea walls were damaged by the flood as the residents of Moorland in North Petherton petitioned the court of Quarter Sessions, in the summer of 1608, regarding the damaged 'sea wall' along their stretch of the river. The order to mend the section of the riverine defences followed quickly thereafter.[41] Notwithstanding this evidence, the burial records at St Mary's Bridgwater and Chedzoy parish church nearby record no unusual numbers of burials in January or February 1607, nor any marginal notes relating to extraordinary events or burials elsewhere.[42] Sadly, the early seventeenth century burial registers for Burnham, Huntspill, Berrow and Brean have all been lost, so they cannot provide any corroborating evidence for deaths by drowning along that part of the Somerset coast.

To the north of Bridgwater, at Burnham, the sea wall was breached by the flood. The Commissioners of Sewers ordered that 500 men repair this section of sea wall. Such was the determination to make good, or perhaps a reflection of the urgency of the situation, that the Commissioners and justices helped with the work 'not with their eyes alone but also with their hands'.[43] Nearby, at Huntspill, comes a heart-rending story of the loss of property caused by the great inundation. William Payne's house had burned down at some point before the flood and it had been recently rebuilt before it was 'overthrown' and his goods carried away. William was granted 40 shillings by the Court of Quarter Sessions.[44] In the same village, Widow Cadwell had survived the flood by clinging to the floating thatch of her cottage. She was 'washed' for three miles before being rescued. At least Payne and Cadwell were more fortunate than the 28 people who were said to have lost their lives in the parish of Huntspill when it was 'quite over-flowne'.[45]

At Berrow, the house of John Stowles was 'throwne downe' by water. Stowles and three or four of his children were drowned, but his wife and one son clung on to the floating thatch of their house and were driven two miles by the wind until they were blown into a hay rick. They clambered on to the hay rick from which they were rescued the next day. The Stowles family may have been the only casualties in the village, since it is stated that there were but five drownings in the settlement. A Berrow milkmaid, surrounded by the flood, survived because she happened to be near a bank which she could climb up where she remained for 24 hours with rats, mice and moles around her. Apparently, she was rescued by some enterprising young men who made a raft from two salting troughs.[46]

It was reported that 26 people were drowned at Brean when seven of the nine houses in the parish were destroyed. One resident, John Good, like others from nearby villages, survived the flood by clinging to the thatch of his house which was driven at least a mile until he came to a bank which saved him. His wife, five children and 'nine or ten' of his servants were amongst the dead. In all, about 30 villages on the Somerset Levels are recorded to have flooded.[47] It is clear that the inundation must have flowed far inland beyond the area of those 30 named villages, as it reached the doors of St Benedict's church in Glastonbury.[48] In St Benedict's church "a record of the terrible inundation was marked on the great arch which divides the nave from the Chancel thus, 'the breach of the sea flood was January 20th 1606' ". The author of this statement was a local vicar, who knew of the location of the inscription. There is no trace of the mark today. Significantly, the comment in the 1808 book is accompanied by the assertion that the flood was caused by a high spring tide accompanied by a strong south-west wind, although no contemporary reference is given to support this comment.[49]

Illustration 9.5: St Benedict's church in Glastonbury, on the western edge of the lower part of the town, is about 10-12 metres above mean sea level. A record survives of the water level reaching 'the doors'; the land 200 metres or so down the street is the same height above sea level, or slightly lower than that flooded at Kingston Seymour (Adrian Webb, 2017)

Further north of Brean, at Uphill, there must also have been a sea wall which was breached and subsequently repaired after the storm. When a ship from Hull was driven into the Axe River in 1611, it was at a time when people were still mending the sea walls (or embankments) in the parish.[50] Given the expense of mending sea walls at Uphill, it is not surprising work was still being carried out four years later. No doubt those who worked on the walls remembered the eleven people reported to have drowned at Uphill in January 1607.[51] At neighbouring Weston-super-Mare, whatever sea walls were in place (perhaps strengthened after the 1607 flood), were severely breached in another storm in 1689, such that £153 was allocated for their repair.[52]

In the narrative of events above there is no reference to damaged ships or vessels brought inland on the flood. Records of such events are most likely to have been made and some would have survived if such occurrences had taken place. There is an account of a shepherd who witnessed his sheep drown, but saved himself by climbing into a tree. He was subsequently rescued by a boat that had been launched for the purpose of finding survivors.[53] The location of this event is not recorded, but it is likely to have been somewhere on the Somerset Levels. Furthermore, it seems that sea-faring men, thieves, came daily in boats and went away richly laden with goods they find swimming upon the waters.[54] There seem always to be some people that profit from the misfortune of others.

The sea walls were certainly overcome further north at Kingston Seymour. Here in the church porch is one of a handful of physical markers indicating the height of the great flood, the others being on the Welsh side of the Bristol Channel. The plaque in the porch (Illustration 9.6) records the event in some detail.

Illustration 9.6: The plaque in the porch of Kingston Seymour church. Note the year 1606 is written but this relates to the Julian calendar.[55] (David Pugh, 2016)

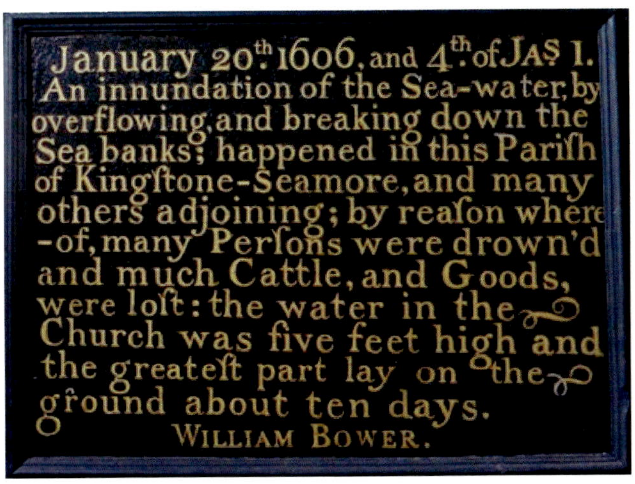

Illustration 9.7: The top step of the medieval cross base at Kingston Seymour gives some indication of the height of the flood in relation to a structure that itself was inundated in January 1607. The base of the cross is 6-7 metres above mean sea level according to the Ordnance Survey. (Garry Holden Photographics, 2015)

Illustration 9.8: Kingston Seymour Church before restoration. Note that there is no cross above the plinth. (J. Rutter, *Delineations of the north western division of the county of Somerset* (Shaftesbury, 1829), 65)

Illustration 9.9: The water around the church today is a drainage moat (David Pugh, 2016)

The flood in this parish also caused one person to relocate, as would be expected with a depth of flooding of this magnitude. The Quarter Sessions held at Taunton in 1616 recorded that Ursula Cox, late of Kingston Seymour, lost £80 or more worth of property in the flood and that she was forced to go and live with her father in Curry Mallet where she was born. She lived with him for four years and then three years after his death the inhabitants would not allow her to continue to live there; she had been sleeping rough in thunder and lightning but the law of settlement and removal had to be obeyed. It was ordered that a decision on her place of residence and who should provide for her should be made.[56] To the north-east of Kingston Seymour, in the parish of Kenn, people and animals took shelter in a large building belonging to Lady Stallinge. Despite this the water level rose above the middle of horses taken there to safety.[57]

The sufferings at Kingston Seymour were soon repeated, as within a generation there was another flood in the parish. On the night of the 27 November 1636 there was a great wind from the south-west on a high spring tide. Many cellars along the quays in Bristol were also flooded and the sea came over the 'walls' at Kingston and Clevedon, with many sheep and cattle being drowned. The flood was reckoned to have been a foot lower than the 1607 flood.[58] Yet again, however, there seem to be no records of damaged ships. Just south of Kingston Seymour lies Puxton, a location recorded to have flooded in January 1607.[59] Recent investigations have revealed archaeological evidence of continuous habitation in the local vernacular houses from medieval to modern times, as well as evidence that the aspect of houses most exposed to the flood stood up to the surge of water. Furthermore, information from estate surveys and leases, indicating family continuity on the agricultural holdings from Tudor to Stuart times, from and after the 1607 flood,

Illustration 9.10: The landward edge of the modern sea wall at Kingston Seymour, with the tower of Woodspring Priory visible in the background, as well as Sand Point at the end of the headland. This image is taken from the inland, lower and older sea wall which would have been rebuilt after the 1607 inundation. (Garry Holden Photographics, 2015)

Illustration 9.11: The seaward bank of the Kingston Seymour sea wall, with sea anglers fishing from the top of it. (Garry Holden Photographics, 2015)

suggests that in this particular parish, many of the homes and families were not damaged in any lasting way.[60]

The flood height was amplified as it funnelled into the Severn and Avon estuaries to such an extent that as it passed up the Avon and into Bristol flooding streets to the depth of about 5 feet. This caused certain citizens of Bristol to sustain great losses.[61] Given that January saw St Paul's Fair in Bristol, the dock warehouses were filled with goods, subsequently rugs and 'packes of wares' were utterly spoiled and 'cast away'. Many of the damaged packs of goods were from Ireland.[62]

Illustration 9.12: Today there are extensive drainage systems around Kingston Seymour (David Pugh, 2016)

Part 4: Scientific analysis of the causes of the 1607 flooding

For our scientific investigations, there is a frustrating lack of exact information about the levels reached. However, in some cases the flood levels were marked by church plaques and subsequent surveying has quantified the approximate depth of the flood waters. Boon calculated the water level at Goldcliff, Newport to be 7.14 metres above Ordnance Datum (A.O.D.),[63] and Williams gave the height at Kingston Seymour, Somerset, as 7.74 metres A.O.D.[64]

Tide and weather on 30 January 1607

A prediction of the astronomical tide in the Bristol Channel for January 1607 is possible since we know the periodicities of the astronomical forces. Figure 9.4 shows the tidal elevation at Avonmouth (with respect to Ordnance Datum Newlyn) for the period. This is a shorter but similar plot to Figure 9.1, showing the transition from neap to spring tides.

The greatest amplitude is 7.86 metres that should have occurred at 09:00 hours on 30 January 1607. Times of exceptional semi-diurnal forcing are tabulated by Pugh and Woodworth;[65] March 2020, October 2020, March 2024 and September 2024 are also predicted to have very high tides predicted. To appreciate the magnitude of the 1607 tide it is worth noting that predictions for Avonmouth on 20 March 2007 give the maximum elevation A.O.D. as 7.78 metres, which is 8 cms less than the estimated high water level on 30 January 1607. Astronomical

Figure 9.4: Tidal curve for Avonmouth, 23 to 31 January 1607.

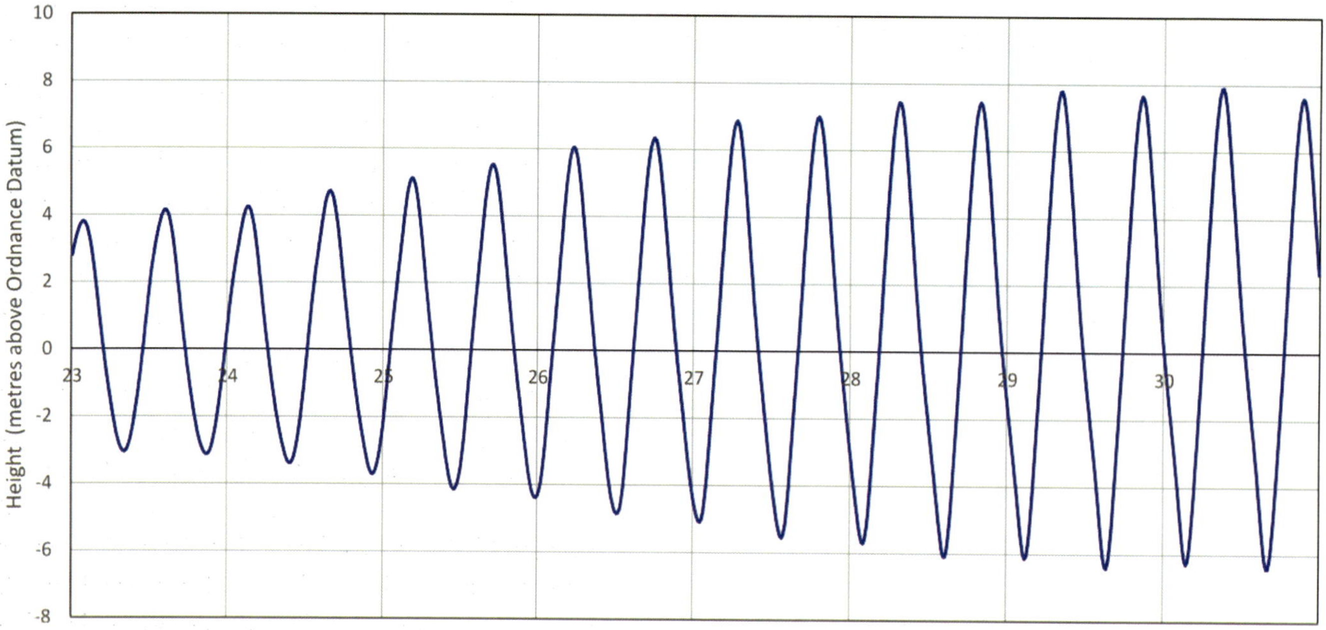

conditions in September 1922 were especially favourable for large tides with the new Moon occurring within one day of the equinox. The peak prediction for Avonmouth on 22 September 1922 was 8.04 metres A.O.D.

The weather preceding and during the flooding provides the key to the possibility of a storm surge. On 26 January 1606/7, John Paul, Vicar of Almondsbury recorded:

> But the yeere 1606, the fourth of King James, the ryver of Severn rose upon a sodeyn Tuesday mornyng the 20 of January beyng the full pryme day and hyghest tyde after the change of the moone by reason of a myghty strong western wynd.[66]

At Barnstaple it was recorded that 'This storme begane at 3 of clock in the morninge and continewd tyll 12 of clock of the same daye'.[67] However, the most authoritative account is that of the annalist John Stow in 1631[68] who noted that a westerly wind blew for 16 hours; Stow was also aware that it was a spring tide. Camden recorded that a strong south-west wind blew for three days without intermission.[69] All known contemporary references to weather conditions are collected in Table 9.4. Taking all material into consideration, the most likely weather was a severe storm with gale force westerly or south-westerly winds, precisely those conditions required for local surge generation in the Bristol Channel.

Flooding due to this weather event was not restricted to the Bristol Channel. There is reliable evidence of flooding on the east coast of England the same day. Stow recorded that great damage was done in Norfolk,[70] whilst reports of flooding at Kings Lynn, Wisbech and other villages in the Bishopric of Ely when 20 kms of the coastline was breached. From these accounts, it appears that the east coast flooding occurred on 30 January 1607, but at night. High water along the East Anglian coastline would have been around 21:00 hours that evening, when the weather system may have moved eastwards and winds veered to the northwest. One source mentions damage in Kent, but it is not unambiguously clear that the writer is referring to the same event.[71]

Table 9.4: Weather conditions for 30 January 1607 from contemporary sources.

	Reported weather	Source
1	Stormy	*A true report* (1607)
2	Vaguely implies fine weather	*God's Warning to his people of England* (1607)
3	Stormy	*Lamentable newes out of Monmouthshire in Wales* (1607)
4	Stormy	Camden, *Britannia* (1789)
5	Stormy	*Walter Yonge's Diary* (1848)
6	Stormy	Barnstaple, Devon parish register
7	Stormy	Arlingham, Gloucestershire parish register
8	Stormy	Stow, *Annales* (1631)

Simulation of the 1607 flood

We now show that superimposing a realistic Bristol Channel storm surge on the astronomical tide for 30

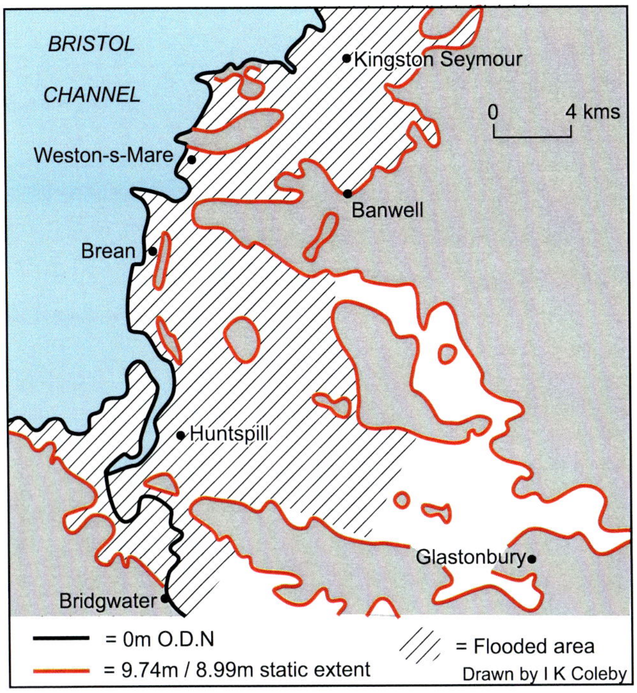

Illustration 9.13: A sketch of the modelling of the inundation extent, for the astronomical tide of 30 January 1607, plus a 2.3 metre surge. The red line shows the maximum level potentially reached in the model, but because of the hydrodynamics of spreading, the flood extends only to the shaded area, receding before reaching the maximum extent. The modelled levels at Kingston Seymour exceeded those actually observed by 1.3 m, showing that the 1607 flood levels could have been reached by a smaller surge than the 2.3 m used in the model (redrawn from Horsburgh and Horritt, 2006).

January 1607 provides sufficient water level to inundate the towns and villages indicated in Illustration 9.13, assuming that whatever flood defences existed were either breached or simply overtopped.

Tidal curves for Avonmouth and Hinkley Point were derived in order to correctly impose tidal heights along the estuary. The realistic surge chosen for comparison was from 27 October 2002. The spatial and temporal variability of the surge was extracted from an archive of numerical model results maintained at the National Oceanography Centre. The 2002 surge had a maximum height of 2.3 metres which was added to the tidal curve over a full tidal cycle centred on high water. We have assumed the worst case, of the peak surge coinciding with high water but the level of this particular surge event varied by only 0.15 metres over a five-hour period, so similar results would be obtained even if the peaks did not coincide. Finally, the surface elevation was adjusted for the long-term variability in mean sea level.

The total water level was then used as a dynamic imposed elevation input condition for the flood plain inundation model LISFLOOD-FP.[72] The model represents the coastal floodplain as a grid of square cells. This is a simplistic approach, but is capable of capturing important features of dynamic flood events, such as topographic influences and the advance or retreat of the wetting front. Models for both Somerset and Welsh levels were run with a grid spacing of 200 metres. Ground elevation data was derived from Ordnance Survey Profile data, sampled from an original resolution of 10 metres to the 200 metres required for the model. The vertical accuracy of ±1 metre is adequate for this study, allowing for the effects of basin shapes and large scale topographic features to be modelled. Smaller features such as dykes, ditches and flood defences will not be present in the model and hence their hydraulic effects cannot be taken into account, but model results are still broadly representative of how a flood wave would propagate across the levels in response to a surge event.

There is likely to have been significant morphological change since 1607, both from natural causes and improvement works on the levels. The Ordnance Survey data should, however, still be representative of the wider morphology of the particular coastal area. The results for the Somerset Levels are shown in Illustration 9.12.

For the Welsh levels, and the Somerset levels north of Weston-super-Mare (with the divide being formed by the Mendip Hills), the flood extents predicted by LISFLOOD-FP are very similar to those predicted by simply extrapolating a level surface at the maximum water elevation (solid lines). For these areas, dynamic effects are unimportant and over the period where high tide and surge combined the flood wave velocity is such that the basin is filled. However, south of Weston-super-Mare dynamic effects are significant, with the flood propagating only partially into the basin. Dynamic effects may actually be more significant than these results suggest, as real flood events may be controlled by flow over sea defences, rather than by water levels alone. However, as much of the drainage and improvement work was carried out after 1600, the level of protection in the sixteenth century is likely to have been far lower than today, and hence inundation more rapid. It was also possible to extract the depth of the water for those sites where the reported 1607 levels were reduced to datum: the depth at Kingston Seymour (illustration 9.12) was 9.02 metres A.O.D. (compared with the 7.74 metres surveyed) whereas at Goldcliff across the Channel, the modelled flood was 9.44 metres A.O.D. (compared with 7.14 metres surveyed). Even allowing for topographic changes, and inaccuracies in the placement of the commemorative plaques, it appears from these results that the inundation of 30 January 1607 could have been brought about by a more modest surge than that selected here (or alternatively, the peak of a surge need not have coincided with high water).

Conclusion

We have shown that the tide and probable weather at the time were capable of generating a surge that is totally consistent with the observed inundation, without needing to invoke high river levels due to previous rainfall (although one contemporary source refers to a 'land-floude',[73] implying that river flow in the Severn was high). This event is of scientific interest since it may represent the worst combination of high spring tide and locally generated surge in the Bristol Channel. The extent and depth of the flooding is well reproduced by superimposing a nominal surge of 2.3 metres on the tidal conditions of 30 January 1607. The sixteenth and seventeenth centuries appear to have been exceptionally windy. Lamb records 128 North Sea flood events for the seventeenth century.[74] His tentative climatic reconstruction suggests constant gales for western Britain. One candidate for causing these windy conditions would be the southward displacement of the jetstream, causing a corresponding shift in depression tracks to lower latitudes.

Had the flooding been caused by a tsunami,[75] then one might expect the original writings to have made reference to damage caused along the coasts of Cornwall, southern Ireland and west Wales where the model run demonstrates that the wave effects are similar. There is no reference to any of these locations in the four primary sources. Furthermore, it is clear that a tsunami of this origin cannot propagate into the North Sea, or have any significant impact around the Wash. The flooding in East Anglia can only have been caused by a combination of tide and surge.

The event of January 1607 provides a reminder of the destructive capability of storm surges, and was probably responsible for a greater loss of life in the UK than in the North Sea surge of 1953. The latter prompted the UK government to protect vulnerable areas: the Thames barrier was installed in 1982 and the Storm Tide Forecasting Service at the Met Office now provides operational flood warning to the Environment Agency. This service uses the tide-surge computer models employed in this account, meteorological models from the Met Office and real-time data from tide gauges to give surge warnings up to 36 hours ahead.

There are many questions surrounding the lasting social and economic impacts of the flood of January 1607. It is difficult to assess how long it took for all coastal and riverine flood defences to be re-strengthened or improved along the Somerset coast, how long the pastures took to recover from the salt water inundation, how long farm incomes took to recover, how long impoverished persons continued to wander the byways of the county after losing homes or family. The shock of the flood would have been passed down from generation to generation around the hearths of the householders.

The parishioners of Kingston Seymour who survived the 1607 flood must have been doubly shocked, since there was a repeat event in 1636. Child survivors of the 1607 flood must have wondered deeply about the sufferings of life, since many would later live through the negative experiences, challenges and horrors of the English Civil War including loss of agricultural land through abandonment and the excesses of soldiers living in their village.[76]

Acknowledgements

We acknowledge access to the sea level data at Avonmouth and Hinkley Point, afforded by the British Oceanographic Data Centre, Liverpool. The scientific modelling of the 1607 event first appeared in The Royal Meteorological Society journal Weather, Volume 61, October 2006, in an account *The Bristol Channel floods of 1607– reconstruction and analysis* by Kevin Horsburgh and Matt Horritt. We are grateful for permission to reproduce some of their figures here. Rose Hewlett, University of Bristol, who is researching the response and recovery aspects ofthe 1607 flood, has provided some valuable guidance on contemporary sources. Finally, encouragement and guidance from the volume editor, Dr Adrian Webb, has helped us to bring together in this account, for the first time, both the historical and scientific aspects of the 1607 event.

References

1 By the seventeenth century the Julian calendar was ten days out of step with the passage of the seasons since 365.25 days is a slight over-estimate of the true length of a year. To correct this, the Gregorian calendar was introduced in 1582 but was not adopted by England and her colonies until 1752. The same Act of Parliament in 1752 also changed the official start of year date to 1 January. Previously, the Civil or Legal Year in England began on 25 March (referred to as "Old Style" by historians). In this article, we use the New Style date of 30 January 1607 to describe the event, apart from when quoting contemporary accounts which would have referred to 20 January 1606.

2 A.J. Webb, *Charts and sailing directions of the Somerset coast c.1350-1824*, Somerset Record Society 97 (2014).

3 A more detailed discussion of the tidal dynamics can be found in D.T. Pugh and P.L. Woodworth, *Sea Level Science* (Cambridge, 2014).

4 R.A. Flather, 'A numerical model investigation of the storm surge of 31 January and 1 February 1953 in the North Sea' in *Quarterly Journal of the Royal Meteorological Society* 110 (1984), 591-612.

5 Sea level data are collected and made available through the British Oceanographic Data Centre (B.O.D.C.), and from the International Permanent Service for Mean Sea Level (P.S.M.S.L.). Both are located at the National Oceanography Centre, Liverpool.

6 Sea levels are either measured above Admiralty Chart Datum, an extreme low water level, or relative to Ordnance Datum Newlyn, a mean sea level approximation.

7 Pugh and Woodworth, *Sea Level Science.*

8 Pugh and Woodworth, *Sea Level Science.*

9 Gao C. and T.A.A. Adcock, 'The characteristics of storm surges in the Bristol Channel' in *International Society of Offshore and Polar Engineers. The 26th International Ocean and Polar Engineering Conference, 26 June-2 July, Rhodes, Greece* (2016).

10 R. Proctor and R. A. Flather, 'Storm surge prediction in the Bristol Channel – the floods of 13 December 1981' in *Continental Shelf Research* 9 (1989), 889-918.

11 There is a valuable central database of extreme UK marine flooding events at Surgewatch www.surgewatch.org accessed 1 May 2017.

12 S.L. Bradley, G.A. Milne, I. Shennan and R. Edwards, 'An improved glacial isostatic adjustment model for the British Isles' in *Journal of Quaternary Science* 26 (2011), 541-52.

13 C. Ross (ed.), *Cartulary of St Mark's Hospital, Bristol*, Bristol Record Society 21 (1959), 133.

14 M. Williams, *The draining of the Somerset Levels* (Cambridge, 1970), 83.

15 Rev. S. Seyer, *Memoirs historical and topographical of Bristol and its neighbourhood* (Bristol, 1823), 202.

16 Seyer, *Memoirs*, 290.

17 *Calendar of State Papers Domestic Charles II* 6, 213.

18 D. Defoe, *The novels and miscellaneous works* (London, 1855) 316, 356-9, 374.

19 Plaque in Kingston Seymour church porch.

20 Defoe, *Novels*, 316, 356-9, 374.

21 L. Clarke, *Exposition on the common prayer*, 1737, no. 28, 23 Jan. 1737, 3.

22 C. Durnford and E. Hyde-East, *Reports of cases argued and determined in the court of the King's bench 1798-1800* 8 (Dublin, 1800), 313.

23 Williams, *Somerset Levels*, 44-5, 88, 119.

24 E. Baker (ed.), *A true report of certain wonderful overflowings of waters in Somerset, Norfolk and other parts of England A.D. 1607* (Weston-super-Mare, 1884).

25 W. Oldys, and T. Park, *The Harleian Miscellany* 3 (1809), 64-71.

26 O. Morgan, 'Goldcliff and the ancient Roman inscribed stone found there' in *Monmouthshire and Caerleon Antiquarian Association Papers* (1882).

27 R. Gough, translated and edited, W. Camden, *Britannia* (London, 1789).

28 J. Stow, *Annales, or a general chronicle of England* (London, 1631), 889.

29 G. Roberts (ed.), *The diary of Walter Yonge esq, justice of the peace and M.P. for Honiton written at Colyton and Axminster*, Camden Society 41 (1848), 13-14.

30 D. Keys, 'The great flood of 1607' in *B.B.C. History Magazine* 6 (2005), 46-7.

31 Anon, *More strange newes of wonderfull accidents hapning by the late overflowings of waters in Somerset-shire, Gloucestershire, Norfolke and other places* (London, 1607).

32 P. Ashford, 'The rise and fall of the Bristol Channel herring fishery with especial reference to Porlock, Somerset, 1580-1830' in *Mariner's Mirror* 92:1 (2006), 23-4.

33 S.H.C., D\P\m.st.m/2/1/1, Minehead registers of baptisms, marriages and burials, late sixteenth and early seventeenth century.

34 S.H.C., Q/SR/4/1 Quarter Sessions award, n.d.

35 S.H.C., Q/SR/6/42-43 petition to the Court of Quarter Sessions, 25 Apr. 1609; E. Bates (ed.), *Quarter sessions records for the county of Somerset 1607-1625*, S.R.S. 23 (1907), 45, 47.

36 Anon, *More strange newes.*

37 S.H.C., D\P\stogs/2/1/1 Stogursey burial register.

38 S.H.C., Q/SR/4/97 Court of Quarter Sessions examination.

39 S.H.C., DD/X/W1, 34 Survey and maps of the Manor of Weeke Fitzpaine.

40 Roberts, *The diary of Walter Yonge*, 13-14.

41 S.H.C., Q/SR/3/168 and 3/151 Court of Quarter Sessions petition and order.

42 S.H.C., D\P\bw.m/2/1/1 Bridgwater St Mary's burial register; D\P\chez/2/1/1 Chedzoy burial register.

43 Anon, *More strange newes.* This information is retold in Williams, *Somerset Levels*, 88.

44 S.H.C., Q/SR/3/36-37 Court of Quarter Sessions order, 15 Sep. 1607.

45 Anon, *More strange newes.*

46 Anon, *More strange newes.* The story of the milkmaid is repeated in A. Powell, *The ancient borough of Bridgwater*, (Bridgwater, 1907), 12. The names of the animals quoted

here derive from Powell. The original chap book uses animal names which are not commonly known.

47 Anon, *More strange newes.*

48 S.H.C., DD\SAS/C795/SE/84/3 notes and news cuttings regarding various matters in the Wells area.

49 J. Williamson, *Glastonbury Abbey: its history and ruins* (Wells, 1862), 55. Many nineteenth-century guide books have the exact quote about the breach, being in the church, the earliest reference is in a book of 1808 (Anon, *The Avalon guide to the town of Glastonbury* (London, 1808), 9). The breach is not mentioned in Rack's survey of the church undertaken in the 1780s, but it is possible that he may have missed it, nor does he mention it in his account of Kingston Seymour (M. McDermott and S. Berry, ed., *Edmund Rack's survey of Somerset* (Taunton, 2011), 125, 146-8.

50 S.H.C., Q/SR/11/57-8 Court of Quarter Sessions certificate, *c.*1611. When the Brue Drainage Act of 1801 was passed it delineated the area to be covered as that where there were records of earlier floods. One result was that the commissioners proceeded to remove the markers of the more extreme flood levels, including the one inside St Benedict's church, Glastonbury, in order to reduce their liability. (Information from Neill Bonham, Glastonbury Antiquarian Society, July 2017).

51 Anon, *More strange newes.*

52 G. Farr, *Somerset harbours* (London, 1954), 71.

53 Baker, *A true report.*

54 Anon, *More strange newes.*

55 The text on the board shown here which hangs in the porch of Kingston Seymour church is also to be found on a map of the manor of Kingston Seymour dated 1784 (S.H.C., DD/MKG/12/3/1). A shorter version of the text appears in the preface to the parish register of 1727 (S..H.C., D/P/k.sey 2/1/1), presumably taken from a previous record. We are grateful to Dr Adrian Webb and Rose Hewlett for directing us to these sources.

56 Bates, *Quarter Sessions 1607*-1625, 180-1.

57 Anon, *More strange newes.*

58 Seyer, *Memoirs*, 290.

59 Anon, *More strange newes.*

60 S. Rippon, *Landscape, community and colonisation: The north Somerset Levels during the 1st and 2nd millennia AD* (2006), 299-301 found at https://ore.exeter.ac.uk/repository/handle/10036/30003 (accessed October 2016).

61 Anon, *More strange newes.*

62 Baker, *A true report.*

63 G.C. Boon, '*Caerleon and the Gwent Levels in early historic times*' in F.H. Thomson (ed.), *Archaeology and coastal change*, Society of Antiquities Occasional Papers No.1 (London, 1980), 24–36.

64 Williams, *Somerset Levels*, 288.

65 Pugh and Woodworth, *Sea Level Science.*

66 Gloucestershire Archives, D674a/L39 Almondsbury parish register.

67 North Devon Record Office, 3054A/PR/1/1 Barnstaple parish register.

68 Stow, *Annales.*

69 Camden, *Britannia.*

70 Stow, *Annales.*

71 Baker, *A true report.*

72 P.D. Bates, and A.P.J. De Roo, 'A simple raster-based model for flood inundation simulation' in *Journal of Hydrology* 236 (2000), 54-77.

73 Baker, *A true report.*

74 H.H. Lamb, *Climate: present, past and future. Volume 2 climatic history and the future* (London, 1977), 835.

75 E.A. Bryant and S.K. Haslett, 'Was the AD1607 coastal flooding event in the Severn Estuary and Bristol Channel (UK) due to a tsunami?' in *Archaeology in the Severn Estuary* 13 (2002), 163-7.

76 J. Wroughton, *An unhappy Civil War* (Bath, 1999), 248-9; D. Underdown, *Somerset in the Civil War and Interregnum* (Newton Abbot, 1973), 90-1.

Index of Vessel Names

Index of Personal Names

Index of Place Names